CHRISTIAN THEOLOGY IN ASIA

The majority of the world's Christians now live outside Europe and North America, and global Christianity is becoming increasingly diverse. Interest in the history and theology of churches in non-western contexts is growing rapidly as 'old world' churches face this new reality. This book focuses on how Asian Christian theologies have been shaped by the interaction of Christian communities with the societies around them and how they relate to the specific historical contexts from which they have emerged. The distinctiveness of Asian Christianity is shown to be the outcome of dealing with various historical challenges. Questions addressed include:

- How does Asian Christianity relate to local socio-cultural, religious and political environments?
- What is distinctive about the historical development of Asian theologies?
- How have Asian theologies contributed to contemporary theological discussions within world Christianity?

SEBASTIAN C. H. KIM is Professor of Theology and Public Life at the Faculty of Education and Theology, York St John University. His publications include *In Search of Identity: Debates on Religious Conversion in India* (2003).

CHRISTIAN THEOLOGY
IN ASIA

EDITED BY
SEBASTIAN C. H. KIM

CAMBRIDGE
UNIVERSITY PRESS

CAMBRIDGE UNIVERSITY PRESS

Cambridge, New York, Melbourne, Madrid, Cape Town, Singapore, São Paulo, Delhi

Cambridge University Press
The Edinburgh Building, Cambridge CB2 8RU, UK

Published in the United States of America by Cambridge University Press, New York

www.cambridge.org
Information on this title: www.cambridge.org/9780521681834

First published 2008

Printed in the United Kingdom at the University Press, Cambridge

A catalogue record for this publication is available from the British Library

Library of Congress Cataloguing in Publication data
Christian theology in Asia / edited by Sebastian C. H. Kim.
p.   cm.
Includes bibliographical references and index.
ISBN 978-0-521-86308-7 (hardback: alk. paper) – ISBN 978-0-521-68183-4 (pbk.: alk. paper)
1. Theology–Asia.   2. Asia–Church history.   I. Kim, Sebastian C. H.
BR1065.C42 2008
230.095–dc22   2007050991

ISBN-13 978-0-521-86308-7 hardback
ISBN-13 978-0-521-68183-4 paperback

Contents

v

Contributors

S. WESLEY ARIARAJAH is Professor of Ecumenical Theology at Drew University School of Theology, Madison, New Jersey, USA. Before joining Drew, he served the World Council of Churches, Geneva, Switzerland for sixteen years as Director of the Interfaith Dialogue Program and as Deputy General Secretary of the Council. His publications include *Hindus and Christians – A Century of Protestant Ecumenical Thought, The Bible and People of Other Faiths, Not without My Neighbour – Issues in Interfaith Relations* and *Axis of Peace – Christian Faith in Times of Violence and War.*

CHOONG CHEE PANG is Visiting Professor at Beijing University and the Chinese University of Hong Kong. He was Principal of Trinity Theological College, Singapore and the Academic Consultant of the Lutheran World Federation. His latest publication includes a two-volume *Chinese Commentary on John.*

SATHIANATHAN CLARKE is Professor of Theology, Culture and Mission at Wesley Theological Seminary in Washington DC, USA. He taught theology for many years at the United Theological College in Bangalore, India. Dr Clarke has published numerous academic articles and is the author of *Dalits and Christianity: Subaltern Religion and Liberation Theology in India* (1998). He also co-edited *Religious Conversion in India: Modes, Motivations, Meanings* (2003).

HWA YUNG is Bishop of the Methodist Church in Malaysia. He was Principal of Malaysia Theological Seminary and, later, the founding Director, Centre for the Study of Christianity in Asia at Trinity Theological College, Singapore. His writings have been mainly in the area of Asian missiology and theology, including *Mangoes or Bananas? The Quest for an Authentic Asian Christian Theology* (1997).

JACOB KAVUNKAL is Professor and Coordinator of Postgraduate Studies at the Pontifical Athenaeum Seminary, Pune, India. He is a member of the Society of the Divine Word, holds a Licentiate and Doctorate in Missiology from the Gregorian University, Rome and has published extensively on missiological topics. His latest publication is *Vatican II: A Gift and a Task* (2006). He has initiated a project to publish a one-volume *Encyclopedia of Christianity in India*. He is also the founder of the Fellowship of Indian Missiologists.

NAMSOON KANG is Associate Professor of World Christianity and Religions at Brite Divinity School, Texas Christian University, USA. Her expertise is in constructive theology, postcolonialism and feminism, world religions and ecumenics. She was one of the plenary speakers at the Ninth Assembly of WCC in 2006, Porto Alegre, Brazil. She is the author of 'Who/What is Asian?: A Postcolonial Theological Reading of Orientalism and Neo-Orientalism' in *Postcolonial Theologies: Divinity and Empire* (2004) and numerous books in Korean.

SEBASTIAN C. H. KIM is Professor of Theology and Public Life in the Faculty of Education and Theology of York St John University, UK. He is a Fellow of the Royal Asiatic Society and the author of *In Search of Identity: Debates on Religious Conversion in India* (2003). He was formerly Director of the Christianity in Asia Project and taught World Christianity at the Faculty of Divinity of the University of Cambridge. He is founding and current Editor of the *International Journal of Public Theology*.

ARCHIE C. C. LEE is Professor at Chung Chi College of the Chinese University of Hong Kong and author of many articles relating to interpretation, hermeneutics and contextual readings of the scriptures. He is currently involved in research projects on cross-cultural hermeneutics, and comparative scriptural studies in cultural contexts.

NOZOMU MIYAHIRA is currently Professor of Christian Theology and American Thought at Seinan Gakuin University, Fukuoka, Japan. His books written in Japanese include *Contemporary American Theological Thought: Ideas of Peace, Human Rights and Environment* (2004), *The Gospel according to Matthew: Translation and Commentary* (2006), *Gospel Essence: Five Stories Presented to You* (2004) and *Gospel Forum: Five Stories Presented to You* (2007).

ISRAEL SELVANAYAGAM, from the Church of South India, has taught at Tamilnadu Theological Seminary, Madurai, India, and at Wesley College, Bristol and the Queen's Foundation, Birmingham, UK. For nearly six years he was Principal of the United College of the Ascension, one of the Selly Oak Colleges in Birmingham. At present he is the Interfaith Consultant for the Methodist Church, based in Birmingham.

M. THOMAS THANGARAJ is the D. W. & Ruth Brooks Associate Professor of World Christianity at the Candler School of Theology, Emory University, Atlanta, Georgia, USA. After serving as a Minister in the Church of South India in the Tirunelveli area, Professor Thangaraj moved to teach at the Tamilnadu Theological Seminary, Madurai, India from 1971 to 1988, before joining Emory. He has published widely both in English and in Tamil, including *The Crucified Guru: An Experiment in Cross-Cultural Christology* (1994), *Relating to People of Other Religions: What Every Christian Needs to Know* (1997) and *The Common Task: A Theology of Christian Mission* (1999).

DAVID M. THOMPSON is Professor of Modern Church History in the University of Cambridge, and a Fellow and former President of Fitzwilliam College. Recent publications include: *Baptism, Church and Society in Modern Britain* (2005); contributions to volumes 8 and 9 of the *Cambridge History of Christianity* (2006); *Protestant Nonconformist Texts, volume 4: the Twentieth Century* (with J.H.Y. Briggs and J. Munsey Turner) (2006); and *Cambridge Theology in the Nineteenth Century: Enquiry, Controversy and Truth* (forthcoming).

JOHN A. TITALEY is Professor of Theology at the Graduate Program in Sociology of Religion in the Faculty of Theology, Satya Wacana Christian University in Salatiga, Indonesia. He was the chairperson of the Association of Theological Schools in Indonesia 1994–2004. In autumn 2006 he was a Visiting Professor at the Graduate Theological Union in Berkeley, California. Among his many writings are *Toward a Contextual Theology of Religion* and *Asian Models of Religious Diversity: The Uniqueness of Indonesian Religiosity*.

Preface and Acknowledgements

> Perhaps the most striking single feature of Christianity today is the fact that the church now looks more like that great multitude whom none can number, drawn from all tribes and kindreds, people and tongues, than ever before in its history. Its diversity and history lead to a great variety of starting points for its theology and reflects varied bodies of experience. The study of Christian history and theology will increasingly need to operate from the position where most Christians are, and that will increasingly be the lands and islands of Africa, Asia, Latin America and the Pacific.[1]

As Andrew Walls rightly points out above the rise of world Christianity has led to much greater diversity, and also generated interest in the history and theology of churches in non-western contexts. The purpose of this volume is to examine the emerging forms and themes of theologies in Asian Christianity, which have been shaped by the Christian communities in their interaction with the societies around them. The question this volume wishes to address is not how the churches in Asia have expanded in terms of numbers but how they have sustained their identity by developing their own theologies.

The focus of this volume is on the relation of these distinctive theologies to the specific historical contexts from which they have emerged. Considerable study has been done, both in English and vernacular languages, on the history of Christianity in different Asian countries. There are also a number of works on the theologies of particular countries in Asia. The particular appeal of this volume to contemporary readers is the way it relates theology to local socio-cultural, religious and political environments. The forms and themes of distinctive Asian Christianity are shown to be the outcome of dealing with various historical challenges.

---

[1] Andrew F. Walls, *The Cross-Cultural Process in Christian History: Studies in the Transmission and Appropriation of Faith* (Maryknoll, NY: Orbis Books, 2002), p. 47.

The volume is divided into two parts. The first part explains the emergence of Christian theologies in different countries of Asia: India, Indonesia, China, Japan and South Korea. Using an historical framework, contributors identify theological trends and responses to the problems Christianity faces and highlight major areas of debate. The second part deals with theological themes emerging out of Asian Christian experience: namely, religious pluralism, hermeneutics, Asian feminism, ecumenical and communal conflict, mission and evangelism, and subaltern theologizing. The authors discuss topics with special reference to particular regions or movements, and also interact with the main protagonists of these themes.

In examining the forms and themes emerging from Asian theologies, the contributors identify five questions for Asian theologies. First, whether a particular theology or way of Christian thinking is *distinctive* or *different* from others. Christian theologies in Asia are unique in the sense that they have arisen out of a particular context. However, the question is whether they are essentially different from 'traditional' theology, and in what sense they are making new ground. Beside the distinctiveness drawn from its unique environment, a theology may need to exhibit something qualitatively unique in its ideas and insights.

Second, whether a particular theology is *contextual*. In one sense every theology is contextual: it reflects a particular context. The question the contributors of the volume ask is whether a particular theology has a dynamic nature which will enable it to continue to be relevant to people in a context which is always changing. In what way does a given theology authentically arise from the particular context? And what is the nature of the interaction between the Christian text and the context? This does not mean disregarding rich insights from other religious texts, but Christian theology requires constant engagement with Christian scripture in an on-going process.

Third, whether a theology fulfils its *prophetic role*: in other words, not only should theology be contextual, arising from a given situation, but it should also provide tools and a framework for people to act. Does it change people and society? Does it challenge the social norms? Does it formulate any new thinking and ethic for both the Christian community and the wider society? Or does it go along with authorities and remain content with the *status quo* or even give moral justification for an unjust system? In time of crisis, prophetic voices both within and outside the church become instruments of God for transforming unjust systems.

Fourth, whether a theology is *ecumenical*. Here the meaning of ecumenical is in its wider sense – interacting with and sharing resources with communities other than one's own across a variety of boundaries.

Just because theology is contextual, that does not mean it should not be shared. It should make a contribution to other communities who may be experiencing similar struggles. Furthermore, the emphasis on being contextual is not an excuse to avoid the scrutiny of the tools of theological and historical method and criticism, which have been developed through the centuries. These need to be actively employed for the furtherance of theological thinking in Asia.

Fifth, whether a theology addresses the questions of *transcendence and mystery* people are asking. The emphasis of Asian theologies on either liberation from socio-political and economic injustice on the one hand or inculturation of Christian faith and practice on the other needs to be balanced by addressing Asian people's desire for the transcendental aspects of life. Questions of truth, spirit-worlds, sin, death and evil do not evaporate in modernity or post-modernity but revisit people either in their desperation or in their affluence. Asian theology, with its rich religious and cultural resources, can draw out a new appreciation of transcendence and mystery.

This volume is a product of the Christianity in Asia Project (CAP) at the Faculty of Divinity in the University of Cambridge. Three Directors have each contributed: Archie Lee initiated the idea of a publication, Namsoon Kang developed it and the present Editor has shaped it in its present form. I would like to express my gratitude to David Thompson for his leadership as the Director of the Centre for the Advanced Theological Studies (CARTS), and to David Ford for his sustaining support and encouragement as the Chair of the CARTS committee, and to Rosalind Paul, formerly Coordinator of CARTS. At York St John University, I wish to thank Dianne Willcocks, David Maughan-Brown, John Spindler, Pauline Kollontai and Richard Noake for their support and Esther MacIntosh for her efficient editing work. I also would like to acknowledge those who helped in various ways: Kirsteen Kim, Sue Yore, Richard Andrew, Joshua Kalapati, Peter Ng and Alan Suggate. Kate Brett and Elizabeth Davey of Cambridge University Press have provided much inspiration and advice for the book project.

The contributors to this volume discuss the distinctive characteristics of Christianity in Asia: its concepts, historical setting and its place in the religion and society of Asia. It is hoped that it will provide a prospect for conversation between Asian Christian theologians and those in other parts of the world, identifying some commonalities and diversities, and suggesting methodologies for further interaction.

Sebastian C. H. Kim, Editor

I

Formation of Christian theologies in Asia

CHAPTER I

Introduction: mapping Asian Christianity in the context of world Christianity

David M. Thompson

The time has long since gone when Asian Christianity could be regarded as simply a development of what happened in Europe. The twenty-first century is much more aware than perhaps the twentieth of the fact that Asian Christianity is either as old as or older than European Christianity. Quite apart from the fact that the Holy Land is part of Asia, there is now greater appreciation of the fact that Christianity spread east as rapidly as it did west, reaching India probably in the first century and China by the sixth or seventh. That is roughly contemporaneous with the second conversion of the British Isles (the first being before the withdrawal of the Romans from Britain). The distinctive context of Asia has been that Christianity has always existed alongside other major world faiths and religious traditions.

Nevertheless the legacy of western imperialism and its relationship to the missionary activities of European and North American churches has also been significant in shaping the current situation. This Introduction considers the significance of the difference between the way in which theology is tackled in the academic context as distinct from the church context, and reflects on the way in which theology has been differently perceived in different regions of the world at different times.

ACADEMIC AND ECCLESIASTICAL THEOLOGY

The underlying approach adopted here is essentially historical, rather than that of the systematic theologian.[1] A systematic theologian usually feels

---

[1] Because of my own limitations it is also confined to works translated into English, which is a significant disadvantage. There is an invaluable book edited by J. C. England and others, *Asian Christian Theologies: A Research Guide to Authors, Movements, Sources: vol. 1: Asia Region, South Asia, Austral Asia* (New York, 2002). Much use has been made of anthologies such as that produced by

drawn to presenting a picture which is universally true; indeed it is rather difficult within the discipline of systematic theology to find a way of acknowledging that the relative importance of different aspects of the truth may vary from time to time or place to place. By contrast a historian is accustomed to making relative statements. The very variety of different points of view, even when based on the same evidence, forces historians to acknowledge that their discipline is concerned with relative truths. This has not, of course, prevented some historians from time to time affirming that their view is the right one, or indeed the only right one; but generally speaking a historian is more at home in the world of relativities. Thus the variety of interpretations which has to be acknowledged in relation to different periods can very easily be extended to different places in the same period. It does not necessarily mean abandoning hope of reaching absolute truth in relation to certain matters; but it is a fact of life in the history of ideas that some things seem more important in some times and places than others, and the significance of this has to be acknowledged.

Such changes in relative importance may be illustrated by the difference between academic and ecclesiastical (or ecclesial) theology. There was a time when there was no difference. The medieval European universities had Faculties of Theology in which the teachers were approved by the Church; and what they taught was essentially what the Church taught. The change which came was a result first of the Reformation and then of the Enlightenment. In Protestant countries the direct control of the Church over the universities was weakened, and particularly in eighteenth-century Germany, where professors were employed by the state rather than the Church, a difference between academic and ecclesiastical theology gradually opened up.[2] This difference became most apparent as a result of the development of biblical criticism; and in the nineteenth century books were written by some scholars which horrified many churchmen. The classic example was David Strauss's *Life of Jesus*, written in 1835–6. Strauss lost his job at Tübingen because of this; having secured a position in Zürich in January 1839, he lost it almost immediately as a result of a cantonal referendum, but was able to establish that he was

the Programme for Theologies and Cultures in Asia: J. C. England and A. C. C. Lee (eds.), *Doing Theology with Asian Resources* (Auckland, 1993). There is a good short introduction to the situation in India and East Asia in chapters 3 and 4 of J. Parratt (ed.), *An Introduction to Third World Theologies* (Cambridge: Cambridge University Press, 2004).

[2] See T. A. Howard, *Protestant Theology and the Making of the Modern German University* (New York: Oxford University Press, 2006); W. Clark, *Academic Charisma and the Origins of the Research University* (Chicago: University of Chicago Press, 2006), chap. 7.

entitled to his salary for life; so he never taught again![3] But although Strauss is the most obvious example, there were other theologians whose work caused great anxiety to many in the churches, such as F. C. Baur or J. Wellhausen. This happened more rarely in England because many university professors hoped for and secured promotion to bishoprics. This had two consequences: their university careers were shorter than those of their German colleagues, and they were often more anxious to ensure that they retained a reputation for theological orthodoxy. J. B. Lightfoot and B. F. Westcott stand out as scholar bishops in that tradition, though each spent much longer in the university than some of their predecessors. In the twentieth century it became less common for scholars to become bishops, and university posts in theology were opened to scholars from all churches, though this happened more recently at Oxford and Cambridge than in other universities.

What is more important, however, is that the agenda of academic theology is now significantly different from that of the Churches. The doctrines of the Church, the sacraments, salvation and justification are much less important for academic theologians than they are for the Churches. By contrast academic theologians are more interested in the way in which the Bible should be understood, the way in which biblical insights relate to theology more generally, and the way in which theology relates to contemporary science and philosophy. When that extends to economics and social questions, there may be a new intersection between academics and church leaders; but this depends very much on the view that is taken, as issues relating to contraception, abortion and economic justice demonstrate. That difference, however, is still very much charac- teristic of the west – Europe and North America. Indeed in North America, because of the separation of church and state, theology is usually taught in divinity schools, which are separate from universities, rather than in faculties of divinity as in Europe; university departments in North America tend to be departments of religious studies. However, in other respects the difference of agenda between academic and ecclesiastical theology remains true in North America. Very often when people refer to a western-dominated theological agenda, they are referring to the agenda of western universities, and it helps to understand that relationship in any discussion of the responsibility of the churches. Furthermore the sense that others, whoever the others may be, are determining the agenda is not

[3] D. F. Strauss, *The Life of Jesus Critically Examined* (London: SCM, 1973), p. xxxvi; H. Harris, *David Friedrich Strauss and his Theology* (Cambridge: Cambridge University Press, 1973), pp. 58–65, 123–33.

unique to Asia, Africa or Latin America; sometimes in Britain it is felt that the theological agenda is determined by Germany, France or the USA.

The churches in the west have been largely content to accept the academic agenda, whilst reserving the right to discuss more specifically ecclesiastical concerns in their own way. The most significant exception to this are the Orthodox Churches, although Orthodox scholars with academic posts in western universities will usually work within the framework of the academic agenda. Moreover, the contribution of Orthodox theology and tradition has generally been welcomed as an important contribution to a broader understanding of theology, even though the methods of the interpretation of scripture in the Orthodox tradition perhaps raise more questions than have yet been answered. One important aspect of the western theological tradition that deserves a little more comment is precisely the issue of the way in which scripture is used. Within the Roman Catholic Church the teaching authority of the Church has generally remained decisive for Roman Catholic theologians.[4] Protestants, however, rejected that form of teaching authority for the Church, and instead turned to scripture. Although in the sixteenth-century context there was never any intention that scripture would be anything other than a corporate authority, in practice it proved extremely difficult to prevent more individual interpretations appearing, not least because of the right of private judgement that was affirmed in several churches of the Reformation. The consequence was that over time it became possible for individuals to appeal to scripture to support their particular theological viewpoints, regardless of the extent to which these were shared by the Church as a whole. When this tendency was reinforced by the suggestion in the nineteenth century that the text of the prophetic books of the Old Testament was generally older than that of the books of the Law or history, the idea that a prophetic appeal to the Word of the Lord was likely to count for more than anything that the Church might say proved almost irresistible. The significance of this development for particular styles of Protestant theology in the twentieth century can scarcely be under-estimated.

This point may be illustrated with a Latin American example. Gustavo Guttiérez, a Peruvian Roman Catholic priest working with the poor in Lima, achieved fame as a theologian by his development of 'liberation theology'. His book *A Theology of Liberation* (1971) was based on a paper

---

[4] Thus the valuable report of the Pontifical Biblical Commission is entitled *The Interpretation of the Bible in the Church* (Rome: Libreria Editrice Vaticana, 1993); cf. the constitution *Dei Verbum* of the Second Vatican Council, 1965.

originally given in Chimbote, Peru, in July 1968, entitled 'Notes on a Theology of Liberation', and given in a revised form to the Consultation on Theology and Development organized by the joint committee on Society, Development and Peace in Cartigny, Switzerland, in November 1969. The original paper was a few months before the epoch-making Latin American Bishops' Conference at Medellín, which described the new epoch in the continent as 'a time of zeal for full emancipation, of liberation from every form of servitude, of personal maturity and of collective integration'.[5] Guttiérez was reacting against the predominant view that economic development was the way forward for the poorer countries of the world by pointing out that there were fundamental injustices in the societies, which could not just be developed away. Instead a more dramatic break with the past was needed, and Guttiérez used the idea of liberation from slavery in the Old Testament as a dominating theme, or *leitmotiv*, in scripture, over against more traditional understandings of theology within the Church. In this way he sought to identify the Church with the situation in which many of the Latin American poor found themselves, and to offer a tangible demonstration of what it might mean to speak of God's preferential option for the poor. The Latin American bishops' conference was persuaded to follow this line, and initially the Vatican did not condemn it because it picked up on a sermon of Pope John XXIII.[6] Subsequently liberation theology attracted many followers in Asia and Africa as well as the West. Moreover, this became as much part of the Church's theological agenda as that of academic theologians. As such it may stand as an early example of the twentieth-century wish to read theology in the light of a particular perspective – the action-reflection model, rather than the deductive model. The 'base communities', which had already been initiated in Latin America, were attempts to create meeting places within larger parishes, where Christians would talk together about the implications of their theology, instead of simply listening to sermons.

CONTEXTUAL THEOLOGY

The example of liberation theology leads into the second area of discussion – the extent to which theology has different emphases according to

---

[5] Quoted in G. Guttiérez, *A Theology of Liberation*, Introduction to the revised edn (London: SCM, 2001), p. 5.

[6] 'In the face of the underdeveloped countries, the church is, and wants to be, the church of all and especially the church of the poor', John XXIII, Address of 11 September 1962: Guttiérez, *Theology of Liberation*, p. 17.

where Christians live. There was a particular relevance in the development
of liberation theology in Latin America. Virtually all the Latin American
countries were dominated by the Roman Catholic Church in the 1960s,
and many of them were political dictatorships. The theology of liberation
had inevitable political implications, which were immediately appreciated. Moreover the Roman Catholic Church had scarcely ever found itself
on the side of political revolution – Belgium in 1830 is the most obvious
exception. It had indeed been more common for Protestants to find
themselves backing political revolution, though the extent to which this
was so should not be exaggerated, notwithstanding the example of the
English Civil War. But the theological issue was not so much the question
of political revolution as such, as the question of whether and to what
extent the state should follow the moral teaching of the Gospel. From this
point of view the fact that theologies of the state were often based on the
example of the Old Testament monarchy was something of a weakness.
The New Testament contained various injunctions by the Apostle Paul
concerning respect for authority, teaching by Jesus which was often
somewhat obscure – the classic example is 'Render to Caesar what is
Caesar's and to God what is God's' (Matthew 22:21), where what is due to
each is not defined – and an apocalyptic picture in the Book of Revelation. The result of putting all this together was not so clear as, for
example, a simple appeal to Micah:

> He shall judge between many peoples,
> and shall arbitrate between strong nations far away;
> they shall beat their swords into ploughshares,
> and their spears into pruning-hooks;
> nation shall not lift up sword against nation,
> neither shall they learn war any more. (Micah 4:3)

At first theologians from Asia studied in Europe or North America –
this was true of a whole generation of Indians. The situation in East Asia
was rather different. Here the very point at which things were opening up
further west was when things closed down in the east. The Communist
revolution in China in 1949 put an end (albeit not immediately) to more
than a generation of hopes about the future for Christianity in East Asia.
Japan was still recovering from the Second World War. The Korean War
in 1950–3 disrupted the peninsula, though ultimately the outcome made
possible Christian growth in South Korea. Before the war the strength of
Christianity in Korea had been in the north. South Korea moved towards
democracy between 1987 and 1992. Indo-China was to be involved in war

until the United States withdrew from Vietnam in 1975. The Philippines had secured political independence, but were under a dictatorship until 1986, or 1992 (depending on whether the date of the first multi-party elections is regarded as crucial). Indonesia became the largest Muslim state in the world.

The story of a specifically contextual Asian theology is largely a Protestant one. This is not to minimize the significance of the Roman Catholic Church. But in the pontificate of Pius XII there was still a suspicion of anything which might be called modernism. After John XXIII and the Second Vatican Council the atmosphere eased, but the international character of the Church, and specifically of its theological education, meant that the opportunities for a truly contextual theology were more limited. Among the Protestant churches, however, the gathering pace of effective independence from western missionary domination created new opportunities for the development of indigenous theologies.

The pace was originally set by India. The Church of South India (1947) and later the United Churches of North India, Pakistan and Sri Lanka (1970) provided contexts for the development of an Indian theology. It is true that many of those who took the lead in these developments in fact received their theological education in the west. But the World Council of Churches was particularly supportive of such people, and also encouraged the formation of the Ecumenical Association of Third World Theologians in 1976.[7] Stanley Samartha was Director of the Karnataka Theological College, the United Theological College and Serampore College in India, before going to Geneva to be the first Director of the Dialogue Programme of the World Council of Churches. He subsequently returned to India to the South Asia Theological Research Institute in Bangalore. His book, *One Christ – Many Religions*,[8] suggested a revised Christology in the light of the contact between Christianity and other world religions; but it was far more than that. Out of ten chapters, the last five concerned the construction of a new Christology and its implications for mission; the first five considered the general issues for Christianity in a situation of religious pluralism and dialogue.

The lead in East Asian Christianity in the later twentieth century was taken by Korea. This was partly due to a long-standing tradition in Korea of sending missionaries outside the country, going back to the beginning

---

[7] See the brief account in the Introduction to K. C. Abraham, *Third World Theologies: Commonalities and Divergences* (Maryknoll, NY: Orbis Books, 1990), pp. xv–xvi.

[8] Maryknoll, NY: Orbis Books, 1991.

of the twentieth century. It was also related to the tangled situation following the Korean War and an increasingly ambiguous relationship with the USA as the main supplier of foreign missionaries. The Korean Churches had been divided as a result of the Japanese occupation, when ecumenism was discredited by association with the Kyodan – the United Church of Christ in Japan – which the Korean churches had been expected to join. Then the strong links between anti-communism and evangelicalism on the part of US missionaries in the 1950s and 1960s complicated the internal dynamics of the Korean churches.[9] One reaction to this situation was the development of minjung theology, which began as a simple telling of the stories of those who were suffering under the South Korean dictatorship.[10] It should be emphasized that this was not simply an imitation of what was happening elsewhere; it was rather an attempt to see how similar insights related to the rather different economic and political situation in Korea. This was also a theology with politically revolutionary implications.

The political relaxation in China made it possible to see what had been happening to the Chinese church while it was concealed from western eyes. The Church of Christ in China early in the twentieth century united most of the major Protestant churches on a federal model. Under communism in 1954 this was transformed into the Three-Self Patriotic Church (self-supporting, self-administering and self-propagating).[11] The insistence that the Church should not acknowledge any authority outside the Chinese state presented problems for the Roman Catholic Church, but not to the Three-Self Movement. Indeed the three selves could be traced back to the early missionary thinking of Henry Venn of the Church Missionary Society and Rufus Anderson of the Overseas Board for Foreign Missions in the nineteenth century.

One overwhelming reality, which the Christian Gospel had to address, was war and the consequent suffering. Asia suffered even more from war than Europe in the twentieth century. Troops were recruited from

---

[9] I have learned much about the Korean churches from my research student, K. S. Ahn, who is writing a dissertation on the development of the Presbyterian Church in Korea in the twentieth century.

[10] A classic source for this is D. Kwang-sun Suh, *The Korean Minjung in Christ*, 2nd edn (Hong Kong: Commission on Theological Concerns, 2002).

[11] P. L. Wickeri, *Seeking the Common Ground: Protestant Christianity, the Three-Self Movement, and China's United Front* (Maryknoll, NY: Orbis Books, 1988); P. Freston, *Evangelicals and Politics in Asia, Africa and Latin America* (Cambridge: Cambridge University Press, 2001), pp. 101–5; R. L. Whitehead (ed.), *No Longer Strangers: Selected Writings of K. H. Ting*, Maryknoll (NY: Orbis Books, 1989) pp. 9–10.

western imperial territories to fight in the First World War, but Asia was not a major theatre. Asian politics followed a different track with the consequences of inner turmoil in China after the fall of the Qing dynasty in China in 1912. A developing Japan took advantage of this in launching the Sino-Japanese War in 1937, after the occupation of Manchuria from 1931. Japan's political ambitions made it ready to take advantage of the British and French distraction after 1939 to attack western imperial territories, most memorably Singapore in 1942 following the attack on the US Navy in Pearl Harbour in 1941. Even after the final defeat of Japan with the first use of atomic weapons by the western allies in 1945, war persisted in Korea until 1953 and in Indo-China until the 1970s. The scale of casualties in these wars is only paralleled by those on the Russian front in the west.

The Japanese theologian Kazoh Kitamori published his book *Theology of the Pain of God* in 1946 and it was translated into English in 1965. Described as 'the first strictly theological Japanese book to be introduced in the English-speaking world',[12] it was written in the aftermath of Hiroshima. Although strongly influenced in certain respects by the categories of Lutheran systematic theology, it nevertheless also represented an engagement with Buddhist ideas, not least in the particular understanding of pain. Kitamori's approach was re-appraised by Kosuke Koyama in his *Water Buffalo Theology* (1974). He also engaged with Buddhism, in his case in Thailand, in order to discuss the possibilities of 'theological re-rooting' for those brought up in different cultural and religious *milieux*.[13] Koyama did so in order to affirm what he took to be Kitamori's main point, that what Christ achieved went beyond the categories of Christian theology alone. Is that religious pluralism or a new kind of Christian imperialism?

Politically and economically Asia shared some characteristics of Latin America and Africa, but was in other respects strikingly different. The most obvious common feature was poverty, which affected as much as eighty per cent of the population in some countries such as Bangladesh and the Philippines. When it is remembered that Asia has nearly sixty per cent of the world's population, both the relative and the absolute significance of poverty is clear. With the partial exception of Japan, even

---

[12] K. Kitamori, *Theology of the Pain of God* (London: SCM, 1966), p. 7.

[13] K. Koyama, *Water Buffalo Theology*, revised edn (Maryknoll, NY: Orbis Books, 1999), pp. 82–9. (Readers should be warned that in new on-line library cataloguing systems the title of the first edition is usually *Water-Buffalo Theology*, which does not necessarily appear if the hyphen is omitted.)

the economic success stories of Asia, such as South Korea and Singapore, have proved to be vulnerable to cyclical downturns. Asia also shared colonial and post-colonial experiences in the sense that even those countries that had never been politically part of western empires were dominated by the economic influence of the West. Thus another major reality was the poor. If Christianity was not good news for the poor, it would not be good news for anyone.

This was the context for both dalit theology in India and minjung theology in Korea. The term 'dalit' refers to those often previously referred to as 'untouchables', the lowest rank in the Indian caste system. The earliest western missionary efforts in India were usually directed at the upper castes, with relatively limited success. Christian evangelization among the Dalits took the form of mass conversions in various parts of India in the mid to late nineteenth century, and became really significant in the 'mass movements' in the 1920s and 1930s.[14] After independence the Indian government, and more particularly the state governments in certain states, supported the maintenance of caste distinctions either for reasons of principle or political expediency. From the same period, in part also due to political independence, there was an increasing emphasis on the experience of Dalits as most authentically representing those to whom Jesus brought good news.[15]

Minjung theology in Korea emerged in the 1960s and 1970s, with an agenda closely tied to the achievement of human rights, democracy and social and economic justice. It assimilated Marxist insights (an example of another western influence) and was also opposed to the alliance between Korea, Japan and the USA.[16] But it did not die when some of the political goals of democratization in Korea were achieved; if anything, it was emphasized as a more universal insight affecting not only Asia but the world. Thus Kim Yong Bock wrote, 'It is a central understanding of biblical wisdom that the life of victims, the minjung (the poor, oppressed, outcast and alienated, orphans and widows etc.) has pride of place in the sharing of the gospel. The life of the minjung has been the parable of the whole of cosmic life.'[17] From this he drew seven missiological affirmations, the common feature of which is an opposition to economic

---

[14] A brief account may be found in J. C. B. Webster, *The Dalit Christians: A History* (Delhi: ISPCK, 1992).

[15] There is a comprehensive collection of examples in V. Devasahayam (ed.), *Frontiers of Dalit Theology* (Delhi: ISPCK, 1997).

[16] Abraham, *Third World Theologies*, pp. 27–8.

[17] Kim Yong Bock, 'Sharing the Gospel among the Minjung in the 21st Century' in P. L. Wickeri, *The People of God among all God's Peoples: Frontiers in Christian Mission* (Hong Kong and London: CWM, 2000), p. 116.

globalization. It is significant that the Presbyterian Church of Korea, in its response to the World Council of Churches Faith and Order Commission's Statement on *Baptism, Eucharist and Ministry*, pointed out that 'the church has a mission not only to offer salvation to sinners (all humankind), but especially liberation to oppressed people'.[18] The Theology Committee of the National Council of Churches in Korea was even more trenchant:

The document [*Baptism, Eucharist and Ministry*] does not speak to the desperate realities of the third world, nor indicate the responsiveness of the first-world churches to the rest of the world. It seems that the document is mainly concerned with doctrinal differences, and therefore shows very little concern about the divided and suffering world to which the church is to minister... The third-world theology has risen as a movement of liberation for the poor and oppressed from their suffering in the unjust and oppressive structures. Spiritually and culturally, the movement of third-world theology was born out of the struggle for rediscovery of self-identity; self-identity which was crushed by the domineering Western religions and cultural influences. It should be pointed out that the document does not address these genuine, meaningful struggles of the theologians and the people of God in the third world.[19]

A third striking feature of the Asian context is the presence of other world faiths. Whereas in Africa and Latin America it may be claimed that the majority of people are Christian, in Asia Christians are the lowest proportion of the population in any continent. Only in the Philippines do Christians constitute a majority of the population; and only there and in Korea is there a significant Protestant presence.[20] Although Christianity has been present in Asia from the beginning of the Christian era and has a long history in India and China, it is the Christianity planted by western missionaries which has dominated in the twentieth century. Moreover in various ways other Asian world faiths such as Hinduism and Buddhism have undergone renewal as a result of being confronted with a missionary Christianity. Political independence for many former western colonies has also led to a change in the status of Christianity in many countries. Asian Christians have therefore sought to understand all world faiths as being in some way vehicles of God's self-revelation: in this respect they asked questions similar to those asked by western missionaries.[21] Almost inevitably this

---

[18] M. Thurian, *Churches respond to BEM*, ii (Geneva: WCC, 1986), p. 163.
[19] M. Thurian, *Churches respond to BEM*, vi (Geneva: WCC, 1988), p. 135. (It should be noted that by this time the National Council of Churches in Korea represented a minority of Korean Christians.)
[20] Freston, *Evangelicals and Politics*, p. 59.
[21] See, for example, the discussions at the World Missionary Conference at Jerusalem in 1928, which contrast interestingly with the emphasis ten years later at Tambaram.

has raised questions about Christology, for it is here that the most obvious stumbling blocks in the relations between Christianity and other faiths present themselves. Comparisons between Jesus and Krishna or Buddha seem to require abandonment of any Christian claim that God is uniquely revealed in Jesus Christ.[22] This in turn raises the question of whether Christianity was distorted as it was expressed in Hellenic culture, particularly in the doctrinal definitions between Nicaea (325) and Chalcedon (451). Such theological questions are not, of course, new; they were pressed in Europe during the eighteenth-century Enlightenment. But the thrust of the question is different in the context of other world faiths; and although it is presenting itself in the west as well at the present time, in East Asia it is inescapable. C. S. Song, for example, states categorically that 'Even the creeds of the early ecumenical councils have no absolutely binding power over members of the church in succeeding generations.'[23]

A fourth characteristic of Asia, which is shared to a different extent with Africa and Latin America, is the position of women. At the Conference of Third World Theologians in Oaxtepec, 1986, Sun Ai Park, an ordained woman minister from Korea, said:

Women in Asia have been made voiceless, with no identity of their own in male-dominated societies ... If one views women's domination not within the context of Western civilization but within the context of patriarchy, then the cultural structures of women's oppression can be generalized. But the domination of women is not done in only one manner. It is done in different combinations of economic, political, cultural, and religious categories. Therefore, Asian women's oppressions are characterized as double, triple or quadruple.[24]

In the quarter of a century since then Asian women have taken their part in presenting those issues in Christian theology. There was a Consultation on Asian Women's Theology on Christology at Singapore in 1987; and there are two essays in Sugirtharajah's *Asian Faces of Jesus*, one by Chung Hyun Kyung, who caused a stir by her address at the World Council of Churches Assembly at Canberra in 1991 and the other by Virginia Fabella from the Philippines. Both in different ways offer criticisms of more traditional Christologies.

Such issues raise once more the question of authority or, viewed from a different perspective, methodology in theology. The implications of this

---

[22] See, for example, the essays on these themes in R. S. Sugirtharajah (ed.), *Asian Faces of Jesus* (Maryknoll, NY: Orbis Books, 1993), pp. 9–61.

[23] C. S. Song, *Third-Eye Theology: Theology in Formation in Asian Settings* (Maryknoll, NY: Orbis Books, 1979), p. 12.

[24] Abraham, *Third World Theologies*, pp. 150–1.

may be well illustrated in relation to one issue concerning the understanding of scripture. Since the 1970s the historical–critical approach to scripture has been challenged by other ways of reading, particularly those based on literary critical approaches and socio-cultural readings. Indeed that historical–critical approach has even been characterized as a western attempt to take over the way in which scripture is to be understood.[25] Not surprisingly the socio-cultural readings have offered the opportunity to read scripture in the same way as the scriptures of other world faiths.

Kim Yong Bock has written an interesting essay on the way in which Korean Christians have read the Bible.[26] He noted that Nestorian Christianity may have entered Korea from China and that Roman Catholic Christianity certainly entered Korea from China in the seventeenth century. In each case the Christian message was conveyed in Chinese script. It was not until the first Korean Bible was translated with the assistance of John Ross and other missionaries in Manchuria in the 1880s that Christianity entered the Korean vernacular. (The new Research Guide to *Asian Christian Theologies* suggests that by the end of the eighteenth century a library of Christian writings had developed in Korea numbering almost 150 items in both original works and translations from the Chinese, but it may be that these remained the preserve of an elite group.)[27] The nineteenth-century vernacular Bible made an impact upon the people, the minjung, which was subversive of the Confucian social order of the leadership of Korean society. The first Korean Christian community, Sorae Church, was established in North Korea in 1885, independently of foreign missionaries. With the establishment of Japanese rule, the key text for Korean Christians became the Book of Exodus, with its message of liberation. One result was a series of conflicts between western missionaries, who wished to secure their missions against accusations of political subversion, and the Korean tradition. After the Second World War a similar set of conflicts developed as minjung theology in its modern sense began in the 1960s and 1970s under the influence of Kim Chan Guk and Ahn Byung Mu. The key insight of minjung theology was that it regarded the minjung as the subject of history: 'The historical eye of the minjung perceives the real gospel of liberation … It was not for the official churches to discern the message of the Gospel in a kairotic

---

[25] E. W. Conrad, 'How the Bible was Colonized' in P. L. Wickeri (ed.), *Scripture, Community, and Mission* (Hong Kong and London: CCA & CWM, 2002), pp. 94–107.

[26] Kim Yong Bock, 'The Bible among the Minjung of Korea: Kairotic Listening and Reading of the Bible' in Wickeri, *Scripture, Community, and Mission*, pp. 72–93.

[27] England, *Asian Christian Theologies*, pp. 59–63.

sense. The churches read the Bible doctrinally, religiously and politically to protect their established interests.'[28]

This may be contrasted with various essays written by Archie Lee on cross-textual hermeneutics. He has argued that 'the biblical paradigm of the Exodus story, which has been widely accepted by liberation theologians for understanding the liberation of people from injustice and oppression, needs to be seriously reconsidered'.[29] The implications of its ratification of the conquest of the Promised Land are much more difficult to accept today. He developed this in a second paper, in which he drew attention to the significance of the fact that the Book of Deuteronomy disrupts the flow of the Pentateuch from Numbers to Joshua. The canonical form of the text took shape in the Exile, when the possession of the land was 'not a present reality, but a promise yet to be realized'.[30] He went on to discuss the way in which other traditions are reflected elsewhere in the text; in other words, there is not one single view, and choices have to be made. This was developed in a third essay, entitled 'Polyphonic Voices in the Bible'.[31] Taking this polyphony as given, Lee used it to reinforce the argument he had advanced in other places that Christians should be ready to interpret their own scriptures in dialogue with the scriptures of other faiths. Another approach suggested by C. S. Song was that the politics of the resurrection should be the ultimate criterion of a 'liberation theology'.[32] Bishop Ting was even more critical: 'The poor are not the Messiahs of the world, as if it were only necessary to liberate the poor and they would then liberate the world ... We must not idealize or absolutize the poor ... We have had a taste of this during the ten years of the Cultural Revolution.'[33] Nevertheless Ting appreciated liberation theology in its own context, and like Song affirmed the liberating nature of the Gospel of the Resurrection.[34]

It is not surprising that this issue should emerge so clearly in an Asian religious context. But it is related to the kind of issue referred to at the beginning of this Introduction in relation to the controversies of the Reformation. Before then the way in which the Old Testament should be interpreted in a Christian perspective was clearly laid down by the

---

[28] *Ibid.*, pp. 82–3.
[29] Archie Chi Chung Lee, 'Plurality and Mission in the Bible' in *The People of God among all God's Peoples* (Hong Kong and London: CCA & CWM, 2000), p. 66.
[30] Archie Chi Chung Lee, 'Refiguring Religious Pluralism in the Bible' in P. L. Wickeri, J. K. Wickeri and D. M. A. Niles (eds.), *Plurality, Power and Mission* (London: CWM, 2000), p. 225.
[31] Archie Chi Chung Lee, 'Polyphonic Voices in the Bible' in P. L. Wickeri, *Scripture, Community, and Mission* (Hong Kong and London: CCA & CWM, 2002), pp. 182–97.
[32] Song, *Third-Eye Theology*, pp. 243–59.
[33] Whitehead, *No Longer Strangers*, p. 18.
[34] *Ibid.*, p. 50.

church. When scripture was made into an authority independent of the church, it became possible to interpret it in other ways. There are various political issues in the contemporary world, not least the conflict in the Holy Land, where the Christian view of any notion of a 'promised land' needs to be affirmed. But the Christian understanding of the Old Testament, as distinct from a Jewish, Muslim or purely academic understanding is a much more complex question today. It reintroduces the question of the relative authority of scripture and church. One of the risks of inter-scriptural comparison, however fascinating it can often be, is that it presumes that the way each religious tradition regards its scriptures is the same. That is far from self-evident.

What also emerges from this reflection is that those who refer primarily to scripture often do so because of a distrust of the church – the hermeneutics of suspicion. Byung Mu Ahn's essay 'Jesus and People', as a classic text of minjung theology, illustrates this perfectly. He treads a relatively familiar path in contrasting Paul's Christology unfavourably with the picture of the historical Jesus in the gospels – familiar, that is, in the sense that the early nineteenth-century German quest for the historical Jesus followed a similar road in seeking to prioritize the gospels over the epistles. Ahn also commented unfavourably on the twentieth-century western reaction to the quest, which emphasized the difficulty of getting behind the original *kerygma*. 'The Christology in this Kerygma has greatly served as an ideology to preserve the church, but at the cost of silencing Jesus.'[35] No church historian could suggest that the church has never pursued its own interests at the expense of the gospel. Nevertheless the Christian task is constantly to recall the church to the gospel, and the possibility of abandoning the church in order to pursue the gospel is a mirage. This emphasizes the importance of pursuing these questions ecumenically, wherever possible. It also means, ultimately, that there are limits to the extent to which the church can pursue one theology in one part of the world and a different theology in another.

PENTECOSTALISM

There is another side of these developments. Some years ago it was noted that as liberation theologians were preaching the option for the poor in

---

[35] Byung Mu Ahn, 'Jesus and People (Minjung)' in Sugirtharajah, *Asian Faces of Jesus*, p. 166; cf. Byung Mu Ahn, 'Jesus and the Minjung in the Gospel of Mark' in R.S. Sugirtharajah, *Voices from the Margin: Interpreting the Bible in the Third World*, 2nd edn (London: SPCK, 1995), pp. 85–104.

Latin America, the poor were opting for the Pentecostal churches. The same phenomenon is present in Asia as well. The Theology Committee of the National Council of Churches in Korea, in responding to *Baptism, Eucharist and Ministry*, noted that the common characteristic of the liturgical practices of the Protestant Churches in Korea was freedom from liturgical forms 'due to the influence of the Pentecostal movement'. This was another reason why they felt that *BEM* was of very little concern to most of the churches in Korea: to disregard that situation and to continue to discuss and implement the document was to ignore the third-world churches and impose 'the theological agenda of the first-world churches on the rest of the people of God in the world'.[36] But the influence of pentecostalism in Korea is very significant: the Yoido Full Gospel Pentecostal Church with a membership of 800,000 was the largest congregation in the world in 1996, having grown from an initial membership of five in 1958.[37]

It has sometimes been argued that pentecostalism essentially represents the expansion of North American influence, and that it is a religious manifestation of globalization. There is some truth in this view. However, there is also abundant evidence of the indigenization of pentecostal spirituality. Harvey Cox has even argued that in the Korean case the expansion of pentecostalism represents the development in Christian clothes of traditional shamanism.[38] This may or may not be a helpful analogy. It is important not to confuse what may happen in the first generation with the long-term results. For example, Pope Gregory I advised St Augustine, when he was engaged in the evangelization of England at the beginning of the seventh century, that it was permissible to use the sites of previous Anglo-Saxon pagan worship, provided that they were consecrated to God; and there is considerable evidence from the evangelization of northern Europe that traditional sites and occasionally rites were taken over and used for Christian worship. In Rome itself the Pantheon had been converted into a Christian church. This could be regarded as a sensible strategy to indigenize Christianity. It would be fanciful to argue that anyone in England or Rome today still associates the main centres of Christian worship with their pre-Christian past. But 1,500 or more years of Christian history have passed since the original changes.

---

[36] Thurian, *Churches respond to BEM*, vi, p. 135.
[37] H. Cox, *Fire from Heaven: The Rise of Pentecostal Spirituality and the Reshaping of Religion in the Twenty-First Century* (London: Cassell, 1996), p. 221.
[38] *Ibid.*, pp. 225–41.

The perception is not the same for those who are much closer to a pre-Christian past, and indeed may not have been so in Europe *circa* AD 800.

The real question, however, is how to relate such pentecostal manifestations of theology to the kind of theological agenda sketched so far. They cannot simply be ignored because an alternative theological emphasis is preferred: they are an inescapable part of the map. This is the more true for East Asia because it is clear that a strand within the Chinese Church, and probably the largest, has been firmly evangelical and almost pentecostal in emphasis for many years. Bishop Ting in China did not turn to a liberationist Christology, partly because of his own beliefs about Christ and also because the unity of the church in China could not be maintained on such a basis 'because of the strength of Christian fundamentalism among many ordinary believers'.[39] The nature and concerns of the house church movement in China are quite as important on the theological map as the Three-Self Patriotic Movement. Consequently it is misleading to suggest that authentic Asian theology represents a different range of theological options from that found in the West.

CONCLUSION

In what ways, therefore, does the map of Asian theology differ from that of the rest of the world? From one point of view it is reassuring to discover that the same range of theological options exists as in the west. There is a different balance, and a different set of priorities. Such priorities may not be more important than those in Europe; but there is no doubt that they are more important in Asia. On the other hand it is still necessary to pay attention to the theology, which is spoken, as it were, with the local accent. All theology is contextual, and the particular aspects of the Asian context which have been discussed are increasingly important further afield. The multi-religious setting of Asian theology, for example, is especially significant in the contemporary world, and has much to offer to the increasingly multi-religious context of contemporary Europe. Not for the first time, therefore, Europe will have something to learn from Asia.

A map is a tool for travellers. An old map has little interest, except for historians; indeed it can be positively misleading to have an old road atlas. So the mapping of theology is not an end in itself. It enables us to see where we are; it will also be a guide for the continuing journey. For the

---

[39] Whitehead, *No Longer Strangers*, p. 17.

one thing which is certain, from a historical point of view, is that there
will be more changes to come.

BIBLIOGRAPHY

Abraham, K. C., *Third World Theologies: Commonalities and Divergences*, Maryknoll,
    NY: Orbis Books, 1990.
Ahn, Byung Mu, 'Jesus and People (Minjung)' in R. S. Sugirtharajah (ed.), *Asian
    Faces of Jesus*, Maryknoll, NY: Orbis Books, 1993.
    'Jesus and the Minjung in the Gospel of Mark' in R. S. Sugirtharajah (ed.), *Voices
    from the Margin: Interpreting the Bible in the Third World*, 2nd edn., London:
    SPCK, 1995, pp. 85–104.
Clark, W., *Academic Charisma and the Origins of the Research University*, Chicago:
    University of Chicago Press, 2006.
Conrad, E. W., 'How the Bible was Colonized' in P. L. Wickeri (ed.), *Scripture,
    Community, and Mission*, Hong Kong and London: CCA & CWM, 2002,
    pp. 94–107.
Cox, H., *Fire from Heaven: The Rise of Pentecostal Spirituality and the Reshaping of
    Religion in the Twenty-First Century*, London: Cassell, 1996.
Devasahayam, V. (ed.), *Frontiers of Dalit Theology*, Delhi: ISPCK, 1997.
England, J. C. and Lee, A. C. C. (eds.), *Doing Theology with Asian Resources*,
    Auckland: Pace Publishing for the Programme for Theology and Cultures
    in Asia, 1993.
    (ed.), *Asian Christian Theologies: A Research Guide to Authors, Movements,
    Sources: vol 1: Asia Region, South Asia, Austral Asia*, Maryknoll, NY: Orbis
    Books, 2002.
Freston, P., *Evangelicals and Politics in Asia, Africa and Latin America*, Cambridge:
    Cambridge University Press, 2001.
Guttiérez, G., *A Theology of Liberation*, revised edn., London: SCM, 2001.
Harris, H., *David Friedrich Strauss and his Theology*, Cambridge: Cambridge
    University Press, 1973.
Howard, T. A., *Protestant Theology and the Making of the Modern German
    University*, New York: Oxford University Press, 2006.
Kim, Yong Bock, 'Sharing the Gospel among the Minjung in the 21st Century' in
    P. L. Wickeri, *The People of God among all God's Peoples: Frontiers in
    Christian Mission*, Hong Kong and London: CCA & CWM, 2000, p. 116.
    'The Bible among the Minjung of Korea: Kairotic Listening and Reading of
    the Bible' in P. L. Wickeri (ed.), *Scripture, Community, and Mission*, Hong
    Kong and London: CCA & CWM, 2002, pp. 72–93.
Kitamori, K., *Theology of the Pain of God*, London: SCM, 1966.
Koyama, K., *Water Buffalo Theology*, revised edn., Maryknoll, NY: Orbis Books,
    1999.
Lee, Archie Chi Chung, 'Plurality and Mission in the Bible' in P. L. Wickeri
    (ed.), *The People of God among all God's Peoples*, Hong Kong and London:
    CCA & CWM, 2000, pp. 57–66.

'Polyphonic Voices in the Bible' in P. L. Wickeri (ed.), *Scripture, Community and Mission*, Hong Kong and London: CCA & CWM, 2002, pp. 182–97.

'Refiguring Religious Pluralism in the Bible' in P. L. Wickeri, J. K. Wickeri and D. M. A. Niles (eds.), *Plurality, Power and Mission*, London: CWM: 2000, pp. 225–37.

Parratt, J. (ed.), *An Introduction to Third World Theologies*, Cambridge: Cambridge University Press, 2004.

Pope Paul VI, Dogmatic Constitution on Divine Revelation, *Dei Verbum*, Second Vatican Council, Rome: Vatican Observatory Publications, 1965.

Pontifical Biblical Commission, *The Interpretation of the Bible in the Church*, Rome: Libreria Editrice Vaticana, 1993.

Song, C. S., *Third-Eye Theology: Theology in Formation in Asian Settings*, Maryknoll, NY: Orbis Books, 1979.

Strauss, D. F., *The Life of Jesus Critically Examined*, London: SCM, 1973.

Sugirtharajah, R. S. (ed.), *Asian Faces of Jesus*, Maryknoll, NY: Orbis Books, 1993.

Suh, D. Kwang-sun, *The Korean Minjung in Christ*, 2nd edn, Hong Kong: Commission on Theological Concerns, 2002.

Thurian, M., *Churches respond to BEM*, vol. 2, Geneva: WCC, 1986.

Webster, J. C. B., *The Dalit Christians: A History*, Delhi: ISPCK, 1992.

Whitehead, R. L. (ed.), *No Longer Strangers: Selected Writings of K. H. Ting*, Maryknoll, NY: Orbis Books, 1989.

Wickeri, P. L., *Seeking the Common Ground: Protestant Christianity, the Three-Self Movement, and China's United Front*, Maryknoll, NY: Orbis Books, 1988.

CHAPTER 2

The Mystery of God in and through Hinduism

Jacob Kavunkal

INTRODUCTION

The church, the community of the disciples of Jesus Christ, is continuity in discontinuity. It is the continuation of the mission initiated by Jesus Christ, but a discontinuity in so far as this mission implies the fulfilment of every culture, as Jesus came to fulfil and not to destroy. The history of the Indian church, heir to a 'tradition that sought God with a relentless search', is a manifestation of the church's hot and cold relationship to the religious and cultural traditions of India. Whereas the earliest community, the St Thomas Christians, considered each religion salvific to the followers of the religion, the age of Inquisition would tolerate nothing of it.

Today Christians in India along with the rest of the Asian Christians are becoming increasingly aware of the Asian roots of Christianity. Though they are largely compromised to a Christianity that has come to Asia in its western form, there is increasing talk of the need to rediscover the Asianness of the gospel teachings and thought patterns.

PART I HISTORICAL CONTEXT

A context of pluralism

Traditional Asian thought, while sharing western abstract thinking, is very much context-dominated. The abstraction is not free from the context in which it is made, the reality of the experience. As the Japanese thinker Hajime Nakamura writes:

Europeans generally think of the abstract notion of an abstract noun as constructed solely by means of the universal meaning which is extracted from daily experience, so that they represent it in the singular form; on the contrary the Indians think of the abstract notion as what is included within experienced facts so fused with them that the essential principle is often represented in plural form.[1]

Traditional Indian openness to pluralism is ingrained in its very understanding of the Ultimate Mystery. In contrast to the Christian understanding of God as uniquely revealed to the biblical tradition and thus considered as an exclusive privilege to be this God's only people, the Indian seers present the Ultimate Reality as an inexhaustible ocean into which many rivers flow or as an immense mountain to which many roads lead. The rivers and roads are compared to different religions, none of which can claim the monopoly of the Reality. This is not a question of syncretism, or passive relativity, as it is generally understood. The focus is not on religions, as though they are all the same, but on the inexhaustibility of the Reality that no religion can exhaustively explain. Hence we have the acceptance of the pluralism of religions. As to themselves, the Hindus consider their religion as the *Sanatan Dharm* (eternal religion not traceable to any founder). They, thus, do not entertain syncretism. However, they were open to other religions and hence they welcomed them as they came to India either to propagate themselves, like Christianity, or to flee from persecution, like Zoroastrianism, or those who came as traders or conquerors like the followers of Islam.

Along with the understanding of the Mystery goes also the Asian epistemology that works not so much on the principle of contradiction as on the principle of relationship. Whereas the principle of contradiction advocates separation and isolation, the principle of relationship places one in the web of relationship with others as the mark of meaning. The principle of contradiction emphasizes that a thing has to be what it is. It cannot be at the same time A and non-A. The meaning of A is derived from the fact of its being in opposition to others. Hence there is room for uniqueness, in so far as what one is, the other is not. The Christian understanding of God and revelation is considered to be unique in so far as others do not have that revelation and that understanding of God. Christian identity is defined in terms of negation to others concerning what Christianity alone is. In contrast with this the Asian epistemology understands the meaning of a thing by relating it with others. Meaning is

[1] Hajime Nakamura, *Ways of Thinking of Eastern Peoples: India-China-Tibet-Japan* (Delhi: Motilal Banarsidass Publishers, 1991), p. 46, cited by F. Wilfred, *From the Dusty Soil* (Madras: University of Madras, 1995), p. 23.

derived from the relationship, by reaching out and identifying with others. In this sense being and non-being are the characteristics of the Ultimate Reality. *Sat* (being) and *asat* (non-being) are the qualities of the unknowable Brahman. Reality cannot be conceived in terms of either-or but of both-and.

Due to this fact, a religious person cannot be indifferent to the followers of other religions, and far less by negating their religious value. What one has experienced is touching the person in that person's totality at the deepest roots. It is something specific and cannot be traded with others. Thus, the Asian religious traditions are open to religious pluralism with an attitude of acceptance of all religions. Commitment to one's faith implies also respect for others leading to interrelationship.

The Mystery of God in Hinduism

The earliest Vedas present the Ultimate Mystery as one Power seen with different names and forms by humans (*Ekam sat, vipra bahuda vadanti,* Rig Veda 1.164.46). The whole universe is the manifestation of the same Power at the physical, psychological and spiritual level. However, the material phenomena began to be identified in isolation, concentrating on the qualitative aspects of matter and identified as the reality. This is due to ignorance (*avidya*). The basic Power is presented through the symbol of fire, which is physical in so far as it is the energy that works through the universe, and yet psychological, the fire of life, and it is the manifestation of the Supreme and thus spiritual as well.

This Supreme Spirit is Brahman, that which holds the universe together. Brahman manifests through the whole universe. It is that which grows, wells up, swells. It is the word uttered in the sacrifice, expressing the meaning of the sacrifice. The seers of the Upanishads, the last part of the Vedas, which are actually esoteric teachings on the Vedas, in their meditation saw how Brahman, the Power of the universe, was actually the Power within each person. Brahman is consciousness. Brahman is *atman* (the individual self). Eventually the whole universe is conceptualized as a person, *Purusha*, the Supreme Person who fills the whole creation.

The idea of the Cosmic Man (*Purusha*) begins in the renowned *Purushasukta* in the Rig Veda. The passage describes the Cosmic Man in whom the whole world is to be found. 'This purusha is all that has been, and all that will be, the Lord of immortality' (RV 10.90). The sacrifice of this Cosmic Purusha led to the creation of the world (RV 10.90).

Later, the Brihadaranyaka Upanishad speaks of existence of the Atman in the form of the Purusha (1.4.1) and the Katha Upanishad presents Purusha as the summit of all creation (3.11). He is the Cosmic Lord in whom all become immortal (Svetasvatara Up. 3.7). He is the Lord of Lords, God of Gods, the Lord of the world, the adorable (Svet. 6.7).

The Bhagavad Gita presents the Cosmic Purusha as the origin of all, the guardian of the ever-lasting law (*Sanatan Dharma*), the immortal person (BG 11.18–19). Hinduism stresses the underlying unity of all existence. Equally, there is the awareness of the presence of the divine power in all things, the multiplicity. They are only manifestations of the One Reality, the Formless One. They are the 'names and forms' of the One Reality, the One without a second. Brahman is the source and end of all existence. 'That from which beings are born; that by which when born they live; that into which when dying they enter; that you shall desire to know. That is Brahman' (Taittiriya Up. 3.1).

The formless (*a-rupa*) Brahman can be recognized and worshipped in every kind of form (*sarva rupa*). He is the un-name-able and the possessor of every name. There is nothing that cannot manifest God to the soul which is open to him in deep awareness of itself. Everything is a sign of God, his *linga* (sign).[2] A *jnani* realizes how any approach to God ends up in a sort of 'alas!' in so far as humans know God only when they realize that they know nothing about God.

> When you think I know well –
> Truly it is but little that you know . . .
> He who knows him not, knows him;
> He who understands him, has not understood . . .
> It is through an awakening that he is found . . .
> As when the lightning flashes . . . the eye blinks . . .
>
> (Kena Up. 2.1–4; 4.4)

The knowledge of God implies that one gives up everything, including one's self; otherwise one remains at the stage of talking about God, a theologian, a *brahmavadin*. A knower of God is a contemplative, a seer, a *brahmavid*. For such a person there is no more I and Thou, setting oneself apart from God or others. 'For he who knows the supreme Brahman truly himself has become Brahman' (Mundaka Up. 3.2.9).

---

[2] Swami Abhishiktananda, *Saccidananda: A Christian Approach to Advaitic Experience* (Delhi: ISPCK, 1974), p. 5.

This awareness comes to one only when one enters into the innermost being of oneself, the cave of one's heart, in contemplation.

> In this city of Brahman (the heart of man)
> There is an abode, within it a small lotus flower;
> Inside, a little space;
> What there is within,
> It is that one must seek,
> That one must desire to know!
>
> (Chandogya Up. 8.1)

The identification of the Ultimate Reality (Brahman) and the individual self (*atman*) is brought out by the Upanishads through certain short formulas known as *mahavakhyas* (great utterances). The three most important *mahavakhyas* are: 1. *ayam atma Brahma* (atman is Brahman) (Mandukya Up. 2); 2. *aham Brahmasmi* (I am Brahman) (Bri. 1.4.10); and 3. *Tatvam asi* (That thou art) (Chan. 6.8.6). Through these utterances the Upanishads summarize the experience of the identification of the individual self and the Brahman, the one without the second (*a-dvaita*). It can be experienced only by those who have reached the experience of that stage of existence.

The Upanishads describe the Absolute in three-fold images; that is, in terms of pure existence (*sat*) (Katha Up. 6.12), consciousness (*cit*) (Mandukya Up. 2.2.11) and bliss (*ananda*) (Taittiriya Up. 2.1). In the compound form it becomes *Saccidananda.* The awareness of God is to be had not by discussions but rather by plunging deeper and deeper *within*, as Abishiktananda would say,[3] so that one is led to discover the mystery hidden in the depths of one's being, 'set in the cavern (of the heart), beyond the firmament, that splendour into which the saints pass' (Kaivalya Up. 1.3).

One comes to the true awareness by going beyond all that is known and all that is not known, beyond all becoming and non-becoming (Isa Up. 10.14), beyond all words, all thoughts, all distinctions, all qualifications (Mandukya Up. 7). Then one will have conquered fear, old age and death itself in order to become *Atmavid*, a knower of the Self (Chandogya Up. 7.1). Abhishiktananda writes:

It would seem as if India, moved by the Spirit, invites the Christian to seek the mystery of God, Creator and Saviour, no longer outside or alongside himself, but in the profoundest depths of his own heart.[4]

---

[3] *Ibid.*, p. 11.   [4] *Ibid.*, p. 13.

PART 2 THE CATHOLIC RESPONSE

Intellectual approaches to the Mystery

Roberto de Nobili (1577–1656)

In the following pages we shall present the description of the Mystery of God by some of the mystical theologians whose writings have inspired the emergence of an Indian Catholic Theology. We begin with a brief reference to Roberto de Nobili, the Italian Jesuit, who could rightly be described as the trail-blazer of an Indian theology.

De Nobili, the first one to take the road to the contemplative experience of the Mystery, reached South India in 1605. He realized the role of the Brahmins in making Christian inroads into Indian society. The Brahmins were prejudiced against Christianity as a religion of the low castes. Hence at a time when other religions were 'anathema' (condemned) in the Christian world view, de Nobili learned Hinduism in Sanskrit and attempted to meet the Hindu world in its own religious sources. 'He sought for a point of insertion of the Gospel message in the world of Hinduism by making the Gospel intelligible to the Indian mind',[5] comments Wilfred.

Through his efforts to present the Christian gospel in the language and thought patterns of the Brahmins, he evolved a Christian theological vocabulary and thus laid the foundation for today's inculturation. He was convinced that the life-style of a sannyasi was the best way to make Christianity acceptable to people of the upper castes and to implant the church into Indian soil. According to the Indian church-historian Joseph Thekkedath, he evolved a theological structure for communicating the Christian faith and coined a terminology for Christian theology in the Indian context.[6]

De Nobili's attempts, however admirable they were, were embroiled in the inter-congregational rivalries spinning off accusations and counter-accusations, leading to the eventual banning of all experiments with local cultures by a papal bull in 1754. This explains the absence of any Catholic initiative to produce a local theology in any part of the colonial world.

---

[5] F. Wilfred, *Beyond Settled Foundations: The Journey of Indian Theology* (Madras: University of Madras, 1993), pp. 15–16.

[6] J. Thekkedath, *History of Christianity in India, vol. II* (Bangalore: Theological Publications of India, 1982), p. 73, cited by W. Teasdale, *Toward a Christian Vedanta* (Bangalore: Asian Trading Corporation, 1987), p. 27.

Brahmabandhab Upadhyay (1861–1907): a Hindu–Catholic
Interestingly, the seminal ideas for an Indian Christian theology in modern times were sown by a group of reform-minded Hindu scholars, foremost among whom were Raja Ram Mohan Roy (1774–1833) and Keshabcandra Sen (1838–84) of Bengal. These thinkers had a profound impact on a young Brahmin, Bhabanicaran Bandyopadhyay, later assuming the name Brahmabandhab (Theophilus = friend of God) Upadhyay, at the time of his baptism in 1891. Upadhyay, who 'made a significant contribution to the shaping of the new India', was described by Rabindranath Tagore, his contemporary, as 'a Roman Catholic ascetic yet a Vedantin'.[7]

Upadhyay's orthodox Hindu tradition as a Brahmin and his unflinching nationalism oriented him to move towards giving shape to a 'Hindu–Catholic' faith, constructed on the Advaitic philosophical theology and an idealized understanding of the caste system. He was convinced that becoming a Catholic did not imply adopting a foreign life-style. Rather, he made it known how he was a Catholic by faith without ceasing to be a Hindu by culture.[8] He wanted to articulate his faith in such a way that it could be receptive to Hindus so that he could bring educated India to Christ. Hence he set out to indigenize the Catholic faith by synthesizing east and west in a new spirituality. To this end he turned to the Advaita system of Shankara, the eighth-century philosopher–theologian. Advaita, both as the theory of the Ultimate advocated by the Upanishads and as the philosophical and theological system developed by Shankara, was considered as the core of religious Hinduism.

He was convinced that Vedanta could serve as a source of theism in conformity with Christianity. Following the Thomistic distinction of nature and grace, Upadhyay took Vedanta as the nature on which the divine revelation, Christianity, is to be constructed. He writes:

It is on account of the close connection between the natural and the supernatural that we have taken to ourselves the task of expounding the Hindu scripture systematically and of fishing out the theistic truths from the deluge of pantheism, idolatry and anthropomorphism and thus glorify him who enlightens every man who comes into the world.[9]

Keeping with the distinction between the natural and the supernatural, he upholds the preparatory role of Hinduism which is to be fulfilled in

---

[7] J. J. Lipner, *Bhahmabandhab Upadhyay* (Delhi: Oxford University Press, 1999), p. xv.
[8] M. M. Thomas, *The Acknowledged Christ of the Indian Renaissance* (London: SCM Press, 1969), p. 107.
[9] Bhahmabandhab Upadhyay, 'Christianity in India', *The Tablet* 69 (1903), p. 8, cited in S. Sumithra, *Christian Theologies From an Indian Perspective* (Bangalore: Theological Book Trust, 1995), p. 70.

Christianity. The task of philosophy is to support, defend, clarify, expound and develop revelation and show how it is relevant for life. In the west Aristotelian philosophy served this purpose at the hand of Thomas Aquinas. However, that system is alien to the Indian mind and hence must be replaced by Vedanta, Upadhaya argued, 'because the Hindu mind is synthetic and speculative, and not analytic and practical'.[10] Vedanta must be made to 'hew wood and draw water for the Catholic Church', he believed. In the process, as Lipner rightly points out, he is not developing an indigenized Catholic faith by implanting Christian concepts into Vedanta soil, but only replacing Thomism with Vedanta.[11]

Making use of the Upanishadic understanding that described the Absolute in terms of the *sat, cit* and *ananda,* Upadhyay held that the essence of the divine being that was understood by neo-Thomistic reasoning could be expressed as *sat, cit* and *ananda* of classical Vedanta.[12] The Supreme Being, *parabrahman*, is essentially *sat*; that is, whose nature is to exist in and for itself. It is the first cause of all. It is self-sustaining. Thus, the *parabrahman* of the Vedanta and the God of the neo-Thomistic philosopher is one, infinite and eternal. It is also *cit*; that is, consciousness in the form of self-awareness, as self-productive. Hence, it alludes to the procession or generation of the Son from the Father. Thus, the Upanishads prefigure the Christian revelation.

Thus, according to Upadhyay, Vedanta provides to India the natural basis to receive the supernatural Christian truth, which is not to be identified with the European garb. The European garb of Christian truths makes it unintelligible to the Hindus. Hence, the Vedantic tradition would serve as the vehicle to present Christian truth, the truth regarding the Trinitarian nature of God, to India.

Upadhyay described Brahman, the Supreme Being, as pure Being, pure act and thus intrinsically self-contained and unrelated. Using the structure and terminology of Shankara, Upadhyay shows how Shankara can serve as the metaphysical foundation for a Christian understanding of the divine nature and its relation to the world.

God, in God's supernatural, intrinsic aspect, is separate from creation. Once we realize this distinction with all its implications, humans can live an appropriate natural existence with the liturgical practices and beliefs derived from Christian revelation. Shankara, according to Upadhyay, was granted some form of divine dispensation which enables Advaita and his commentary freedom from subtle errors.[13] From the transcendental standpoint, the

[10] Lipner, *Bhahmabandhab Upadhyay*, p. 187. [11] *Ibid.*, p. 188. [12] *Ibid.*, p. 191. [13] *Ibid.*, p. 268.

Supreme Being is *nirguna* (not impersonal, but attributeless), whereas from the perspective of creation, the Supreme Being is *saguna,* having attributes. Further, Upadhyay insists, Shankara has not held that Brahman is unknowable; rather he is knowable as bliss, intelligence and so on.[14]

Commenting on creation and the principle of *Maya,* in the Advaita understanding, Upadhyay writes:

Shankara teaches that the individual soul is different from the highest Self (Para Atman) as well as non-different from it. If *abheda* means '*absolute* identity' as M. Thibaujt supposes, then the individual soul can never be said to be distinct from the Supreme Being in the face of their declared non-difference.[15]

According to Upadhyay, Shankara means that the individual soul is a reflection (*adhyasa*) of Brahman and thus creation is a sort of communication by the Supreme Being, participating in his being. This communicating and this participating is a mysterious activity. It is similar to the sun's reflection in different water-bodies, which have a type of dependence on the sun, without affecting it in any way. This communication is called *Maya. Maya* affects the communicated things, but not Brahman. Thus, the individual soul is different from Brahman as its reflection, as a result of the mysterious communication of Brahman. It is not-different from Brahman in as much as Brahman is the substratum of the individual soul. *Maya,* thus, is not illusion, but the principle of creation. It is neither real nor unreal.

Maya can be an occasion for sin, in so far as it can lead to distortion of nature and reality, bestowing on the world a reality that it does not deserve.[16] Further, *Maya* expresses the Christian understanding of creation in the following aspects: (a) that God does not necessarily create; (b) that created things come into existence from prior non-existence; and (c) that the infinite perfections are contained in the finite in a pre-eminent way.

Christ through Vedanta

The legacy, bequeathed by Brahmabandhab Upadhyay, of developing an Indian theology through the mould of Advaita died out with his death in 1907 (aged 46), due to the high-handedness of the then papal delegate. Interest among the later generation begins with three Jesuit scholars, G. Dandoy, J. Bayart and P. Johanns. They were encouraged by Upadhyay's disciple, Animananda, to interpret Christianity, especially the understanding of Jesus Christ, through the philosophical tradition of India.

---

[14] *Ibid.* [15] *Ibid.* [16] *Ibid.*, p. 270.

The main argument of the trio is that the Indian philosophical tradition is the natural base for Christianity in India. The Vedantic tradition
is the preparation that finds its fulfilment in Jesus Christ. Johanns argues
contentiously that there is nothing that St Thomas writes that is not
somehow anticipated in Advaita.[17] The Vedantic systems, thus, pave the
way for a true Christian theology.

Mystical approaches to the Mystery

Thus far we have concentrated on the intellectual methodology of the
Indian tradition, represented by Advaita. We turn now to the insight that
a genuine encounter of Christianity with the soul of India can take place
only through India's mystical tradition.

Abbé Jules Monchanin (1895–1957): the land of the Trinity

Abbé Monchanin, belonging to a French religious missionary congregation,
reached India in 1939, with the mandate, as he acknowledged, given to him
by his theologian friend, Henri de Lubac, 'to rethink everything in the light
of theology and to rethink theology through mysticism'.[18] This inspired
Monchanin to launch a sannyasic-monastic movement in India in 1950,
founding, with another French missionary, Dom Henri Le Saux, the
renowned Saccidananda Ashram on the banks of the holy river Kavery.

Although, following Upadhyay, he named the ashram as Saccidananda,
the name for Trinity, he was careful not to identify the Advaita notion of
the Absolute with the Christian understanding of the Trinity. In a lecture
in 1956 he states:

Christian mysticism is Trinitarian or it is nothing. Hindu thought, so deeply
focused on the Oneness of the One, on the *kevalin* in his *kevalatva*, cannot be
sublimated into Trinitarian thought without a crucifying dark night of the soul.
It has to undergo a noetic metamorphosis, a passion of the spirit.[19]

Yet, he believed that at the depth of the mystical experience the two could
meet and he worked for the reconciliation of the two traditions.

His contemplative theology and his life focused on the Trinity. He
writes: 'It is because of the mystery of the Trinity – Alpha and Omega –
that I am a Christian.'[20] The Saccidananda Ashram was the expression
of Monchanin's relentless search for the Absolute. He believed that

---

[17] Wilfred, *Beyond Settled Foundations*, p. 40.   [18] Teasdale, *Toward a Christian Vedanta*, p. 29.
[19] *Ibid.*, p. 31.   [20] *Ibid.*

Christianity could strike roots in India only if it met the innermost soul of India in the mystery of interiority, mysticism and contemplation.

The object of the contemplation where both Christianity and Hinduism can meet is the mystery of God as Trinity. He proceeds from the events of the incarnation, death and resurrection, and concentrates on the Triune God, the fulfilment of the Hindu experience of God as Saccidananda.[21] Christian faith, on the other hand, must rethink the understanding of person and creation in line with the Hindu experience of Saccidananda. Trinity, as opposed to the individualism suggested by person, is a being for the other. A sannyasi should transcend concepts and concentrate on God the Father as *Sat*, on the Son as *Cit* and on the Holy Spirit as *Ananda*. Such a vision leads him to qualify India as 'the Land of the Trinity'.

Abhishiktananda (1910–73): meeting the Mystery at the cave of the heart
Dom Henri Le Saux, a French Benedictine, came to India in 1948, led by the desire to integrate the Indian contemplative tradition into the Christian monastic ideal as a meeting point of Christianity and the eastern religions. For this he joined hands with Abbé Monchanin in founding the Saccidananda Ashram and adopted the much-researched name Abhishiktananda (joy in the anointed one; that is, Jesus Christ). He was of the view that the western intellectual formulations of Christianity could not adequately express the spiritual reality of the Christian faith; for this we have to turn to the Upanishads which offer experience based on the spirituality of wholeness.

Abhishiktananda, convinced as he was that for a meaningful dialogue with India the church has to enter into its mystical traditions, develops his theology based on this mystical dimension. He became the first Catholic priest to sit at the feet of Hindu Gurus when he made himself a disciple of Sri Ramana Maharsi and Swami Gnanananda, who introduced him to the Hindu contemplative tradition.[22] At their feet he learnt what it means to enter into the cave of one's heart.

He holds that the great primitive Upanishads, like the Chandogya and the Brihadaranyaka, are incomparable witnesses to the awakening of the soul to the Mystery of being and of the self, and these earliest formulations of that experience have never been surpassed.[23] Hence, he starts from the

---

[21] Wilfred, *Beyond Settled Foundations*, p. 50.
[22] Swami Abhishiktananda, *Guru and Disciple* (London: SPCK, 1974), p. 87.
[23] Swami Abhishiktananda, *Hindu-Christian Meeting Point* (Bangalore: CISRS, 1969), p. 51.

Upanishadic relationship of the Atman and Brahman, which for him ensures a solid foundation for the Christian encounter with traditional Indian thought. The Christian turns to Vedanta, according to Abhishiktananda, as an encounter between the Word of God communicated by means of speech and thought on the one hand, and on the other, as an inner experience springing from those levels of the Spirit that transcend words and concepts.[24] Hence it is only in the highest experience of the Spirit that the Christian can come to terms with and crown the Vedantic experience. While in the Bible God's inaccessibility is symbolized by turning to heaven (Our Father who art in Heaven, Matt. 6:9, RSV), the Indian tradition expresses the same by emphasizing the need to enter ever deeper within (Kaivalya Up. 1.3).

According to Abhishiktananda, the Johannine prologue, through its identifications and its deeper penetration into the Mystery of God, recalls the Upanishadic experience. Abhishiktananda shows how John, as in the case of the Upanishads, starting from God and proceeding to the lowest level of the creature, discovers the presence of the Mystery of God in each stage.[25]

John, using the Greek concept of the Logos, the principle of order and continuity, presents the Word as God. Further, Logos-God-Life-Light is identified with the man born on earth. This way, all that was said in the Upanishads is in reality said of Christ. Hence, in John we have not only the Upanishadic method, but also the fundamental themes contained therein.

The 'I am' statements in John remind us of the Upanishadic *maha-vakyas* (great sayings) such as 'I am Brahman'. Jesus simply identifies 'I' with being. Here we are not using the Bible to understand the Indian scriptures, but our knowledge of the Indian texts enables us to interpret the Bible. We come across the reciprocity and communion of love which is the very foundation of the unity and non-duality of being. Based on Matthew 11:25, 'No one knows the Son except the Father, just as no one knows the Father except the Son and those to whom the Son chooses to reveal him', Abhishiktananda believes that the knowledge in which the Father begets the Son and in which the Son receives existence from the Father is the 'revelation' of God within himself which the Son came to make known to the world, inviting whoever 'receives' this revelation to share in his own divine sonship (John 1:12; 18).[26] As the Father and Son are one, so the Son and his own are one. Ultimately, in him, they are one with God. Similarly, the Father has given the Father's glory to the Son

---

[24] Abhishiktananda, *Saccidananda*, p. 11.
[25] Abhishiktananda, *Hindu-Christian Meeting Point*, p. 86.   [26] *Ibid.*, p. 94.

from the beginning (John 17:5) and it is given to them as well. Just as there is only one glory, there is only one life; the life that was in the bosom of the Father from the beginning (John 1:4). Through other concepts like joy (John 17:13), name (17:26) and love (John 17:23), Abhishiktananda concludes that just as in the inner silence the sages of India hear the primordial OM, the murmur of *Sat-cid-ananda*, so in the depths of the silence of the Spirit, springing up from the Word, the Christian hears deep within his or her own soul the echo of the same *Sat-cid-ananda*.[27]

One who has never experienced the non-duality of being cannot understand the Mystery of God manifested in Jesus Christ. As long as we look upon God or Jesus Christ as another, we cannot grasp what God is or what we are. For Abhishiktananda 'the Ultimate Mystery lies at the very heart of non-duality. The Spirit of unity alone silently teaches that essential reciprocal Gaze of Love in the depths of Being of which all earthly "otherness" is simply a sign.'[28]

The Christian knows how God is in all things; and in order to meet God one has to plunge deep within oneself and within all things in pursuit of his final secret. But in this search the soul finds that every atom of it is ablaze with the glory of God and the 'I' and the 'Thou' disappears like a person shipwrecked in a high sea, tossed from wave to wave that sweeps him away. Abhishiktananda adds, 'Soon there will no longer be any *I* to be conscious of any experience whatever, still less to be aware that all possible experiences are now finished.'[29] Just as it is only at the very heart of Being that the loneliness of the Monad can transcend, so also it is only in the heart of God that the antinomy of created existence can and must be resolved. 'In the end', he points out, 'it is in the mystery of the essential koinonia of the divine Being that man can rediscover himself as simultaneously one with God and yet present to him.'[30] The Christian jnani knows in truth that in the Mystery of God, at the very heart of Being, the Son and the Spirit proceed from the Father, alike in the non-duality (*advaita*) of nature and in the threefold communion (*koinonia*) of Persons. The Vedanta experience of Self leads to the Trinitarian experience of *Saccidananda*. However, the Christian experience of *Saccidananda* transcends that of Hinduism. Whereas in Hindu understanding everything stops with Being, the indivisible and attributeless Brahman (Mundaka Up. 2.2.11), the Christian passes on to the communion in love, within the indivisibility of unity of being. However, it is a mystery of faith.[31]

---

[27] *Ibid.*, p. 96.   [28] *Ibid.*, p. 102.
[29] Abhishiktananda, *Saccidananda*, p. 64.   [30] *Ibid.*, p. 104.   [31] *Ibid.*, p. 198.

Abhishiktananda rightly holds that though there are several texts in the Hindu scriptures articulating the Vedantic experience, it is in the lives of saints like Sri Ramana Maharshi and Sri Gnanananda that we encounter it concretely.[32] The whole Indian spirituality is shaped on the basis of sages' intuition of the Self within, the call of which can be heard only from within. It is the realization that who one is does not depend on the changing external circumstances of bodily and mental existence, but is at the kernel of one's consciousness and cannot be identified with any external circumstance.

Christianity, with its experience of the Spirit, can accept what is essential in the Advaitic experience and penetrate to its very heart. In the process it may find itself anew 'precisely in those ultimate depths of the Spirit to which advaita recalls it', Abhishiktananda insists.[33] He goes on to say that, whether we like it or not, we are faced with the fact of India's religion and spiritual experience and we are challenged to define our faith and present it in the presence of this experience. It is in this spirit that Abhishiktananda and others have attempted to define the Christian experience of the Mystery from the Indian perspective.

Likewise, he points out, Christianity has a universal definitive service of manifesting God's love made present in Jesus Christ.[34] To do this it will have to integrate whatever is true and good, wherever it is found, to itself. If Christianity is incapable of assimilating the spiritual traditions of India, it will cease to be an agent of universal service, in so far as the truth of the Vedanta in itself is unassailable.

As Gispert-Sauch shows, one of Abhishiktananda's concerns is to go beyond (or below) the *namarupa* (world of multiplicity) to Reality itself.[35] In the spirit of the Upanishadic tradition, he had a distrust of all mental forms, which he considered as belonging to the realm of *maya*, entering the realm of the Real. Towards the end of his life he acknowledges the relative value of the realm of *vyavaharika* (world of senses), which loses its significance when the Absolute Truth (*paramartha*) dawns in the heart of the world of multiplicity and history. The *vyavaharika* is left behind when the *paramartha* dawns, as one leaves behind the boat that one has used to cross the river.

What about the Christian faith – does it not belong to the vyavaharika? For Abhishiktananda, though much of the Christian faith was part of the vyavaharika, the deepest Mystery of Jesus who said, I AM, the pure being

---

[32] *Ibid.*, p. 19.   [33] *Ibid.*, p. 47.   [34] *Ibid.*, p. 48.
[35] G. Gispert-Sauch, 'Christ and the Indian Mystical Tradition' in J. Mattam and K. C. Marak (eds.), *Blossoms From the East: Contribution of the Indian Church to World Mission* (Mumbai: St Paul's, 1999), pp. 112–27 at p. 116.

of non-duality, is interiorized and is seen as one with the Godhead. He writes in his diary on 28 May 1972, about a year before his death:

Saving mystery can only emerge from the cave, from the depth of consciousness. 'Christianity believes that salvation comes from outside, through thoughts, rites, "sacraments". The level of *namarupa*.' But actually, in truth, Christianity is first of all Upanishad, correlation, not direct teaching. Direct teaching only gives *namarupas*. Correlation causes the spark of experience to flash, that alone gives fulfilment ... The pure act of love or service, that is what awakens one to oneself. That is what awakens one to God, not to the God of *namarupas* but to God in himself! It is on this inner experience that all *real* religion should be based, not on ideas that come and are passed on to us from outside.[36]

What is happening in Jesus the Incarnate One is his awakening to the Father's intimate presence in him. This Jesus Christ is the *Satpurusha* in whose awakening the awakening of all are included. Just a few months before his death he writes: 'There is in truth only one act by which Jesus – every human being – goes to the Father (to use biblical terminology): *it is the act of awakening* [italics added]. As soon as you awake, on account of the essential connectedness of all human beings, you awake with, on behalf of all.'[37] The Paschal Mystery is an impressive symbol of the awakening of Human Being to himself or herself.

In short, Abhishiktananda's understanding of the Ultimate Mystery evolves out of his grasp of the Upanishadic traditions as well as his Christian Faith.

A new vision of reality: Bede Griffiths (1906–93)
Bede Griffiths, a British Benedictine with an Anglican background, who came to India in 1955, carried forward the tradition Abbé Monchanin and Abhishiktananda left behind. As can be gleaned from his autobiography, from childhood he was blessed with a mystical sense and a spirit of contemplation that generated in him a regard for cosmic revelation.[38] His exposure to Hindu and Buddhist mysticism convinced him of the need to develop a valid and creative synthesis of the inner encounter of Christianity and Hinduism, relating the Oriental tradition to Christianity.[39]

He was influenced also by modern science, especially Fritjof Capra, David Bohm, Ilya Prigogine and others. He was attracted by the scientists' advocating a cosmic whole, as the vedic revelation sees it.[40]

[36] *Ibid.*, p. 120.   [37] *Ibid.*, p. 121.
[38] Bede Griffiths, *The Golden String: An Autobiography* (Springfield: Templegate, 1980), p. 10.
[39] *Ibid.*, p. 64.
[40] Bede Griffiths, *A New Vision of Reality: Western Science, Eastern Mysticism and Christian Faith* (London: Collins, 1989), p. 27.

Hence he asserts:

The one divine Mystery is beyond word and thought, reveals itself in different ways in each religious tradition. Each religion manifests the one Reality, the one Truth, under different symbols, a symbol being defined [as] a sign in which the reality is really present. In this sense it is true to say that Jesus Christ is a symbol of God.[41]

Beyond the physical world of differences there is a deeper dimension, the world of the transcendent. Bede Griffiths writes:

This we find, in the great revelations. There what is revealed is not merely the physical or the psychological or psychic world but rather there takes place an intuitive insight into the ultimate, the transcendent. All the great revelations are, as it were messages from that transcendent world ... transcendent reality.[42]

This revelation he describes in terms of the myths understood as the mystical. All religions have their origin in some sort of mystical experience.[43] This experience as such is incommunicable, though the religions do communicate it through myths and symbols. Hence he describes myth as 'the symbolic expression of the one Reality experienced as a living unity in an undivided consciousness'.[44] In fact, even the biblical books, according to him, gain their meaning from the mythical elements they contain.[45] It is the myth that relates the events contained in the Christian Bible to the eternal drama of human salvation.

In the Christian tradition this One Reality is known as the Father, the Source of the Godhead. The Father signifies the Absolute from which every thing originates. Griffiths writes:

The understanding is that from this ground, from this source, there springs a Word, a wisdom, an image of the Godhead, and that is this cosmic Person, who reveals the Father, the Source. In that cosmic Person, in the Word or Son, all the archetypes of all created beings are contained. The archetype of every being in the universe is contained eternally in the Word, in the Godhead.[46]

His Word, his image, the Cosmic Person, Jesus Christ reveals the Father, the source. In the Son all created universe is contained as the archetype, unfolded.

---

[41] Bede Griffiths, 'Reflections and Prospects' in Michael von Bruck (ed.), *Emerging Consciousness for a New Humankind* (Bangalore: Asian Trading Corporation, 1985), pp. 123–4, cited by Teasdale, *Toward a Christian Vedanta*, p. 73.

[42] Griffiths, *A New Vision of Reality*, p. 267.

[43] Bede Griffiths, *The Marriage of East and West* (Springfield: Templegate, 1983), pp. 174–5.

[44] *Ibid.*, p. 30.

[45] Bede Griffiths, *Return to the Centre* (Springfield: Templegate, 1982), p. 79.

[46] Griffiths, *A New Vision of Reality*, p. 269.

As the Word/Son is the source of all forms in creation, so the Spirit is the source of all energy. 'It is the uncreated energy', Griffiths says, 'which flows forth eternally from the Godhead and which then brings into being the energies of matter and of nature.'[47] Thus, the universe is an overflow of the energy of the spirit, the energy of love. In other words, the Spirit is the love-energy of God. God calls into being the whole creation to manifest God's self, to manifest God's love and to bring forth that love in the creation. The Spirit flows out in this love to effect the creation and the Word organizes all those energies of matter and creation gradually bringing it back to its source in the cosmic Person, Purusha. The Spirit is active throughout history, and at work in all religions. As part of this cosmic process at times certain centres, like Israel, are formed, in and through which the cosmic process of redemption is consummated. Through Israel, the organizing power of the universe, the archetypal man, Jesus, manifests to overcome the power of sin and death. Through his resurrection the redemptive power of the Spirit is poured out to the world. The Spirit's coming on the church is part of that outpouring, though the Spirit is everywhere and not limited to the church.

The church is the centre for the regeneration of humankind, the Spirit rebuilding humans into the likeness of Christ and uniting all in the love of the Father from which everything comes. So the universe and humanity return to the divine unity and each element and each person discovers its original archetype. So he writes: 'In love the whole universe is pouring out and that love is drawing it all back to itself.'[48] All are reintegrated into the one. All are held together in Christ, the supreme Person, and all become persons in the Person. However, it is not a matter of dissolving into the One. As Hinduism says, rather it is a reintegration into the One in total unity. It is an eternal and infinite reality, and all of us, even now, are interwoven and interpenetrating in that one reality. Yet, Bede Griffiths reminds us:

The Absolute itself is beyond all human comprehension and we use words, images and concepts taken from everyday finite experience in order to direct our mind, our will and our heart towards the Infinite and to allow that Infinite to enter into our lives and transform them.[49]

Bede Griffith's contemplative theology springs from his spirituality, mystical experience and reading and reflection on the sacred texts of eastern religions and the Bible. Thus, it can be qualified as 'theological

---

[47] *Ibid.*, p. 270.   [48] *Ibid.*, p. 273.   [49] *Ibid.*, p. 275.

epistemology'[50] paving the way for a new world order through religions renewing themselves in relation to one another.

CONCLUDING REMARKS

What I have attempted in this chapter is the presentation of one stream of reflection on the Ultimate Mystery, which, while it is the most prevalent, is not the only one. The Indian church is surging ahead in its theological reflection. Not denying the acuteness of the dehumanizing poverty in which millions live, one could still say that the major issue the church in India faces is how to cope with the vibrant religions with their ancient wisdom expressed in the lived spirituality of the Indian masses. The originality of Indian Catholic theology is to be found above all in the writings and lived spirituality in response to this religiosity of India. Though most Indian theologians have something to say about the Ultimate Mystery, most of the time what they say is from the perspective of understanding Jesus Christ as the only medium of salvation and articulating the mission of the church emanating from that understanding.

A characteristic that the Indian mystical tradition has brought out is that theology is not solely a science of God as an abstraction, but it is for and in relation to humans. Humans constitute as much importance as God in theology. Humans exist in the world and thus there can be no theology divorced from the world. The world is the arena in which humans struggle to grapple with the problems which derive their meaning in relation to God. The search for God takes place in the context of lived reality. This makes the Indian search not just a conceptual clarification but an encounter with the Ultimate Reality in the context of *atmasashatkar* (self-realization).

Even in the midst of globalization, frequently we lack the readiness to accept others and respect the space of others. The Indian approach to the Ultimate Mystery can serve as a corrective to this tendency to exclusivism. Equally, it is a corrective to another spin-off from market-oriented globalization: a trade mentality with respect to others and to the world – how to make the best of them for one's own advantage. The Indian approach insists on a sort of detachment (*nishkamakarma*) in the pursuit of interests, keeping the Ultimate Reality in focus, in the midst of the relative reality (*maya*) of the world of senses (*namarupa*). The Indian approach reminds us of the need to concentrate on the experience of the

[50] Teasdale, *Toward a Christian Vedanta*, p. 41.

Ultimate Mystery, which is all-pervading and thus invites us not only to be tolerant but respectful of others. Here religions will have to underplay doctrinal expressions but must concentrate rather on the Mystery itself, which unites all. The Mystery is greater than the representation of it. This implies an inward orientation, the gift of interiority with which India was blessed, leading to the state when 'God may be everything to every one' (1 Cor. 15:28), the state of convergence of existence in its crystal purity and limitless plenitude in the experience of the Ultimate Mystery, the pure non-duality.

BIBLIOGRAPHY

Abhishiktananda, S., *Guru and Disciple*, London: SPCK, 1974.
   Hindu-Christian Meeting Point, Bangalore: CISRS, 1969.
   Saccidananda: A Christian Approach to Advaitic Experience, Delhi: ISPCK, 1974.
D'Lima, E. and Gonsalves, M. (eds.), *What does Jesus Christ Mean?*, Bangalore: ITA, 1999.
Gispert-Sauch, G., 'Christ and the Indian Mystical Tradition' in J. Mattam and K. C. Marak (eds.), *Blossoms from the East: Contribution of the Indian Church to World Mission*, Mumbai: St Paul's, 1998, pp. 112–27.
Griffiths, B., *The Golden String: An Autobiography*, Springfield: Templegate, 1980.
   The Marriage of East and West, Springfield: Templegate, 1983.
   A New Vision of Reality: Western Science, Eastern Mysticism and Christian Faith, London: Collins, 1989.
   Return to the Centre, Springfield: Templegate, 1982.
Lipner, J. J., *Bhahmabandhab Upadhyay*, Delhi: Oxford University Press, 1999.
Panikkar, R., *The Trinity and the Religious Experience of Man*, London: Darton, Longman & Todd, 1973.
Sumitra, S., *Christian Theologies from an Indian Perspective*, Bangalore: Theological Book Trust, 1995.
Teasdale, W., *Toward a Christian Vedanta*, Bangalore: Asian Trading Corporation, 1987.
Thomas, M. M., *The Acknowledged Christ of the Indian Renaissance*, London: SCM Press, 1969.
Wilfred, F., *Beyond Settled Foundations: The Journey of Indian Theology*, Madras: University of Madras, 1993.
   From the Dusty Soil, Madras: University of Madras, 1995.

CHAPTER 3

Waters of life and Indian cups: Protestant attempts at theologizing in India

Israel Selvanayagam

INTRODUCTION

The words in the title are deliberately chosen. Those who know the famous phrase 'the water of life in an Indian cup' attributed to Sadhu Sundar Singh, one of the most well-known lay theologians of India, would realize the twist. It challenges straight away a few traditional assumptions about the nature of the so-called Indian Christian theology. First, to claim that there is a single theology or even a cluster of theologies produced in India is far from the truth. Partly, such a claim is the result of imitating the western way of naming theology, which is basically a reasoning or talking about God. Although there are particular theological constructions made in the west within defined frameworks of certain philosophies, today we realize the variety of methods and plurality of perspectives from which theology is approached. Second, 'the water of life in an Indian cup' suggests that the 'water of life' has come from elsewhere and the cup, a single cup, is only a receptacle. If Sundar Singh's other image 'channels' is preferred, again it means what India has is nothing more than an instrumental value. Third, in spite of several attempts having been made, India has yet to produce a systematic theology that is constructive, consistent, coherent and relevant.

It is rather modest to say that some Indian Christian thinkers have made serious attempts to reflect the Christian faith in the context of challenges facing their country. As it will become clear in this chapter, most of them were fresh converts from the major religious tradition called Hinduism. They were evangelistic and apologetic while reclaiming their national heritage with a sense of protest against western ways of thinking and the western image of the church in India. This unique fact raises questions about definitions of theology in relation to mission. In fact the

Indian theological reflections obscure, if not obliterate, the boundaries between missiology and theology, including what is known as contextual theology. What is theologically significant, however, is that they have been indirectly revolting against the Syriac captivity of the Syrian Church, which has been in existence from the early centuries of the Christian era and which appeared to be a special caste without any passion for sharing the gospel with their Hindu neighbours; so also against the Latin captivity of the Catholic Church, which started to take root in Indian soil from the beginning of the sixteenth century, although some radical attempts (for example by Robert de Nobili) were made to indigenize the mission in the seventeenth century. Such a captivity gripped Protestant traditions also which operated within the colonial and cultural domination of the west; the only difference was that theological formulations and liturgical forms were available in European languages, mainly English.

DIFFERENT STYLES AND MODELS OF INDIAN CHRISTIAN THEOLOGIES

We have space here only to illustrate the major approaches, about which several preliminary points should be made. First, many of the influential theologians of Protestant circles in India were non-professionals with claims to first-hand religious experience, and they came up with random reflections. This could be best illustrated with the approach of Sadhu Sundar Singh (1889–1929). As a convert from the Sikh tradition through a mystical encounter with Christ, Sundar Singh joined a divinity school but soon walked out, finding it a laboratory where students analysed scripture rather than aspire to drink it as milk. As a wandering monk he preached the gospel both in India and abroad, and he impressed some well-known leaders like Tagore and Gandhi and theologians like A. J. Appasamy in India, and B. H. Streeter, F. Heiler, N. Söderblom and F. von Hügel in Europe. Many in India and in the west found in him the message of the New Testament embodied, the living Christ reflected and the missionary passion personified. Singh did not make a contribution to what is known as theology so much as to a new definition of theology. He was not against any critical approaches to the study of the Bible and theology but he insisted that they could never be a substitute for prayer and living in Christ. As Heiler has pointed out, Singh had a special mission to Christian theology and to the Christian Church of the west: 'Theological research needs to be constantly balanced by living Christian piety if it is not to degenerate into presumptuous speculation, destructive criticism, or empty dialectic. Theology without prayerful piety is like a fountain whose waters have dried up.'[1]

Singh's reflections on Christian themes[2] like sin, salvation, Christ, church and sacraments would certainly compare with others in general. What is distinctive, however, is that the reflections are illustrated with personal experience and tolerance of different viewpoints. For example, he was thoroughly christocentric and believed salvation is through Christ alone, but he held that people of other faiths also are illumined by the Sun of Righteousness, living in Christ and breathing the Holy Spirit. What was manifested in Jesus Christ is the highest point. More uniquely, he used images, metaphors and parables of everyday life. For example, just like diving to find a pearl, one has to dive into the spiritual depths to have the inner joy; just as a mother bird allowed herself to be burned by a wildfire to save her chicks, Jesus died for us. Somewhat similar was the Anglican priest Nehemiah Goreh (1825–95), who won another famous convert from the same Brahmin community, Pandita Ramabai (see below). While calling the people of his country to a new life in Christ, who came as both grace and judgement, Goreh regarded Hindu ideas about divine miracles and incarnation as a preparation for the Christian gospel. The very titles of Goreh's books, such as *A Rational Refutation of the Hindu Philosophical Systems* (1862), suggest his exclusive position and apologetic approach but with authentic knowledge and experience of the Hindu tradition.[3]

Second, going beyond the boundaries of the above, some tried to develop a definitive approach to the Indian religious traditions and their resources. For instance, in connection with a discussion on the place of the Old Testament in comparison with the scriptures of the Indian religious traditions, A. J. Appasamy points out: 'If Jesus blames His contemporaries for not listening to the voice of Moses, with equal power and vehemence will He condemn us for not listening to Rāmānuja, Māṇikkavācakar, Tukārām and Chaitanya, who have left behind them teaching of such undying value, pointing the way to Christ.'[4] But how this was done is a different question. Some stopped with slogans and others did not move beyond a certain point. Moreover, some were captured by the spirit of nationalism while others experimented with new combinations – either with Indian thoughts and practices or with secular ideologies.

---

[1] F. Heiler, *The Gospel of Sadhu Sundar Singh* (Delhi: ISPCK, 1989), p. 259.
[2] Dayanandan Francis, *The Christian Witness of Sadhu Sundar Singh – A Collection of his Writings* (Madras: Christian Literature Society, 1989).
[3] B. A. M. Paradkar, *The Theology of Goreh* (Madras: Christian Literature Society-CISRS, 1969).
[4] A. J. Appasamy, *Christianity as Bhakti Mārga* (Madras: Christian Literature Society, 1930), pp. 165–6.

Third, some theologians tried to establish points of contact with Hinduism and used concepts as interpretive tools for presenting the Christian message, such as Appasamy, Chakkarai and Chenchiah, whom we will discuss later. Fourth, a few attempted to create a coalescence between Christianity and Hinduism, such as Mark Sunder Rao (d. 1980), who wrote: 'The idea of a confluence of two streams of thought and faith, *sangam* of West and East, in the heart of the Indian Christian had then taken firm grasp of my thought and life.'[5] It should be asked whether this is the experience of a few individuals or of all Indian Christians irrespective of their particular historical and religious contexts. Certainly there are examples of such coalescence, particularly in the vernacular attempts, as we will see later. Fifth, some theologians, like M. M. Thomas and others we will encounter later, have made a dialogical response to an Indian renaissance and acknowledged Christ. Sixth, the contemporary scene has a new awakening to distinctive identities such as those of women, dalits, tribals and children. We will point out examples of these theologies, which attempt to take the contemporary situation seriously.

India today as a sub-continent with over one billion people has its unique diversity and challenges. Christians form a tiny minority in India and are placed in the midst of many religious traditions. According to the 2001 census, the percentage of Hindus is 80.5, Muslims 13.4, Christians 2.3, Sikhs 1.9, Buddhists 0.8, Jains 0.4 and others, including Parsees, 0.6. Of the Christian population, Protestants represent about half. On the whole, India illustrates a strange combination of plurality and contradictions. In the tenth largest industrial nation, with some of the wealthiest persons in the world, more than twenty-five per cent of the Indian population live below the poverty line. Known as the laboratory of interfaith dialogue, India has not been without its explosive moments. In spite of the immense diversity of traditions, both ancient and modern, with their long past of mutual interaction and influence, communal harmony is still the cry of leaders and thinkers. Social stratification based on the hierarchical caste system not only often implicitly segregates communities but also has produced the most heinous practice of untouchability. While continuing to be the largest democracy in the world, the illiterate masses of India have been subjected to political manipulation and personality cults.

In such a context with a vast land, a long history, a variety of traditions, numerous theologians and an immense wealth of literature, it is not easy

---

[5] Quoted in C. Duraisingh, 'Indian Hyphenated Christians and Theological Reflections – A New Expression of Identity', *Religion and Society*, XXVI/4 (1979), pp. 95–101 at 95.

to bring together all that has been said by Indian Christian thinkers in Protestant circles. The most difficult matter is to distinguish between serious theological reflections and expositions, devotional reflections and missionary appeals on the one hand, and socio-economic analysis on the other. What is possible is to consider only those reflections which are most original and distinctively Indian. Ours is a historical survey of phases, groups, approaches and major issues identified. We are compelled to be ruthlessly selective and tantalizingly brief.

THE MISSIONARY CONTRIBUTION TO INDIAN CHRISTIAN THEOLOGIZING

Western missionaries came to India with a definite mandate to preach the gospel of light to heathens. But some of them had startling experiences when they encountered natives who had a high sense of morality and undertook fascinating acts of religious devotion. This happened to the first Protestant missionary, Barthalomaeus Ziegenbalg (1682–1719), who was sponsored by a Danish king, sent by the pietistic Halle Mission, and landed on the east coast of southern India in 1706. Startled by the religious life of the Hindus around him, even before he brought out the first New Testament in the Tamil language in 1714, he made a field study of their beliefs and practices. Although he uses phrases like 'foolish heathenism', 'heathenish darkness' and 'blind heathens', he appreciated the Hindu belief in one Supreme God Almighty. In this regard he wondered 'how much further they have gone in his knowledge, by the light of nature, than the heathens of Rome'. But the light, he continues, 'has been quite obscured by their ancient poets and Brahmins, who have written many fabulous stories, and introduced a confused idol worship, out of which they cannot easily extricate themselves'.[6] This initial appreciation of positive elements in Hinduism, while pointing out the negative side, later gave way to more accurate perceptions.

Of the missionaries, G. U. Pope (1820–1907)[7], Thomas Slater (1840–1912)[8], Robert Hume (1847–1929)[9], John Jones (1847–1916)[10], Bernard Lucas

[6] B. Ziegenbalg, *Geneology of South Indian Gods* (New Delhi: Unity Book Service, 1984), p. 22.
[7] G. U. Pope, *The Tiruvacagam* (Oxford: Clarendon Press, 1900).
[8] T. E. Slater, *The Higher Hinduism in Relation to Christianity: Certain Aspects of Hindu Thought from a Christian Standpoint* (London: Elliott Stock, 1902).
[9] R. A. Hume, *Missions from the Modern View* (New York: Fleming H. Revell Co., 1905).
[10] J. P. Jones, *India: Its Life and Thought* (New York: The Macmillan Company, 1908).

(1860–1921)[11], J. N. Farquhar (1861–1929), C. F. Andrews (1871–1940) and E. Stanley Jones (1884–1973) are most remarkable for their positive approach to India and its heritage. They affirmed the universal witness of God, studied the Indian religious traditions and pointed out visions and ideas akin to Christian ones. Some of them developed the model of the fulfilment in Christ of what is in Hinduism. Farquhar made extensive studies of Hindu traditions, scriptures and modern religious movements and the fulfilment model is particularly associated with him. His famous book *The Crown of Hinduism* demonstrated how Christianity was the fulfilment of all types of religions and particularly the crown of evolutionary Hinduism. Taking insights from the theory of evolution and Jesus' insistence that he came 'not to destroy but to fulfil', Farquhar declared that

Christ is already breathing life into the Hindu people. He does not come to destroy. To him all that is great and good is dear: the noble art of India, the power and spirituality of its best literature, the beauty and simplicity of Hindu village life, the love and tenderness of the Hindu home, the devotion and endurance of the ascetic schools.[12]

He held that the New Testament must be the central sun, in the light of which all other scriptures and teachings should be assessed. Though he allowed that the great scriptures were set like stars around the sun and could be considered as supplementary to the Hebrew Bible, he did not want to lose the historical connections and significance of its message.

Andrews worked in close association with great figures like Tagore and Gandhi at the height of the national movement and Indian renaissance. Fascinated by every aspect of India, he took a pro-Indian stance in his writings and advocated that Christianity would have to be stripped bare 'of its present foreign accretions and excrescences' if it was to become indigenous; 'otherwise it will remain an exotic plant, unacclimatised and sickly, needing the continual support and prop of the West'.[13] Setting an agenda for creative Indian theology to develop, he suggested a combination of unity and transcendence, firmly held by Muslims and divine immanence and incarnation, which the Hindus sought to realize. Like Andrews, E. Stanley Jones found Christ was already in India, particularly in the hungry, thirsty, naked and sick. He gave an exposition of Jesus' 'Nazareth Manifesto' in the light of the Indian reality suggesting concrete programmes for the most depressed class of people. Jones encountered

---

[11] B. Lucas, *The Empire of Christ: Being a Study of the Missionary Enterprise in the Light of Modern Religious Thought* (London: Macmillan, 1908).
[12] J. N. Farquhar, *The Crown of Hinduism* (London: Oxford University Press, 1913), p. 54.
[13] C. F. Andrews, *North India* (London: A. R. Mowbray, 1908), p. 223.

freshly 'the Christ of the Indian road', which is the title of his first book. He held that Jesus is universal; that he can 'stand the shock of transplantation' and 'appeals to the universal heart'. He urged the Indian Christians 'to interpret him through their own genius and life' so that 'the interpretation will be first-hand and vital'.[14]

A. G. Hogg (1875–1954) was perhaps the most influential figure of his time. He was the mentor of great figures like S. Radhakrishnan. He criticized the radical discontinuity proposed by Hendrik Kraemer at the 1938 World Missionary Conference held at Tambaram, Madras, on the one hand and the fulfilment model presented by Farquhar on the other. He was upset by the typical Hindu attitude of neither acceptance nor rejection. 'The Christian message to the Hindu', Hogg wrote, 'must never be merely a Christianised version of Hinduism, but it does need to give to the authentic Christian faith a truly Indian form of expression.' But he submitted that this could be done only by the Indian Church, although foreign missionaries have a subsidiary role to play by helping 'that Church to see to it that what is presented to India is the full challenge of the ancient Christian Gospel in all its distinctiveness'.[15] In some ways Hogg's position was replicated by one of the last group of missionaries, Lesslie Newbiggin (1909–98), who did not allow himself to be carried away by the radical re-thinking of Christianity that was developing in his working context, but emphasized the ancient Christian Gospel in all its distinctiveness.

The contribution of Western missionaries to the development of Indian theological reflections should not be underestimated. Robin Boyd (b. 1924) studied the attempts of major theologians and produced the monumental book *An Introduction to Indian Christian Theology*, published first in 1969, with several subsequent impressions.[16] This and his later books[17] reflect penetrating insights of a missionary theologian into exciting moments of the history of Indian Christian thought and spin a thread bringing together relevant themes. By making concurrent connections and comparisons with theological positions of the West, Boyd has made Indian reflections somewhat respectable and worth consulting. Besides Boyd, Eric Lott (b. 1934) and David Scott (b. 1938), the last in a

---

[14] E. S. Jones, *Christ of the Indian Road* (Lucknow: Lucknow Publishing House, 1925), pp. 6–7.

[15] E. Sharpe, *The Theology of A. G. Hogg* (Madras: Christian Literature Society, 1971), p. vi.

[16] R. H. S. Boyd, *An Introduction to Indian Christian Theology* (Delhi: ISPCK, 1969).

[17] Including R. H. S. Boyd, *India and the Latin Captivity of the Church – The Cultural Context of the Gospel* (London: Cambridge University Press, 1974); *Manilal C. Parekh, 1885–1967, Dhanjibhai Fakirbhai, 1895–1967: A Selection* (Madras: Christian Literature Society, 1974); and *Khristadvaita – A Theology for India* (Madras: Christian Literature Society, 1977).

line of missionary theologians in India, based in the United Theological College, have also made valuable contributions to Indian Christian theology through their study of Indian religious traditions and their interaction with a community of scholars, both Christian and non-Christian.

POINTS OF CONTACT AND THE CHRISTIAN
USE OF HINDU CONCEPTS

S. K. Datta (1878–1942) and S. K. Rudra (1861–1925) in the North, and K. T. Paul (1876–1931) and V. S. Azariah (1874–1945) in the South, in general terms, sharing some of the ideas of the missionary theologians mentioned above, presented Christ as a window to God and vision for humanity, as well as a source of inspiration to raise the moral consciousness of Indians.[18] But they were divided on the question of the value and theological validity of the institutionalized church in India. The last two made a great contribution to the union movement of the Church of South India – the first united church of its kind – formed in 1947, the year of Indian independence. They viewed the church union as a mark of achieving national selfhood and a starting point to make the church truly Indian. Subsequently, the Church of North India was formed in 1970 and its formation and other developments in the area of church union were not unconnected with independent commitment to mission and fresh theological reflection in the Indian context.

Aiyadurai Jesudasen Appasamy (1891–1975), Vengal Chakkarai (1880–1958) and Pandipeddi Chenchiah (1886–1959) would best represent those who identified points of contact for the Christian message in the Hindu religious traditions. Appasamy, a scholar, bishop and a close friend of Sundar Singh, was impressed by the original, indigenous contributions of some vernacular poets. Their outpouring of devotion to Christ, appropriating ideas of their original Hindu traditions, testified to Appasamy's interpretation of Christianity as *bhakti marga* (the way of devotion) and clarification of the meaning of *moksha* (liberation).[19] Instead of interpreting Jesus' sayings, such as 'I and my Father are one', as identical with the Upanishadic formula 'Thou art That' on which the non-dualist Vedānta was built, he saw them in the light of the 'qualified non-dualism'

[18] M. M. Thomas, *The Secular Ideologies of India and the Secular Meaning of Christ* (Madras: Christian Literature Society-CISRS, 1976), pp. 241–84.
[19] A. J. Appasamy, *Christianity as Bhakti Marga: A Study of the Johannine Doctrine of Love* (Madras: Christian Literature Society, 1930); *What is Moksa? A Study in the Johannine Doctrine of Life* (Madras: Christian Literature Society, 1931).

of Ramanuja. Accordingly, the oneness between Jesus and his Father was not ontological but moral, 'a union in love and work and not an identity in their essential nature'.[20] Such is the harmony of the individual soul with the Divine soul in liberation.

Appasamy used the word *antaryāmin* for the immanent Word (*logos*) and indwelling Spirit, which pervade the whole universe always. The popular Hindu word *avatāra* he found a useful conceptual category for interpreting the incarnation of Christ but stressed the distinctive nature of it as a one-time manifestation of the wholeness of God in a concrete human form in a particular time in history. He emphasized that 'The sacrifice on Calvary is the uttermost expression of the love of God', the supreme power who 'forgives and redeems, exerts its irresistible influence' on every human being.[21] To the three-fold basic sources of authority (*pramānas*) held by Christianity and the Hindu traditions in common – scripture (*śruti*), reason (*yukti*) and experience (*anubhava*), Appasamy adds the source of church (*sabha*), where there is authoritative teaching revealed by God in contrast to Hindu religion, which is very individualistic. And he finds the Upanishadic idea of Brahman as food (*anna*) to be a useful tool to interpret the Eucharist through which 'the living Christ enters into us and forms a part of our inmost self in the same organic way in which food and drink become a part of our being'.[22] This interpretation suits Ramanuja's idea of Brahman as the inner controller of the whole universe, which is his body, including the human souls who realize him in absolute surrender in loving devotion. However, Appasamy never fails to recognize the church as Christ's body in a special way, where the reciprocal relationship of divine revelation and devotees' obedience to God's will continue.

Chakkarai, whose conversion was effected by the inspiration of Jesus' cry of dereliction on the cross, was a key member of the Madras group known for *Rethinking Christianity in India*. He combined his commitment to sharing the gospel with educated Hindus with active participation in the nationalist movement, social service as a lawyer, and at one time being mayor of Madras. He introduced 'the Christhood of God' in the sense that Jesus typified the real nature of God. He believed the immanent God (*antaryāmin*) took a special form in Christ's incarnation and now the new experience of his devotees is having his whole person seated in their hearts as teacher and inspirer. More than anyone else

[20] A. J. Appasamy, *The Gospel and India's Heritage* (London: SPCK, 1942), p. 38.
[21] A. J. Appasamy, *Christianity as Bhakti Mārga* (Madras: Christian Literature Society, 1930), pp. 125, 112.
[22] A. J. Appasamy, *Christianity as Bhakti Mārga* (Madras: Christian Literature Society, 1930), p. 142.

Chakkarai made a thorough study of the Hindu understanding of *avatāra* and contrasted it with incarnation. Christ's *avatāra* was not a theophany, nor was it static, but 'the Incarnation advanced from stage to stage, from the historical to the spiritual, from the external to the internal, from time to eternity'.[23] Chakkarai applied to Jesus several terms known in the Hindu tradition to signify that Jesus was the true and supreme person. While he acknowledges the descriptions of the Holy Spirit in John's gospel as the comforter and indweller, in a strange way, Chakkarai identifies Christ with the Spirit and declares that 'the Holy Spirit in human experience is the Incarnation of Jesus Christ'.[24] His book *The Cross and Indian Thought*[25] represents a brilliant study bringing together Western and Indian interpretations of the cross and stressing it as signifying the perpetual and sacrificial love of God. By sacrificing his ego to the Being of God and merging into the Spirit, Jesus revealed a new kind of oneness which was based not on a mystical experience but on a historical event. In the ongoing dynamic movement of this oneness, the Christian devotees too have a share.

Chenchiah, brother-in-law of Chakkarai, a chief justice and the most distinguished member of the group 'Rethinking Christianity', stood on the threshold of linking the Hindu tradition and modern scientific thinking. His was the first critical review of Kraemer's famous book, *The Christian Message in a Non-Christian World*, prepared for the third World Missionary Conference held in Tambaram, Madras, in 1938.[26] He showed in this review that most of the Barthian theology represented by Kraemer was totally irrelevant to the Indian context of many religions with Hinduism as a major one. He also criticized the ecclesiastical battles of the West fought in India in the name of church union. For him loyalty to Christ did not contradict a reverential attitude towards Hindu heritage. He gave primacy to the 'raw fact' of experience of Christ and tested church tradition, including creeds and doctrines, in its light. Drawing from Aurobindo's integral yoga and theory of evolution, Chenchiah affirmed Jesus Christ as not simply a perfect man but as the New Man and True Man produced by God and Man. As he saw it, a new quality of life and a new energy has been injected into the world and human life, as Jesus was the first man (*ādi-purusha*) of a new creation and order, that is,

---

[23] V. Chakkarai, *Jesus the Avatār* (Madras: Christian Literature Society, 1930), p. 114.
[24] V. Chakkarai, *Jesus the Avatār* (Madras: Christian Literature Society, 1930), p. 124.
[25] V. Chakkarai, *The Cross and Indian Thought* (Madras: Christian Literature Society, 1932).
[26] H. Kraemer, *The Christian Message in a Non-Christian World* (London: International Missionary Council, 1938).

the Kingdom of God.[27] According to Chenchiah, organized church and organized evangelism are unbiblical and ineffective for the mission of reproducing Jesus in India. He suggests a base in an ashram and active involvement in society to penetrate and infect the new life with a vision for the evolution of the whole cosmos.

Chenchiah was knowledgeable in science, philosophy and comparative religion. He had no fear of change and mutation as they are the facts of an evolving life. He calls for the self-awareness of every religion and a willingness to change towards a new fusion. The following is his desire or vision:

The revelation of God, now bottled up in different religions, should coalesce. The light that shone through Geeta, Zendavest, Buddha, Christ, and Muhamud – shall confluence and man shall be baptised in this confluence of spiritual rivers and come out as the Son of God . . . This is not eclecticism. This is the faith that God will be all in all to all of us.[28]

For Chenchiah this vision is not in any way in contradiction of the biblical vision, the life in Christ and growth in the process of salvation, which is not 'sinlessness' but 'lifefullness'. His interpretation of the Christian message was so original that it calls for a new approach to traditional views and interpretations.

Following the above, efforts to relate the Christian message to Hindu conceptual categories continued as evident in a number of studies and publications undertaken by younger scholars. Most notable of them is K. P. Aleaz (b. 1946), who has made an extensive study of those who have tried to use the non-dualist (*advaita*) categories to interpret the person and work of Jesus. In his own attempt he has reconsidered the constitution of the person of Jesus and features of his work. The life and work of Jesus manifests Brahman, the Supreme Self, as the pure consciousness, witness and self of all; reveals the all-pervasive power; and proclaims the liberative, illuminative and unifying power.[29] Aleaz expounds the meaning of these categories with reference to their Sanskrit roots and their inter-connections as worked out in the system.

---

[27] P. Chenchiah, 'Jesus and Non-Christian Faiths' in G. V. Job, P. Chenchiah, V. Chakkarai, D. M. Devasahayam, S. Jesudason, Eddy Asirvatham and A. N. Sudarisanam, *Rethinking Christianity in India* (Madras: A. N. Sudarisanam, 1938), pp. 47–62 at 60–1.

[28] P. Chenchiah, 'Religion in Contemporary India' in G. V. Job, P. Chenchiah, V. Chakkarai, D. M. Devasahayam, S. Jesudason, Eddy Asirvatham and A. N. Sudarisanam, *Rethinking Christianity in India* (Madras: A. N. Sudarisanam, 1938), pp. 201–15 at 214.

[29] K. P. Aleaz, *Christian Thought Through Advaita Vedānta* (Delhi: ISPCK, 1996), pp. 90–112.

DIALOGICAL RESPONSE TO THE INDIAN RENAISSANCE
AND THE ACKNOWLEDGED CHRIST

Now we turn to recognize a new context. With the opportunity to be exposed to British education and western thinking a group of Hindu thinkers in modern India, including Ram Mohan Roy (1772–1833) and Keshab Chunder Sen (1838–84), were motivated to reform their tradition. They challenged exclusive claims by Christians and their missionaries and reclaimed the positive aspects of their ancient tradition. At the same time, they were different from those who were hostile to Christian mission and cynical about its contribution. They read the Bible with fresh eyes and criticized the western doctrines as twisting and mystifying it. Their perceptions helped some Indian theologians to see the influence of the gospel in unexpected ways, to make their own response and to engage in original thinking. Sen was an original thinker and developed some seminal ideas in a unique way of presentation.[30] He claimed that Jesus was originally an Asian before he was Europeanized and that the western image of the church was a hindrance to unveiling the true person of Jesus. Sen's personal experience of God was of the Trinity. He identified the supreme Brahman of the Vedānta with Logos, the personal shape of which was Jesus of Nazareth who typified the new humanity to be created by the same reality. Sen was the first to expound the meaning of Trinity using the Vedāntic category of Brahman as *Saccidānanda*, a compound word constituted by *Sat* (Truth or Being), *Cit* (Intelligence) and *Ānanda* (Joy). He identified the *Sat* with Father, Creator, the still God, the 'I am', Force and Truth; *Cit* with Son, the Exemplar, the journeying God, the 'I love', Wisdom and Good; and *Ānanda* with Holy Spirit, the Sanctifier, the returning God, the 'I save', Holiness and Beauty. They are three conditions and three manifestations of Divinity.

Sen influenced many people, including other Christian theologians such as Pandita Ramabai (1885–1922), Manilal Parekh (1885–1967) and P. C. Mozoomdar (1840–1905), and also leading Hindus such as Vivekananda, Gandhi and Radhakrishnan. All these persons in a way upset those missionaries and Christian Indians who wanted to emphasize the distinctiveness of the Christian gospel because they presented Hinduism – with reference either to the mystical experience of oneness with the Supreme Being or to the ethical ideal of non-violence – as the 'crown of

---

[30] D. Scott (ed.), *Keshub Chunder Sen* (Madras: Christian Literature Society for CISRS and United Theological College, 1979).

Christianity'. The continued influence of their position is such that no Hindu thinker has thought it necessary to reread the New Testament and review the church in India.

Of those Indian Christian theologians who made a studied and considered response to the Indian renaissance and the perceptions of the Hindu reformers and thinkers on Christ and Christianity, four are most worthy of note: P. D. Devanandan (1901–62), M. M. Thomas (1916–96), Stanley Samartha (1920–2001), and Russell Chandran (1918–2000). With the exception of Thomas, all of them were presbyters of the Church of South India. What is common in these men is that all of them in one way or another were associated with the United Theological College and its neighbour the Christian Institute for the Study of Religion and Society (CISRS) in Bangalore, were exposed to the West either for study or work or for both, and made a significant contribution to the ecumenical movement, particularly through the Christian Conference of Asia and the World Council of Churches. All of them took pains to correct the Hindu tendency to subsume Jesus into its system of thought and to clarify in different terms the distinctive character of Jesus as representing a divine humanity or the human face of divinity.

Devanandan, the founder-director of CISRS, believed 'The real problem in Hindu India is to effect a synthesis between the traditional world-view and contemporary secularism ... it is in relation to this concern that the good news of God incarnate in Jesus Christ will have to be spelled out.'[31] As he saw it, the present world, conditioned by many limitations, is both real and unreal, and without the paralysing limitation of *karma samsāra*, Christians have a glimpse of transformation and a vision of hope. He called Christians to help Hindus 'to redefine the very nature of what is called religion' by dialogical inter-penetration to find out the common goal and strive to achieve it. For him, participation in nation-building was an imperative for every Christian in order to spell out Christ convincingly.

M. M. Thomas, who succeeded Devanandan as the director of CISRS, built on his vision, views and programmes. Echoing the views of senior national leaders and thinkers like Lal Behari Day and Gopala Krishna Gokhale, he expressed a positive view of the colonial impact on modern Asia, which effected what was almost a revolution.[32] At the same time he did not fail to point out the immediate possibility of fall and perversion.

---

[31] P. D. Devanandan, *Preparation for Dialogue* (Bangalore: CISRS, 1964), p. 38.
[32] M. M. Thomas, *The Christian Response to the Asian Revolution* (London: SCM, 1966), p. 29.

It was evident that there was conflict in the process of integration, and crushing poverty in the midst of productivity and industrialization. However, for Thomas, the 'Asian revolution' gives 'the spiritual vision of a more abundant life'. In this context the church in Asia has a unique opportunity to have an encounter with all people of progressive thinking, religious and secular, to present Jesus Christ as critically relevant, and to participate in nation-building and social transformation.

In response to Raymond Panikkar's *The Unknown Christ of Hinduism*,[33] Thomas produced his *The Acknowledged Christ of the Indian Renaissance* (1970), the outcome of an extensive study of the modern Hindu reformers and thinkers we mentioned above. He showed how Christ had not been ignored by those who wanted to reform Indian society, although they had their shortcomings in grasping the full stature and meaning of Christ. Thomas argued that theology should always be 'contextual'.[34] Attaining the self-hood of the church should be seen as an outcome of a theological process of discerning the relevance of Jesus Christ for the situation, and he saw in this connection the achievement of the Church of South India in 1947 as very significant. In the context of the battle to find a true anthropology in dialogue with the modern Hindu reformers and secular humanists, Thomas suggested a new phrase to understand the meaning of salvation, 'salvation as humanization'.[35] Thomas paid tribute to those western missionaries who contributed to the process of humanizing the poor and the untouchable communities of India, through which they found their dignity and became part of a new fellowship.

In parallel to John Hick's *God and the Universe of Faiths*,[36] Thomas published his *Man and the Universe of Faiths*[37] in which he presents the divine humanity of Jesus Christ as a spiritual source of a new community and suggests the possibility of 'secular fellowships' and 'Christ-centred syncretism' motivated by 'a spirituality for combat'. While he found secular ideologies like Marxism to have a vision of society close to the Christian vision, he points out how ideologies can become dogmatic, leading to totalitarian structures and failing to continue the exploration

[33] R. Panikkar, *The Unknown Christ of Hinduism* (London: Darton, Longman & Todd, 1964).

[34] M. M. Thomas, *The Acknowledged Christ of the Indian Renaissance* (Madras: Christian Literature Society, 1976), pp. 309–15.

[35] M. M. Thomas, *Salvation and Humanization – Some Critical Issues of the Theology of Mission in Contemporary India* (Madras: Christian Literature Society (for CISRS), 1971).

[36] J. Hick, *God and the Universe of Faiths: Essays in the Philosophy of Religion* (London: Macmillan, 1973).

[37] M. M. Thomas, *Man and the Universe of Faiths* (Madras: Christian Literature Society, 1976).

into the true nature of human life and its ultimate goal. He evaluated the major secular ideologies of India, focusing on anthropology, and tried to reconceive the secular meaning of Christ. In the end, he affirms the reality of human beings as created in the image of God, but fallen creatures, of 'the Crucified and Risen Jesus Christ as the true man and the source of renewal of human nature and through it of all things'.[38] In his later studies also, Christ was his central concern and he was willing to use the phrase 'Risking Christ for Christ's sake' as the title of one of his last books.[39]

Samartha, after his work in India in various capacities, became known in ecumenical circles when he became the founder-director of the sub-unit on 'dialogue with people of other faiths' of the WCC in 1971, and through several publications. That he started thinking in the same line of Devanandan and Thomas is evident in the titles of his early works.[40] Later on he was warning against a kind of Jesus-cult on the one hand and Christo-monism on the other and emphasized God as the centre and the absolute, whose oneness with Jesus was not ontological but relational, sustained and testified to by the eternal Spirit. With reference to the old debate about a christology from above and christology from below, Samartha presents two contrasting pictures. 'In its attempts to land on the religiously plural terrain of Asia,' he says, 'a *helicopter* christology makes such a lot of missiological noise and kicks up so much of theological dust that people around are prevented from hearing the voice and seeing the vision of the descending divinity. A *bullock-cart* christology, on the other hand, has its wheels always in touch with the unpaved roads of Asia, for without that continuing friction with the ground the cart cannot move at all.'[41] It was this friction that kept Samartha on the ground and helped him look with fresh eyes at a number of theological themes. For example, with an awareness of the multi-scriptural context, his was the quest for a new hermeneutics in Asia, seeing the Bible as a book of dialogue, which has to be read along with other religious scriptures. Furthermore, he suggested the Kingdom of God should be seen in essence as the reign of a Servant-Lord and the identity of the church is primarily a

[38] M. M. Thomas, *Man and the Universe of Faiths* (Madras: Christian Literature Society, 1976), pp. 195–203.
[39] M. M. Thomas, *Risking Christ for Christ's Sake: Towards an Ecumenical Theology of Pluralism* (Geneva: World Council of Churches, 1987).
[40] S. J. Samartha, *The Hindu View of History* (Bangalore: CISRS, 1959); *Introduction to Radhakrishnan* (New York: Association Press; New Delhi: YMCA, 1964); and *The Hindu Response to the Unbound Christ* (Bangalore: CISRS, 1974).
[41] S. J. Samartha, *One Christ – Many Religions: Towards a Revised Christology* (Bangalore: Orbis-SATHRI, 1992), p. v.

servant-community, a community of communities. With regard to a proper theology of religious pluralism, Samartha oscillated between seeing 'religions as different responses to the Mystery' and warning against 'rudderless boats in the waters of relativism'. Also, in the name of an inclusive approach he was careful not to co-opt other faiths into a Christian framework without their permission. What is imperative for him is 'dialogue', which he defines as 'a mood, a spirit, an attitude of love and respect towards neighbours of other faiths. It regards partners as persons, not as statistics. Understood and practised as an intentional life-style, it goes far beyond a sterile co-existence or uncritical friendliness.'[42] In the area of working for social change and protecting the environment, he says, members of different faith communities can work together with proximate goals while continuing dialogue on ultimate goals. It is a pilgrimage, focused in balance by the two eyes of 'commitment and openness'.

Chandran, the longest-serving principal of the United Theological College (about 30 years), known as the father and grandfather of several Indian Christian theologians, was committed to church unity and open to new thinking, including a broad and positive approach to people of other faiths. He pointed out how in the name of religious harmony and unity Vivekananda pushed non-Hindu religions into a subordinate position. Such harmony, he noted, could not be achieved even within and in between the schools of Vedānta.[43] But later Chandran worked out a new integration. He argues that the church in India has forgotten the generosity of even the Hebrew tribes to accommodate other groups, and of the first Christians towards the gentile converts, not requiring them to adopt Jewish rituals and norms. Otherwise, he thinks, more people would have come forward to confess their faith in Christ. Hence his call for 'a new and radical ecclesiology, recognising a multi-faith community as the new body of Christ'.[44]

The above four theologians have influenced many who have continued their line of thinking. For example, K. C. Abraham (b. 1936), building on Thomas, argues for a new method of theologizing within the framework of an orthopraxis, which involves commitment to Christ and creative

---

[42] S. J. Samartha, *Courage for Dialogue – Ecumenical Issues in Inter-religious Relationships* (Geneva: WCC, 1981), p. 100.

[43] J. R. Chandran, 'A comparison of the pagan apologetic of Celsus against Christianity as contained in Origen's *"Contra Celsum"* and the neo-Hindu attitude to Christianity as represented in the works of Vivekananda and an estimate of the value of Origen's reply for Christian apologetics with reference to neo-Hinduism', unpublished B.Litt. thesis, University of Oxford, 1949.

[44] J. R. Chandran, 'The Church of South India Jubilee – 10: A Call to Renewal', *People's Reporter* (16–30 June 1997), p. 3.

action in dialogue and co-operation with people of other faiths and secular ideologies. This is with full awareness of the disastrous effect of globalization on the economic situation of the poor, cultural cohesion and destruction of the creation.[45] Of course, such are the concerns of many, repeated in various forms.

VERNACULAR ATTEMPTS AT THEOLOGIZING

So far we have noted reflections done in English with reference to Sanskrit traditions. It is important to recognize contributions in the vernacular, which display features of originality and spontaneity. For example, Narayan Vaman Tilak (1862–1919), the poet of Maharashtra, was a convert, who became a Christian monk, and who sought to gather round himself a group called 'God's *Darbār*', a brotherhood of the 'baptised and unbaptised disciples of Christ'. Tilak wanted to present Christ to India in his 'naked beauty'. He composed poetry to such a high standard as to be included in the corpus of Marathi literature. His poetry is very devotional and became popular among Christians. Although they are not theological in the sense of reasoned statements, his poems carry the flavour of Indian religious poetry and break new ground in imagining God and Christ. For example, he calls Christ the 'Mother-Guru' and longs for the day when Indians acknowledge this. He drew the attention of western orientalists like J. C. Winslow and N. Macnicol, who collected and commented on his poems,[46] and such studies continue.[47]

Gurram Joshua (b. 1895), a dalit Christian poet called the 'Telugu Poet Laureate', was 'passionately committed to the fight against caste and religious communalism, as well as that to end hunger and oppression'.[48] The imagery of God in his poetry is fascinating, as it is in the writings of many vernacular poets and thinkers. No other language has such rich Christian poetry as Tamil. Drinking from the wells of the ancient Tamil literature and the devotional poetry of the Saiva and Vaishnava traditions, many laid foundations for a Tamil Christian theology, of whom most notable are Vedanayagam Sastriyar (1774–1864) and H. A. Krishna Pillai

---

[45] K. C. Abraham, *Liberative Solidarity: Contemporary Perspectives on Mission* (Tiruvalla: Christava Sahitya Samithi, 1996).

[46] See J. C. Winslow, *Narayan Vaman Tilak: The Christian Poet of Maharashtra* (Calcutta: YMCA, 1930) and N. Macnicol, *Psalms of Maratha Saints* (Calcutta: YMCA, 1919).

[47] See P. S. Jacob (ed.), *Experiential Response of N. V. Tilak* (Madras: Christian Literature Society, 1979).

[48] J. England, *Asian Christian Theologies – A Research Guide to Authors, Movements, Sources*, vol. I (Delhi: ISPCK-Orbis, 2002), p. 217.

(1827–1900). They produced epic poems and lyrics which are very popular among the Tamils[49] and which illustrate the coalescence of Christian and indigenous traditions. For example, Krishna Pillai's is the first lyric that appears in the Tamil 'Hymns and Lyrics'. In this lyric he starts addressing God as *Sat-Cit-Ananda* and in due course calls God 'mother', 'friend', and so on. Echoing the southern school of Viashnavism, which thought of divine grace in the model of cat-kitten as opposed to the northern school's monkey-cub, in one verse he says 'I cannot cling to you but you have clung me, do not leave me.' Poets like Krishna Pillai are deeply perplexed by certain Christian doctrines. Of course this is the experience of most Indian Christian theologians. At the same time, the poet uses the analogy of an ancient practice of a lover self-sacrificing to emphasize the suffering love of God for humanity expressed on the cross.[50] It is interesting to note that these poets were zealously evangelistic and theologically exclusive, but this was also typical of the poet-saints of their original Hindu traditions.

Of those who have encountered Tamil Christian poetry theologically, we will mention three. P. A. Sathiasatchy (1923–2006), himself a poet, preacher and writer, has identified resources in the ancient Tamil literature for a Tamil Christian theology. In concluding an essay calling for Christians to take the Tamil heritage and the recent Tamil renaissance seriously, he writes:

As a result we have a distinctive theology, which will have the fragrance of the Tamil soil, flavour of the natural world and breeze of justice and liberation described in the ancient Tamil poems. It is not like the potted plant idea of theology, which was brought from the West and planted in the Indian soil in the name of indigenisation or inculturation. Its preamble recognises similar plants already grown in the vast Tamil garden with the affirmation of God's universal witness and the cosmic presence of Christ who came definitively in Jesus of Nazareth.[51]

Dayanandan Francis (b. 1932) has done extensive studies on Tamil literature and the Tamil Saiva tradition. He identifies a number of parallel views on God between the Saiva and Christian traditions and points out how Hindu terms have influenced the Christian vocabulary.[52] Through

---

[49] See I. Selvanayagam, *A Dialogue on Dialogue: Reflections on Inter-faith Encounters* (Madras: Christian Literature Society, 1995), pp. 45–66.

[50] See R. S. Sugirtharajah, 'Thinking about Vernacular Hermeneutics Sitting in a Metropolitan Study' in R. S. Sugirtharajah (ed.), *Vernacular Hermeneutics* (Sheffield: Sheffield Academic Press, 1999), pp. 92–115 at 99.

[51] P. A. Sathiasatchy, 'Theology with Fragrance of the Tamil Soil' in I. Selvanayagam (ed.), *Moving Forms of Theology: Faith Talk's Changing Contexts* (Delhi: ISPCK, 2002), pp. 159–65 at 165.

[52] See D. Francis, *The Relevance of Hindu Ethos for Christian Presence: A Tamil Perspective* (Madras: Christian Literature Society, 1989).

his Tamil writings and songs he presents Jesus and his message in a new way, making appeal to those influenced by the recent Tamil renaissance. Thomas Thangaraj (b. 1942) contributed towards 'a singable theology' by composing Tamil Christian songs which reflect a contextual theology that addresses various issues of Tamil society. He tried to build on it a new christological model on the Saiva understanding of guru. Thangaraj compares, contrasts and projects Jesus, 'the crucified guru'.[53] It is not easy to fit Jesus into a system for which liberation is primarily from the bond of *karma samsāra*, and therefore he tries very hard to expand it to cover the socio-economic aspects of liberation, which is the cry of many other theologians.

All these three Tamil theologians (and Francis and Thangaraj are presbyters of the Church of South India) were for some time based in Tamilnadu Theological Seminary, an ecumenical institution for ministerial training and theological education. It was founded in 1969 and is situated in Madurai, known as the centre of Tamil culture and religion. Its first principal, Samuel Amirtham, encouraged the building up of a *gurukulam* model of community living and a pilgrim model of learning that involved students in the life of the neighbourhood in the context of the struggle for survival.[54] His theology is known as wholesome, as a *living theology* of perennial value.[55] Developing Tamil theological reflections in dialogue with Tamil traditions in the form of creative writing and songs has been one of the emphases of the seminary.

A NEW AWAKENING TO DISTINCTIVE IDENTITIES AND FRESH THEOLOGICAL INSIGHTS

'Is Christianity the teaching of Christ or the teaching of a certain body of men?'[56] The learned (*pandita*) Ramabai asked this question. We have already noted her association with Goreh and Sen. As a convert and social activist, particularly committed to the emancipation of hapless widows, she was reacting to sophisticated translations of the Bible with misleading Hindu terms, grand ceremonies and dogmas produced by men using their

---

[53] See T. Thangaraj, *The Crucified Guru – An Experiment in Cross-Cultural Christology* (Nashville: Abingdon Press, 1994).

[54] See S. Amirtham, 'Some New Emphases in Theological Education in Arasaradi' in R. S. Sugirtharajah and C. Hargreaves (eds.), *Readings in Indian Christian Theology*, vol. 1 (London: SPCK, 1993), pp. 14–23.

[55] See I. Selvanayagam, *Samuel Amirtham's Living Theology* (Bangalore: BTESSC/BTTBPSA, 2007).

[56] Quoted in R. S. Sugirtharajah, *The Bible and the Third World* (Cambridge: Cambridge University Press, 2001), p. 99.

authority in the church. She asked for a simple translation of the words of Jesus, which had the power of enchanting the people's hearts. She herself translated the whole Bible from the originals into Marathi. She enjoyed the freedom of interpreting biblical passages (including miracles) in such a way that they prompted liberating action.

After a break in the historical link with Ramabai, in the early 1980s a group of women theologians started to remember her and continue to present a feminist perspective to fundamental aspects of life. There are several groups with apparent splintering based on class and ideological differences. While drawing heavily on the feminist theologians of the west, they try to give an Indian flavour by taking metaphors like power (*śakti*), mother earth and the revenge of the goddess. The Hindu image of the androgynous God Śiva has given them insights to conceptualize God as both male and female. On the whole, they are holistic in their vision and 'eco-feminism' has increasingly become a catch-word.

Gabriele Dietrich (b. 1943), of German origin, based in Tamilnadu Theological Seminary, started her process of immersion into Indian reality at CISRS under the leadership of M. M. Thomas. Her main concern is to see the relationship between capitalism, patriarchy, the destruction of the nature, violence and power. She is associated with a number of women's groups and finds in their revolt against oppression the expression of resurrection. In a few overt theological reflections she identifies the leadership of women in the Bible, highlights the feminine quality of compassion, describes sexuality as 'an equal relationship of love, tenderness and mutual enchantment', and calls for a theological language that transcends sex-stereotypes and a feminine perspective for inter-faith dialogue. As a historian of religions too, she points out how 'depatriarchalising the Christian faith opens up new horizons' with reference to how 'historians of religion have drawn parallels between Hindu Shakti, the God of energy, Sophia, the "Wisdom" of God and the Jewish Shechina, the dwelling of God among people' and how feminist theologians have pointed out that 'Ruach, the Spirit of God is feminine'. 'Yet', she insists, 'all such exercises have to stand the test of how they contribute to the liberation of women in day to day life.'[57] She finds the metaphor of the world as God's body, expounded by Ramanuja and recognized by women writers in the west, helpful in seeing the integral relationship between matter and the spirit, the mutual sustainability of life and a scorporate movement towards wholeness. Aruna Gnanadason (b. 1949),

[57] G. Dietrich, *A New Thing on Earth* (Delhi: ISPCK-Tamilnadu Theological Seminary, 2001), p. 82.

based in the WCC, has guided several women in sharing their stories in forums and groups and in using insights that can inform a new approach of feminist theology in the Indian context.[58]

Dalits ('split' or 'broken' people) are the worst victims of the evil and divisive caste system in India. They have been treated as untouchable and they form about seventeen per cent of the Indian population. They are spread all over the country and are known by different names, while the government continues to use the term introduced by the British, 'Scheduled Caste'. Their awakening is attributed to champions of their liberation, particularly B. R. Ambedkar (1891–1956), whose *mantra* was 'unite, educate and agitate'. Dalit theologians use historical and socio-logical studies to show the magnitude of the age-long suffering and pain of the dalit people. They start with the observation that what is known as Indian Christian theology in the past has been produced by those coming from the Brahmin and non-Brahmin high-caste communities.

Sporadic reflections and initial explorations into the theological significance of the dalit experience found a tangible expression in a consultation on 'Towards a Dalit Theology' held in Chennai (Madras) in December 1986.[59] Since then theological consultations and the resultant literature on dalit theology have established a stable place for one of the most authentic expressions of the Indian liberation theology, which is distinctive because the caste system is unparalleled anywhere in the world. Arvind Nirmal (1936–95), one of the distinguished pioneers of dalit theology, in his seminal essay, defines it as a theology *about, for* and *from* the dalits.[60] For him it is a counter-theology, calling for 'a methodological exclusivism'. 'What this exclusivism implies', he says, 'is the affirmation that the Triune God – the Father, the Son and Spirit – is on the side of the dalits and not of the non-dalits who are the oppressors.' He writes that the unparalleled depth of pathos and misery of the dalits should inform dalit theology, and that those who have experienced that misery are the dalit theologians proper, though non-dalits who can empathize and sympathize with them can contribute.

According to Nirmal, the exodus experience of the dalits, which was even more traumatic than Israel's, is from a non-people to people, to a realization of a humanness, the image of God, and the goal is 'the glorious

[58] A. Gnanadason, 'Feminist Theology: An Indian Perspective' in R. S. Sugirtharajah and C. Hargreaves (eds.), *Readings in Indian Christian Theology*, vol. 1 (London: SPCK, 1993) pp. 59–71.
[59] M. E. Prabhakar (ed.), *Towards a Dalit Theology* (Delhi: ISPCK-CISRS-CDLM, 1989).
[60] A. P. Nirmal, 'Towards a Christian Dalit Theology' in A. P. Nirmal and V. Devasahayam (eds.), *A Reader in Dalit Theology* (Madras: Gurukul, 1985), pp. 53–70 at 58.

liberty of the children of God'. He denounces Hindu gods like Rama who, according to a story, killed a dalit for daring to perform a religious act and argues that 'the God whom Jesus Christ revealed and about whom the prophets of the Old Testament spoke is a dalit God'. That is, 'He is a servant-God – a God who serves', as was Jesus Christ, whom the Gospel writers identified with the Servant of God of Isaiah 53.[61] Jesus, both the Son of God and Son of Man, like the dalits, 'encountered rejection, mockery, contempt, suffering, and finally, death'. He fought for the rights of the excluded in the society, when he cleansed the temple in Jerusalem, and the price was the cross where he cried of God-forsakenness. Nirmal writes, 'That feeling of being God-forsaken is at the heart of our dalit experiences and dalit consciousness in India.'[62] Nirmal left the development of a dalit theology of the Holy Spirit to the younger theologians, who have identified the Spirit with the deep sighs of the dalits and the groaning of the whole creation, which suffers destruction and domination by the powerful. Of the essays of other dalit theologians in the above-mentioned *Reader*, the most notable are those of Devasahayam (b. 1949),[63] who discusses the connection between pollution, poverty and power-lessness, and James Massey (b. 1943), who identifies life-context, history and language as the main requirements of a dalit theology, which he elaborates in a separate book.[64]

Dalit theology is still emerging and promises to be the most authentic and creative theology in India. For example, there are studies of subaltern religion, which show the liberative elements of dalit symbols. The drum is identified as one of the most prominent among a particular dalit community. It represents divine–human communication and the Christic principle of both resistance and emancipation.[65] And there are also attempts to develop a 'systematic' dalit theology.[66] An important question for dalit theology is whether it can be (selectively) inter-faith. This is because, while most of the Indian Christians are dalits, most of the dalits

[61] A. P. Nirmal, 'Towards a Christian Dalit Theology' in A. P. Nirmal and V. Devasahayam (eds.), *A Reader in Dalit Theology* (Madras: Gurukul, 1985), pp. 53–70 at 63–5.

[62] A. P. Nirmal, 'Towards a Christian Dalit Theology' in A. P. Nirmal and V. Devasahayam (eds.), *A Reader in Dalit Theology* (Madras: Gurukul, 1985), pp. 53–70 at 69.

[63] V. Devasahayam, 'Pollution, Poverty and Powerlessness – A Dalit Perspective' in A. P. Nirmal and V. Devasahayam (eds.), *A Reader in Dalit Theology* (Madras: Gurukul, 1985), pp. 1–22.

[64] J. Massey, *Towards Dalit Hermeneutics: Rereading the Texts, the History and the Literature* (Delhi: ISPCK, 1994).

[65] S. Clarke, *Dalits and Christianity – Subaltern Religion and Liberation Theology in India* (Delhi: Oxford University Press, 1998), pp. 163–5.

[66] See C. Singaram, 'Can Dalit Theology be Systematised? A Tentative Proposal' in I. Selvanayagam (ed.), *Moving Forms of Theology* (Delhi: ISPCK, 2002), pp. 126–33.

are registered as Hindus, though originally they did not have anything to do with Brahminic Hinduism.

Dalit woman is known as 'the dalit of the dalit' and 'the thrice alienated', having to experience manifold suffering and pain.[67] If this is the case of women, what about dalit children? In any context children are the most vulnerable and their experience must be taken as an authentic resource for a creative theology. No other victim is as innocent as a child. In an initial attempt, I have observed that 'All types of Christian theology known in history . . . are based on the experience and articulation of the adults, the grown-ups. They are necessarily wordy, prepositional and argumentative.'[68] I have pointed out some of the terrible experiences of children in India like child-marriage, sexual abuse, domestic violence, female infanticide, street-life, child labour and negligence. Jesus put the children in the middle of the adult community and interpreted them as the primary recipients of the Kingdom of God, revealers of God's love and the symbols of powerlessness. Referring to observations made by psychologists and others, I have stressed the importance of becoming children, again and again, for achieving true maturity and wholeness.

Tribal identity also seeks theological expression in India. Along with the dalits, the tribal communities, who account for about four per cent of the population, experience oppression, mainly from invaders from the plains. The central belt and north-eastern regions are the two areas having the greatest concentration of tribals, who are themselves of varied language and customs. The best representative of theologians reflecting on the experience of people in the central belt is Nirmal Minz (b. 1927), a Lutheran bishop based in Bihar. Building on the fruits of anthropological studies and biblical views on covenant, Minz's focus is on land. According to Minz, the corporate ownership of the land gives tribal people a 'sacred' sense of community and a 'harmonious or balanced relationship of man-nature and spirit'.[69] He believes that the generous and accommodative attitude of the tribal people was exploited by the invaders, and the new order introduced by Jesus requires a 'servant-politics' for its full realization within a covenantal relationship. Wati Longchar (b. 1961), a Baptist

---

[67] See R. Manorama, 'Dalit Women: The Thrice Alienated' in M. E. Prabhakar (ed.), *Towards a Dalit Theology* (Delhi: ISPCK-CISRS-CDLM, 1989), pp. 146–50.

[68] I. Selvanayagam, 'Children Laugh and Cry: Authentic Resources for Christian Theology', *Asian Journal of Theology*, 9/2 (1995), 352–66 at 352.

[69] N. Minz, 'A Theological Interpretation of the Tribal Reality in India' in R. S. Sugirtharajah and C. Hargreaves (eds.), *Readings in Indian Christian Theology*, vol. 1 (London: SPCK, 1993), pp. 46–58 at 48.

theologian from Nagaland, may be taken as the best representative of the tribal theologians in the north-east. For him too, the central focus of reflection is land, or 'space', which is integrally connected with God and creation and to the communal living of the people. He believes the task of theology is to 'explore resources for strengthening the interconnectedness of all realities' to 'safeguard the world from destruction and exploitation'.[70] This will lead to a holistic vision of the Triune God, who is integrally connected with the cosmic organism, which moves in history as a whole.

CONCLUDING REMARKS

The complex and multi-faceted reality of India is reflected in the variety of approaches and levels of understanding of theology. Faith-talk or God-talk is interwoven with historical, natural and social realities and passes through different stages. Robin Boyd's assessment of Indian theology after presenting the first stage is noteworthy. Writing in 1969, he says:

To use a familiar simile, the Church in many parts of India has been like a pot-plant transplanted into a garden. At first it grew in its imported soil, and perhaps the assistant gardener who accompanied it forgot to break the pot! The time has come, however, when the plant has taken root in the new environment; the pot has been shattered within and the imported soil has been absorbed and replaced. No longer does the gardener have to bring the water of the Word from a distant source, for the plant has struck its own deep tap-root to the perennial springs. It grows larger and more luxuriant than it ever did in its bleak northern home. And the time for fruit-bearing has come. The western confessions have indeed been channels for bringing the Water of Life, but they are not the only ones and the Indian Church must in time develop its own confession, a development to which many official statements and publications already look forward.[71]

Boyd's observation is fascinating and has gone on to be fulfilled today. Perhaps Sen and Chenchiah would have whispered that the original habitat of the Water of Life was Asia before it was taken to the West and poured into jars and cups of complicated shapes, and that the western confessions were not pure channels but tainted with political domination, commercial interest and a sense of cultural superiority. And Hogg and Sathiasatchy would ask for the recognition of similar plants in the Indian garden with their roots attached to the perennial springs. But what has

---

[70] W. Longchar, 'An Emerging Tribal/Indigenous Theology: Prospect for Doing Asian Theology', *The Journal of Theologies and Cultures in Asia* 1 (2002), 3–16 at 13.

[71] R. H. S. Boyd, *An Introduction to Indian Christian Theology*, revised edn. (Delhi: ISPCK, 1975), pp. 259–60.

failed the hope of Boyd is the Indian Church, which is unable to break the pot that has no attraction for the Indian majority.

The theologians mentioned in this essay have shown great courage and confidence to criticize what was held as sacrosanct and attempt new interpretations of the gospel. Greater has been the confidence more recently in re-reading the Bible with fresh eyes based on the social experience of living in concrete contexts and encountering realities on the ground. For example, Dhyanchand Carr (b. 1938) has launched a movement of re-reading the Bible in the whole of Asia. His interpretations of the Galilean priority of Jesus' ministry and of the Son of Man as the true representative of the victim community has been a great boost to dalit theology. His is an activist's understanding of the Bible as the 'Sword of the Spirit'.[72] Similarly, there have been distinctive biblical reflections in specialized areas such as the dalit movement and theology[73] and relating to people of other faiths.[74]

For most of the theologians studied by Boyd, Hinduism means Vedānta, Vedānta means Advaita Vedānta and that again is that of Sankara! And the Latin captivity referred to at the beginning of this article seems to have been replaced by a Sanskrit captivity! We have a long way to go to recognize a variety of traditions within the pan-mythic Indian religious reality, and the dynamic interaction within and between them, which would greatly inform proper methods in Indian Christian theologies. The present revival within the Hindu fold with the persistent identification of Indianness with that of the Brahminic tradition hardly allows scope to develop a dialogical theology with commitment and openness. At this juncture the attempt of Christopher Duraisingh (b. 1938) needs recognition. Captivated by Sunder Rao's experience and vision of the coalescence of the two streams of west and east providing the inseparable 'co-efficients and co-determinants of the Indian ethos', with a background in the study of Ramanuja and process theology, and referring to the achievement of poets like Krishna Pillai, he presents a rather ideal scheme in a series of articles on 'Indian Hyphenated Christians and Theological Reflections' (1979–80).[75] Duraisingh critically evaluates the earlier attempts of Indian Christian theologians, arguing that theology is not an exercise in ideas and

[72] See D. Carr, *Sword of the Spirit: An Activist's Understanding of the Bible* (Geneva: WCC, 1992).

[73] V. Devasahayam, *Outside the Camp: Bible Studies in Dalit Perspective* (Madras: Gurukul, 1992).

[74] I. Selvanayagam, *Relating to People of Other Faiths: Insights from the Bible* (Tiruvalla: Christava Sahitya Samithi-BTTBPSA, 2004).

[75] C. Duraisingh, 'Indian Hyphenated Christians and Theological Reflections – A New Expression of Identity', *Religion and Society* XXVI/4 (1979), 95–101.

concepts, but more to do with life and liturgy, in which there will be thanksgiving for all the resources of the Indian heritage, including arts and architecture, herbal medicines and yoga. But if the 'total Indian hyphenated Christian ethos' includes 'our classical linguistic and religious sensibilities as well as our socio-economic realities and actions', Brahminic tradition with its ritual and caste system, which has chained masses, may still be at the centre. Even the subaltern traditions have perpetuated fatalistic notions that obstruct process of development. The *Hindutva* (Hinduization) vision of militant Hinduism is no different, even though India is now a fast-changing society in the throes of modernization and globalization.

It should be pointed out that the Indian understanding of the Judaeo-Christian tradition has not been purged of the anti-Semitic attitude of the early western theologies or of Hinduism. Because the worth of the Hebrew Scripture was relegated to the position of mere preparation and promise for fulfilment in Christ, some Indian Christian theologians like Chenchiah and Chakkarai have gone to the confused extent of suggesting the replacement of it with some Hindu scriptures, but without clarifying their axioms. Today we have to take the Jewish–Christian relationship within a continuum, a single process in which God, with mysterious names like Yahweh and Trinity, has specially located himself in the faith journey of a community which had its origin in slavery and liberation, and which experienced extension and renewal. God's struggle with this community, both challenging deviation and taking new initiatives, is uniquely insightful. The significance of Jesus, perceived and confessed in several ways, was originally part of this process, and the development of extended communities by the power and guidance of the Spirit is very important for Indian Christians. They are called not to save their souls only but also to create a transformed and transforming community of equals with collective charisma and commitment to service so that the other Indian communities do not ignore them.

Awakening to and asserting distinctive identities is important for cre-ative theological reflections. But if we are committed to being truly part of the body of Christ all over the world, we should also be able to com-municate and exchange with others. It would be hard to deny that outside observers find much of what is said in India has already been said in their own context, and this needs to be acknowledged within an academic ethos. Moreover, it is time to recognize as universal the shifting combinations of the power of evil in abusing differences between socio-economic status, intellectual capacity, gender and age. The only way out seems to be to recapture Jesus' vision of a powerless yet loving and trusting child with whom God is identified and who symbolizes the universal ethos of the Kingdom of God. The combination, exemplified by persons like Sundar Singh and Ramabai, of prayerful life in Christ, simple life-style and communication, commitment to service, but without giving up reasoning, seems to have perennial appeal to India.

BIBLIOGRAPHY

Abraham, K. C., *Liberative Solidarity: Contemporary Perspectives on Mission*, Tiruvalla: Christava Sahitya Samithi, 1996.

Aleaz, K. P., *Christian Thought Through Advaita Vedānta*, Delhi: ISPCK, 1996.

Amirtham, S., 'Some New Emphases in Theological Education in Arasaradi' in R. S. Sugirtharajah and C. Hargreaves (eds.), *Readings in Indian Christian Theology*, vol. I, London: SPCK, 1993, pp. 14–23.

Andrews, C. F., *North India*, London: A. R. Mowbray, 1908.

Appasamy, A. J., *Christianity as Bhakti Mārga*, Madras: Christian Literature Society, 1930.

What is Moksa? A Study in the Johannine Doctrine of Life, Madras: Christian Literature Society, 1931.

The Gospel and India's Heritage, London: SPCK, 1942.

Boyd, R. H. S., *An Introduction to Indian Christian Theology*, Delhi: ISPCK, 1969.

India and the Latin Captivity of the Church – The Cultural Context of the Gospel, London: Cambridge University Press, 1974.

Manilal C. Parekh, 1885–1967, Dhanjibhai Fakirbhai, 1895–1967: A Selection, Madras: Christian Literature Society, 1974.

Khristadvaita – A Theology for India, Madras: Christian Literature Society, 1977.

Carr, D., *Sword of the Spirit: An Activist's Understanding of the Bible*, Geneva: WCC, 1992.

Chakkarai, V., *Jesus the Avatār*, Madras: Christian Literature Society, 1930.

The Cross and Indian Thought, Madras: Christian Literature Society, 1932.

Chandran, J. R., 'A comparison of the pagan apologetic of Celsus against Christianity as contained in Origen's "*Contra Celsum*" and the neo-Hindu attitude to Christianity as represented in the works of Vivekananda and an estimate of the value of Origen's reply for Christian apologetics with reference to neo-Hinduism', unpublished B.Litt. thesis, University of Oxford, 1949.

'The Church of South India Jubilee – 10: A Call to Renewal', part II, *People's Reporter* (June 1997), 16–30.

Chenchiah, P., 'Jesus and Non-Christian Faiths' in G.V. Job, P. Chenchiah, V. Chakkarai, D. M. Devasahayam, S. Jesudason, Eddy Asirvatham and A. N. Sudarisanam, *Rethinking Christianity in India*, Madras: A. N. Sudarisanam, 1938, pp. 47–62.

'Religion in Contemporary India' in G. V. Job, P. Chenchiah, V. Chakkarai, D. M. Devasahayam, S. Jesudason, Eddy Asirvatham and A. N. Sudarisanam, *Rethinking Christianity in India*, Madras: A. N. Sudarisanam, 1938, pp. 201–15.

Clarke, S., *Dalits and Christianity – Subaltern Religion and Liberation Theology in India*, Delhi: Oxford University Press, 1998.

Devanandan, P. D., *Preparation for Dialogue*, Bangalore: CISRS, 1964.

Devasahayam, V., 'Pollution, Poverty and Powerlessness – A Dalit Perspective' in A. Nirmal and V. Devasahayam (eds.), *A Reader in Dalit Theology*, Madras: Gurukul, 1985, pp. 1–22.

Outside the Camp: Bible Studies in Dalit Perspective, Madras: Gurukul, 1992.

Dietrich, G., *A New Thing on Earth*, Delhi: ISPCK-Tamilnadu Theological Seminary, 2001.

Duraisingh, C., 'Indian Hyphenated Christians and Theological Reflections – A New Expression of Identity', *Religion and Society* XXVI/4 (1979), 95–101.

England, J. (ed.), *Asian Christian Theologies – A Research Guide to Authors, Movements, Sources*, vol. I, Delhi: ISPCK-Orbis, 2002.

Farquhar, J. N., *The Crown of Hinduism*, London: Oxford University Press, 1913.

Francis, D., *The Christian Witness of Sadhu Sundar Singh – A Collection of his Writings*, Madras: Christian Literature Society, 1989.

The Relevance of Hindu Ethos for Christian Presence: A Tamil Perspective, Madras: Christian Literature Society, 1989.

Gnanadason, A., 'Feminist Theology: An Indian Perspective' in R. S. Sugirtharajah and C. Hargreaves (eds.), *Readings in Indian Christian Theology*, vol. I, London: SPCK, 1993, pp. 59–71.

Heiler, F., *The Gospel of Sadhu Sundar Singh*, Delhi: ISPCK, 1989.

Hick, J., *God and the Universe of Faiths: Essays in the Philosophy of Religion*, London: Macmillan, 1973.

Hume, R. A., *Missions from the Modern View*, New York: Fleming H. Revell Co., 1905.

Jacob, P. S. (ed.), *Experiential Response of N. V. Tilak*, Madras: Christian Literature Society, 1979.

Jones, E. S., *Christ of the Indian Road*, Lucknow: Lucknow Publishing House, 1925.

Jones, J. P., *India: Its Life and Thought*, New York: The Macmillan Company, 1908.

Kraemer, H., *The Christian Message in a Non-Christian World*, London: International Missionary Council, 1938.

Longchar, W., 'An Emerging Tribal/Indigenous Theology: Prospect for Doing Asian Theology', *The Journal of Theologies and Cultures in Asia*, vol. I (2002), 3–16.

Lucas, B., *The Empire of Christ: Being a Study of the Missionary Enterprise in the Light of Modern Religious Thought*, London: Macmillan, 1908.

Macnicol, N., *Psalms of Maratha Saints*, Calcutta: YMCA, 1919.

Manorama, R., 'Dalit Women: The Thrice Alienated' in M. E. Prabhakar (ed.), *Towards a Dalit Theology*, Delhi: ISPCK-CISRS-CDLM, 1989, pp. 146–50.

Massey, J., *Towards Dalit Hermeneutics: Rereading the Texts, the History and the Literature*, Delhi: ISPCK, 1994.

Minz, N., 'A Theological Interpretation of the Tribal Reality in India' in R. S. Sugirtharajah and C. Hargreaves (eds.), *Readings in Indian Christian Theology*, vol. I, London: SPCK, 1993, pp. 46–58.

Nirmal, A. P., 'Towards a Christian Dalit Theology' in A. P. Nirmal and V. Devasahayam (eds.), *A Reader in Dalit Theology*, Madras: Gurukul, 1985, pp. 53–70.

Panikkar, R., *The Unknown Christ of Hinduism*, London: Darton, Longman & Todd, 1964.

Paradkar, B. A. M., *The Theology of Goreh*, Madras: Christian Literature Society-CISRS, 1969.

Pope, G. U., *The Tiruvacagam*, Oxford: Clarendon Press, 1900.

Prabhakar, M. E. (ed.), *Towards a Dalit Theology*, Delhi: ISPCK-CISRS-CDLM, 1989.

Samartha, S. J., *The Hindu View of History*, Bangalore: CISRS, 1959.

Introduction to Radhakrishnan, New York: Association Press; New Delhi: YMCA; 1964.

The Hindu Response to the Unbound Christ, Bangalore: CISRS, 1974.

Courage for Dialogue – Ecumenical Issues in Inter-religious Relationships, Geneva: WCC, 1981.

One Christ – Many Religions: Towards a Revised Christology, Bangalore: Orbis-SATHRI, 1992.

Sathiasatchy, P. A., 'Theology with Fragrance of the Tamil Soil' in I. Selvanayagam (ed.), *Moving Forms of Theology: Faith Talk's Changing Contexts*, Delhi: ISPCK, 2002, pp. 159–65.

Scott, D. (ed.), *Keshub Chunder Sen*, Madras: Christian Literature Society for CISRS and United Theological College, 1979.

Selvanayagam, I., *A Dialogue on Dialogue: Reflections on Inter-faith Encounters*, Madras: Christian Literature Society, 1995.

'Children Laugh and Cry: Authentic Resources for Christian Theology', *Asian Journal of Theology* 9/2 (1995), 352–66.

Relating to People of Other Faiths: Insights from the Bible, Tiruvalla: Christava Sahitya Samithi-BTTBPSA, 2004.

Samuel Amirtham's Living Theology, Bangalore: BTESSC/BTTBPSA, 2007.

Sharpe, E., *The Theology of A. G. Hogg*, Madras: Christian Literature Society, 1971.

Singaram, C., 'Can Dalit Theology be Systematised? A Tentative Proposal' in I. Selvanayagam (ed.), *Moving Forms of Theology*, Delhi: ISPCK, 2002, pp. 126–33.

Slater, T. E., *The Higher Hinduism in Relation to Christianity: Certain Aspects of Hindu Thought from a Christian Standpoint*, London: Elliott Stock, 1902.

Sugirtharajah, R. S., 'Thinking about Vernacular Hermeneutics Sitting in a Metropolitan Study' in R. S. Sugirtharajah (ed.), *Vernacular Hermeneutics*, Sheffield: Sheffield Academic Press, 1999, pp. 92–115.

The Bible and the Third World, Cambridge: Cambridge University Press, 2001.

Thangaraj, T., *The Crucified Guru – An Experiment in Cross-Cultural Christology*,
    Nashville: Abingdon Press, 1994.
Thomas, M. M., *The Christian Response to the Asian Revolution*, London: SCM
    Press, 1966.
    *Salvation and Humanization – Some Critical Issues of the Theology of Mission in
    Contemporary India*, Madras: Christian Literature Society (for CISRS), 1971.
    The Acknowledged Christ of the Indian Renaissance, Madras: Christian Literature
    Society, 1976.
    Man and the Universe of Faiths, Madras: Christian Literature Society, 1976.
    The Secular Ideologies of India and the Secular Meaning of Christ, Madras:
    Christian Literature Society-CISRS, 1976.
    Risking Christ for Christ's Sake: Towards an Ecumenical Theology of Pluralism,
    Geneva: World Council of Churches, 1987.
Winslow, J. C., *Narayan Vaman Tilak: The Christian Poet of Maharashtra*,
    Calcutta: YMCA, 1930.
Ziegenbalg, B., *Geneology of South Indian Gods*, New Delhi: Unity Book Service,
    1984.

CHAPTER 4

From abandonment to blessing: the theological presence of Christianity in Indonesia

John A. Titaley

Christianity in Indonesia has gone through a history parallel only to the history of the nation-state itself. As a nation-state made of diverse ethnic groups of old societies and still struggling with its pluralistic identity, Christianity in Indonesia struggles likewise. However, during the short history of the nation state, Christianity has made practical contributions to the creation of a just and egalitarian nation-state. It has been, therefore, the struggle and the call of Christianity to define its role as a blessing to the nation-state theologically.

When Christianity first appeared in the archipelago, the country did not exist yet. The people of the archipelago did not think that they would be united in the future as a nation-state. Smaller kingdoms existed in the archipelago autonomously; the two main kingdoms were Sri Vijaya, a Hindu kingdom in Sumatera from the seventh to the fourteenth century CE, and a Buddhist kingdom called Majapahit in east Java from the thirteenth to the sixteenth century CE. However, a stronger notion of Indonesia as a nation in the twentieth century CE was possible because of the legacy of western colonialism; similarly, western colonialism rooted Christianity in Indonesian society.

CHRISTIANITY: PRE-WESTERN COLONIALISM

The history of Christianity in Indonesia has been associated with western colonialism; however, based upon the history of the Catholic Church in Indonesia, Christianity appeared in the archipelago about the middle of the seventh century CE, especially in Sumatra and Java, where western nations had not appeared in the archipelago. Christianity was introduced by a group of Nestorian Christians after the split between western and eastern branches of the Church in the fifth century CE in Europe. One of the reports in the thirteenth century CE of the eastern church in Baghdad said that there were 707 churches and 181 monasteries scattered among Cyprus, Iraq, Iran, Manchuria, Mongolia, India, Sri Lanka, Sumatra and Java. In Sumatra, Fansur (*Pancur*) is mentioned explicitly, which is a famous port in north Sumatra near *Barus*. However, further records about Christianity during this period no longer exist in the Indonesian archives. They are believed to be part of the Sri Vijaya kingdom of Sumatra, the first major kingdom of the archipelago. This means that after two world religions, Hinduism and Buddhism, Christianity was the third world religion to come to the archipelago.

CHRISTIANITY: WESTERN COLONIALISM

With the development of western colonialism among European kingdoms, Christianity was taken all over the world, including the archipelago (later to become Indonesia). Portugal, Spain, Holland and Britain must be noted in bringing Christianity to Indonesia.

Portugal–Spain

When Portugal found the sea route to Asia for spices, avoiding the Middle East and India, they conquered Malaka, the hub for trade in southeast Asia in 1511. In the same year, they went to Maluku, the source of the wanted spices, where Portugal for the first time reached the archipelago. They conquered Ternate and built a fortress called Sao Paulo in the year 1522. Thus began the process of western colonialism and the spreading of Christianity in the archipelago. A priest was commissioned to preserve the Christian faith of the Portuguese. He was also responsible for spreading Christianity from there southwards to Ambon and northwards up to Morotai.

Meanwhile, between 1519 and 1522, breaking the pope's decree of 1494, Spain reached the Philippines from the Pacific side, which was supposed to be the territory of Portugal, having made stops at Alor, Atapupu and Batu Gede in the Timor islands of the archipelago, but they declined to conquer them, believing them to be part of Portugal's hegemony.

This happened because Majapahit, one of the other major kingdoms, was declining. Islam at the time was on the rise, after the killing of the Majaphit King by one of his sons. Later on there developed the Islamic kingdom of Demak in Central Java. The spreading of Islam in the archipelago during this time was enhanced strongly by Chinese Muslims from the north, although traders from Gujarat in India also introduced Islam into the archipelago. During this period, Portugal had to take into consideration the fact of Islam and the smaller kingdoms of Ternate and Tidore in Maluku, despite the fact that Christianity had grown in the archipelago. The Christians were local people with their indigenous beliefs, who perceived the arrival of Portugal to be their rescue from the spread of Islam, especially by the Ternate Sultanate. In addition to the formation of Christian villages that occurred during the above-mentioned period, in 1558 a Catholic archdiocese was founded in Malaka, in which the presently named Indonesia was included.

However, Portugal was not serious about preserving Christianity during this initial stage of the period. The *padroado* system introduced by the pope did not work as planned. The system requires a Portuguese king to be responsible for nurturing Christianity in the regions that he rules, by appointing bishops, missionaries and so on. The Christians still practised their indigenous beliefs after being baptized into Christianity, and no missionaries were commissioned to work with the people until 1546, when the Jesuit Francis Xavier arrived. Xavier coordinated missionary work in central Maluku, north Maluku and Bacan. Missionary work was reported also in Flores, Solor and Adonara in eastern Nusa Tenggara. The north Sulawesi and Sangihe islands were also included in missionary work, with Spanish assistance from the Philippines. The missionary work ended in Manado in 1643, when the people rebelled against Spain, but, afraid of revenge from Spain, the people in Manado invited the Dutch to come, so that Manado was occupied from 1655.

Portugal attempted to bring Christianity to Java, especially in Blambangan, but was crushed by Islamic forces. One of the reasons why Christianity did not develop under the Portuguese was because the spread of Christianity was not their main interest in coming to the archipelago; they were motivated by economic and political considerations. In addition, the lack of missionaries, language barriers with the locals, and problems with teaching methods were factors also. The work of Portugal and Spain was replaced by that of the Dutch, who came with Protestant Christianity, but their primary motivation was not spreading the gospel of Jesus Christ either; their economic and political motivations were stronger than their mission for God. Consequently, *cuius regio, eius religio* (wherever you conquer your religion should reign), the policy of the time, was not implemented fully.

Holland–Britain

The arrival of the Dutch in the archipelago was motivated also by their interest in spices. When Philip II of Spain announced the union of Spain and Portugal, the Dutch engaged in a sixty-year war with Spain and Portugal, but finally decided to find the spices directly. Hence, the Dutch started their own naval task force and finally defeated Portugal in 1601, and in 1609 they conquered the Portuguese fortress in Ambon; their first territory in the archipelago.

Since their main interests were in trade, in the year 1602 the States General of the Netherlands founded the Dutch East India Company with its monopoly extended out from the Cape of Good Hope to the straits of Magellan in the east. The implications were not just political and economic, but also religious. This was especially true for the Christians (Catholics) resulting from Portugal's missionary work. The Company was granted also the rights of her predecessors to take care of the religious life of the society. The policy of *cuius regio, eius religio* applied to the Dutch as well. They managed to convert most of the Catholics in the archipelago to Protestantism, except for the Catholics in the Flores and the Solor islands, due to the fact that these islands had no economic significance. For about two centuries, the Dutch did not take good care of religious life either. Instead of spreading Christianity with their missionary works (which included Joseph Kam), they intervened too much in the church's life, making it a state church. This continued even after the Company had been liquidated in the 1799 CE. The work of developing Christianity was concentrated especially in Ambon, Bandaneira, north Maluku, north Sulawesi, eastern Nusa Tenggara and the big cities in Java. After two hundred years of Protestantism, at the end of the nineteenth century there were several full congregations; five in the eastern part of the archipelago: Makasar, Ambon, Ternate, Banda and Kupang; three in Java: Jakarta, Semarang and Surabaya; one in Sumatra: Padang; and one in Malaka. The congregations in Java served the Dutch only, while the congregations in the east served the local peoples.

Coinciding with the bankruptcy of the Company, there was an international change of politics in Europe. The Netherlands, now a satellite of the French, had to form a government called the Batavian Republic. The republic dismissed the Company and formed a new Dutch government for the archipelago headed by Governor General Daendels from 1808 to 1811. The Dutch in the archipelago were then defeated by the British and Sir Stamford Raffles ruled the archipelago from 1811 to 1815. When the French were defeated by the British in Europe, the rule of the British in the archipelago was handed back to the Dutch. The Dutch wasted no time trying to restore what had been left by the Company, but it was not until the middle of the nineteenth century that the Dutch tried to expand their occupation. They fought several wars with local people into the early twentieth century.

Although religious freedom was granted to the people, the Dutch reorganized the church according to the Company's model under the decree of King William I. They founded the state church in the form of The Protestant Church of the Dutch Indies, where various denominations like Calvinism and Lutheranism came together. They allowed missionary societies to enter the archipelago under the coordination of the state church. Thus, Christianity was no longer just for the Dutch, but was opened up for local people and others in eastern Indonesia. It was only by this time that Christianity was properly developed.

During this period, missionaries had been invited from the Netherlands to help develop the church. The missionaries, with their pietistic Christianity, converted the locals by preaching the gospel verbally and through a strict spirituality. The conversions usually took place through a conversion of tribal chiefs, followed by members of the whole village. After that, a strict Christian life was enforced including prohibitions on smoking and alcohol. This was the reason why there were many places that Christianity could be found in blocks of areas, especially at the village levels. Hence, Christian villages were created and a stronghold of Christianity can be found in certain areas of the archipelago, especially in the eastern part. The missionaries, with support from the colonial government and from the state church, also founded various forms of social services like hospitals, schools and orphanages. These programmes allowed the locals to become part of the colonial bureaucracy, especially in education. One of the legacies of the western colonial era was the fact that most of the educated locals were Christians.

Thus, during Dutch colonial rule, their openness to invite various mission boards allowed ethnic churches to be developed. Consequently, the desire to separate the church from the state was strong among the local Christians, especially with growing nationalism and education among the people. Ethnic churches were formed out of the state church in the form of the Minahasa Evangelical Christian Church in north Sulawesi in 1934, the Protestant Church of Maluku in 1935 and the Timor Evangelical Christian Church in 1947. Other ethnic churches like the Chinese-speaking church, Javanese churches, the Borneo Evangelical Church and the Batak Christian Church were also formed during this period. In addition, a theological school was founded in 1934 in Jakarta in order to prepare future leaders for the churches, where the leadership was still in the hands of their Dutch masters. Some other schools later on developed in Timor and Makassar in south Sulawesi to train *guru injil* (gospel teachers). The training that the locals received from theological schools was not designed to equip them to be ministers. Henceforth, the locals were not qualified to be leaders of the church. This was not true for local churches, developed out of the influence of the state church, like the churches in north Sumatra and east Java. During the 1930s, the leadership of those two churches was in the hands of the locals. These were churches developed by individual missionaries outside the state church or missionaries not supported by the state church; in that regard, they had more freedom than the state church. The Dutch occupation of the archipelago ended with the Japanese occupation in 1942, in their Pacific Ocean campaign for the east Asian commonwealth.

The theology that was developed during the time was basically similar to that of Portugal and Spain: *cuius regio, eius religio.* They managed to bring Christianity to the locals, including theological schools for the locals. However, the leadership of the church was still in the hands of the Dutch, especially the state church, including the local churches developed out of it. Pietistic theology also has to be mentioned as a legacy of this period. This kind of Christianity and its theology, especially its ties with the state, will be resistant to change and have a strong influence among Indonesian Christians in the future.

CHRISTIANITY: JAPANESE COLONIALISM

The short presence of the Japanese in the archipelago from 1942 to 1945 was a turning-point in the development of the church. Coming with its own agendas for the welfare of Asian people, the Japanese rulers capitalized on the blind spot of the state church of the Dutch, by changing the leadership within the church from Europeans to locals, after the Dutch were driven away.

This changing of church leadership created an awareness among the locals of their responsibilities to their faith. With support from Japanese pastors coming from Japan to assist the church leaders in the archipelago, the church tried their best to survive without European support. It was not easy for the church, but from the broader perspective, this was a period of preparation for the church to take full leadership and future accountability. Included in this survival was also the survival of local Muslims. The Japanese rulers assisted the church in surviving persecution by the Muslims, who had been their long-time nemesis since Christianity had been introduced in the archipelago for the first time.

This kind of preparation set a new tone among the local churches for dealing later with their European counterparts, when Japan was defeated, and the Second World War ended. The defeat of Japan and the proclamation of Indonesian independence created a new awareness among the church leaders. They no longer treated their fellow European pastors as masters, but equals. The European churches with their missionary societies that had been treated as mother-churches later on became equal churches, especially within the ecumenical movements and their missionary workers.

This leadership awareness reached its peak with the proclamation of Indonesian independence in 1945, at the end of the Second World War. Before the arrival of the Japanese the church had been basically western and colonial, but after independence and with leadership in the hands of the local ministers, the churches concern with survival was with economic, social and political independence. Therefore, with the defeat of Japan the return of western ministers to take control of the churches was problematic, although a local theology had not been developed.

CHRISTIANITY: INDEPENDENT INDONESIA

The proclamation of Indonesian independence occurred on 17 August 1945. The name Indonesia was entirely new and was used first for political reasons by students coming from the Dutch East Indies in 1922 in order to designate the people in the archipelago under Dutch colonial rule. The name later on gained political support in the archipelago, when the youth from various parts of the archipelago met in a congress in 1928. They pledged the unity of one People of Indonesia, one Fatherland of Indonesia and to admire the Unified Language, the *Bahasa Indonesia* (Indonesian Language).

Since Indonesia as a nation had not existed previously, the unification of diverse ethnic groups was assisted by the *Pancasila* (Five Basic Principles). The principles are:

1. *Ketuhanan Yang Maha Esa* (Belief in One and Only Lord)
2. *Kemanusiaan yang adil dan beradab* (A just and civilized humanity)
3. *Persatuan Indonesia* (Unity of Indonesia)
4. *Kerakyatan yang dipimpin oleh hikmah kebijaksanaan dalam permusyawaratan/perwakilan* (People-hood based on the wisdom of deliberation and representation)
5. *Keadilan sosial bagi seluruh rakyat Indonesia* (Social justice to all people of Indonesia).

Although the *Pancasila* were supported by the founders of the nation, and have gained a profound acceptance among the people, the problem of interpreting and implementing these principles for social and political life has not been easy.

Indonesia: 1945–9

In the preparation for independence as promised by Japan, the Japanese formed the Investigative Body for the Preparation of an Independent Indonesia on 1 March 1945. Its task was to draft the text of the proclamation and the constitution of the new state. The body was confronted with the problem of a philosophical foundation of the state: would this new state be founded upon a religious basis, specifically Islam, because the majority of Indonesians embraced Islam; or upon a liberal view of human rights in a modern state; or upon nationalism, especially traditional Javanism, the major ethnic group of the new nation-state? Sukarno, later to become the president of the country, made a famous speech on the last day of the meeting, 1 June 1945. He stated that five basic principles should become the foundation (*Weltanschauung*) of this state, known as the *Pancasila*.

However, the *Pancasila* were later on developed into a document called the Jakarta Charter. In this document the principle of Lordship in the *Pancasila* was reformulated with an addition of the clause: *Lordship, with the obligation to carry out the Islamic syari'ah (law) to its adherents*. Based upon this Charter, the text of the proclamation of independence was drafted, called *Pernyataan Indonesia Merdeka* (The Declaration of Indonesian Independence).

However, when Indonesian independence was proclaimed on 17 August 1945 the draft was not used. A new text of proclamation was drafted on 16 August and read on the day of proclamation. A new republic was proclaimed by the name of *Republik Indonesia* (RI) or the Republic of Indonesia. In the process of ratifying the constitution, important amendments were made to the Jakarta Charter, argued for by Christian leaders from eastern parts of Indonesia. They expressed their discomfort with the original Jakarta Charter, because it served only part of the people of Indonesia; hence, the clause '*with the obligation to carry out the Islamic syari'ah to its adherents*' was omitted from the constitution. Consequently, similar amendments were made in the body of the constitution in article 6 section 1 and article 29 section 1, such that the requirement that the president should be a Muslim was omitted. Another significant decision was to replace the word *Allah* in the third paragraph of the preamble with the word *Tuhan* (Lord); this was proposed by a

Hindu from Bali. Thus, the *Pancasila* of the 1945 constitution guarantee the notion of equity for all Indonesians, as does the constitution itself.

The amended constitution guaranteed all Indonesians equal rights, including eligibility for the office of the presidency of the nation state, regardless of his/her ethnic, religious or social background – a basic right of a democratic state, which was denied in the draft of the constitution and also by the Jakarta Charter, in which only Muslims qualified for the office of the presidency. Forming a modern and democratic nation state where the Javanese are the biggest ethnic group and Islam is the dominant religion creates strong tendencies towards an Islamic and Javanistic state, hence the guarantee of equal rights is a great achievement, bringing Indonesia to the level of a modern and civilized nation-state.

During the period 1945–9 internal and external problems haunted this young republic, leading to short-lived governments and rebellions. In addition, the establishment of the new nation-state created tension between the people of Indonesia and the Dutch, who were trying to regain their control following the victory of the Allied Forces against Japan. The Dutch did not recognize the Republic of Indonesia and launched military manoeuvres into Indonesia in 1947 and 1948. Several meetings were arranged to find a solution, but failed, and the people of Indonesia were ready to fight for their independence even though they had limited weaponry. Finally a round-table meeting was scheduled in The Hague in 1949. At this conference the Dutch were Persuaded to recognize the independence of Indonesia in the form of a federal state called *Republik Indonesia Serikat* (RIS) or the United States of Indonesia.

During the period of struggle for independence, the Christians proved that they were part of the new Indonesian nation-state, since many church members died together with their fellow Indonesian brothers and sisters in the wars fought against the Dutch. The Christians also formed their own political party to participate in the democratic state of Indonesia and, while members of the church were participating in the various levels of independent Indonesia, indigenous church leaders were taking over from their Dutch counterparts. Moreover, the seed of Christian practical political theology had started to grow in the soil of Indonesia, evidenced by the rejecting of the Jakarta Charter and its preference for *syari'ah* law.

Indonesia: 1949–50

Established on 27 December 1949, this new nation-state was finally recognized by the international communities in the form of the United

States of Indonesia (RIS). However, most Indonesians, especially the political leaders, were dissatisfied with it. The movement to form a unified state of Indonesia (RI) received strong support from the people of Indonesia and this was decreed on 17 August 1950.

In addition to the related political developments that were taking place in the new nation-state, in 1949 there were meetings between the mission boards and the churches that were gaining independence from their Dutch counterparts, with local ministers demanding full leadership roles.

Indonesia: 1950–9

The return to RI demanded a new constitution. To meet that end, a general election was held in 1955 with the purpose of electing the members of the constituent body who would draft the new constitution. While forty political parties participated in the election, four large parties were clear winners; none however gained a majority. The major parties were the Indonesian National Party, which received forty per cent of the votes, followed by Masyumi (Islam), Nahdatul Ulama (Islam) and the Indonesian Communist Party.

The attempt to draft a new constitution faced the same problems as emerged in 1945, narrowing to a choice between the *Pancasila* of the 1945 constitution and Islam, specifically the Jakarta Charter. The western-modern-secular proponents and the nationalists rallied to oppose the Islamic proponents. Since neither side was able to gain two-thirds of the vote, President Sukarno on 5 July 1959 issued a decree dismissing the constituent body and reinstating the 1945 constitution as the official constitution for the unified Republic of Indonesia (RI).

In 1950, while the country was divided between the issue of federalism (RIS) and unification (RI), the church leaders and the mission boards came together in the second stage of their 1949 meetings. In the 1950 meeting, they decided to form the Indonesian Council of Churches (Dewan Gereja-Gereja Indonesia: DGI) with the sole objective of uniting the churches in Indonesia (*Gereja Kristen yang Esa di Indonesia*). One of the drives for forming the Council was the international ecumenical movement of the World Council of Churches, which had inspired participating Indonesian church leaders to bring ecumenism to the nation. The Indonesian ecumenical movement, however, excluded the Catholics, and most of the Pentecostal churches, especially the churches with an Anglo-American background.

Indonesia: 1959–66

With the return to the 1945 constitution, the full command of the country was in the hands of the president, Sukarno, for the first time. Previously, the 1945 constitution had been implemented as a parliamentary system. Yet Sukarno failed to implement fully the 1945 constitution due to the rising influence of the communist party. This period is known as a period of guided democracy; that is, a democracy in which the various factions of the new nation-state rallied behind Surkarno's leadership in developing a uniquely Indonesian democracy. Unfortunately, the strength of the communist party created a threat to the interests of some others, especially the military, and in an era of cold war between capitalism and communism Sukarno was overthrown in 1966, with the leadership being taken over by Suharto, backed by the military.

Between the two drives to form the National Council of Churches in Indonesia, the drive from the ecumenical movement was stronger than the national drive. During this period the National Council of Churches in Indonesia with its member churches, which constitute most of the Christians in Indonesia, especially the Protestants, was struggling with the idea of forming a united church in Indonesia. Between 1950 and 1967 the leadership of the churches was in the hands of the Indonesians, but the churches in Indonesia failed to achieve the objective of the Council of Churches in Indonesia. In this process, too much energy was spent on identifying with the World Council of Churches' structure and ideas, which did not meet the local reality of Indonesia, which was still struggling with its national unity. The churches in Indonesia neglected the national drive that was apparent in the formation of the Council, and the practical theology that the leaders of the churches had begun in the forming of the Council was not developed effectively. Hence, the churches remained dependent on a theology developed by the World Council of Churches. This kind of approach prevented the churches from developing a theology that was unique. The seed that was planted by demanding the omission of Islamic law from the 1945 constitution and by forming the Council of Churches in Indonesia, as a means to voice a preference for the unification of the nation, was wasted during this process. The churches were preoccupied with the ideas and theologies coming from abroad, reflecting the legacy of colonialism. Similarly, the theological training that leaders of the churches had during this period was also foreign, while theological schools founded by the churches in Indonesia were still running theological curricula inherited from their colonial church. Likewise, those that were trained abroad were strongly influenced by the classical theology of the west, thus neglecting the local context.

Indonesia: 1966–98

This is the period in which the *Pancasila* and the 1945 constitution were, for the first time, fully implemented as the reference for political and governmental activities, although, as a professional soldier, Suharto was ignorant of the ideological debates that had taken place following independence. Thus, he expected the political forces to behave according to the ideas of the *Pancasila*, instituting a New Order to replace the Old Order of Sukarno's guided democracy. Suharto ran the country for a long time, 1966–98, under the mantra of development. Consequently, the country opened up to international investors and, for almost thirty-two years, Suharto's government managed to boost the country's economy. The country's economy was raised from a triple-digit inflation rate under Sukarno to become one of the new economic tigers in Asia by the 1990s.

However, economic development was paid for dearly by sacrificing political freedom, since a solid democracy had not been carefully crafted. During the period 1966–98 six general elections were held, but this does not mean that the country was democratic. Three political parties had been formed, but the winner of all the elections was always *Golongan Karya*, a nationalistic semi-political party formed by Suharto, with strong support from the military. The other two political parties, the United Development Party – a fusion of Islamic political parties before the New Order – and the Democratic Political Party – a fusion of all nationalistic parties, including Catholic and Christian political parties, never won any of the elections.

Meanwhile, ideological strains inherited from the foundational stages of the country were still haunting Indonesia. The intention to promote Islamic ideology was still strong, as can be seen from the heated discussions concerning the Marriage Law in 1973, the bill on the National Education System in 1988, and the bill on the Religious (Islamic) Court for Muslims in 1989. In the Marriage Law it was proposed that marriage be rendered legal via government officials; however, this was protested against by the Muslims in parliament, since they did not want any government intervention in marriage. The Muslims argued that marriage was a religious institution, which religion should be responsible for, and a bill to this effect was finally passed. Similarly, in the case of the bill on the

National Education System, the Muslims proposed that all schools should be required to provide religious education in a particular religion if requested by ten or more students, and that the teacher must be an adherent of the religion taught. One other bill produced during this period was the bill authorizing Islamic Courts and thereby contradicting the desire to implement the *Pancasila* as the only source for Law Enforcement in Indonesia.

Thus, Suharto's interpretation of the *Pancasila* failed to resolve the ideological strains inherited from the time of pre-independence. Nevertheless, for at least thirty years, the Indonesian government did maintain stability; stability that made it possible for the government to launch significant economic reforms and development. However, due to corruption, collusion and nepotism during the last decade of his rule, Suharto was forced to resign and handed over his presidency to his vice president, Habibie, in May 1998. Habibie, at the time, was also the president of the Indonesian Islamic Intellectual Organization, and Indonesia entered a new phase of its history called the Reform Era.

During the period of the New Order, Christianity in Indonesia had been participating in national development at all levels. New Christian churches were enjoying the nation's economic growth, especially the evangelical churches. Islam was growing also, and areas that used to be heavily Christian were changing demographically into areas of Islamic majority, such that only one or two provinces in the country remained predominantly Christian.

Again, the seed of practical theology was neglected, and the churches in Indonesia missed another opportunity to contextualize their theology; that is, participation in the development process was not accompanied by theological development. Hence, while the country managed to a certain extent to develop an idea of national development as an implementation of the *Pancasila*, the churches were unable to use the opportunity to develop a theology from the *Pancasila*. The problem was that, while Suharto's government attempted to make the *Pancasila* the sole basis for political and social organizations, including religious organizations, the religious organizations rejected this on the basis that they were not social organizations. Thus, the Council of Churches in Indonesia changed its form of organization to become the Fellowship of Churches in Indonesia, and the Muslims also reacted negatively. A compromise with religious institutions resulted in the agreement that the implementation of the *Pancasila* would cover only the areas of societal life (*bermasyarakat*), nationhood life (*berbangsa*), and statehood life (*bernegara*), but it would

not cover the area of religious life in Indonesia. However, the problem
then was whether it was possible to distinguish sharply between societal
life and religious life; what society means in this sense remained an
unanswered question.

With the formation of the Fellowship of Churches in Indonesia, its
objective changed from 'to form one Christian Church' into 'to realize
one Christian Church'. Meanwhile, the evangelical churches, which had
grown with the economic support of the USA mission boards, managed
to form their own national council, adding to the diversity of Christianity
in Indonesia. Thus, the churches still failed to develop their own theology
in Indonesia, and, for the evangelical churches in Indonesia, a triumph-
alist theology remains dominant, based upon the great commandments; it
is a theology that ignores the context of the new nation-state.

However, one achievement during this period occurred in 1997, when
the minister of national education officially recognized theology as part of
the national education system; this was what the churches in Indonesia
had been fighting for since the 1950s. The official recognition of theology
in education signifies the legal foundation for the churches to develop
their own theology; however, it was another ten to fifteen years before a
new breed of theologians arose with the capacity to develop contextual
theologies.

Indonesia: 1998–9

With the downfall of Suharto, the *Pancasila* faded. Habibie, aware that
his rise had been propelled by Islamic factions in the country, introduced
what was to be a short-lived Islamic version of civil society, called
Masyarakat Madani, based upon the ideas of the Medina constitution
under Prophet Mohammad's reign in the sixteenth century. Following the
downfall of Suharto, a general election was held in 1999, but the result of
the election did not reflect an Islamic majority as the 1955 election had;
rather, political parties that carried nationalistic ideologies won the
election. The election and the following meeting of the People's Representative Council elected Abdurrahman Wahid as president and Megawati
Sukarnoputri as vice president from 1999 to 2004. During Habibie's rule
the 1945 constitution was amended in favour of a decentralization of
power, including the attempt to reinsert the Jakarta Charter's formulation
on the Islamic law, but this was denied by the members of the People's
Representative Council. After the fall of Suharto clashes between Christians
and Muslims broke out in Posso (Central Sulawesi) in 1998 and in Ambon

(Maluku) in 1999, increasing the dependency of the churches on their western allies.

Indonesia: 1999–2001

As a pluralist and nationalist, Abdurrahman Wahid still related himself to the *Pancasila*, speaking of the *Pancasila* society and promoting inter-religious relationships. Moreover, he even recognized Confucianism as a religion in Indonesia, but his attempts to remove the ban on the communist party and open a trade relationship with Israel sparked a strong rejection from many Islamic organizations. Accused of presidential involvement in the misuse of government funds, he was removed from the presidential office by the People's Consultative Council in July 2001 and was succeeded by his vice president, Megawati Sukarnoputri. Megawati made another amendment to the 1945 constitution, adding articles on human rights. However, the churches were still not participating positively in the reforms; instead, they were still captive to their colonial theology and looked to the west for the solution to internal inter-religious conflict.

Indonesia: from 2001

As a representative of the struggle of the Indonesian Democratic Party (PDIP), which is nationalistic in ideology, Megawati was expected to bring the nation back to its nationalistic path, especially since she is the daughter of Sukarno, the first president of the country. Megawati's rise to power in July 2001 was made possible by a coalition of different political parties. Her first step was to form a coalition government by the name of *Gotong-Royong* (co-operative) Cabinet, following Sukarno's policy, showing her intention to unite the nation under the banner of the *Pancasila*.

Megawati ruled from 2001 to 2004 and the economy grew slowly, although it did not reach its former peak under Suharto in the 1980s–1990s. Under her rule, an amendment was made to allow a direct presidential election to demonstrate the country's move to full democracy, even though this is contradictory to the *Pancasila's* fourth principle: Peoplehood based on the wisdom of deliberation and representation. Under the newly amended constitution, in 2004 Indonesia held its parliamentary and its first direct presidential election. Megawati Sukarnoputri was defeated and replaced by the retired general Susilo Bambang Yudhoyono, supported by a non-religious political party. As had been the case with the

1955 and the 1999 elections, the 2004 election indicated a strong nationalistic ideology among the Indonesian people, with religious political parties again not doing well. In an election with more than thirty political parties a coalition was inevitable, but Indonesian coalitions break as easily as they are made and the unity of the new nation-state remains a problematic issue. Primordial identities have prevented the new nation-state from integrating fully as one nation; hence, there is an urgent need to overcome divisions, and it is with this need in mind that the churches in Indonesia are called to make their contribution to the unity of the Indonesian people.

Christian theology in Indonesia: struggling for a post-colonial theology

Christianity was planted by westerners with their own agendas in an archipelago that would later on become one nation called Indonesia. The question to be asked concerns the direction in which Christianity will grow. The churches in Indonesia have not been able to release themselves from their colonial legacy, unlike post-colonialism in other areas. In a country where world religions were brought to the people of the archipelago, together with political forces that denied the rights of the locals in respect of their indigenous religions, world religions grew. The spreading of Hinduism and Buddhism cannot be separated from the legacy of two major kingdoms of the past, Sri Vijaya and Majapahit; and just as Islam is bound up with the various sultanates of Demak, Makassar, Gowa, Bima, Ternate, Tidore, so Christianity is tied to western colonialism. Clearly, these world religions did not tolerate local and indigenous religions and beliefs; hence, despite the Indonesian government policy on equal rights of religious freedom, violations still occurred.

Violations of religious freedom in Indonesia, which run parallel to the growth of the nation-state, can be seen in the intolerant attitudes of some Christians and Muslims, such as the Islamic Ahmadyah. Furthermore, the indigenous religions like Kaharingan in Kalimantan, Parmalin in north Sumatera, Marapu in Sumba, Boti in Timor, and Aluk Tadolo in Toraja lost their religious status and were regarded merely as local cultures, which had to be affiliated with one of the world religions recognized officially by the Indonesian government, such as Hinduism or Buddhism. The tendency to violate religious freedom started in Indonesia after the fall of Sukarno in 1966 and worsened with the downfall of Suharto in 1998. The period of reform with its idea of democratization did not ease the problem; in fact, the narrow notion of majority rule in a country like Indonesia has caused the Christians to reconsider their theology of living with people of other faiths. Colonial theology needs to be replaced with a post-colonial theology that addresses the Indonesian phenomenon expressed through the will of the Indonesian people in their 1945 proclamation of independence and democracy for all.

Independence was made possible also because of the contribution that Christianity had made in Indonesia. Despite its colonial history, Christianity has given the Indonesian people a sense of human equity regardless of one's religious or racial background. In addition, the churches in Indonesia have made it clear that they are committed to the unity of Indonesia through the formation of the united church in Indonesia (*Gereja Kristen yang Esa di Indonesia*). The contextual drive is stronger than the ecumenical drive, since it is on the issue of human equality that the future of Indonesia rests. One of the problems with implementing equality is the strong sense of exclusivism that is deeply rooted in the monotheism of the Abrahamic religions. When the world is struggling with the resurgence of religions out of secularization, the danger of religious exclusivism is imminent; hence, an Indonesian theology of human equality grounded in Christianity will have an enormous impact.

BIBLIOGRAPHY

Al-Qurtuby, S., *Arus China-Islam-Jawa: Membongkar Sejarah Peranan Tionghoa dalam Proses Islamisasi di Nusantara Abad 15–16*, Jogjakarta: INTI, 2003.

Anshari, E. S., *Piagam Jakarta, 22 Juni 1945*, Bandung: Perpustakaan Salman ITB, 1981.

Bahar, S., Ananda, B. K. and Hudawati, N., *Risalah Sidang Badan Penyelidik Usaha-Usaha Persiapan Kemerdekaan Indonesia (BPUPKI)-Panitia Persiapan Kemerdekaan Indonesia (PPKI) 28 Mei 1945–22 Agustus 1945*, Jakarta: Sekretariat Negara Republik Indonesia, 1995.

Berger, P. L. (ed.), *The Desecularization of the World: Resurgent Religion and World Politics*, Grand Rapids: William B. Eerdmans, 1999.

Boland, B. J., *Pergumulan Islam di Indonesia 1945–1970*, Jakarta: Graffiti Pers, 1985.

Cobb, Jr., J. B., *Transforming Christianity and the World Religions: A Way beyond Absolutism and Relativism*, Maryknoll: Orbis Books, 1999.

Cooley, F. L., *The Growing Seed: The Christian Church in Indonesia*, New York and Wuppertal-Barmen-Jakarta: The Division of Overseas Ministries NCCUSA, The European Commission for Church and Mission in Indonesia, BPK Gunung Mulia, 1982.

Darmaputera, E., *Pancasila and the Search for Identity and Modernity in Indonesian Society*, Leiden: E. J. Brill, 1988.

Dahm, B., *Sukarno and the Struggle for Indonesian Independence*, Itacha: Cornell University Press, 1969.

Hatta, M., *Pengertian Pancasila*, Jakarta: Idayu Press, 1977.

Memoir, Jakarta: Tintamas Indonesia, 1979.

Harun, H. M. S. and Mulkhan, A. M., *Latar Belakang Ummat Islam Menerima Pancasila sebagai Azas Tunggal*, Yogyakarta: Aquarius, 1986.

Hick, J., *God Has Many Names*, Philadelphia: Westminster Press, 1982.

A Christian Theology of Religions: The Rainbow of Faith, Louisville: Westminster John Knox Press, 1995.

Kahin, G. M., *Nationalism and Revolution in Indonesia*, Ithaca: Cornell University Press, 1971.

Lev, D. S., *The Transition to Guided Democracy: Indonesian Politics, 1957–1959*, Ithaca: Cornell University Press, Modern Indonesia Project, 1966.

McCoy, A. W. (ed.), *Southeast Asia Under Japanese Occupation*, New Haven: Yale University Press, Southeast Asia Studies, Monograph Series No. 22, 1980.

Malik, A., *Riwayat Proklamasi Agustus 1945*, Jakarta: Widjaja, 1982.

Pattiasina, J. M. and Sairin, W. (eds.), *Gerakan Oikumene: Tegar Mekar di Bumi Pancasila. Buku Peringatan 40 Tahun PGI* (Ecumenical Movement: Strongly Rooted in The Pancasila Soil. A 40th Anniversary Commemorative Book of the Communion of Churches in Indonesia), Jakarta: BPK Gunung Mulia, 1990.

Pranarka, A. M. W., *Sejarah Pemikiran tentang Pancasila*, Jakarta: CSIS, 1985.

Simatupang, T. B., *Membuktikan Ketidakbenaran Suatu Mythos*, Jakarta: BPK, 1991.

Suharto, H. M., *Pikiran, Ucapan, dan Tindakan Saya: Otobiografi*, as told to G. Dwipayana and K. H. Ramadhan, Jakarta: Citra Lamttoro Gung Persada, 1989.

Sukarno, A., *Dibawah Bendera Revolusi*, Djakarta: Publishing Committee, 1963.

Pancasila Sebagai Dasar Negara, Jakarta: Inti Idayu Press-Yayasan Pendidikan Soekarno, 1984.

Pantjawarsa Manipol, edited by Roeslan Abdulgani, Djakarta: Panitia Pembina Djiwa Pantjasila, 1964.

Ukur, F. and Cooley, F. L., *Jerih dan Juang: Laporan Nasional Survai Menyeluruh Gereja di Indonesia* (Efforts and Struggles: Report of a National Comprehensive Survey of the Churches in Indonesia), Jakarta: Lembaga Penelitian dan Studi DGI, 1979.

van den End, T., *Ragi Carita 1: Sejarah Gereja di Indonesia 1500–1860 (Leaven Story 1: Indonesian Church History 1500–1850)*, Jakarta: BPK Gunung Mulia, 1980.

and Weitjens, J., SJ, *Ragi Carita 2: Sejarah Gereja di Indonesia 1860an – Sekarang (Leaven Story 2: Indonesian Church History 1860s–Present)*, Jakarta: BPK Gunung Mulia, 2003.

Yamin, M., *Naskah Persiapan Undang-Undang Dasar 1945*, Djakarta: Jajasan Prapantja, 1959.

Yasni, Z., *Bung Hatta Menjawab*, Jakarta: Gunung Agung, 1978.

CHAPTER 5

Studying Christianity and doing theology extra ecclesiam in China

Choong Chee Pang

CAN THEOLOGY BE DONE OUTSIDE THE CHURCH (*EXTRA ECCLESIAM*)?

Cyprian (c. 200–58), Bishop of Carthage, insisted that 'outside the church there is no salvation' (*extra ecclesiam nulla salus*). In the context of modern China, the question is now: Is there Christian theology outside the (Chinese) church (*extra ecclesiam*)? This has become an important issue in modern China because non-Christian scholars in the Chinese academia have been seriously involved in studying Christianity and doing theology for about twenty years now. Lo Ping Cheung of the Hong Kong Baptist University has in fact written an article on this issue: 'Can Any Good Theology Come Out of the University?'[1]

Lo writes in response to Wilson Chow and Liu Xiao Feng who hold opposing views on the issue. Chow holds that 'The university has virtually no place for theology. As such, the responsibility for theological studies has landed on the theological college.'[2] On the other hand, Liu Xiao Feng asserts that if the goals and interests of Sino-Christian theology are perceived within the structure of academia, it will have to depend on the university to produce the kind of theologically educated intellectuals who can expand the knowledge of Christian thought as well as having the ability to engage in dialogue on modern thinking. As such, the traditional division between 'humanist theology' and 'church theology' is precisely what is needed for the survival of Christianity in the modern context.

---

[1] P. C. Lo and P. S. Kang (eds.), *University and Christian Studies* (Hong Kong: Centre for Sino-Christian Studies, Hong Kong Baptist University, 2002), pp. 373–89.

[2] Calver Yu (ed.), *Life and Knowledge: Silver Jubilee Anthology of the China Graduate School of Theology* (Hong Kong: China Graduate School of Theology, 2001), pp. 9–12.

Such a division is also required for the development of Sino-Christian
theology.[3]

Lo Ping Cheung attempts to look at the issue from both the perspectives of Chow and Liu and is of the opinion that much depends on
how 'the church' is being understood. Treating the church as an 'institution' is just one way of understanding it. In the more restricted sense,
Lo thinks that those who are engaged in Christian studies in the university
may not necessarily be members of the institutionalized church. On the
other hand the church may also be understood as a communion or
community (*koinonia, Gemeinschaft*, fellowship). In this broader sense,
those who are involved in Christian studies in the university can have
their place in both the university and the Christian community. Lo sees
the church-run theological institution and the university-based Christian
studies having complementary roles to play. As such, there should be a
mutual respect between the two as well as appreciation for each other.[4]

CHRISTIAN STUDIES AND THE '*WEN HUA RE*' ('CULTURAL HEAT') OF THE 1980S

The Christian studies in the Chinese academia which started in the early
1980s must be put in a much broader socio-political context. For nearly
thirty years after the founding of Communist China in 1949, this gigantic
nation with the largest population on earth chose ideologically to live in
isolation from the so-called 'free world' dominated by the west, especially
the United States. Mr Deng Xiao Ping's Open Door Policy, inaugurated
in 1978, marked China's most decisive step towards modernization.
Deng's epoch-making policy was very pragmatic. It was clearly dictated
by economic considerations over the others. In order to modernize, China
had to open its forbidden red door to the outside world. But once this
happened, the socio-political and other implications were obvious.
Throughout the long history of China, the intellectuals were usually
among those who first perceived the changing atmosphere of the nation.
The Chinese intellectuals in the late 1970s were no exception. This new
atmosphere soon generated a kind of 'heat' (*re*), which the Chinese
qualified with the adjective 'cultural' (*wen hua*), hence, 'cultural heat'
(*wen hua re*). The newly generated 'cultural heat' which was felt in the

---

[3] Liu Xiao Feng, *Sino Theology and the Philosophy of History* (Hong Kong: Centre for Sino-Christian
Studies, 2000), pp. 60–3.
[4] *Ibid.*, p. 388.

intelligentsia and academia found two concrete expressions: a revival of Chinese classical learning; and a deep yearning for the world outside the great wall. At the height of this new cultural revival in the 1980s, a most common aspiration and slogan was: 'Let Chinese culture open to the world and world culture to China!'

Having been isolated from the 'free world' for so long it was only natural and understandable that the Chinese, especially the thinking and curious intellectuals, should desire to know what was going on outside the 'great wall'. For Deng the leader and for those who were excited about his enlightened policy, to be open necessarily meant willingness to learn from the outside world, including the capitalist west. For more than a century China's attitude towards the west has remained intriguingly 'love-hate'. Hate, because of the enormous humiliation China suffered at the hands of western 'imperialists', including Japan, since the time of the 'Opium War' (1839–42) until the founding of Communist China in 1949. Love, because the modernization of the west and its many achievements were realities which even the Chinese communists could not possibly ignore or deny. China under Deng was at long last convinced that modernization was the way forward for China. As Deng appropriately and humorously put it: 'Who cares whether the cat is black or white as long as it catches mice!' There was thus a genuine desire to find out and to learn. But for the Chinese intellectuals, learning about and from the west went beyond the economic and industrial levels. Hence, the cultural and spiritual dimensions of the modernization of the 'Christian' west had to be considered and studied also. It was the Open Door Policy inaugurated by Deng Xiao Ping in 1978 that gave the academic disciplines of the humanities, including Christian studies, a new lease of life. Bishop K. H. Ting, the paramount leader of the Three-Self Church, makes the following remarks in a published 1995 letter to the alumni of China's leading theological school, Nanjing Union Theological Seminary:

For more than a decade now the [Chinese] intelligentsia has been treating Christianity with an unprecedented open attitude. However, we Christians are acutely short of those who have the [intellectual] ability to dialogue with the intelligentsia on equal footing. We are therefore in desperate need of a group of respectable Christian intellectuals from different professions and levels. They should not be church-goers only, but should also get themselves involved in different levels of the leadership of the 'two councils'.[5] They are also expected to join organizations of their respective

---

[5] The 'two councils' are the China Christian Council (CCC) and The Council for Three-Self Patriotic Movement (TSPM).

professions ... discussing with them about faith, as well as upgrading the level of their own professions ... These professions include creative and performance arts as well as religious studies ... We must also form a contingent of theologically well-educated intellectuals who are strong, distinctive and insightful, to speak for Christians of our motherland which is committed to socialism with Chinese characteristics, in international theological circles.[6]

China in the 1980s began to witness the loosening of the ideological grip in academia, creating a moral and spiritual vacuum which could not be filled simply by material things, despite the newly acquired wealth and opportunities in the market economy. In an international symposium held in Beijing in October 2001, Gao Shi Ning of the Chinese Academy of Social Sciences spoke on Christian belief and ethical values in which she made three observations: traditional ethical values in modern China are gradually diminishing; current ethical values have become increasingly pluralistic; and social values which are sub-cultural and vulgar are becoming more and more widespread. Gao held that in the midst of all these changes Christian values had become a viable option for some intellectuals as well as a deterrent force against moral erosion, although its influence was still rather limited at the present time because of certain existing socio-political constraints.[7]

INSTITUTIONS AND SCHOLARS INVOLVED IN CHRISTIAN STUDIES IN CHINA

Chen Jian Ming of Sichuan University has put those Chinese institutions which are engaged in Christian studies under four categories: institutes for Religious Studies in the Chinese Academy of Social Sciences as well as academies in the provinces and cities; research units in charge of religious studies under the various governmental departments; seminaries of the Chinese Christian Church (CCC); and various religious studies institutes under the various departments in the universities and other institutions of higher learning.[8]

There are broadly three categories of scholars and students who are involved in Christian studies, according to Chen Chun Fu of Zhejiang

---

[6] K. H. Ting, *Anthology of K. H. Ting* (Nanjing: Yi Lin Chu Ban She, 1999), pp. 371–2.

[7] Zhuo Xin Ping and Josef Sayer (eds.), *The Christian Religion and Contemporary Society* (Beijing: Religious Culture Publisher, 2003), pp. 282–3.

[8] Lo and Kang (eds.), *University and Christian Studies*, p. 175; Chen lists sixteen Chinese universities which have Christian studies in the year 2002, including leading universities such as Beijing, Tsinghua, Fudan, Ren Min, Nanjing, Zhejiang and Zhongsan.

University: those who approach Christian studies purely from an academic perspective, treating it just as a subject of serious inquiry (primarily from universities and government-sponsored institutions); those who treat Christian studies and the Chinese Church socio-politically (including scholars, policy-makers and policy-implementers whose research institutions are closely linked to the State Administration for Religious Affairs (SARA) as well as other governmental departments); and 'freelance' scholars who are not attached to any institution but nonetheless take a keen interest in Christian studies.[9]

Generally speaking, it would be quite right to think that there are scholars and students in the first and third categories who also combine academic studies with some kind of a personal spiritual quest. In the last two decades or so, a relatively new, but somewhat controversial and enigmatic term, 'cultural Christians' (*wen hua ji du tu*), has been used, apparently for want of better words, to describe those who possess a certain amount of 'faith' in Christ or subscribe to some Christian beliefs, values, 'spirit' (*jing sheng*) and 'ideal' (*li xiang*). This has become a new kind of *cultural* phenomenon, hence 'cultural Christians'. Some 'cultural Christians' have eventually 'crossed over' to the side of the Christian community, while a great many more remain outside the organized church. There are obvious reasons, some of which are socio-political (such as, party membership), and others, religio-cultural (such as, formal church membership which requires baptism and so on), to explain why they remain outside the church (*extra ecclesiam*). Christian attitudes toward such an apparently strange phenomenon vary a great deal.[10]

Naturally, there are also those who would declare their non-Christian position quite openly, and yet honestly admit that certain aspects of the Christian faith or a particular piece of Christian literature has become part of their 'philosophy of life'.

CHRISTIAN STUDIES, PUBLICATIONS AND READERSHIP

The publication of works written by Chinese scholars who are not Christians as well as by the so-called 'cultural Christians' has been quite impressive both quantitatively and qualitatively.[11] Zhao Dun Hua's *Ji Du*

---

[9] Chen Chun Fu, 'A Survey of the Cultural Christian Phenomenon and Reflection', *Wei Zhen Xue Kan*, 4:1 (1996), 14–33.

[10] See Liu Xiao Feng, *Wen Hua Ji Do Tu: Xian Xiang Yu Lun Zheng [Cultural Christians: Phenomenon and Argument]* (Hong Kong: Institute of Sino-Christian Studies, 1997).

[11] See Lo and Kang (eds.), *University and Christian Studies*, pp. 185–93.

Jiao Zhe Xue Yi Qian Wu Bai Nian [*Fifteen Hundred Years of Christian Philosophy*], first published in 1994 by the prestigious People's Press, has been reprinted many times.[12] The translation of Christian classics and other Christian literature in mainland China has also been considerable, with the Institute of Sino-Christian Studies in Hong Kong making a significant contribution in this area.

Equally significant has been the changing attitude of Chinese scholars toward Christian literature. One of the best known authorities on Nestorianism in China was undoubtedly the late Professor Zhu Qian Zhi, who taught at Beijing University and later worked at the Chinese Academy of Social Sciences, where he passed away in 1972 at the age of 73. Zhu's work on *Zhong Kuo Jing Jiao* [*Chinese Nestorianism*], which was completed in 1966, was only published posthumously in 1993. Zhu's own *Preface*, written in 1968, during the early years of the Chinese 'Cultural Revolution' (1966–76), when compared with the *Introduction* by his close colleague Professor Huang Xin Chuan, written in 1991, fifteen years after the end of the Cultural Revolution, reveals the drastic change in the attitude of Chinese intellectuals toward Christianity in the last couple of decades. In his 1968 *Preface*, Zhu claimed that his study was more 'scientific' than his predecessors because his was conducted 'under the guidance of the Marxist history of science' and he concluded his book with this remark:

The demise of Nestorianism in China and elsewhere does not necessarily mean the end of Christianity in China ... The Jesuit missionaries who came during the late Ming and early Qing dynasties and the arrival of Protestant missions after the Opium War were all in the steps of the Nestorians and they were connected with the colonial system of the West.[13]

Writing in 1991, thirteen years after the inauguration of Deng's Open Door Policy, Professor Huang Xin Chuan wrote in his *Introduction*:

Before the 'Great Cultural Revolution' Christian studies in the mainland of our country were very weak. From 1949 to 1978, for nearly thirty years, not a single book on the subject was published; only some forty articles appeared. This was due to the influence of extreme leftist thinking. Writings on religions in general, and Christianity in particular, during this period adopted a very critical and negative attitude, so that even Mr Zhu was not quite free from such influence.[14]

---

[12] Zhao Dun Hua is the current Head of the Departments of Philosophy and Religious Studies in Beijing University.

[13] Zhu Qian Zhi, *Zhong Guo Jing Jiao* [*Chinese Nestorianism*] (Beijing: Dong Fang, 1993), p. 222.

[14] Another noted scholar, Professor Luo Er Gang, writing about seven years after the inauguration of the Open Door Policy, remained convinced that 'historical science was committed to class struggle,

Since Mr Zhu had passed away, we were not able to change the contents of his book or judge him according to the academic yardstick of today. After 1978 our Government has adopted a reform and open door policy which has created a situation where many diverse views of the academia can find expressions. Religious studies have since been given a new lease of life and are now gradually moving towards the right direction.[15]

While Huang had earlier lamented the absence of a single published book on Christianity from 1949 to 1978, a modern Chinese scholar, Wang Xiao Zhao of Tsinghua University, was very pleased to inform the fifth annual meeting of Chinese scholars in Christian and other religious studies in Boston, USA, in June 2000, that from about 1980 to 2000 no less than a thousand Chinese books, translation works and articles on Christianity were published.[16]

In an international symposium held in Beijing in October 2001, Wang Xiao Chao confounded the participants with his suggestion that '[Modern] Chinese society has already accepted Christianity.'[17] What Wang actually meant was that the Chinese, especially the intellectuals, have never been so open and fair to Christianity as they are now. Historically and culturally speaking there is a great deal of truth in what Wang said.

Liu Xiao Feng of Zhongsan University observes that while the publication of Christian books was sporadic in the late 1980s, it has certainly become more organized since the early 1990s. What is even more significant is the fact that some of the most serious works have actually been produced by state-owned publishers. This is rather rare even in Taiwan and Hong Kong.[18]

Li Ping Ye, a Chinese Government official now based in Hong Kong, thinks that an understanding of Christian civilization especially since the Reformation is essential in an age of globalization, and a comparison

---

so that the work of historical studies must provide political service to the proletariat'; *Tai Ping Tian Guo Shi [A History of the Taiping Heavenly Kingdom]* (Beijing: Zhong Hua Shu Ju, 1991), pp. 9–11.

[15] Zhi, *Zhong Guo Jing Jiao*, pp. 10–11.

[16] Wang Xiao Zhao, 'A Review and a Vision: Christian and Religious Studies in China', paper presented at the fifth annual meeting of Chinese scholars in Christian and Religious Studies, Boston, USA (2–5 June 2000).

[17] Wang elaborates: 'Personally, we could say that the Chinese individual accepts Christianity as his own faith and spiritual pillar; culturally ... the Chinese culture accepts Christianity as an important ingredient and stimulant for its own renewal and change; socially ... the Chinese society accepts Christianity as an important force for its own stability and development. Ever since the time of China's current reform the Government has repeatedly stressed the need to utilize the positive social function of religions which necessarily includes Christianity'; Ping and Sayer (eds.), *The Christian Religion and Contemporary Society*, pp. 53–4.

[18] Feng, *Wen Hua Ji Du Tu [Cultural Christians]*, p. 65.

between eastern and western cultures would be beneficial to the Chinese in their search for a direction on their way to modernization.[19] Zhao Dun Hua, Dean of the Departments of Philosophy and Religious Studies of Beijing University and author of the now popular book *Fifteen Hundred Years of Christian Philosophy* (1994), states that the purpose of his writing is to help readers understand western culture comprehensively; to help readers compare Chinese and western philosophies and cultures; and to help readers think more rationally.[20]

Zhuo Xin Ping of the Chinese Academy of Social Sciences thinks that Christianity is not only the largest world religion but also the most socially influential. He believes it is quite impossible to understand the history of human civilization and current world development without some basic knowledge of Christianity. Zhuo is convinced that with the arrival of the new millennium, studies on the development of Christian intellectual culture have become more important and urgent.[21]

It was largely along similar lines of thinking that China's top academic institution, Beijing University, which began to offer religious studies in 1982 in the Philosophy Department, formally established a Department of Religious Studies in 1996 with the following aim:

The Department commits itself to academic study and interdisciplinary research of religions as well as cultures in general, with a scientific approach and rigorous attitude. It places emphasis on an objective, unbiased evaluation of the history and reality of the major religions of the world. The Department's tasks are to educate students with broad, basic knowledge of religion, philosophy and other relevant disciplines and to train specialists and intellectuals to meet the country's needs in the areas of religious studies, public administration and social activity.[22]

THE GROWTH OF THE CHINESE CHURCH AND THE 'CHURCH AND STATE' ISSUE

That the non-Christian academia in China has now committed itself so enthusiastically to Christian studies is certainly unprecedented in the long history of the nation where Christianity has failed repeatedly to take root socio-culturally since AD 635. The current unique situation must also be

[19] Li Ping Ye, *Zhong Jiao Gai Ge Yu Xi Fang Jin Dai She Hui Si Chao [The Reformation and the Modern Social Thinking of the West]* (Beijing: Jin Ri Zhong Guo, 1992), p. 12.
[20] Zhao Dun Hua, *Ji Du Jiao Zhe Xue Yi Qian Wu Bai Nian [Fifteen Hundred Years of Philosophy]* (Shanghai: People's Press, 1994), pp. 17–18.
[21] *Ji Du Jiao Yan Jiu [Christian Studies]*, vol. I (Beijing: She Hui Ke Yue Wen Xian, 1999), p. 1.
[22] Peking University, *Department of Religious Studies Catalogue* (1996), p. 8.

viewed in the context of the phenomenal growth of the Chinese Christian population during the same period of time. It is already the largest Christian community in Asia and one of the most numerous in the world. This fact has been used by Bishop K. H. Ting apologetically to defend the Chinese government's religious policy. His rhetoric is:

People know that the ruling party of our country is atheistic. Some people abroad have consequently inferred with great passion that the Communist party and the government are antagonistic to religions and are determined to eliminate them. These people have indeed disregarded the actual fact. Christianity, for instance, has witnessed the increase of three churches daily since the end of the 'Cultural Revolution' for more than ten years now ... The number of Bibles which has been distributed by the church has already exceeded ten million, and church-run seminaries now number thirteen ... Although certain aspects in the implementation of the policy of religious freedom are still not satisfactory, what are the real grounds for the allegation that the [communist] party and the government are antagonistic to religions, according to what has been shown above?[23]

The new attitude of the Chinese government toward Christianity in the last two decades has also been confirmed by Zhuo Xin Ping of the Chinese Academy of Social Sciences (CASS), which is the leading think-tank of the Chinese government. Speaking on the role of the Chinese church in modern Chinese society in the October 2001 international symposium in Beijing, Zhuo states:

(1) Following China's 'open door' policy there has been an unprecedented opportunity for the church to accommodate itself more harmoniously to Chinese society. Through positive dialogue and reciprocal efforts, relations between the two have seen a far-reaching breakthrough.

(2) The mainstream ideology of China is now taking a more positive and objective view on the socio-ethical function of the Chinese church in a changing Chinese society. On the other hand, the Chinese church has also responded to the new situation and attitude by highlighting its belief in and practice of Christian love ... This new emphasis has given the church a new lease of life. Its spirit of selfless service and sacrifice, of forgiveness and universal brotherly love, could now have a significant contribution to make to the reconstruction of the 'spirit' (*Jing shen*) of the Chinese people.

(3) The Chinese church must see to it that it serves as a unifying force rather than a divisive element in modern Chinese society. Only an

---

[23] *Anthology of K. H. Ting*, p. 371.

inclusive Christian community will be welcome by the Chinese and consequently will have a contribution to make.

(4) To be true to its witness and mission the church has to play the roles of servant as well as prophet. However, in view of the present socio-political dynamics of China, the church has wisely chosen to play the role of servant rather than prophet. This is because the present Chinese society is not quite ready to accept the 'prophetic' mission of the Church, especially its more critical aspects.[24]

It is worth noting that while symposium participants did generally endorse Zhuo's analysis of the Chinese situation, some also wished to see the Chinese church assuming both the biblical roles of servant as well as prophet. In reply, Zhuo seemed to think that the church's present choice for the servant's role is out of pragmatic consideration. Hopefully the time will come when the church can play the two roles effectively.

Despite its continuous growth, not much theology was done in the organized Chinese church in the first two decades following Deng's Open Door Policy, until the so-called 'theological re-construction' became a prominent agenda of the leadership of the Three-Self Church. This is perhaps one of the 'many problems' which Bishop Ting has in mind in his 1995 letter to the alumni of Nanjing Union Theological Seminary when he says quite openly that 'We should not be satisfied with these figures [growth of churches and so on]. Problems that Chinese Christianity faces are many, which should demand the great concern and deep reflection of the old alumni.'[25]

Bishop Ting was apparently quite supportive of Christian studies in the Chinese academia in its early stages, regarding it as being supplementary to the very limited work which the organized church was trying to do. However, such positive attitudes have changed drastically in recent years for at least two reasons. First, after about two decades of continuous development and expansion, Christian studies in Chinese academia have become more or less a free-for-all, so that its direction and contents are perceived by Ting to be increasingly detached from the main concerns of the organized church. Secondly, in the organized church there is now a young generation of clergy as well as some educated laity who are keen to upgrade themselves academically. With its very limited resources the organized church is clearly not able to meet such a need. In the last few years several leading Chinese universities have responded to the need for

[24] Ping and Sayer (eds.), *The Christian Religion and Contemporary Society*, pp. 247–53. [25] *Ibid.*

Christian studies by providing special postgraduate courses for those who are highly motivated. Again, the theological as well as ideological orientation and direction of those university-run courses are obviously different from those of the organized church. In a society where the church leadership is insecure, there are causes for concern. (We will return to this later.)

CHRISTIAN STUDIES IN AN INTERDISCIPLINARY CONTEXT

Christian studies in China are conducted currently in the interdisciplinary environment and context of academia; thus, its contact with and impact on other academic fields should be recognized. In his paper 'Christian Studies and its Significance for Chinese Academia', He Guang Hu shows convincingly that recent Christian studies have enriched Chinese academia in three particular areas: in encouraging critical thinking; in distinguishing the transcendental from the mundane; in providing a holistic and three-dimensional approach as well as a sense of the 'holy' to the study of humanities.[26] In a similar article, 'The Significance of Christian Studies for Contemporary Chinese Universities', He Guang Hu suggests that Christianity, being the 'spiritual core' (*jin sheng he xin*) of western civilization, could have a significant contribution to make to the 'quality education' (*su zhi jiao yu*) of Chinese universities.[27] Zhang Qing Xiong of the Christian Study Center of Shanghai's Fudan University regards the cultivation of the student's 'humanist spirit' (*ren wen jin sheng*) and 'ultimate concern' (*zhong ji guan huai*) as the basic principles of Christian studies in the university.[28]

Fudan University in Shanghai, which established a Christian Study Center in 1996 in the Philosophy Department, was authorized by the State Administration for Religious Affairs (SARA) of China as early as 1986 to run training courses for its senior officials (party cadres).[29] In Beijing, Fudan and a couple of other universities, Christian studies have in fact gone beyond interdisciplinary concerns within the university itself. Since 2001 they have even been providing further education for the 'Three-Self' as well as the 'house' and other Chinese churches. While Fudan University is doing this in cooperation with the official church of the Shanghai area, others, like Beijing and Ren Min Universities, are conducting their postgraduate courses for Christian pastors and lay

[26] *Ibid.*, pp. 150–2. [27] Lo and Kang (eds.), *University and Christian Studies*, pp. 156–8.
[28] *Ibid.*, pp. 199–201.
[29] Xu Yi Hua and Zhang Qing Xiong (eds.), *Ji Du Jiao Xue Shu* vol. I (Shanghai: Shanghai Gu Ji Zhu Ban She, 2002), pp. 1–2.

leaders quite independently, much to the displeasure of the Three-Self top leadership. The universities involved are able to generate quite considerable income from their unique programmes. The two-year programmes aim at broadening the scope and horizon of the candidates' knowledge in the social sciences, humanities, theology and philosophy, with a much broader perspective than the church seminaries. This is bound to have a lasting impact on the mindset of candidates who have gone through an ideologically rigid system of education both within and outside the church. Unlike their previous theological education, which was given almost exclusively by church-related teachers, they are now being taught by academics of the university, the great majority of whom are not Christians. English is part of the core curriculum, and it is hoped that the level of English which the candidates obtain may eventually help them gain access to the literature and media of an exceedingly new world. These candidates should eventually be more equipped than their elders in the vital enterprise of theological 're-construction' in the post-Mao era.

The present theological re-construction of the organized church, which is under the leadership and control of Bishop Ting and his associates, does not seem to appeal to the ordinary clergy and laity. It is often perceived to be more ideological than theological in its effort to adapt the church to 'socialism with Chinese characteristics', so that the church could better serve its 'social function'. The theological task that the Chinese church faces is thus daunting and delicate: how to respond to the socio-political realities of modern China seriously and yet remain true to its Christian identity and mission. It remains to be seen if those who are currently doing theology outside the organized Chinese church could eventually have something significant to contribute to the challenging task of theological 're-construction'.

THINGS 'CHINESE' AND THINGS 'FOREIGN' ARE NO LONGER POLARIZED

All foreign missions in the past, from the time of the Nestorians in the seventh century, through the Catholic missions in the sixteenth and seventeenth centuries, and down to the Protestant missions in the modern period, had to face the long cultural traditions of China. Hence, different ways and forms of contextualization/indigenization/inculturation had been tried out, yet without much success. The 'foreignness' or 'strangeness' of Christianity remained a great stumbling block to the great majority of the Chinese. From the perspective of mission, Chinese communism was even harder for Christianity to deal with. As such, the basic assumption was that the more 'Chinese' Christianity appeared, the more attractive and appealing it would be to the Chinese. However, a new phenomenon since the late 1980s seems to have rendered such assumptions questionable.

Modern Chinese, especially the young and educated (and fashionable), who grow up with the 'market economy', have often been attracted to Christianity, not due to its affinity with traditional Chinese culture, but because of its 'foreignness'. Newly 'liberated' Chinese are not particularly interested in things which China already has, or presumes to have, such as Chinese religions and socio-ethical systems like Confucianism, but rather in things which China does not possess, including things 'Christian'. Such 'foreign' things may include Christmas celebrations and a wedding ceremony in the 'special atmosphere' of the church. This new attitude and mentality could hardly be disassociated from the whole Open Door Policy of China, which has already turned some fundamentals upside down. Many things which were formerly despised, discarded, even officially forbidden and condemned, have now become the very objects of people's search and inquiry, including Christianity.

CONTACT AND NETWORKING THROUGH CHRISTIAN STUDIES

Christian studies in China, perhaps more than other academic disciplines, bring those who are engaged in it into close contact with the outside world, including Chinese scholars in the diasporas. The Centre for the Study of Christianity in the Chinese Academy of Social Sciences was formally launched in May 1998. Besides having broad networking relationships with other academic institutions in the country, it has established links with some top universities abroad, including Oxford, Harvard and Munich.[30] The universities and academic institutions in Hong Kong have played a significant role also. This ever-widening contact and networking with the global community has provided enormous opportunities for mainland scholars to broaden their horizons and constantly upgrade their knowledge and academic credentials, including the acquisition of respectable doctoral degrees in theology whether at home or abroad. A small number of the official seminaries have also engaged some

---

[30] Zhuo Xia Ping, *Ji Du Jiao Yan Jiu [Christian Studies]*, vol. I (Beijing: She Hui Ke Yue Wen Xian, 1999), p. 19.

university academics to help teach in some of the theological and social science courses.

IMPLICATIONS FOR CHRISTIANITY IN EAST ASIA

Implications for China and the Chinese diasporas

As mentioned earlier, those who are interested in Christianity, especially the better educated, have to depend largely on work produced by scholars who are outside the church (*extra ecclesiam*). Not only that, even educated Chinese Christians, including those in the Christian ministry and seminaries, often have to rely on the non-Christian market for the supply of literature on Christianity. There are obviously both positive and negative aspects to such a strange phenomenon. Positively, writings produced outside the church provide the readers with views and perspectives rarely found within the church. Negatively, such literature can unwittingly misrepresent and misinterpret biblical faith. Moreover, a high percentage of those who are writing seriously have a highly theoretical and philosophical approach, which may not have much to do with the life and witness of the Christian readers. It is due to the lack of training in the biblical languages, Hebrew and Greek, that few Chinese scholars have attempted serious writings in biblical studies. However, Hebrew is taught at Beijing University and elementary Greek has been offered by a couple of visiting professors at a few leading universities. Nevertheless, both the positive and negative aspects of Christian studies in the Chinese academia have caused concern amongst conservative leaders of the Chinese church.[31]

Perhaps only God knows how many Christians there are in China today. The estimate ranges from a conservative 15 million to an (obviously exaggerated?) 70 million. Some observers think that some way between the two figures (around 40 million?) may be a more reasonable and intelligent guess. This is an enormous figure, although in proportion to the total Chinese population of 1,300 million it is still rather small. Nevertheless, it is reasonable to assume that the number of Christians who worship on an average Sunday in China may far outnumber those in Britain, Germany and France put together. Furthermore, the potential 'market' for Christian literature must be viewed from the perspectives of the total population of China.

---

[31] For different views on a similar issue, see Lo Ping Cheung's article, 'Can Any Good Theology Come Out From the University?' in Lo and Kang (eds.), *University and Christian Studies*, pp. 373–89.

Implications for China's immediate neighbours in East Asia

Both culturally and linguistically, the Koreans and the Japanese have the best background and greatest advantage to appreciate literature written in the Chinese language, respectively called 'Kanji' (literally the words of the *Han* people) by the Japanese and 'Hanmun' (literally the language of the *Han* people) by the Koreans. The Chinese language had for centuries been a kind of *lingua franca* for the whole of East Asia, including Vietnam. Even to this day, it is still common to find older and educated Japanese and Koreans who are well versed in Chinese language and culture. In direct response to a rising modern China, there has been a revived interest in recent years in the learning of Chinese among younger Koreans and Japanese.[32] Again, here is a potential market for Christian writings produced by Chinese scholars outside the church (*extra ecclesiam*). Many young Koreans and Japanese are eager to learn both English and Chinese. The Korean or Japanese scholars who can write in the Chinese language will, at least potentially, have nearly a quarter of the human race as their market, one that is much larger than the Korean and Japanese markets put together.

In the last couple of decades Korean Christians have been very active in their mission outreach to China, especially in the north-eastern part where the great majority of *Chao Xian* people are living. They are ethnically the same as the Koreans. On the other hand, there are also a considerable number of *Chao Xian* Christians from China who have received their theological education and training in South Korea. Such contacts and networking are expected to increase.

RELIGIOUS ISSUES REMAIN SOCIO-POLITICALLY SENSITIVE AND FLUID

In case what has been said above appears too rosy, an important article in the February 2000 issue of the Hong Kong-based monthly *Cheng Ming* may serve as a reminder that religious issues remain socio-politically sensitive and fluid in modern China. According to the *Cheng Ming* article 'Zhong Gong Zhong Jiao Zheng Ce Xin Wen Jian' ['A New Document of the Chinese Communist Party on Religious Policy'], a clear directive

---

[32] See Choong Chee Pang's paper, 'An Inquiry into the Possibility of the Han [Chinese] Language Becoming a *Lingua Franca* of East Asia', presented at an international conference organized by Nanyang Technological University, Singapore (23–25 June 2004).

was given to the directors of all religious affairs bureaux in their meeting in Beijing on 10 January 2000. The directive is contained in a document which was issued by the central committee of the Party together with the state department called 'Guan Yi Tang Qian Zhong Jiao Gong Zuo Ruo Gan Zheng Ce Wen Ti' ['Some Policy Matters Regarding the Present Work on Religions']. Its three main aims are: (1) to strengthen the work of the 'united front' among top leaders of the various religions by inculcating in them a strong sense of patriotism, national unity, security, stability and national pride; (2) to deepen political infiltration into the various religions by increasing the percentage of 'progressive and active' non-party members from the present three per cent up to nine per cent (in the case of Protestantism and Catholicism) and to upgrade the quality of the political thinking of cadres in the religious affairs bureaux and to instil in their minds a stronger sense of duty; and (3) to be constantly on guard against hostile religious activities, especially those with foreign connections, which seek to infiltrate Chinese religious circles in order to control them.[33]

The document also refers to some religious leaders' involvement in 'anti-social and anti-party' activities under the guise of religion. Some of them are allegedly 'agents' of foreign political powers who engage in sectarian and subversive activities. It holds that both history and the present situation can testify to the fact that the west is used to interfering in the internal affairs of China under the pretext of religion. This view is shared by Jiang Ze Min, who sternly warns against the 'politicization' of religion and the 'westernization' of China's value system. In the Party document Jiang gives clear instructions that cadres who participate in religious activities must either leave the Communist Party voluntarily or face expulsion. The participation of cadres in Christian activities is believed to be particularly widespread, especially in developing cities. In the January 2000 Beijing meeting, the figures for the major religions in China were officially released for the first time: Buddhists, more than 150 million; Protestants, more than 25 million; Catholics, 3.2 million; Muslims, more than 11 million; and Taoists, more than 5.5 million. But the figures given by the Public Security Department are much bigger: Protestants, 35 million; Catholics, more than 8.5 million. Moreover, the Christians are thought to be more educated than the followers of all other major religions and they are also proportionally more numerous in the knowledge-based sectors and in educational institutions.

---

[33] Communist Party, 'Guan Yi Tang Qian Zhong Jiao Gong Zuo Ruo Gan Zheng Ce Wen Ti' ['Some Policy Matters Regarding Present Work on Religions'] (2000), pp. 19–20.

CHRISTIAN STUDIES IS INSEPARABLE FROM THE 'RELIGION AND STATE' ISSUE

In a conference on 'Religion and the Rule of Law', which was held in Shanghai in the summer of 2004, there was a great deal of discussion on the old and complicated issue of 'religion and state', or what is more commonly referred to in the west as 'church and state'. While practically all participants upheld the separation between religion and state as a good and broad principle, some academics had also asked for a critical re-examination of the traditional Marxist view on religion, and a review of the Chinese Constitution on religion and the government's religious policy as well as its implementation. There is concern that while the religious communities in China are constantly asked not to meddle with politics, the state seems to be interfering too much in religious affairs. However, the Chinese simply have to accept the reality that religion will continue to be a major concern of the government in the foreseeable future, so that religious studies, especially Christian studies, will have to operate within this purview and parameter.

A 'Bible Show' was held in Hong Kong in early August 2004 and reported by a local Singapore daily, *The Straits Times* (7 August 2004), under the title, 'China Opens HK Bible Show' with the sub-title, 'Exhibition is seen as an attempt to polish Beijing's image before next month's [Hong Kong] legislative elections'. The news in Hong Kong states:

Mixing religion and politics, China's state-sanctioned churches have opened a Bible exhibition here [Hong Kong] that appeared to be aimed at helping Beijing's allies in upcoming legislative elections. In a rare sight, dignitaries from the officially atheist government bowed their heads during a prayer – part of the ceremony that analysts say was intended to polish Beijing's image in a heated political season ... Hong Kong chief executive Tung Chee Hwa and Beijing's top representative here, Mr Gao Siren, attended the opening ceremony on Thursday, along with the director of China's State Bureau of Religious Affairs, Mr Ye Xiaowen.

CONCLUSION: GUARDED OPTIMISM

The Hong Kong-based Institute of Sino-Christian Studies (ISCS) has established a very broad network in the last ten years, not only with the Chinese academia involved in Christian studies, but also with many respectable institutions internationally. As a Hong Kong-based institute it obviously enjoys much greater freedom than its mainland counterpart to monitor and critically assess the development of Christian studies in the

Chinese academia. Certain points which have been raised in the latest issue (2004) of the Institute's Newsletter are very insightful and revealing. In the lead article, 'Sino Theology in the Academia of Mainland China: Present and Future', He Guang Hu of Beijing's Ren Min University and a research fellow of the ISCS, gives a candid survey of Sino theology in the last decade and makes the following points succinctly.

First, the emphasis on 'Sino theology' in the last ten years has been largely justified. Sino theology has now become part of the 'academic language' system of the humanities in China. However, a certain amount of polarization still exists between those who are basically satisfied with just the introduction of western theology to China and those who believe in full commitment to China's own contextualized/indigenized theology (literally, 'theology with local [Chinese] colours'). These two extremes must obviously be avoided and there have been some encouraging signs in recent years that there is a working towards a healthy balance between the two positions. Secondly, while some Chinese scholars continue to translate western theological works into Chinese, a great deal more are producing Chinese works in more creative ways. Practically every scholar who is seriously involved in Christian studies is actively writing, so that just within the last five months more than thirty serious works (both original and translation) as well as over fifty scholarly papers have been published. Thirdly, there are still some basic problems facing Chinese scholars in Christian studies: how to catch up with the rapid cultural and academic developments in a fast-changing modern China; how to meet the needs of the growing Christian population in China; and the fact that the gigantic society in mainland China has practically all the basic features of pre-modernism, modernism and post-modernism co-existing at the same time, but the gaps between them are widening. Economic development and the market economy continue to create problems in the areas of social injustice, inequality, exploitation, abuse of powers, civil rights and the ecological crisis. All these must be addressed theologically. Fourthly, most crucial of all is perhaps the need for the academics who are engaged in Christian studies to constantly keep in touch with the harsh realities of people's life and existence. For Sino theology to be relevant and credible it must be contextual and existential. Fifthly, there is the problem of 'aging' among those who are engaged in Christian studies or Sino theology in the Chinese academia.

I have no difficulty endorsing the above points of He Guang Hu, except the last one about 'aging'. In my opinion Professor He's concern is quite unnecessary at the present time because the average age of those who are leading in the field is in their fifties. Moreover, much larger in number are those who are between thirty and fifty, and a high percentage of them are even better educated than their seniors, at least in terms of paper qualifications.

Besides the lead article of He Guang Hu, the editorial of Daniel Yeung, Director of the Institute of Sino-Christian Studies, is equally insightful. 'Is the movement of Sino-Christian studies a mere slogan, and has it constructed anything and achieved something that is substantial?' asks Director Yeung rhetorically. First, he responds, as part of religious studies in the Chinese academia Christian studies has continued to prosper in recent years, particularly in the contacts and exchanges between scholars in mainland China, Hong Kong and abroad. The same period has also witnessed the emergence of younger scholars in the field. Secondly, as the work of translation is not just a matter of language, it is also a necessary process through which knowledge is transmitted, received and spreads; it will continue to be needed as part of the foundation-building exercise. The ultimate aim is naturally to think, write, and read creative works in the Chinese language, so that Sino-Christian theology can become an integral part of the life-experience and cultural tradition of modern China. Thirdly, the original agenda of Sino-Christian studies was proposed by those who first conceived of the need to conduct and promote Sino-Christian studies in the Chinese language back in the 1990s. Over the years Sino-Christian studies have gradually been incorporated into other disciplines and have become increasingly multifaceted and pluralistic. Sino-Christian studies are now being recognized as a component of the whole academic system of modern China. In the last 1400 years since Christianity first came to China this is the first time that Chinese scholars have taken the initiative to study Christianity with a positive and objective attitude. Fourthly, as Chinese scholars who are deeply involved in Christian studies, we have in fact taken the awful responsibility of providing the resources for Christian thought of the different ages from Jewish Christianity, through Catholicism and Eastern Orthodoxy, right down to Protestantism. We are doing this not in isolation but in close contact and cordial relation with other disciplines both at home and abroad, with the sincere hope of making this a truly open, multifaceted and global project.

The current state of Sino-Christian studies, as portrayed in the latest Newsletter of the ISCS, looks encouraging and promising, thus offering hope that the laudable and noble goals above can eventually be realized.

BIBLIOGRAPHY

Communist Party, 'Guan Yi Tang Qian Zhong Jiao Gong Zuo Ruo Gan Zheng Ce Wen Ti' ['Some Policy Matters Regarding the Present Work on Religions'], (2000).

Feng, L. X., *Sino Theology and the Philosophy of History*, Hong Kong: Centre for Sino-Christian Studies, 2000.

Wen Hua Ji Do Tu: Xian Xiang Yu Lun Zheng [Cultural Christians: Phenomenon and Argument], Hong Kong: Institute of Sino- Christian Studies, 1997.

Fu, C. C., 'A Survey of the Cultural Christian Phenomenon and Reflection', *Wei Zhen Xue Kan*, 4:1 (1996), 14–33.

Gang, L. E., *Tai Ping Tian Guo Shi [A History of the Taiping Heavenly Kingdom]*, Beijing: Zhong Hua Shu Ju, 1991.

Hua, X. Y. and Xiong, Z. Q. (eds.), *Ji Du Jiao Xue Shu* vol. I, Shanghai: Shanghai Gu Ji Zhu Ban She, 2002.

Hua, Z. D., *Ji Du Jiao Zhe Xue Yi Qian Wu Bai Nian [Fifteen Hundred Years of Philosophy]*, Shanghai: People's Press, 1994.

Institute of Sino-Christian Studies, 'Newsletter', Hong Kong (2004).

Lo, P. C. and Kang, P. S. (eds.), *University and Christian Studies*, Hong Kong: Centre for Sino-Christian Studies, Hong Kong Baptist University, 2002.

Pang, C. C., 'An Inquiry into the Possibility of the Han [Chinese] Language Becoming a *Lingua Franca* of East Asia', conference paper presented at Nanyang Technological University, Singapore (23–25 June 2004).

Peking University, *Department of Religious Studies Catalogue* (1996).

Ping, Z. X., *Ji Du Jiao Yan Jiu [Christian Studies]*, vol. I, Beijing: She Hui Ke Yue Wen Xian, 1999.

Ping, Z. X. and Hui, E. (eds.), *Study of Christianity*, Beijing: She Hui Ke Xue Wen Xian Chu Ban She, 1999.

Ping, Z. X. and Sayer, J. (eds.), *The Christian Religion and Contemporary Society*, Beijing: Religious Culture Publisher, 2003.

The Straits Times, 'China Opens HK Bible Show', Singapore (7 August 2004).

Ting, K. H., *Anthology of K. H. Ting*, Nanjing: Yi Lin Chu Ban She, 1999.

Ye, L. P., *Zhong Jiao Gai Ge Yu Xi Fang Jin Dai She Hui Si Chao [The Reformation and the Modern Social Thinking of the West]*, Beijing: Jin Ri Zhong Guo, 1992.

Yu, C. (ed.), *Life and Knowledge: Silver Jubilee Anthology of the China Graduate School of Theology*, Hong Kong: China Graduate School of Theology, 2001.

Zhao, W. X., 'A Review and a Vision: Christian and Religious Studies in China', paper presented at the fifth annual meeting of Chinese scholars in Christian and Religious Studies, Boston, USA (2–5 June 2000).

Zhi, Z. Q., *Zhong Guo Jing Jiao [Chinese Nestorianism]*, Beijing: Dong Fang, 1993.

CHAPTER 6

Christian theology under feudalism, nationalism and democracy in Japan

Nozomu Miyahira

Christian theology in Japan takes a number of forms, but still it is meaningful to talk of Japanese Christian theology. On the one hand, Japanese Christian theology could be understood negatively as a nationalistic and introverted theology in Japan; on the other hand, it could be understood positively as an indigenous and original theology in Japan. Moreover, Christian theology in Japan is not merely the theology of Japanese theologians; it is also the theology of Japanese Christians and at the same time Christian theology conducted, while living in Japan, by those who are not Japanese. The reality of Christian theology in Japan will be seriously biased if any one of these categories is missing or is under-represented.

The first stage of Christian theology in Japan begins with the introduction of Catholic Christianity under feudalism in which feudal lords governed society. In this period non-Japanese Christian theology, or western Christian theology brought by missionaries, as well as the theological education of Japanese Christians, are the dominant features. The second stage develops through the introduction of Protestant Christianity, and the reintroduction of Catholic theology under nationalism, within a modernized nation of Japan. While some Japanese theologians emerged from under the nationalistic system, others conformed to it. The third stage begins with the avalanche of missionaries of various denominations who engaged with the process of the democratization of Japan, following its defeat in 1945. Since then the study of western theology and the indigenization of Christian theology have been undertaken in many ways.

CATHOLIC TRADITIONAL THEOLOGY AND KIRISHITAN SYNCRETISTIC THEOLOGY UNDER FEUDALISM (1549 TO 1865)

The arrival of Christianity in Japan dates back to 1549, when the Jesuit priests Francis Xavier (1506–52) and Cosme de Torres (1510–70) landed in

Kagoshima, Kyûshû. While committed to the basic tenets of Catholic Christianity, they endeavoured to accommodate the language and customs of the mission field – a method that became the standard model for subsequent missionaries. The missionaries built schools as well as churches, so that they might lead the Japanese to become 'Kirishitan', the Japanese pronunciation of the Portuguese *Christão*, meaning Christian.

Alexandro Valignano (1539–1606), a Jesuit visitor, came to Japan in 1579 and played a crucial role in establishing the Christian teaching system. He planned to found seminaries (Seminario) to follow the catechistic education given to children at church schools, and in 1580 two seminaries were set up, one in Azuchi (near Kyoto) and the other in Arima (Shimabara Peninsula, Kyûshû). The seminaries were intended to train boys to become priests and lay leaders. The curriculum included Japanese and Latin, classical literature and music, as well as Christian doctrine, church history and moral education. Later, in 1580, a preparatory novitiate (Novisiado) was founded in Usuki, Kyûshû, for the graduates from the seminaries. In 1582 a professional college (Collegio) was started in Funai (now Ôita), Kyûshû, in order to teach theology and philosophy to candidates for the Jesuit priesthood. A plan to establish a more comprehensive university was aborted, because in 1587 the feudal lord Hideyoshi Toyotomi ordered the expulsion of the Christian missionaries. Then, in 1614, the seminaries were closed down in accordance with the isolation policy of the Tokugawa government, which tightened restrictions on Christianity out of fear of western colonization and ideological subversion within Japan.

During this short and adverse period, however, essential theological works were published and used as textbooks by Jesuit priests. The catechism was edited by Francis Xavier and subsequent missionaries. From 1580 Valignano began to edit *Catechismus Iaponensis*, in collaboration with some Japanese Kirishitans who had formerly been Buddhist monks, finally publishing it in Latin in 1586. This book expounds *Deus* the Creator against Japanese religions, and explains Christian doctrines, including the Ten Commandments, the sacraments, grace, everlasting life and judgement. In 1591 the definitive version of the catechism, *Doctrina Christam*, was published in Japanese and in 1592 it was authorized in Nagasaki Province. This catechism includes teaching on being a Christian, the Cross, the Lord's Prayer, the Apostles' Creed, the Ten Commandments, canon law, sin and the sacraments. Buddhist terminology was partially employed to translate some of the basic doctrinal terms, and the principle of accommodation was clearly adopted in that Japanese local customs and circumstances were taken into serious consideration.

In 1593 Pedro Gomes (1535–1600), the Principal at Funai college and the Jesuit Vice Provincial in Japan, wrote a college textbook, *Compendium catholicae veritatis*, published first in Latin and subsequently in Japanese in 1595. This book consists of an introduction to western natural science, Aristotelian philosophy of the soul interpreted by Thomas Aquinas (1225–74) and the Catholic doctrines explicated by the Council of Trent (1545–63). In 1601 Luis de Cerqueira (1552–1614), a Jesuit Bishop, founded a seminary for candidates for parish priests in Nagasaki. One of the seminary's main textbooks, edited and published in 1605 by Cerqueira as *Manuale ad Sacramenta Ecclesiae ministranda*, covered the sacraments, the church calendar and Gregorian chant. Another influential textbook was *Flosculi ex Veteris*, edited and published in 1610 by Manuel Barreto (1564–1620), Jesuit secretary to Cerqueira. This book is a collection of excerpts from the Old and New Testaments, classical literature and biographies of the Church Fathers. Both of these books provided practical help to priests engaging in the ministry and preparing sermons.

In addition to the books written by missionaries, an apologetic theological work, *Myôtêmondô*, was written by an intellectual Japanese Kirishitan, Fucan Fabian (1565–1621). He was baptized in Kyoto in 1583 and then studied at a seminary, a novitiate and a college. In 1590 he was summoned by Valignano to attend the second Council of the Jesuits at Kazusa in Shimabara Peninsula, where missionary policy and the education of the Japanese Kirishitans was discussed by the missionaries, who included Gomes, Gnecchi-Soldo Organtino (1533–1609) and Luis Frois (1532–79), as well as by the Japanese Kirishitans. Following his critical study of Buddhism written in Nagasaki, Fabian wrote *Myôtêmondô* in Kyoto in 1605. This book, which takes the form of dialogues between a Buddhist nun and a Kirishitan woman, refutes Buddhism, Confucianism and Shintoism, and then propounds Christianity. Through this book Fabian points out the empty and irrational theories of these traditional Japanese religions, over against which he argues that Christianity enjoys the absolute and only God, the sovereign Creator, who is utterly different from Buddha and the Japanese gods. Then, in 1606, Fabian entered into a controversy with a celebrated Confucian scholar, Razan Hayashi (1583–1657), in Kyoto Nanbanji church. Hayashi, academic adviser to the Tokugawa government, wrote *Haiyasho*, which argued for the Confucian understanding of heaven and earth and refuted the view, as explained in *Tenshu Jitsugi* (True Teaching of the Heavenly Lord), published by the Jesuit Matteo Ricci (1552–1611).

But in 1608 Fabian left the Jesuits, along with a Kirishitan woman, and began sending letters that criticized the Jesuits to Pedro Morejón (1562–1639),

successor to Organtino in Kyoto. Finally he cooperated with the
Tokugawa government in its persecution of Christians in Nagasaki in 1619.
In the following year he published *Hadaiusu* (*Deus* destroyed), with a
dedication to General Hidetada Tokugawa. In order to take issue with
Christianity in this book, Fabian deployed the same methodology with
which he had once refuted the Japanese religions; that is, he highlighted
Christian doctrines he considered to be irrational.

On the one hand, Catholic Christianity permeated Japan gradually and
intellectually through churches and schools; on the other hand, it spread
over some local areas massively and authoritatively through conversions of
their Daimyô, or feudal lords. Some of the Daimyô in Hizen (now
Nagasaki), such as Sumitada Ômura (1533–87) and Harunobu Arima
(1561–1612), became interested in Christianity, partly in expectation of the
potential benefits from the economic and military support of Portugal.
Ômura was baptized in 1563 by Torres, becoming the first Kirishitan
Daimyô, and Arima was baptized in 1580 by Valignano. Arima later
founded a seminary in his territory. Sôrin Ôtomo (1530–87), Daimyô
in Bungo (now Ôita), met Xavier in 1551 and, following the disruption
of war, was baptized in 1578 by Francisco Cabral (1533–1609), the successor to Torres. Ôtomo subsequently founded a novitiate and a college in
his territory. In 1582 Ômura, Arima and Ôtomo, following Valignano's
advice, dispatched a mission, including four Japanese boys, to Pope
Gregory XIII (1502–85) at Rome. The boys returned to Japan in 1590 with
western news and goods.

Ukon Takayama (1552–1615), Daimyô in Settsu (now Osaka), is famous
for his faithful life. In 1564 he was baptized by Lourenzo (1526–92), a
Japanese Jesuit. He contributed devotedly to the construction of Kyoto
Nanbanji, a representative church which was finally completed in 1578.
He also founded a seminary in Azuchi and in 1581 he celebrated Easter
with Valignano on a grand scale. He was consistently dedicated to
Christian evangelism, but in 1614 the Tokugawa government banished
him from Japan, with other Kirishitans and missionaries including those
of orders other than the Jesuits. He died later in Manila. The Franciscans
had already visited Japan in 1593, with the Dominicans and Augustinians
following in 1602.

A Daimyô's conversion to Christianity was often followed by the mass
conversion of his territory. In the early seventeenth century there were
about three hundred and seventy thousand Kirishitans in Japan; that is,
over one per cent of the population as it was then, and about two hundred
and fifty churches. However, the number of missionaries competent to

educate and edify newborn Kirishitans was far from enough. From 1549 to 1644, when Manshiyo Konishi (1600–44), the last Japanese priest, was arrested and martyred, the foreign and Japanese missionaries numbered only several hundred. Besides which the official proscription of Christianity, issued in 1612 by the shogunate government, caused such recurrent predicaments as the persecution, martyrdom, banishment and proselytism of Kirishitans and missionaries.

For about two hundred and thirty years, until 1873 when the official proscription of Christianity was removed, Kirishitans were left without any leading priests or supporting Daimyô. In 1708, the Jesuit Giovanni Battista Sidotti (1688–1714) landed in Yakushima, Ôsumi (now Kagoshima), in an attempt to re-evangelize Japan, but he was soon arrested and, in 1709, sent to Edo (now Tokyo), where Hakuseki Arai (1657–1725), an influential Confucian politician, interrogated him to find out whether the Christian countries of the west were planning to expand their territories into Japan. Although the lack of such a plot relieved the fundamental reason for the isolation policy of the shogunate government, the government remained closed to missionaries.

Nevertheless, risking their own lives, Kirishitans had already organized underground communities, called *Confraria* or *Companhia*, in an effort to hand their teachings and rituals over to the next generations by themselves. But, given the lack of priests, they developed their Christian beliefs and practices in syncretism with local conventional religions and customs, including Buddhism and Shintoism. Once, some of the Kirishitans were taught traditional Catholic Christianity with such spiritual vademecums as the Japanese version (1607) of *Exercitia Spiritualia* by Ignatius Loyola (1491–1556), founder of the Jesuits, the accurate Japanese translation (1596) of *Imitatio Christi* ascribed to Thomas à Kempis (1379–1471) and the abridged Japanese translation (1599) of *Guia de Pecadores* by Luis de Granada (1504–88), a Dominican theologian. However, their tradition, which had to depend to a great extent on their memory, became necessarily subject to change and eventual oblivion.

One of the rare extant written materials which demonstrates the syncretistic belief of Kirishitans at that time is *Tenchi Hajimari No Koto*, or *Beginning of Heaven and Earth*, which is supposed to have originated from a Kirishitan in Nagasaki during the eighteenth century. This book, circulated among underground Kirishitans, records the doctrines of creation, angels, original sin, Mary, the life of Christ and eschatology. It quotes largely from the Old and New Testaments, but it includes Buddhist concepts and local legends and dialects as well; for instance, heaven is associated with the twelve heavenly beings of Buddhism, God is called 'Hotoke' or Buddha, and Christ is once called 'Oshô' or Buddhist priest.

A Buddhist element is found also in the Kirishitans' 'orasho'; their pronunciation of *oratio* or prayer. Some orasho derives from Gregorian chants taught by missionaries; however, when they pray orasho now, it sounds more like sutras chanted by Buddhists than like Christian prayer. For Kirishitans, orasho gradually became monotonous and nebulous out of fear of being overheard by others. Kirishitans had to disguise their Christianity in a variety of ways; hence, almost all Kirishitans belonged to a Buddhist temple or a Shinto shrine. There remains an interesting shrine, Karematsu Shrine, in Sotomechô, Nagasaki Prefecture, where an evangelist named San Juwan has been worshipped.

The underground Kirishitans, called 'Senpuku Kirishitan' in Japanese, followed two different courses when Catholic Christianity was reintroduced to Japan after the mid-nineteenth century. Some Kirishitans returned to the Catholic Church to have the non-Christian elements shaved off their beliefs and practices. Later, in 1896, the returners, unlike those who held onto their syncretistic customs, were referred to as 'Fukkatsu Kirishitan', or Resurrected Kirishitan, by Francisque Marnas (1859–1932). The syncretized Kirishitans were usually called 'Kakure Kirishitan', or Hidden Christians, although they did not need to hide themselves as strictly as before. Today, a few hundred Kakure Kirishitan households remain, mainly in Nagasaki Prefecture. Most Kakure Kirishitans in Ikitsuki, Nagasaki Prefecture, belong to a Buddhist temple or a Shinto shine, and the items regarded as their divinities include relics and pictures of saints hanging on a wall.

PROTESTANT EVANGELICAL AND LIBERAL THEOLOGIES UNDER NATIONALISM (1865 TO 1945)

The re-introduction of Christianity into Japan can be traced back to the mid-nineteenth century when western European powers launched into treaties of commerce and amity with Japan, accompanied by Catholic and Protestant missionaries engaged in evangelism. In 1865 Bernard Thadée Petitjean (1829–84), a Catholic missionary of the Société des Missions Etrangères de Paris, found the remaining Kirishitans at Ôura Cathedral (Nagasaki) dedicated to the twenty-six saints (twenty Japanese Kirishitans and six Franciscan missionaries) who were martyred by crucifixion in 1597 in Nagasaki, and he devoted himself to guiding them and other Japanese citizens towards Catholic Christianity. Later in the same year, James

Hamilton Ballagh (1832–1920) of the Reformed Church in America baptized the first Japanese Protestant Christian, and in 1872 the Christians baptized by him formed the first Protestant church, Nihon Kirisuto Kyôkai (Church of Christ, Japan), in Yokohama. These Christians, called the 'Yokohama Band', attempted to establish an evangelical, non-denominational and self-governing church.

From this group emerged Masahisa Uemura (1858–1925), who was baptized by Ballagh in 1873. His family belonged to a samurai class which had declined as the new Meiji government (1868–1912) began to replace feudalism by returning the feudal territories to the Meiji Emperor in 1869. Uemura sought social advancement, through the new regime, by learning western academic disciplines, including theology taught in Yokohama by Ballagh and Samuel Robbins Brown (1810–80) of the Reformed Church in America. In Yokohama, during Ballagh's sermon, Uemura had a religious experience in which his soul was overwhelmed by the only and true God who is omnipresent, holy and gracious. After studying at Tokyo Icchi Shingakkô (Union Theological Seminary, Tokyo, later Meiji Gakuin University), Uemura was ordained in 1880 by the Nihon Kirisuto Icchi Kyôkai (The Union Church of Christ in Japan, later Church of Christ in Japan), which was founded in 1876 by the Reformed and the Presbyterian churches.

While engaging in evangelism as a pastor, Uemura published *Sinri Ippan* (*A View on the Truth*) in 1884, the first theological book to come from a Japanese Protestant. In his book he considered issues such as the nature of religious truth, the existence of God, human spirituality and Christ's apologetic as set against the Japanese social background of atheistic and materialistic Enlightenment thought. In 1887 he founded Banchô Icchi Church (later Fujimichô Church, Tokyo) and all his work centred around this church, while also committing himself to journalism by publishing such journals as *Fukuin Shinpô* (Gospel News) and *Nihon Hyôron* (Japan Review), and also to theological education at Tokyo Singaku Sha (Tokyo Theological School, later Tokyo Union Theological Seminary), which he founded in 1904. His theology was based on an evangelical faith in the incarnation of Jesus Christ as the Son of God and in the redemption of human sins by the death and resurrection of Christ on the cross; in addition, he thought that Christianity could purify Japanese social justice as found in samurai ethics.

Another Christian group, the 'Kumamoto Band', was formed in 1876 when Japanese students with a highly nationalistic, Confucianistic and samurai spirit, taught by Leroy Lansing Janes (1837–1909), an American educationalist at Kumamoto Yô Gakkô (Kumamoto Western School), took an oath to the effect that they would dedicate their lives to Christianity and its mission. But later in the same year Kumamoto Yô Gakkô had to be closed because of its Christianization, and the students were transferred to Dôshisha Ei Gakkô (Dôshisha English School, later Dôshisha University), Kyoto, which had been founded in 1875 by Jô Niijima (1843–90), a Japanese missionary from the American Board. In 1886 the American Board organized Nihon Kumiai Kyôkai (The Associated Churches in Japan), which shared the characteristics of congregationalism and an independent spirit.

Danjô Ebina (1856–1937), one of the students of the Kumamoto group, was baptized by Janes in 1876. When Janes explained prayer as the obligation of those created to the Lord of all, Ebina, who was from a samurai family that collapsed following the Meiji Government, found in God the new lord whom he should obey and serve. He finished studying at Dôshisha and was ordained in 1879 to become pastor at Annaka Church, Gunma and others. He was known as an influential pastor (1897–1920) at Hongô Church (later Yumichô Hongô Church), Tokyo, and as the directive Chancellor (1920–28) at Dôshisha. In 1900 he began to publish a journal, *Shinjin* (New Man). His theology originates from a religious experience in which the baby of God was born in his heart, and its ultimate goal consists in the realization of the Kingdom of God by expanding the ideal human character of the God-man union to the realms of society, the nation and the world.

A serious theological controversy ensued between Ebina and Uemura from 1901 to 1902, surrounding a liberal theology called 'Shin Shingaku' (New Theology). The New Theology, brought into Japan from the late 1880s by missionaries of the Allgemeiner Evangelisch-Protestantischer Missions-verein, the American Unitarian Association and the Universalist General Convention, influenced the Associated Churches in Japan. Such influence was possible because the Associated Churches in Japan were quite independent of the original foreign mission of the American Board, in sharp contrast to the Nihon Sei Kô Kai (Japan Holy Catholic Church), founded in 1887 by the American Episcopal Church; the Society for the Propagation of the Gospel; the Church Missionary Society; Nihon Mesojisuto Kyôkai (Japan Methodist Church), built in 1907 by three American Methodist Churches; and other denominations such as the Baptist and the Lutheran churches. Ebina was not the only one to be attracted to this New Theology, which denied the traditional Christian doctrines; in addition, Michitomo Kanamori (1857–1945) transferred from the Kumamoto group and was baptized in 1876 by Niijima.

Uemura regarded the New Theology as highly problematic and potentially destructive for Japanese churches. By applying the theology of the History of Religion School to the Japanese context, Kanamori argued that religious truth was not confined to one religion; on the contrary, he claimed that religions with truth and life would prevail, but that the stories of miracles, rituals, abstinence and interdenominational strife in Christianity were hindrances to the Japanese. Kanamori relativized and reduced Christianity to an open religion by denying the infallible and unique revelation of God in the Bible and the traditional views on the divinity and redemption of Christ. Over against the New Theology as found in Kanamori, Uemura maintained in 1891 in his *Japan Review* that Christianity was the absolute religion based on the historicity of Jesus Christ as described in the Bible and that Christianity without miracles, including the resurrection, did not deserve its name; although he accepted some of the fruits of biblical criticism.

Furthermore, Uemura in his *Gospel News* took issue with Ebina over such doctrinal points as the relation between God and Christ and the incarnation of Christ. Ebina in his *New Man* clarified the religious truth found in the doctrines of the divinity of Christ and the Trinity, but stressed the vital relation between the Father and the Son over the doctrines. Ebina understood this relation on the basis of the Confucianist familial ethics expressed as paternal affection and filial piety, which was in keeping with his own religious experience. Thus, for Ebina Jesus Christ was the ultimate realization of filial piety directed towards paternal affection, and it was through this realization that Christ became God. Ebina also considered the religious consciousness found in Jesus to be universal to all humans, who thereby enjoyed some divinity whether they were Confucianist or Shintoist.

In order to counter Ebina's argument, Uemura pointed out that the Christian doctrines originated from the faith of the original Christians, and he argued that Christ could not redeem sinners if the divinity of Christ and the divinity of humans were relatively continuous with each other. By referring to the New Testament, Uemura attempted to demonstrate that the divinity and the incarnation of Christ vouchsafed his saving power for sinners in this world, although Uemura depended on the term subordination for expressing the Son's relation to the Father in this inchoate period of theological history in Japan.

Hiromichi Kozaki (1856–1938), who was from a Confucian samurai family, accepted Christianity under the influence of the Kumamoto group who had not succumbed to persecution, and of Janes at Kumamoto

Western School, who advised him to pray to God so that the Spirit of
God might assist him in understanding Christianity. Baptized by Janes in
1876, Kozaki finished studying at Dôshisha in 1879 and went on to
establish a number of churches, including the Reinanzaka Church,
Tokyo. In 1880 he organized the YMCA with Uemura in Tokyo,
becoming its first President and the founder of its *Rikugô Zasshi* (Rikugô
Journal). In the journal he introduced Karl Marx (1818–83) to Japan, in
1881, for the first time. In 1886 Kozaki clarified his understanding of the
relation between Confucianism and Christianity in his *Seikyô Shinron*
(New Essay on Politics and Religion). According to his book, the Confucian spirit which points out human sins is confined to particular areas
and supports the discriminative social order, whereas Christianity with
the gospel of salvation reaches all countries and stresses the equality of all
humans. This means that Confucianism leads the Japanese to Christianity, as Judaism was the background of Christianity. In this sense
Christianity is the fulfilment of Confucianism and Christianity is con-
ducive to the modernization of Japan, just as Confucianism informed
Japanese feudalism.

In 1889 Kozaki delivered a lecture on the inspiration of the Bible at
Dôshisha, in which he argued that the inspiration of the Bible did not
mean its infallibility but pointed to the Spirit's guidance of its authors.
Furthermore, in 1903 he contended that the theory of evolution is not
contradictory to the Bible; he showed that the Holy Spirit cultivates the
Church and he likened the kingdom of God to a growing seed. Although
he was open to some aspects of liberal theology, Kozaki defended what he
called progressive evangelicalism against the New Theology in his 1911
book, *Kirisutokyô no Honshitsu* (The Essence of Christianity). He critiqued the New Theology for separating the theology of Paul from the
Gospel of Jesus and failing to recognize the serious need for sinners to
repent and be born again. Since he understood the doctrine of the Trinity
as the development of the original Gospel by spiritually purified human
reason, he thought of the theology of Paul as the appropriate development
of the Gospel of Jesus and championed the redemption of Christ. After
Niijima he assumed the Chancellery of Dôshisha (1890–98) and then
returned to Reinanzaka Church (1898–1931) as a pastor.

The other Christian group, the 'Sapporo Band', was established
under the influence of William Smith Clark (1826–86), an American
agronomist at Sapporo Nô Gakkô (Sapporo Agricultural School, later
Hokkaidô University). After studying western disciplines at Tokyo,
Kanzô Uchimura (1861–1930), with a samurai spirit and Confucian ethics,

entered the School in 1877, signing the 'Covenant of Believers in Christ' written by Clark and being baptized in 1878 by Merriman Colbert Harris (1846–1921), an American Methodist Episcopalian. After this, Uchimura determined to delve into the mystery of the universe created by God, while wrestling with the theory of evolution in its relation to Christian theism, and also the difficulties of loving two Js (Japan and Jesus) by reconciling patriotism with a Christian worldview. After struggling with the gap between the sin in himself and the ideal holy life before God, under the guidance of Julius Hawley Seelye (1824–95), President at Amherst College, Massachusetts, to whom he was introduced by Niijima in 1886, Uchimura realized that he should focus on Christ who died on the cross for his sin. After studying at Amherst College and Hartford Theological Seminary, Connecticut, he engaged in teaching and journalism in Japan. In 1891 he had to resign his teaching post at the Daiichi Kôtô Chûgakkô (The First High School, later part of Tokyo University), because he refused, on the grounds of his Christian faith, to bow to a page of the Imperial Precept on Education which had been signed by the Emperor. He published an autobiography, *How I Became a Christian: Out of My Diary*, in English in 1895.

From 1900 Uchimura took the initiative in issuing a monthly journal, *Seisho no Kenkyû* (The Biblical Study, with the subtitle '*Pro Christo et Patria*'), and in creating Mukyôkai, or the Non-Church Movement and its groups, which focused its mission on Bible studies in house meetings, underpinned by the view that clergy and sacraments are counter-productive to the Christian faith. According to Uchimura, *ecclesia* means assembly or gathering; thus, Christ intended to form a spiritual assembly based on voluntary faith in him rather than an institutional church with rules and regulations. In 1901 he advised Sapporo Christ Church (later Sapporo Independent Christ Church), founded in 1882 by the Sapporo group which included Uchimura, to abolish the Eucharist and baptism in order for the congregation to learn salvation by faith in Christ, not by the administration of the sacraments. What he endeavoured to clarify is that the authentic church is non-church as the Kingdom of God in this world, in the sense that there is no sacrament nor clergy in heaven. The authentic church, for members of the non-church, is the universe itself, created directly by God, with the sky as the ceiling, grass as the floor, birds as the musicians, mountains as the pulpit and God as the preacher.

In 1917 Uchimura expressed his faith in the Second Advent of Christ, organizing its movement in the following year, in collaboration with Holiness churches in Japan. Then in 1930 Uchimura left a note to the effect that his non-church movement is not for the non-church itself but for faith in Christ on the cross. His theology is evangelical in his attempt to construct it on the basis of his biblical study, and also indigenous in his attempt to mediate Japan and Christianity.

The Yokohama, Kumamoto and Sapporo groups produced Christian leaders of the first generation, who further influenced various quarters of church and society in Japan.

Following the Ebina and Uemura controversy (1901–2), the conference of the Fukuin Dômeikai (Evangelical Alliance in Japan) held in 1902 approved evangelicalism with faith in Jesus Christ as the incarnate God of human salvation, a view closer to Uemura's, but within ten years the evangelical tenets were no longer taken up as the agenda of the Alliance. Ebina's liberal Christianity, with its positive understanding of human progress, stimulated social movements. Sakuzô Yoshino (1878–1933), who belonged to Hongô Church ministered by Ebina during his student days, became Professor at Tokyo Imperial University (later Tokyo University) in 1914. In accordance with the imperialistic polity of the 1910s, he championed a democracy which balanced the ruler's obedience to the people's will and the people's obedience to the ruler's spiritual guidance. Shigeru Nakajima (1888–1946), who also belonged to Hongô Church as one of the students of Yoshino, began to teach jurisprudence from 1917 at Dôshisha. In 1928 he formed Dôshisha Rôdôsha Mission (Dôshisha Labourers Mission, later Japan Labourers Mission in 1929) with Toyohiko Kagawa in order to realize the new Japan, and then he started the movement of Social Christianity in 1930. The main point of focus for Social Christianity is the concept of the kingdom of God. The kingdom of God is the community of God based on personal and voluntary relationships, which underlie the association of members of an institution with regulations and obligations. Such a community does not evolve from class struggles, as Karl Marx argued, but from the development of interpersonal solidarity. Hence, Nakajima understands social practice in terms of the redemptive love of Christ. The love of Christ functions in actual society in such a way that humans do not seek individual salvation, but social reform on the basis of cooperation and service, as Jesus as Christ did to the utmost.

For five years, from 1930, Toyohiko Kagawa (1888–1960) organized and activated 'Kami No Kuni Undô' (The Kingdom of God Movement), a nationwide evangelistic movement with its main emphasis on social reforms for factory workers and farmers. He was baptized by Harry White Myers (1874–1945) of the Presbyterian Church in the United States

(South) in 1904, studied at Meiji Gakuin (1905–7) and graduated from Kobe Theological Seminary (1907–11). In 1909 he moved to the under-privileged area in Kobe to serve and evangelize and then to Tokyo to help those suffering from the Kantô Great Earthquake in 1923. He also studied at Princeton University and Theological Seminary from 1914 to 1917. During his years in Kobe and Tokyo, he made an extensive contribution to the improvement of social conditions by establishing unions of labourers, farmers and consumers. While the Kingdom of God Move-ment was partly stimulated by the American Social Gospel, this social practice was closely connected with his personal conviction that Jesus' love consists in redeeming the missing people.

Tokutarô Takakura (1885–1934), one of the disciples of Uemura, rose up against Social Christianity. He was baptized by Uemura in 1906 and studied at Tokyo Theological School until 1910. After pastorates in Tokyo, Kyoto and Sapporo, he began to teach at the School in 1918. From 1921 he continued his research at Edinburgh, Oxford and Cambridge and was influenced, in particular, by the theology of Peter Taylor Forsyth (1848–1921). On returning to Japan, in 1924, he started his house church (later Shinanomachi Church, Tokyo) and became President at the School. Originally he approached Christianity in order to seek an answer to problems of the self, whereby he came to see that the grace of God was transcendent over the self and that salvation was by faith alone. He put a balanced emphasis on the need for a newborn experience as an evangelical person and also on the need for the reborn event of culture via the arrival of the kingdom of God.

In his main work, *Fukuinteki Kirisutokyô* (Evangelical Christianity, 1927), Takakura clarified what he means by evangelical Christianity against stereotyped orthodoxy, liberalism, pietism and Catholicism. That is, evangelical Christianity is the religion of the Bible, beginning with the Prophets in the Old Testament, incorporated into the New Testament and enlivened by the Reformers. This Christianity is in sharp contrast with Catholicism and liberalism, which have been amalgamated with non-Christian elements.

Another disciple, influenced and baptized by Uemura, is Seiichi Hatano (1877–1950), a philosopher of religion who later belonged to the church ministered by Takakura. He studied western philosophy under Raphael von Koebel (1848–1923) at Tokyo Imperial University, further under Adolf von Harnack (1851–1930) in Berlin and under Wilhelm Wind-elband (1848–1915) and Ernst Troeltsch (1865–1923) in Heidelberg from 1904 to 1906, becoming Professor at Kyoto Imperial University in 1917.

His works include *Kirisutokyô no Kigen* (The Origin of Christianity, 1908), *Shûkyô Tetsugaku* (Philosophy of Religion, 1935) and *Toki to Eien* (Time and Eternity, 1943). He produced pioneering work in the philosophical interpretation of religious experience and regarded religious experience as the crowning personal event in which the transcendent God encounters the self. Humans reach this event through natural life in which they objectify others, cultural life in which they conceptualize others and religious life in which they enjoy interpersonal relations with God and others as thou. He also expressed human love, kept in relation to God and others, as the unification of faith already given and hope yet to be realized, and he found eternity in this love.

In 1929 Toraji Tsukamoto (1885–1973), one of the disciples of Uchimura but independent of him because of his own excessive Non-Churchism, engaged in evangelism by means of his journal *Seisho Chishiki* (Knowledge of the Bible, with the subtitle 'There is salvation outside the church'). In 1928 he published articles of severe anti-churchism in *The Biblical Study*, edited by Uchimura, with the result that he entered into controversy on ecclesiology with Sôichi Iwashita (1889–1940), a Catholic priest. Iwashita was baptized in 1901 by Émile Heck (1868–1943), Professor of French Literature at Tokyo Imperial University. He studied under the influence of Koebel and was led by Heck into the Catholic faith, studying further in Paris and Rome and then being ordained in 1925. Tsukamoto rejected the Catholic view that the Church was built on Peter and maintained that the Protestant churches did not stand on Peter's confession: 'You are the Christ, the Son of the living God' (Matt. 16:16 RSV). Iwashita argued that the faith of Non-Church, while supported academically by the higher criticism of the Bible, is subjective without the objective authority of the Church as the pledge of truth. Then Tsukamoto contended that the infallibility of the Pope is false and regarded the direct revelation of the Holy Spirit as the rule of faith.

In the 1930s dialectic theology began to infiltrate into the work of Japanese theologians. In 1932 Hidenobu Kuwada (1895–1975), later President at Tokyo Union Theological Seminary, announced his conversion from liberal theology to the theology of Karl Barth (1886–1968). Yoshitaka Kumano (1899–1981), one of the disciples of Uemura and later Professor at Tokyo Union Theological Seminary, enriched the scheme of his theology with recourse to dialectic theology. In 1934 Enkichi Kan (1895–1972), Professor at Rikkyô University, who once studied under Hatano and was a leader of the Student Christian Movement (closely related to Social Christianity), became a dialectic theologian. Keiji Ashida (1867–1936), Professor at Dôshisha University, converted to the theology of Barth and introduced it by translation. However, most of them did not develop fully a theology of resistance against Japanese nationalism and the system of Emperors, thereby failing to apply to the Japanese context the criticism which the Theology of the Word of God hurled at Nazism, beside which the liberal theology as found in Ebina, Kozaki and Kanamori tended towards a Christianity religiously compromised by Japanese nationalism.

Some of the disciples of Uchimura steered a more critical course. Shigeru Nanbara (1889–1974), Professor of Politics at Tokyo Imperial University, wrote *Kokka to Shûkyô* (Nation and Religion, 1942), critical research into the nationalism of the Nazis. Tadao Yanaihara (1893–1961), Professor of Economics at Tokyo Imperial University, critiqued the aggressive Japanese foreign policies in Asia so severely that he was compelled to resign his professorship in 1937, although he became Chancellor of Tokyo University in 1951, succeeding Nanbara.

Although the Japanese Imperial Constitution stipulated the freedom of religion in 1889, this freedom was defined on the condition that it should not infringe upon the national order and the duty of the subjects. Thus, the Christian pacifists, pastors and educators against nationalism experienced various levels of oppressions and persecutions. Japanese Christendom itself was finally incorporated into nationalism by the Shûkyô Dantai Hô (Religious Organizations Act), which the Imperial Diet passed in 1939, with a view to ruling over all religious organizations, including Christian churches. More than thirty Protestant denominations, in contrast with the Catholic Church as one body, were incorporated into Nihon Kirisuto Kyôdan (The United Church of Christ in Japan) in 1941, and their pastors had to minister to the churches under the aegis of the Imperial government in order to support the Japanese wartime regime. This system, however, ended up virtually suppressing the other Asian Christians by forcing them to worship gods at the Japanese Shinto shrines, while the Japanese nationalistic ideology was explicated in the propaganda of the United Church of Christ, insisting that this Church was the authentic and ideal form of Christianity in Japan, replacing western-derived Christianity. When Japan surrendered unconditionally in 1945, some churches were beginning to separate themselves from the United Church of Christ, in order to return to previous denominations or to organize new denominations, whereas others remained within it.

WESTERN THEOLOGY AND INDIGENOUS
THEOLOGY UNDER DEMOCRACY

The third rise of Christianity in Japan comes after the war. The full freedom of religion in the new Japanese Constitution of 1947 boosts Christianity again in Japan, as part of the process of democratization instigated by the American occupation policies.

Independently of the reintroduction of Christianity, an ingenious Japanese theology emerged from within the painful situation of defeat; that is, *Theology of the Pain of God* (1946) by Kazô Kitamori (1916–98). As Professor of Systematic Theology at Tokyo Union Theological Seminary, with a background in the Lutheran church, he expounded the cross of Christ as the event of the pain of God on the basis of a systematic interpretation of the Bible and of Japanese sentiment, while criticizing both Barthian theology for lacking the concept of embracing God and liberal theology for its emphasis on divine love without pain. By the pain of God he does not mean a concept of Sabellian Patripassianism, as he argues that not the Father but the Son suffered on the cross and the Father experienced the pain because of the death of the Son. The pain of God consists essentially in the Father begetting the Son and then leading him to suffer and die on the cross, and in God forgiving unforgivable sinners, based on events on the cross. Therefore, the pain of God is not a substantial concept but rather a relational concept between the Father and the Son, and God and sinners.

Katsumi Takizawa (1909–84) wrestled with the Japanese Buddhist mindset and expounded a theology of Immanuel. He was a follower of Kitarô Nishida (1870–1945), a Japanese philosopher who set forth a theory of the self-identity of absolute contradiction, or of contradictory concepts being complementary to each other. Through Nishida's recommendation, Takizawa became the first Japanese student of Karl Barth in 1934 at Bonn University, and then from 1947 to 1971 he taught philosophical theology at Kyûshyû University. According to Takizawa's theology of Immanuel, the first contact of God and humans is expressed as God being with us through Christ; a point stressed by Barth and also an example of the self-identity of the transcendent God and immanent humans. The second contact is realized when humans become enlightened as to the first contact, whether they are Christian or Buddhist. In other words, Buddhism as well as Christianity consists in the original fact of Immanuel and as such these two are equally true religions based on different perspectives.

In dialogue with Buddhism and also Takizawa himself, Seiichi Yagi (1932–), a New Testament scholar and philosopher of religion, attempts to seek a common ground in which Christianity and Buddhism can share religious experiences and understandings. Yagi realized that there is a parallel phenomenon between his conversion to Christianity and his enlightenment in Zen Buddhism; in both experiences the deliverance from something conceptual plays a central role. Therefore, he holds in high esteem immediate experiences taking place before the conceptualization by means of subject–object differentiation. He reads and interprets the New Testament from this viewpoint to clarify the meaning of central biblical ideas. Further, theoretical study of the religious dialogue between Christianity and other religions has been rigorously undertaken by Yasuo Furuya (1926–), who taught at the International Christian University which was founded in 1949. He has developed a *Theology of Religions* (1985) that seeks to balance the normativity of the Christian revelation and the equal value of all religions. That is, his theology consists of exclusiveness and inclusiveness and of particularity and universality in Christianity.

The indigenization of Christian theology in an Asian or a Japanese context has been unfolded more directly by Masao Takenaka (1925–2006), a Christian ethicist at Dôshisha University. He is a specialist in Asian Christian art as well as Christian ethics, and as such he has endeavoured to share a common Christian way of life and understanding in Asia. Taking into account rice as the staple food in almost all Asian countries, Takenaka defines God as the rice of life in the Asian context, not the bread of life in the biblical and Mediterranean context. Moreover, Nozomu Miyahira (1966–) has attempted to reconstruct Christian theology in a manner both consistent with the Christian theological tradition and appropriate to the Japanese cultural climate. His theology of the Concord of God begins with reformulating the doctrine of the Trinity as three betweennesses and one concord, by applying the Japanese concepts of human beings and their community to the divine Trinity and Unity. In addition, the Japanese interpretation of the doctrine of the Holy Spirit has been extensively elaborated by Masaya Odagaki (1929–); the first Japanese person who, in his *Hermeneutical Theology* (1975), explains God in terms of nothingness. By nothingness he means that God or the divine being cannot simply be objectified as something to be comprehended, so that this theology is not atheism but non-theism. In this sense God can be defined as both being and nothingness. This divine duality also takes place in the divine being and in human beings. The Holy Spirit is appropriated to this duality through the Trinitarian context in which the Father as the divine being and the Son as human being are united by the Holy Spirit.

In relation to Japanese society the works of the following theologians are of equal importance: *Theology of Leisure* (1988), by Toshio Satô (1923–), a specialist in nineteenth-century theology, offers a Christian theological counterpoise to the workaholic Japanese society; Hideo Ôki (1928–), a systematic theologian especially interested in the Puritans, Emil Brunner (1889–1966) and Karl Barth, published *Ethics of the New Community* (1994), which delineates from a Christian perspective the new creative community over against the old closed Japanese community; *Theological Thought of Democracy* (2000), written by Katsuhiko Kondô (1943–), which traces the tradition of freedom in Protestantism, which is indispensable to Japan where democracy is a relatively foreign newcomer; finally, cutting-edge research on the relation between Christianity and communities suffering discrimination in Japan is expounded theologically by Teruo Kuribayashi (1948–) in his *Theology of the Crown of Thorns* (1986).

Protestant theologians constructing indigenous theology or relating theological thought to the Japanese context have been dealt with above in this section, but theology unique to Japan begins to emerge on the Catholic side as well. Through his dialogue with Buddhism, Kakichi Kadowaki (1926–) points out that religious disciplines like silent meditation and austere practice are characteristic of Japanese religions, and thus for the Japanese the way of Christ is followed, rather than learned, through such disciplines. Further, Yôji Inoue (1927–) attempts to transplant western Christianity into Japan, expressed in the substantial language of the 'field', which plays a central role in the Japanese way of life. For instance, when Jesus calls God the Father, there is no division between the Father and the Son, rather a 'field' is created in which they share an experience of love that embraces them as one. Additionally, influenced by Nishida, Isao Onodera (1929–) focuses on field-oriented theology rather than persona-oriented theology and thus on the significance of mother earth rather than that of heavenly Father, with the result that he attempts to base his Catholic spiritual theology on the Trinitarian field, in which the Holy Spirit on earth empowers human beings to say that Jesus is Lord.

Whereas some Japanese theologians are in the process of indigenizing Christian theology, other historical theologians are looking forward to the future of Christianity in Japan by delving into problems of past

Christianity within Japan as well as in Europe. In relation to this, it is important to note that in 1967 the United Church of Christ in Japan, followed by the other denominations, began to admit responsibility for their wartime collaboration with the government. Mitsuo Miyata (1928–), an influential scholar of political and theological thought at Tôhoku University, has produced various works on wartime nationalism in Japan and Germany, and, in particular, his analysis of church and state is of essential value for contemporary Japan, in which a nationalistic ambience is still dominant in those who think that the democratic Constitution and foreign Christianity have been imposed on them. Moreover, taught by Tetsutarô Ariga (1899–1977), a scholar of patristics who clarified the hayatology (deriving from the Hebrew verb in Exodus 3:14: I am who I am) of Hebrew thought by contrast with the ontology of Greek thought, Akio Dohi (1927–), a prominent Christian historian well-versed in both Japanese and western Christian history at Dôshisha University, has also produced extensive analysis of the problems of Japanese Christianity in relation to its wartime collaboration with the government, the Emperor system and the structure of discrimination. The works of these two theologians help to fix the eyes of Japanese Christians, still one per cent of the population, not merely on Europe academically or Japan nationalistically, but rather on Asia as their neighbour.

BIBLIOGRAPHY

Breen, J. and Williams, M. (eds.), *Japan and Christianity: Impacts and Responses*, Basingstoke: Macmillan, 1996.

Cary, O., *A History of Christianity in Japan: Roman Catholic, Greek Orthodox, and Protestant Missions*, Rutland: Charles E. Tuttle Company, 1976.

Dohi, A., 'Christianity in Japan' in T. K. Thomas (ed.), *Christianity in Asia: North-East Asia*, Singapore: Christian Conference of Asia, 1979, pp. 35–66.

Drummond, R. H., *A History of Christianity in Japan*, Grand Rapids: Eerdmans, 1971.

Furuya, Y. (ed.), *A History of Japanese Theology*, Grand Rapids: Eerdmans, 1997.

Iglehart, C. W., *A Century of Protestant Christianity in Japan*, Tokyo: Charles Tuttle Publishing, 1959.

Ikado, F. and McGovern, J. R. (eds.), *A Bibliography of Christianity in Japan: Protestantism in English Sources (1859–1959)*, Tokyo: International Christian University, 1966.

Inoue, Y., *The Face of Jesus in Japan*, Tokyo: Kindai-Bungeisha, 1990.

Kadowaki, K., *Erleuchtung auf dem Weg: Zur Theologie des Weges*, Munich: Kosel-Verlag, 1993.

Kitamori, K., *Theology of the Pain of God*, London: SCM Press, 1966 [1946].

Lee, R., *Stranger in the Land: A Study of the Church in Japan*, New York: Friendship Press, 1967.

Michelson, C., *Japanese Contributions to Christian Theology*, Philadelphia: Westminster Press, 1959.

Miyahira, N., *Towards a Theology of the Concord of God: A Japanese Perspective on the Trinity*, Carlisle: Paternoster Press, 2000.

Miyata, M., *Der Politische Auftrag des Protestantismus in Japan*, Hamburg-Bergstedt: Herbert Reich Evang. Verlag, 1964.

Mullins, M. R., *Christianity Made in Japan: A Study of Indigenous Movements*, Honolulu: University of Hawaii Press, 1998.

Phillips, J. M., *From the Rising of the Sun: Christians and Society in Contemporary Japan*, Maryknoll: Orbis Books, 1981.

Takenaka, M., *God is Rice: Asian Culture and Christian Faith*, Geneva: World Council of Churches, 1986.

Takizawa, K., *Das Heil im Heute: Texte einer Japanischen Theologie*, Göttingen: Vandenhoeck and Ruprecht, 1987.

Turnbull, S., *The Kakure Kirishitan of Japan: A Study of Their Development, Beliefs and Rituals to the Present Day*, Richmond: Japan Library, 1998.

Yagi, S. and Ulbrich, L. (eds.), *Gott in Japan*, Gütersloh: Chr. Kaiser/Gütersloher Verlagshaus, 1973.

CHAPTER 7

The Word and the Spirit: overcoming poverty, injustice and division in Korea

Sebastian C. H. Kim

INTRODUCTION

Christianity first arrived in Korea not through foreign missionaries but through a Korean scholar. In the eighteenth century Lee Seng-Hoon went to China to study, where he met a Jesuit missionary. Lee eventually became a Christian and was baptized in Peking in 1784. He returned to Korea and started to share his Christian faith, which led to many conversions. In 1789, when Jesuit missionaries first entered Korea, they discovered that there were already about four thousand Catholic Christians on the Korean peninsula. The Catholic Church grew rapidly, but between 1801 and 1867 it faced great persecution because of the refusal of Christians to practise ancestor veneration or worship, which was regarded as essential for national stability, and because of accusations that the Christians were in contact with European imperial powers. The persecution of 1866 was especially severe; about eight thousand Christians were martyred, and almost the same number later starved to death when they fled to the mountains. The country remained closed to the outside world until the Japanese imposed a trade agreement in 1876.

While the Korean peninsula was still closed, several Protestant missionaries who were working in China became interested in Korea. In 1832 K. A. Gützlaff briefly visited Korea, as did Robert Thomas in 1865 and 1866 (suffering martyrdom on his latter visit). The reports of their encounters drew the attention of other missionaries, who ventured into this hidden kingdom. The first official Protestant missionaries came to Korea in 1885 from North America and were soon followed by others. As they started work in many different parts of Korea, together with Korean evangelists, the church began to grow through a series of revivals, the most significant of which was the great revival in Pyeungyang in 1907.

Christians suffered persecutions again during the latter part of the period when Korea was under Japanese rule (1910–45). The Japanese authorities imposed worship at Shinto shrines, persecuted the Christians who refused, and burned down many churches. After independence in 1945, the Korean church had to face yet another persecution, this time by the Communists. During the Korean War (1950–53), Christians in Communist-held areas were accused of being pro-American or capitalist, and many were persecuted by the Communist army and local militias.

After the war the churches in South Korea, both Catholic and Protestant, grew very rapidly through their engagement in evangelism and church planting. According to the 2005 census, 29.2 per cent of the population are Christians (Protestants, 18.3 per cent; Roman Catholics, 10.9 per cent). Christianity has become a major religion, not only in numbers, but also in its influence on society in terms of education, medical work and social reform. The majority of Protestants are Presbyterians, but there is also a strong presence of Methodist, Baptist and Holiness churches; altogether there are 230 different denominations and groups. The Sunday morning worship services in most denominations of Protestant churches are quite formal, structured and male-led, whereas the rest of the services on Sundays and other days are either conducted in the form of scripture exposition or various activities involving the whole congregation.

The aim of this chapter[1] is to discuss the major characteristics of Korean Protestant theology, but not to provide a comprehensive survey of Korean theologians, as this has already been done by others.[2] For the purposes of clarity, I divide it into five major strands: the initial establishment of Korean Christianity as 'Bible Christianity' by the early Protestants; 'revival Christianity' in the 1950–60s; 'liberation Christianity' in the 1960–80s; 'folk Christianity' in the 1970–90s; and 'reconciling Christianity' in the 1990s. Though these theological strands are most prominent in particular eras, they are not exclusively limited to that particular period but continue to form distinctive strands of contemporary Korean theological thought patterns.

BIBLE CHRISTIANITY: ARDENT COMMITMENT TO THE TEXT

Among many modes of missionary activity, the translation and distribution of the Bible was a central concern for Protestant missionaries in

---

[1] In this chapter, I shall give the titles of Korean books in English translation.
[2] Protestant theology is surveyed in the following: Ryu Tong-Shik, *The Mineral Veins of Korean Theology*, revised edition (Seoul: Tasan Kulbang, 2000) (first published 1982); Choo Chai-Yong, *A History of Christian Theology in Korea* (Seoul: The Christian Literature Society of Korea, 1998); and Han Sung-Hong, *Streams of Korean Theological Thought*, 2 vols. (Seoul: Presbyterian College and Theological Seminary Press, 1996).

the nineteenth century.[3] For those who were involved in this type of work, their missionary work in this period was regarded as essentially 'Bible-centred' in three ways: the Bible was the source of inspiration for the missionaries, the basis of the worship of the church, and a means of evangelism in itself.[4] The growth of Protestant churches in Korea is due to this missionary endeavour, but Korean Christians have taken it much further in applying the Bible to daily activities and making it key to Christian living.

The most important figures in the translation of the Korean Bible were John Ross and John MacIntyre, who were sent to Manchuria by the Scotland Bible Society in 1872. Through the help of the Korean translators, Lee Eung-Chan and Baek Hong-Jun, Ross and MacIntyre were eventually able to complete the Korean New Testament (*Yaesu Seongkyo Junseo*) and published it in China in 1887. Portions of the Bible and the New Testament in Korean were soon distributed to Koreans in Manchuria and Japan as well as in Korea by colporteurs who carried them from village to village.[5] The significance of the activities of the early Korean Protestant Christians for this study is that they were motivated to preach the Christian message to their own people in China and in the peninsula and that the Bible was the key medium of their activities. Ross and MacIntryre were the ones who organized and pursued the translation, and their contribution to Christianity in Korea is immense, but the efforts of the Korean scholars who were involved in the whole process and the Korean colporteurs are also important to notice.[6]

The growth of the Korean church has to be understood in the light of the socio-political circumstances of the Korean peninsula in the second half of the nineteenth century and not just of the availability of the Bible.[7] However, it is clear that Bible studies contributed to the characteristics of

---

[3] Stephen Neill, *A History of Christian Missions* (London: Penguin, 1990), p. 209.

[4] Eric Fenn, 'The Bible and the Missionary' in S.L. Greenslade (ed.), *The Cambridge History of the Bible* (Cambridge: Cambridge University Press, 1963), p. 383.

[5] The Institute of Korean Church History Studies, *A History of Korean Church* I (Seoul: Korean Literature Press, 1989), pp. 142–8; Lak-Geoon George Paik, *The History of Protestant Missions in Korea: 1832–1910* (Seoul: Yonsei University Press, 1929), pp. 148–53; Min Kyoung-Bae, *History of the Christian Church in Korea* (Seoul: Christian Literature Society of Korea, 1982), pp. 147–8; Yi Mahn-Yol, *Korean Christianity and Unification Movement* (Seoul: Institute of Korean Church History, 2001), pp. 175–211; *A Study of History of the Reception of Christianity in Korea* (Seoul: Durae Sidae, 1998), pp. 60–94.

[6] Min Kyoung-Bae, *History of the Christian Church*, pp. 168–74; H. Underwood, *Korea Mission Field* (Sept. 1908), pp. 131–2; William Scott, *Report of British and Foreign Bible Society* (1916), p. 294.

[7] See: Bong Rin Ro and Marlin L. Nelson (eds.), *Korean Church Growth Explosion*, revised edition (Seoul: Word of life Press, 1995).

the Korean church and its revival, especially because it was translated using Korean script (which was regarded by scholars as inferior to Chinese script), thus making it widely available to women and ordinary people.[8] In fact, the tradition of Bible study was so much the hallmark of early Korean Christianity that one missionary called it 'Bible Christianity'.[9] The distinctive mark of Korean Christianity as Bible Christianity was due to the fact that the Korean education system was heavily influenced by the Confucian traditional method of teaching and learning. Confucian learning was highly systematized and people of the ruling and middle classes were required to learn Confucian texts by heart. People were taught to accept Confucian texts as the authority for socio-political principles as well as the daily practice of ethics and moral conduct. There was no critical evaluation of the texts, nor of their validity in the context of Korea, but they were regarded as given authority by the king and his forefathers. People read them aloud or memorized them and recited them, and tried to follow their teaching literally. In the period when Protestant Christianity was introduced in Korea, Confucian philosophy was largely questioned by educated people, due to the corruption of the government and the division and infighting between different Confucian schools. Nevertheless, the mode of learning it through inculcation is dominant in the Korean education system even to the present day.

When the Bible was introduced to the Koreans, and once Korean Christians accepted it as the sacred text, it was reverenced as the authority above others. And they employed the Confucian method of learning as they studied the Christian scripture. They tended to accept the literal meaning of the text and tried to put it into practice in their daily lives. In this conservative approach, any new understanding or interpretation of the text has to be scrutinized by the traditional understanding of the text. This approach has in turn shaped the Korean church in that there is a strong commitment to applying the scriptures, which has contributed to the rapid growth of the Korean church.

This emphasis on the importance of the text, coupled with pietistic ethics and a great zeal for evangelism, continues to be characteristic of mainstream Protestant Christianity in Korea. The most prominent church leader and theologian was Kil Sun-Joo, who was one of the first ordained Presbyterian ministers in Korea and who led the Pyeungyang

---

[8] William N. Blair and Bruce Hunt, *The Korean Pentecost and the Sufferings which Followed* (Edinburgh: The Banner of Truth Trust, 1977), p. 67.
[9] *Report of British and Foreign Bible Society* (1907), p. 70.

revival movement in 1907. His conservative theology was based on his belief in the imminence of the second coming of Christ. He encouraged Christians to attend early morning prayer meetings, made reading of the Bible a priority and rejected any form of modern biblical criticism. Though his theology owed much to evangelical missionaries from North America, who tended to preach an escapist gospel, his enthusiasm for scripture and spiritual renewal was a motivation for Korean Christians in the midst of political turmoil. He himself became one of the thirty-three signatories of the Declaration of Independence in 1919.

Owing to a rigid commitment to the text, any liberal interpretation of the Bible provoked a strong reaction from both the church leadership and theological circles. More open to the modern biblical interpretation, Nam Kung-Huek, Professor at Pyeungyang Seminary, contributed his New Testament commentaries, particularly on the Pauline epistles, and on the continuity and unity of the teachings of Jesus and the theology of the apostle Paul in response to liberal interpretations. Similarly, Byuen Hong-Kyu, influenced by the neo-orthodoxy of the wider theological circle, saw holiness as the key to understanding the God of the Hebrew Bible, which is expressed as four dimensions: ritual, ethical, personal and spiritual. The liberal interpretation of scripture was much debated in the Korean churches in the 1930s, concerning three issues: the Mosaic authorship of the Pentateuch; the translation into Korean of the Abingdon Bible Commentary, which was regarded as liberal; and the inerrancy of scripture. The conservative section of the church was led by Park Hyeung-Ryong, who held the theological position of 'plenary inspiration', and insisted that doing theology in the Korean church meant not creating something new, but continuing to uphold the apostolic traditions. This conservative and evangelical approach to the text was also reflected by many leading theologians, such as Park Yeon-Sun and Lee Jong-Seong.[10]

Although the strong commitment to the Christian scripture made a significant contribution to the growth of the Korean church, this rigid and radical affirmation of the text also limited the development of Korean Christianity in various ways. Korean Christians tend to take the text literally and are reluctant to accept any new interpretations. The method of interpretation of the Bible by the missionaries which came with the introduction of the scripture was 'accepted as the norm' or held as 'authority'. Therefore any other interpretation had to be measured by this original interpretation. This is not to say that the Koreans accepted the

[10] See: Choo, *A History of Christian Theology in Korea*, pp. 152–73.

interpretation of the early missionaries simply because they brought a text, but rather Koreans accepted that particular version of Christianity and they wanted to maintain their initial commitment. 'Bible Christianity' could lead into biblicalism in which there could be no interpretation but only transmission of the text. This attitude contributed to a fundamentalist approach to the Christian faith, to other scriptures and to people of other faiths. This preoccupation with the study of the Bible as the only authoritative text of Christian living tends to lead Korean Christians to be less concerned about the actual application of the teaching. In other words, this lack of interpretation of the text hinders any experiment with creative approaches to the text, and as a result the text becomes law, which either demands the literal obedience of Christians or puts Christianity in danger of becoming irrelevant to contemporary Korean society. Nevertheless, this eagerness to study the Bible and follow literally what it teaches has been a source of strength for Korean Christianity, especially in times of persecution and turmoil during the nineteenth century, the Japanese occupation and the Korean War.

REVIVAL CHRISTIANITY: THE GOSPEL OF HOLISTIC BLESSING

Revival has been described as a key characteristic of Korean churches: anyone wishing to understand the Korean church has to understand its revivals. A series of revivals, led by Kil Sun-Joo and other evangelists from the early twentieth century, has resulted in several dynamics in the practices of the Korean church in which Korean Christians experience an outpouring of the Holy Spirit, genuine repentance and forgiveness, and this gives them confidence to preach the gospel and keep the faith in times of difficulty. One of the most distinctive characteristics of Korean churches, resulting from the revivals, is the prayer meeting with *tongsung kido* (the whole congregation praying aloud individually but simultaneously). These take place daily in the early morning, in weekly house groups and all night long on Fridays. The revival meetings were to do with seeking blessings, such as forgiveness of sins and personal and national salvation. Studies suggest that during the time of the Japanese threat to the Korean peninsula many of the western missionaries tried to direct the Korean Christians' attention to 'spiritual matters' rather than to a political struggle which they foresaw would inevitably end in Japan's favour.[11] The message of the preachers and

---

[11] See: Min, *Korean Christianity and Reunification Movement*, pp. 59–114.

the expectations of congregations were directed toward something beyond this world.

When Korean society went through depression under the Japanese occupation, there was a frustration that the Christian leadership were preoccupied with either the liberal–conservative debates or hierarchical positions in the church. There was much criticism of the church and also a desire for renewal. In response to this, the revivalist Lee Yong-Do insisted on the need for spiritual renewal and started to lead revival meetings all over Korea from 1928. Crowds gathered at churches and at various prayer and spiritual renewal activities and this continued even after his sudden death in 1933. His theological basis was the personal experience of oneness with Christ, by which the believer could experience the transformation of the life and spirit of Jesus. This required complete self-denial and identification with Christ's suffering. Lee's methods evoked Korean mystical and shamanistic religiosity. He claimed that Jesus Christ had defeated the spirits and demons of popular Korean belief, and engaged in healing and exorcism.

The tendency of the Korean church to depend on spiritual revival coupled with forgiveness of sins and eternal salvation was challenged particularly after the Korean War. The three-year War resulted in the death of over two-and-a-half million soldiers and three-and-a-half million civilians, three million refugees were created and over ten million families were separated. The peninsula was devastated and the people left in extreme poverty. In this situation, as people were desperately looking for a way to meet their material needs that was both eschatological and experiential, they were seeking the eternal kingdom in the reality of the present situation.[12] There was a rapid increase in revival meetings and the messages preached were to meet the people's need of material blessing and healing. This gospel of holistic blessing became dominant in Korean Christianity as these meetings became popular and various religious groups grew up soon after the War. There were also a growing number of 'prayer mountains' where people stayed for prayer and fasting, and where supernatural events and healing were often reported. It was indeed a time of great turmoil and testing for Korean Christians. People were confused and yet they wanted to see God's blessings here and now rather than rely on a future eschatological hope. It was not that they didn't care about matters of belief, ethics and ultimate destiny but, as they had recently faced the challenge of life and death in a real sense, their faith had to be

---

[12] Min, *History of Korean Christianity*, pp. 470–1.

met by the immediate result of supernatural events and healings and above all by liberation from desperate poverty.

The man who epitomises this approach is David (Paul) Yong-Gi Cho of the Full Gospel Church in Seoul. The story is of the remarkable transformation of a church which started meeting in a tent in 1958. Yonggi Cho, in his often-quoted book, *The Fourth Dimension*, described the struggle of hundreds of thousands of Koreans who were living in extreme poverty after the Korean War, and saw their poverty as the work of the Satan. In this time of struggle, Cho often satisfied 'his hunger with nothing other than three meals of porridge given him by an American evangelist' and 'battled poverty along with the members of his congregation' as he 'called out to God for messages appropriate for such harsh reality'. It was this harsh reality that brought Cho to seek the meaning of the gospel and adopt the theology of 'three-fold blessing': 'spiritual well-being, general well-being, and bodily health'.[13]

The gospel of holistic blessing is not limited to the Full Gospel Church, indeed it is found across whole sections of the Korean churches. As revival is characteristic of the Korean church regardless of denomination, so the message of the expected blessings for those who seek is common to most mainline Korean churches. Good news to the poor in the Korean context in the 1950s and 1960s was seen as this gospel of three-fold blessing and it seemed that the message prevailed. However, there has been considerable opposition to this gospel of holistic blessing, commonly known as *kibock sinang*, from both moderate and conservative sections of the Korean church. In fact, most of the articles written on *kibock sinang* in Christian academic or popular journals condemn this approach.[14] They have various reasons. First, they see it as unbiblical and influenced by shamanism, which they regard as this-worldly, unethical, anti-historical and temporal. Second, they object to *kibock sinang*'s belief that poverty is a curse and the result of wrong actions and attitudes toward God. Third, they interpret *kibock sinang* worship, offerings to God and good deeds as performed in expectation of receiving from God something in return. Fourth, they blame *kibock sinang* for contributing to the lack of political participation of the Korean church and a slowness to share their resources

---

[13] Y. Cho, *The Fourth Dimension* (Seoul: Seoul Logos, 1979), pp. 9–14; *The Fourth Dimension II* (South Plainfield, NJ: Bridge Publishing, 1983), pp. 137–8. See also: Wonsuk Ma, William W. Menzies and Hyeon-sung Bae, *David Yonggi Cho: A Close Look at His Theology and Ministry* (Seoul: Hansei University Press, 2004).

[14] See the articles on *kibock sinang* in the special editions of *Sinang Saekae* (April 1989), *Kidockyo Sasang* (March 2000), *Pulbit Mockhea* (September 1996), and *Mockhea wa Sinhack* (December 1999).

with others. It was described as a 'corrupted faith' and 'making Christianity a lower religion'. In addition, some claim that biblical blessings are not meant to be material and that the gospel of Jesus is a gospel of suffering not blessing. Believing in Jesus, they claim, is for eternal salvation and the gospel is the gospel of the kingdom of heaven, of righteousness and forgiveness rather than material blessing.

The critics focus on the negative outcome of an excessive seeking of blessings, seen in the revival meetings and services. They criticize the revival preachers for their unethical approaches, such as offering material blessings and healing. It is not uncommon to see revival meetings dominated by stories and testimonies of those who have received blessings of wealth, healing and success. There is an excessive drive to increase church membership and construct new church buildings or church prayer halls in the mountains, often by borrowing money from the bank in 'faith' that God will fulfil his promise. The critics are right in that the extravagant demonstration of material blessings in church buildings and membership has become a problem in the Korean church. It encourages a materialistic and mechanical approach to faith.

However, these critics have their own biased perspectives. First, the critics focus on the fact that *kibock sinang* is somehow related to Korean traditional religiosity, shamanism, and they uncritically condemn shamanism as unethical, selfish, materialistic, this-worldly, temporal and non-historical. The fact that Korean Christianity has been influenced by a shamanistic understanding of traditional Korean religiosity is not necessarily a negative point. The religious tradition of the Korean people, including shamanism, cannot be just dismissed as unworthy. This interpretation is rather the result of a Christian missionary understanding of the religiosity of the people as something inferior, unacceptable, or even evil, and labelling anything to do with it as syncretism. While conservative theology may meet the need of spiritual fulfilment and eschatological hope, *kibock sinang* has harnessed the people's desire for dream-fulfilment in the present context. In Korean religiosity, the desire for something better, both spiritual and material, is expressed as seeking blessings. It is the humble desire of those who have not experienced fullness of life and who are constantly facing despair and poverty.

Second, it seems that the critics are emphasizing the other-worldly aspect of the Christian gospel and also stressing the example of the suffering of Christ and the Cross. It may be appropriate to preach on suffering, the Cross, inner spirituality and future hope to those who are experiencing material blessing, but the poor are suffering and carrying a cross.

A message of deliverance and liberation from poverty, and the promise of God's blessing in the here and now, is also part of the Christian gospel – often expressed as *shalom*, the peace and well-being of God's people. The tendencies to make blessing in the next world more desirable than blessing in this world have been consistent in Christian tradition, but *kibock sinang* challenges them. In the context of post-War Korea, many of the Korean church leaders responded to the problem of the poor by tapping into traditional religiosity and also interpreting the gospel as seeking holistic blessing.

Though the difficulty remains that the gospel of holistic blessing often threatens the principle of the Cross by employing the unethical methods of 'the end justifies the means', nevertheless it represents one way the Korean church has responded to the problem of poverty, and many testify that it has indeed been good news to the poor.[15] It provided the people of Korea with hope here and now through Christian faith, and resilience to endure hardship and to persevere through the turmoil of post-War Korea.

LIBERATION CHRISTIANITY: STRUGGLING FOR JUSTICE FOR THE POOR AND OPPRESSED

During the 1960s to 1970s South Korea witnessed the rapid rise of the *jaebul*, or family-run mega-companies (with the help of government policy), which started to dominate the Korean economy. As a consequence, there was serious exploitation of factory workers in regard to their working conditions as well as to their wages. The majority of pastors saw this problem as a simply matter of the 'process' of development and concentrated on their emphasis on church growth. In this period, *jaebuls* and mega-churches rose in parallel and the church leadership believed that the growth of the Christian population and the growth of the national economy went hand-in-hand.

However, in the context of 1970s Korea, others realized that there was a need for a new theological paradigm to meet the needs of the urban poor who were victims of the highly competitive capitalist market. The philosophies of *kibock sinang* and evangelistic campaigns did not seem to have the mechanism to deal with this problem of 'process' in modern Korean society. The problem of poverty was not just an individual matter or to do with Christian congregations but it had to do with the structure of the

---

[15] Charles Elliott, *Sword and Spirit: Christianity in a Divided World* (London: Marshall Pickering, 1989), pp. 19–53.

Korean economy and society. At this point, some Christian intellectuals realized that the poor were not just poor in the sense of lacking material things, but they were also exploited and unjustly treated, and that the gaps between the poor and the rich and between employee and employer were widening. The minjung movement was sparked when Jun Tae-Ill set himself on fire in November 1970 as his protest against the exploitation of fellow factory workers. The incident shook the country and soon some socially concerned Christian leaders took this as major issue and stood up for and with the poor and exploited. This meant challenging the *status quo* of the government and the capitalist market economy of the *jaebul*. In 1973, they issued 'The Korean Christian Manifesto', which says:

We believe in God who, by his righteousness, will surely protect people who are oppressed, weak and poor, and judge the power of evil in history. We believe that Jesus, the Messiah, proclaimed that the evil power will be destroyed and the kingdom of the Messiah will come, and this kingdom of the Messiah will be a haven of rest for the poor, oppressed and despised.[16]

Two years later, Suh Nam-Dong, among the most well-known of minjung theologians, presented his thesis arguing that Jesus identified with the poor, sick and oppressed and that the gospel of Jesus is the gospel of salvation and liberation. For him, this is manifested in the struggle with those evils and so liberation is not individual or spiritual but rather communal and political. Suh systematized his minjung theology in the following years, seeing the minjung as subjects of history and introducing *han*, or anguish and despair, as the key theme for theology in the Korean context.[17] Ahn Byeung-Moo, another well-known minjung theologian, asserted that Jesus identified with the people in such a way that 'Jesus is minjung and minjung is Jesus'. He shared his life with the minjung to such an extent that the event of the Cross was the climax of the suffering of the minjung.[18] Therefore the presence of Christ is not when the word is preached nor when the sacrament is conducted but when we participate with or in the suffering of the minjung. Jesus is God becoming flesh and blood, which is a matter of material being and reality in everyday life, not of ideology or philosophy. Therefore he argued that the minjung are the

---

[16] Rhie Deok-Joo and Cho Yee-Jei (eds.), *Creeds and Confessions of Korean Church* (Seoul: Han Deul, 1997), pp. 270–6.

[17] Suh Nam-Dong, 'Toward a Theology of Han' in Kim Yong-Bock (ed.), *Minjung Theology: People as the Subjects of History* (Maryknoll, NY: Orbis Books, 1983), pp. 51–65.

[18] Ahn Byeung-Moo, *The Story of Minjung Theology* (Seoul: Korea Institute of Theology, 1990), pp. 31–7.

owners of the Jesus community. This is fundamentally a 'food community' – a community sharing food; the concept of a worshipping community came later.[19]

Minjung theologians captured the people's imagination and brought the issue of poverty and exploitation into the church. Here we see minjung theology as a 'protest' theology on behalf of the minjung against injustice and exploitation. Their interpretation of 'the poor' is not in isolation from others but it is relational. The poor are poor not necessarily because they are sinners or do not have a 'right' relationship with God, but because of the greediness of some others and the unjust system of modern capitalism. Therefore the theologians' main concern was not dealing with individual poor people but rather to do with social process and the system which prevents the minjung from coming out of their misery. In this respect, as they try to deal with economic and political injustice, the minjung theologians' concern was more with anything anti-minjung than with the minjung themselves. Minjung theology made a great contribution to the Korean church and society through its rediscovery of the gospel of liberation and justice, and by showing the poor and oppressed that they are not or should not be the objects of exploitation and that their protest was a legitimate one. Minjung theology has been good news to the poor and, like the gospel of holistic blessing, it was intended to uplift the poor. However, in its identification of the problem and the way to deal with it, it is vastly different from the latter.

There have been some critiques of minjung theology in two areas.[20] First: Is minjung theology by the minjung or of the minjung, or is it a theology by elites for minjung? Second: Who are the minjung in contemporary Korea and how do they see themselves? Are they only a conceptual group which is created by theologians for the purpose of their argument? On the question of the identity of minjung theologians, and therefore of minjung theology itself, minjung theologians did identify themselves with the minjung by participating in sufferings with them. Many theologians went to prison and went through hardship. Because they identified with Jesus and the minjung in their theology, they suffered with the minjung and so the minjung theologians, at least in the first generation in the 1970s,

---

[19] Ahn, *The Story of Minjung Theology*, pp. 87–185.
[20] See: Moon Dong-Hwan, '21st Century and Minjung Theology', *Shinhack Sasang* (Summer 2000), pp. 30–54; Na Young-Hwan, 'Minjung Theology from the Evangelical Perspective', *Mockhea ywa Sinhack* (Aug. 1992), 40–50. For a hermeneutical critique of minjung theology, see Im Tae-Soo, *Minjung Theology towards the Second Reformation* (Seoul: The Christian Literature Society of Korea, 2002).

became minjung.[21] However, when we come to the second generation in the 1980s, this claim is not so firmly founded. The issue for the former was mainly the socio-economic problem of poor workers and farmers, and for the latter it was political and ideological tensions in relation to democracy. At least the first generation identified with and mobilized the 'mass' of workers and farmers over against the employers and land-owners. But the second generation of minjung theologians had only minority support because they rather uncritically adopted a Marxist ideology in theologizing. Particularly after the Kwangju massacre in 1980 by a military-backed government, minjung theologians shifted their attention to ideological issues, taking a socialist–communist line, favouring North Korea, and confronting what they perceived as the illegitimate government of the South, which was in association with the USA. This caused a large gap between the minjung who were not prepared to be on the side of the North and those who tried to integrate minjung theology into their ideological combat.[22]

The second question of the identity of the minjung is a more difficult one. The term minjung, which is a Chinese word for 'ordinary people' or 'citizens', was quite a new and unfamiliar one for contemporary South Koreans. In addition, people found it difficult to identify themselves with this heavily loaded term without definite or immediate benefits. In a rapidly changing society like contemporary Korea, people were not prepared to commit themselves to such a static concept as minjung and for the cause of the minjung, but in contrast they rather wished to rise out of the minjung.[23] The fact that many articles were devoted to defining the minjung indicates that, unlike black theology, feminist theology and dalit theology, minjung theologians had difficulties identifying this term with a concrete and tangible group.

Nevertheless, in spite of these problems, minjung theology has made a vital contribution to the identity of the minjung and encouraged them to stand and speak. Though Latin American liberation theology made the point that the poor and oppressed are the ones who need to be liberated, minjung theology further asserted that the minjung are the subjects of this liberation as well as the subjects of the history and culture of their particular

---

[21] Baek Nak-Chung, 'Who are Minjung?' in *Essays on Minjung* (Seoul: Korea Theological Study Institute, 1984), pp. 13–28.

[22] Kim Sun-Jae, 'Yesterday, Today and Tomorrow of Minjung Theology', *Shinhack Sasang* (Spring 1998), 8–9.

[23] Park Sung-Jun, 'Reflection on Minjung Theology in the Context of 21st Century', *Shinhack Sasang* (Summer 2000), 70–89.

contexts. This led to the idea of 'Jesus as the minjung and the minjung as Jesus' – the former is acceptable to most theologians but the latter is a problem for many.[24] But minjung theologians, particularly the third generation of the 1990s, asserted that the minjung have to be understood as an experiential entity identified with the event of Jesus in his life and words, especially in the Cross. 'The minjung as Jesus' does not mean for them an ontological identification, but that by participating in the life and death of Jesus the minjung are part of the Jesus event. It does not mean that they are equal with him in an ontological sense, but that they are experiencing the Jesus event and therefore able to be in Jesus and part of his mission in this world. This has further consequences: that being minjung requires being in Christ for others – it is being part of God's transformation for others.[25] On the whole, minjung theology has been a major instrument of the minjung or civil movement that challenged both the church and society to deal with the problems of socio-economic and political injustice, brought democracy to Korea in the late 1980s, and certainly played a 'prophetic' role in Korean history.

FOLK CHRISTIANITY: INTEGRATING THE GOSPEL WITH KOREAN CULTURE AND RELIGIOSITY

In its history Korea has known a succession of religions, which have been closely associated with rulers or the dominant class as state religions. Accordingly, the religions that are out of favour have suffered unfavourable treatment and even persecution by the state. Contemporary South Korea guarantees freedom of religion; the state does not favour any particular religion, but this is almost unique in Korean history. The dominant belief system in ancient Korea was shamanistic. Shamans were intermediaries who contacted the ancestors, who, with the spirits and demons, were regarded as present in every object in the world, seen and unseen. With the introduction of Buddhism and Confucianism, shamanism faded away from the public domain, but the beliefs were assimilated into the organized religions and became deeply rooted in the religiosity of Koreans.

Buddhism was introduced in AD 327. It soon became the state religion of the three kingdoms and was regarded as giving spiritual endorsement to the authorities. During the Koryeo dynasty in particular, Buddhism

---

[24] Ahn Byung-Mu, 'Jesus and Minjung' in Kim Yong Bock (ed.), *Minjung Theology: People as the Subjects of History* (Maryknoll, NY: Orbis Books, 1983), pp. 138–51.
[25] See: Choi Hyeung-Mook, 'Some Issues of Minjung Theology in the 1990s', *Sidae wa Minjung Theology* (1998), 345–69.

received strong support from the monarchy and the aristocrats and produced rich art, literature and architecture. Though Buddhism suffered under the hands of the policies of the Confucian leaders of the Choson (Yi) dynasty and was forced to the periphery of the political and urban life of the people, it has remained the dominant religion for Koreans. In more recent years, Buddhism has been experiencing a revival among the younger generation.

Although Confucianism was introduced to Korea as early as the Three Kingdoms period, it became the official ideology only during the Choson dynasty, which developed a Confucian system of education, public ceremonies and civil administration. Toward the end of the dynasty there was criticism of the close integration of government officials and Confucian scholars, which was contributing to corruption, and of the internal rivalry between different schools, which hampered the smooth operation of government. However, Confucianism, with its philosophical and cultural vigour, has recently been reintroduced into the modern and diverse society of South Korea.

Due to the close association of a particular religion with the political authority in any given historical period, there has been relatively little interaction and conflict between the different religious communities in Korea. Furthermore, the majority of Korean Protestant Christians, due to their evangelical and conservative orientation, have had very little experience of interacting with and expressing interest in other religions – although as we have seen they are subconsciously influenced by Confucianism, Buddhism and shamanism in their beliefs and practices. There have been various theological explorations by progressive theologians to relate Christianity to other religions, or to translate the Christian message into the concepts of other religions, but their theologies have not made much impact on the life of the church or have been harshly rejected by the majority of Christians.

Choi Byeung Hyeun was a pioneer of the indigenization of the Christian message in Korean religious traditions, especially Confucianism and Buddhism. He tried to explain how Christianity could be expressed in the religious frame of Koreans in his series of articles on comparative religions in the academic journal *Sinhak Sekae* between 1916 and 1920. His sources were Eastern philosophies, the Bible and the Wesleyan tradition, and his theological emphasis was on the fall of the human race and salvation through Christ. He distinguished Christ from Christianity because, he reasoned, a religion has continuity with other religions and therefore cannot claim absolute truth. But he saw a clear discontinuity between the gospel of Christ and other religions and concluded that Christ was the fulfilment of all religious aspirations. He was not asserting the dogma of the Christian message over against other religions, nor on the other hand did his apologetics hold the position of modern relativism. But he wished to introduce the Christian message for the salvation of people and social reform.

The integration of Christianity and Korean religiosity was much discussed in the 1960s; the two foremost theologians in this field were Ryu Dong-Shik and Yoon Sung-Bum. Ryu in his thesis on 'Tao and Logos' suggested that the use of the Eastern philosophy of the Way is necessary for conveying the message of the Christian gospel in Asia. According to him, Koreans have maintained in their ancient culture and religiosity the three aspects of *han* (oneness), *mot* (beauty) and *sam* (life), which are essential to the Korean spirit. These were integrated in the classical philosophy of *pungnyu-do* in the sixth century, from which he takes his *pungnyu* theology. *Pungnyu* literally means 'wind and flow', evoking the inspiration of Korean thinkers through creative retreat in the fresh air and by the pure streams of the beautiful mountains. Ryu suggests that Korean theology has diverged in three directions according to this paradigm: conservative fundamentalist theology (*han*), which affirms the authority and greatness of the one in heaven and develops the inner sanctification of personal faith and revival movements; cultural liberal theology (*mot*), which is interested in the harmony of nature and various traditions and the indigenization of any new thought brought into Korea; and progressive social involvement theology (*sam*), which tries to overcome the present sufferings by actively participating in the affairs of this world.[26] He also describes the dynamics of the development of Korean theology as the result of a constant interaction between paternal and maternal movements of the Holy Spirit, where the former is rooted in the Confucian tradition and leads to the conservative and hierarchical aspects of Korean church life, and the latter embraces a shamanistic approach to the faith and is closely related to the revival movements and Pentecostal churches in Korea.[27]

Yoon Sung-Bum believed that Korean theology would blossom through a creative exploration of the religious meaning of the Tankun myth – the story of the origin of the Korean people from the union of the

[26] Ryu, *The Mineral Veins of Korean Theology*, pp. 14–35.
[27] Ryu, *The Mineral Veins of Korean Theology*, pp. 414–26. For a comprehensive evaluation of Ryu's approach, see Kirsteen Kim, 'Holy Spirit Movements in Korea – Paternal or Maternal? Reflections on the Analysis of Ryu Tong-Shik (Yu Tong-Shik)', *Exchange* (35/2, 2006), 147–68.

son of heaven and a female bear – in the light of Christianity.[28] He then further argued that there are elements of the Trinity in the myth because there are three figures referred to in the story. He insisted that Confucianism provided the background for Korean thinking, and so was an indispensable tool for Korean theology. In his 'theology of sincerity', the Chinese word '*seong*' refers to a combination of word and deed. He regarded sincerity as having the meaning of *logos* or revelation. He argued that sincerity could integrate dichotomic concepts in traditional theology, such as law and gospel, sacred and secular.[29]

There are various other approaches to the interaction of Christian theology with the different religions in Korea.[30] One of the most dramatic and creative was the incorporation of Korean shamanism into Christian theology in the presentation by Chung Hyun Kyung at the Canberra Assembly of the WCC (1991), which evoked varied responses. As she invoked the Holy Spirit, Chung also called on the spirits of people in the past and even the spirits of nature. For Chung, the work of the Holy Spirit is carried out through the spirits: 'They [the spirits] are the icons of the Holy Spirit who became tangible and visible to us. Because of them we can feel, touch and taste the concrete bodily historical presence of the Holy Spirit in our midst.' Chung's method is a combination of liberative political action and spiritual exorcism (after the manner of a Korean shamanist) to release the oppressed spirits and set the creation free. She called participants at Canberra to welcome the Spirit and dance with her, 'letting ourselves go in her wild rhythm of life'.[31] Chung has opened a creative possibility of exploring Korean religiosity in Christian theology but she has also drawn much criticism from within Korea and thus demonstrated the difficulties of dealing with the issue of religious pluralism in the Korean context.

Folk Christianity employs Korean traditional religions in order to make sense of Christian theology in Korea. Although much creative thinking and theology have been suggested by progressive theologians in the interests of the indigenization of the Christian message, their radical

---

[28] Yoon Sung-Bum, *Korean Religious Culture and Korean Theology* (Seoul: Kamsin Publications, 1998), pp. 313–62.

[29] Yoon Sung-Bum, *Korean Confucianism and Korean Theology* (Seoul: Kamsin Publications, 1998), pp. 15–45.

[30] For example, Heup Young Kim, *Christ and Tao* (Hong Kong: Christian Conference of Asia, 2003).

[31] Chung Hyun Kyung, 'Come, Holy Spirit – Renew the Whole Creation' in Michael Kinnamon (ed.), *Signs of the Spirit: Official Report of the Seventh Assembly of the WCC, Canberra* (Geneva: WCC, 1991), pp. 37–47.

approaches are usually rejected by mainline church leaders. This is due to the fact that the vast majority of the Korean churches are conservative evangelical churches, emphasizing revival, personal experience, eschatological hope, exclusive truth in Christ and the numerical growth of the church. Since there is a strong connection between theology and the church in the Korean context, most theologians are working in a seminary setting. On the one hand, it is a strength of Korean theology that it always tries to be relevant to the church, but on the other hand, creative theological exploration is limited by this constraint.

RECONCILING CHRISTIANITY: SEEKING TO UNIFY A DIVIDED KOREA

The conflict between the two Koreas is certainly the most pertinent and dominant concern for Koreans and has affected the lives of Koreans ever since the division of Korea, which began straight after the Japanese occupation was ended in 1945 by US and Russian forces. Though the desire for reunification has been the most important agenda item for political leaders, the ways to achieve the goal have differed widely, as the two Koreas were at the forefront of the Cold War ideological conflict. In this context, the churches in South Korea have gone through various stages in attempting to deal with the issue and often made a significant impact by formulating theological thinking as well as by participating in peace and reconciliation movements. Even before the Korean War, Korean Christians held a negative attitude toward the communist ideology because of its anti-religious stance, and this was confirmed by the persecution of churches by the government in the North and even greater suffering during the War. As a result, during and after the War, Christians tended to be at the forefront of anti-communist movements, to be against the ceasefire, and to regard communists as evil.

This rigid and hostile attitude toward the North was soon countered by a more sympathetic acceptance of the people of the North as same-blood relations. This coincided with the rise of the *minjung* theology movement, increasing the awareness of Christians' role in peace and reconciliation, and with the sustaining support of the World Council of Churches for peace and reconciliation. An initiative was taken by a group of overseas Korean Christians who met North Korean Christian delegates in the early 1980s, and this created fresh new beginnings. However, the declarations after the meetings were heavily critical of the South Korean and US governments and supportive of the North, and therefore they were rejected by the South Korean media and the general public, and did not really make any impact.

In 1988 the KNCC issued the 'Declaration of the Korea National Council of the Churches toward the unification and peace of the Korean people', which made a significant impact both within the church and on the whole nation.[32] The KNCC declaration was welcomed by many Christians but also generated a heated discussion among them. However it did raise the issue of peace and reconciliation within the churches, which motivated conservative Christians to participate in the debate. The declaration started with the affirmation that Christ came to earth as the servant of peace and proclaimed the kingdom of God, which represented peace, reconciliation and liberation. It claimed that, accordingly, the Korean church was trying to be with people who were suffering. In the main thesis, the declaration acknowledged and confessed the sins of mutual hatred, of justifying the division of Korea, and of accepting each ideology as absolute, which was contrary to God's absolute authority. The declaration, while affirming the three principles expressed in the Joint Declaration (1972), added the priority of humanitarian practice and the participation of the *minjung*, who were the victims of a divided Korea, in the process of unification discussions. The document made practical suggestions to both governments, including: the change of the existing 'agreement for ceasefire' to 'agreement of peace' and, after a peace treaty was signed and the guarantee of the peace and security of the peninsula by the international community, the withdrawal of the US army and the dismantling of the UN head office. The Declaration then proclaimed the year 1995 as a jubilee year for peace and unification when Koreans could celebrate the fiftieth anniversary of the liberation from Japan. It set down practical steps toward the jubilee year including: church renewal, the church becoming a faith community for peace and reconciliation, and working together with all the churches, employing all the necessary means toward peace and reconciliation.

The declaration was welcomed by many South Korean churches and also by the Council of Chosun Christian Church in the North, but provoked severe criticism from the conservative sections of the Korean church. However, the Declaration brought the issue of reunification on to the main agenda of Korean Christians and challenged many conservative sections of the church to rethink their traditional approaches toward the North, moving from evangelism or relief to partnership for the common

---

[32] Rhie and Cho (eds.), *Creeds and Confessions of Korean Church*, pp. 396–409.

goal of peace and reconciliation. Furthermore, the Declaration has expressed the vital concerns not only of Christians but also of the whole nation on the issue, and set the future direction of the Korean church. In spite of its limitations and shortcomings, the Declaration was a most significant landmark in the Korean Christian attempt to bring peace and reconciliation. It seems the gap between the conservative and liberal approaches toward reunification has been as deep as that between North and South Korea. However, the changing policy of the South Korean government since the early 1990s and also the increasing voices from younger generations mean that the church leadership is no longer saddled with the old pattern of the conservative and liberal dichotomy, but has to work together regardless of denominational and theological differences.[33]

Several theological themes need to be explored more deeply for understanding the church's involvement in peace and reconciliation.[34] First, the implications of the jubilee principle in the present context of a divided Korea. The biblical jubilee principle has several dimensions: sabbatical, restoration of ownership, and liberation of slaves. When the KNCC declared 1995 as the year of jubilee, it focused on the third aspect of liberation and also more on the proclamation than the actualization of unification in any particular year. Though many sincerely expected and wished that it could be achieved, the important point was that the jubilee was proclaimed. It was the proclamation of the liberation of the Korean people from the bondage of ideological hegemony and from political systems which hinder the formation of a common community. This theme is also related to the remembering of God's grace in spite of the present situation, so that Christians are called to hold faith in confidence.

Restoration of community identity by employing the concepts of *koinonia* and *oikoumene* is another important theme. The separation of the people in the North and South for over sixty years in two very different socio-economic and political systems means that there are very few shared identities. What could be the contribution of theology in this context? Perhaps, as Ahn Byeung-Mu insists, the early church in Acts was primarily a food community, which shared the basic needs of humanity with others, rather than a worshipping community. The restoration of

---

[33] See: Yi, *Korean Christianity and Unification Movement*, pp. 351–414.

[34] See: Noh Jong-Sun, *Toward a Theology of Reunification: Third World Christian Ethics* (Seoul: Hanul Publishing Co, 1988); Park Soon-Kyeung, *The Future of Unification Theology* (Seoul: Sakaejul, 1997); David Kwang-Sun Suh, *The Korean Minjung in Christ* (Hong Kong: The Christian Conference of Asia, 2002), pp. 177–88; Min Young-Jin, *Peace, Unification and Jubilee* (Seoul: The Christian Literature Society of Korea, 1995).

this concept of *koinonia* between the South and North is most urgent, especially as this is a time of severe economic hardship and even starvation in the North. Sharing of resources is a theological imperative that the church should be actively engaged in. It is a central affirmation of Christian faith that the people of God are catholic or universal. It is in this sense that the Greek word *oikoumene* – the household of God – has been taken up by the ecumenical movement to express its mission for the unity of the church and humanity. Since God is one, the household of God must be one and this is not limited just to Christians but includes all the people of North and South Korea. This gives us a great hope and vision that, in God's sustaining power, we may experience oneness, and at the same time we rejoice in the diversity of our cultures and societies in the wider household of God.

The themes of the Cross and resurrection could be explored in order to overcome *han*. Koreans have experienced *han* through the constant cycle of hope and despair during the last half century and still there is no immediate sign of improvement in the relationship between the two nations. Koreans understand and identify in a national way with the story of Israel in Old Testament times and with the meaning of the Cross. The separation is understood as the Cross which Koreans have to bear, and it is through this experience of bitter conflict and division that Koreans understand the reality of human nature and yet find the seed of hope in the midst of despair.[35]

CONCLUSION

I have examined the five strands of Korean theology in relation to their socio-historical backgrounds and their theological discourse as each has made a distinctive contribution to the life of the churches and society in Korea in response to the problems of poverty, injustice and division. The choice of theologians discussed here is by no means comprehensive but selective, in order to demonstrate the emerging forms and themes of theology in the Korean context. 'Bible Christianity' and 'revival Christianity' represent the dynamics of the occasional *sakyunghoe* (Bible examining meetings) and *buhoenghoe* (revival meetings), and the weekly home group meetings, which include Bible study, sharing of testimony and prayers. These are key aspects of faith for most Christians, and often

---

[35] See: C. S. Song, *Third-Eye Theology: Theology in Formation in Asian Settings* (London: Lutterworth Press, 1980), pp. 146–7.

result in the revival of their faith and the deepening of their commitment. The collective interpretation of scripture and the earnest prayer-support of fellow believers made a significant contribution to the growth of the church, as well as becoming a positive characteristic of the Korean churches.[36] 'Bible Christianity' and 'revival Christianity' have been instrumental in the growth and strength of the Korean Protestant churches, and these aspects of Christian life are common to all denominations. The latter three theological approaches – 'folk Christianity', 'liberation Christianity' and 'reconciling Christianity' – have made significant impacts on Korean politics and society. However, the churches particularly associated with each approach are not in the mainstream of Korean Christianity. On the surface, the majority of Protestant Christians are not associated with the three approaches we have discussed, but in reality the life and practice of ordinary Christians is significantly influenced by these three movements.

Both 'revival Christianity' (the gospel of holistic blessing) and 'liberation Christianity' (minjung theology) can be described as two major contextual theologies intended to address the problems of poverty and injustice in the second half of twentieth-century South Korea. The former integrates traditional religiosity and Christian teaching on blessing to address the problem of poverty, and the latter employs socio-political tools developed in the west and articulated in Latin America to meet the question of injustice. The gospel of holistic blessing focuses on the individual poor and helps people in the context of post-War Korea to hope for material blessings by committing themselves to God, who is understood as being ready to bless his people. Minjung theology was formulated in the 1970s as a protest theology against both conservative evangelical theologies and *kibock sinang*, on the one hand, and against the unjust system of modern and divided Korea, on the other. These two approaches are products of the search for an answer to a particular problem in a particular time and context, therefore they both have their limits. Nevertheless, they are the outcomes of sincere quests by Koreans to solve what are perhaps the most difficult issues for the Christian church: poverty and injustice.

Philip Jenkins asserts that the churches in the South are 'not just a transplanted version of the familiar religion of the older Christian states: the new Christendom is no mirror image of the Old. It is a truly new and

---

[36] Jong Chun Park, *Crawl with God, Dance in the Spirit! A Creative Formation of Korean Theology of the Spirit* (Nashville, TN: Abingdon Press, 1998), pp. 18–23.

developing entity.'[37] Though his usage of the term 'the next Christendom' is problematic, Jenkins is right in that theologies from the South have distinctive characteristics. Korean Christian theology emerges from her turbulent history as the 'queen of suffering'.[38] Choo Chai-Yong suggests that the future direction of Korean theology should aim to be ecumenical by engaging with churches and other Christian organizations and dialoguing with other religions and non-religious groups, which are so divided.[39] Ryu Dong-Shik envisages Korean theology overcoming another divide: that between personal or socio-political salvation, by moving in the direction of a unifying religio-cosmic theology.[40] With the changing situation of economic growth (as the world's eleventh economy) and the establishment of democracy, although the problems of poverty and injustice still remain, some of the distinctive theologies of the second half of the twentieth century have less relevance in contemporary South Korean society. There are emerging challenges concerning the integrity of the church: a lack of authentic spirituality in church leadership and a lack of social and personal ethics. The ecological crisis and globalization also feature highly in contemporary concerns. However, the issue of peace and reconciliation in the Korean peninsula is still the most urgent matter for the Korean churches. Also, articulating a relevant theological discourse which can be accepted by both liberal and conservative sections is an imperative. Korean theology, while embracing these aspects, needs to continue to challenge the church and society, while also being open to scrutiny from the church and the general public, if it is to make an authentic and yet relevant contribution to the lives of the Korean people.

BIBLIOGRAPHY

Ahn, Byeung-Moo, *The Story of Minjung Theology*, Seoul: Korea Institute of Theology, 1990.
Ahn, Byung-Mu, 'Jesus and Minjung' in Kim Yong-Bock (ed.), Minjung *Theology: People as the Subjects of History*, Maryknoll, NY: Orbis Books, 1983, pp. 138–51.
Baek, Nak-Chung, 'Who are Minjung?' in *Essays on Minjung*, Seoul: Korea Theological Study Institute, 1984, pp. 13–28.

[37] Philip Jenkins, *The Next Christendom: The Coming of Global Christianity* (New York: Oxford University Press, 2002), p. 214.
[38] Ham Sok Hon, *Queen of Suffering: A Spiritual History of Korea* (trans. E. Sang Yu) (London: Friends World Committee for Consultation, 1985).
[39] Choo, *A History of Christian Theology in Korea*, pp. 413–21.
[40] Ryu, *The Mineral Veins of Korean Theology*, pp. 427–40.

Blair, William N. and Hunt, Bruce, *The Korean Pentecost and The Sufferings Which Followed*, Edinburgh: The Banner of Truth Trust, 1977.

Cho, Yong-Gi, *The Fourth Dimension*, Seoul: Seoul Logos, 1979.

The Fourth Dimension II, South Plainfield, NJ: Bridge Publishing, 1983.

Choi, Hyeung-Mook, 'Some Issues of Minjung Theology in the 1990s', *Sidae wa Minjung Theology* (1998), 345–369.

Choo, Chai-Yong, *A History of Christian Theology in Korea*, Seoul: The Christian Literature Society of Korea, 1998.

Chung, Hyun Kyung, 'Come, Holy Spirit – Renew the Whole Creation' in Michael Kinnamon (ed.), *Signs of the Spirit: Official Report of the Seventh Assembly of the WCC, Canberra*, Geneva: WCC, 1991, pp. 37–47.

Elliott, Charles, *Sword and Spirit: Christianity in a Divided World*, London: Marshall Pickering, 1989.

Fenn, Eric, 'The Bible and the Missionary' in S. L. Greenslade (ed.), *The Cambridge History of the Bible*, Cambridge: Cambridge University Press, 1963.

Ham, Sok Hon, *Queen of Suffering: A Spiritual History of Korea* (trans. E. Sang Yu), London: Friends World Committee for Consultation, 1985.

Han, Sung-Hong, *Streams of Korean Theological Thought*, 2 vols., Seoul: Presbyterian College and Theological Seminary Press, 1996.

Im, Tae-Soo, *Minjung Theology towards the Second Reformation*, Seoul: The Christian Literature Society of Korea, 2002.

Jenkins, Philip, *The Next Christendom: The Coming of Global Christianity*, New York: Oxford University Press, 2002.

Kim, Heup Young, *Christ and Tao*, Hong Kong: Christian Conference of Asia, 2003.

Kim, Kirsteen, 'Holy Spirit Movements in Korea – Paternal or Maternal? Reflections on the Analysis of Ryu Tong-Shik (Yu Tong-Shik)', *Exchange* (35/2, 2006), 147–68.

Kim, Sun-Jae, 'Yesterday, Today and Tomorrow of Minjung Theology', *Shinhack Sasang* (Spring 1998), 8–9.

Ma, Wonsuk, Menzies, William W. and Bae, Hyeon-Sung, *David Yonggi Cho: A Close Look at His Theology and Ministry*, Seoul: Hansei University Press, 2004.

Min, Kyeung Bae, *Korean Christianity and the Reunification Movement*, Seoul: Korean Institute of Church History, 2001.

Min, Kyoung-Bae, *History of the Christian Church in Korea*, Seoul: The Christian Literature Society of Korea, 1982.

Min, Young-Jin, *Peace, Unification and Jubilee*, Seoul: The Christian Literature Society of Korea, 1995.

Moon, Dong-Hwan, '21st Century and Minjung Theology', *Shinhack Sasang* (Summer 2000), 30–54.

Na, Young-Hwan, 'Minjung Theology from the Evangelical Perspective', *Mockhea wa Sinhack* (Aug. 1992), 40–50.

Neill, Stephen, *A History of Christian Missions*, London: Penguin, 1990.

Noh, Jong-Sun, *Toward a Theology of Reunification: Third World Christian Ethics*, Seoul: Hanul Publishing Co., 1988.

Paik, Lak-Geoon George, *The History of Protestant Missions in Korea: 1832–1910*, Seoul: Yonsei University Press, 1929.

Park, Jong Chun, *Crawl with God, Dance in the Spirit! A Creative Formation of Korean Theology of the Spirit*, Nashville, TN: Abingdon Press, 1998.

Park, Soon-Kyeung, *The Future of Unification Theology*, Seoul: Sakaejul, 1997.

Park, Sung-Jun, 'Reflection on Minjung Theology in the Context of 21st Century', *Shinhack Sasang* (Summer 2000), 70–89.

Rhie, Deok-Joo and Cho, Yee-Jei (eds.), *Creeds and Confessions of Korean Church*, Seoul: Han Deul, 1997.

Ro, Bong Rin and Nelson, Marlin L. (eds.), *Korean Church Growth Explosion*, revised edition, Seoul: Word of Life Press, 1995.

Ryu, Tong-Shik, *The Mineral Veins of Korean Theology*, revised edition, Seoul: Tasan Kulbang, 2000.

Scott, William, *Report of British and Foreign Bible Society* (1916).

Song, C. S., *Third-Eye Theology: Theology in Formation in Asian Settings*, London: Lutterworth Press, 1980.

Suh, David Kwang-Sun, *The Korean Minjung in Christ*, Hong Kong: The Christian Conference of Asia, 2002.

Suh, Nam-Dong, 'Toward a Theology of Han' in Kim Yong-Bock (ed.), *Minjung Theology: People as the Subjects of History*, Maryknoll, NY: Orbis Books, 1983, pp. 51–65.

The British and Foreign Bible Society, *Report of British and Foreign Bible Society* (1907).

The Institute of Korean Church History Studies, *A History of Korean Church* I, Seoul: The Korean Literature Press, 1989.

Underwood, H., *Korea Mission Field* (Sept. 1908), 131–2.

Yi, Mahn-Yol, *A Study of History of the Reception of Christianity in Korea*, Seoul: Durae Sidae, 1998.

   Korean Christianity and Unification Movement, Seoul: Institute of Korean Church History, 2001.

Yoon, Sung-Bum, *Korean Confucianism and Korean Theology*, Seoul: Kamsin Publications, 1998.

   Korean Religious Culture and Korean Theology, Seoul: Kamsin Publications, 1998.

II

Theological themes of Christianity in Asia

CHAPTER 8

Religious pluralism, dialogue and Asian Christian responses

M. Thomas Thangaraj

The major thrust of this chapter is to discuss the theological themes and challenges raised by the encounter between Christianity and other religious traditions of Asia, and how Asian Christians have responded to those challenges.[1] Asia is a vast geographical area covering many diverse nations and peoples. It is also an area that houses a variety of religious traditions and languages. These religions include Hinduism, Jainism, Christianity, Sikhism, several forms of Buddhism, Confucian traditions and Islam. A nation like India has its own rich diversity in terms of cultures, languages and religions. Thus this chapter's project is a formidable task in relation to the geographical vastness of Asia and the diversity of religious traditions within Asia. Therefore I have – purely out of my limited knowledge and for the sake of a sharper focus – decided to rely mostly on illustrative materials from India. One can easily draw similar examples from other parts of Asia.

Two introductory surveys are helpful to our task here. First our discussion is best introduced by offering a demographic and statistical portrait of religious pluralism in Asia. Though each of the nations within Asia may have a different dominant religion, all nations within Asia are multi-religious in their makeup. For example, in nations such as Indonesia, Bangladesh and Pakistan more than eighty per cent of the people belong to Islam. Yet, in each of these nations there are a significant number of Christians, Hindus, Buddhists and people who practice tribal religious traditions. In India and Nepal, more than eighty per cent of the population is Hindu and there again one notices a significant variety of religious traditions within these two nations. In Japan, Vietnam, Thailand, Myanmar and Sri Lanka, a

---

[1] My initial research for this essay was carried out as the William Paton Fellow at Selly Oak College, Selly Oak, Birmingham, UK (autumn 2001), and was supported by the Lilly Theological Research Grant of the Association of Theological Schools in the United States for the year 2001–2.

great majority of the population belongs to one of the varied Buddhist traditions, while other religious traditions coexist along with Buddhism.

There is indeed a variety in terms of the composition of religious populations within each country. Yet, one thing common to all the nations of Asia is that Christians form only a very small minority within each nation; for example, less than three per cent in India, ten per cent in Indonesia, eight per cent in Sri Lanka, less than one per cent in Bangladesh and Japan. The Philippines is the only exception, since eighty-two per cent of the population of the Philippines are Roman Catholic. Another important fact to bear in mind is that the kind of religious plurality that exists in Asia is not a product of any recent demographic changes; it is unlike the way religious plurality has come about in some European nations and the United States of America through recent migrations of people. Furthermore, religious plurality in Asia has existed for many centuries. This means that the question of religious pluralism is not something new to Asian Christians. From their historical beginnings, Asian Christians lived with religious plurality around them and had to encounter questions – theological or otherwise – with regard to their role and place within such religiously pluralistic settings.

Secondly, even though Christians in Asia, for centuries, encountered on a day-to-day basis the fact of religious plurality, the types and forms of their encounter have had significant variations. A helpful way to expound this, I consider, is to outline a set of models or typologies of encounter. These models are theological models and not chronological or regional. The chronological and regional concerns go beyond the parameters of this essay because to bring in illustrative examples from both a variety of geographical areas and a variety of periods, to substantiate each model, is a Herculean task. The discussion of models will be followed by a pointed discussion of four theological themes raised by the encounter between Asian Christianity and the religious pluralism of Asia. These four do not exhaust the wide array of challenges; rather this list highlights some of the most important ones among them.

MODELS OF ENCOUNTER

It is not difficult to discover, even with a cursory glance, the otherness of Christianity in the midst of the religions of Asia. The historical beginnings of Christianity are very different from those of Hinduism, for example. Hinduism may even claim not to have any historical beginning and it calls itself *sanatana dharma*, meaning 'the eternal order'. The theological underpinnings of Christianity are significantly different from those of Buddhism, which in its original form is 'atheistic'. Similarly, the rituals and practices of the Christian faith are markedly different from those of Asian religions, even though Christian rituals and practices have taken on an Asian flavour in many places of Asia. This means, then, that when Asian Christians encounter the other religions of Asia, the question of the 'other' becomes crucial and the perception and view of the other plays an important role in defining the goals and the processes of the encounter. This is one of the reasons why we first look at some of the models of encounter before we address the theological themes that arise out of the encounter.

THE OTHER AS AN ENEMY OF GOD

Christians in Asia belong to all the three confessional families of the Christian faith; namely, Eastern Orthodox, Roman Catholic and Protestant. The Eastern Orthodox Christians belong to the earliest Christian communities of Asia. Their entry into the Christian faith was not as dramatic as the conversion of people in India and other parts of Asia during the eighteenth and nineteenth centuries through the work of the Roman Catholic and Protestant missions from the west. For example, the early Syrian Orthodox community in Kerala, India, positioned itself comfortably within the Hindu community in India.[2] The Protestant converts, on the other hand, had a dramatic break from the Hindu community and such a break led to the perception of the Hindu 'other' as an enemy of God. In some settings, the early Christians were persecuted by the Hindu or Muslim communities. For example, a new town, called Mudalur (First Town), came into being in South India as a way of protecting the early converts from their Hindu neighbours.[3] Settings like these promoted a posture that saw the other as an enemy of God. This would entail viewing the other as a worshipper of demons rather than of God.

THE OTHER AS A POTENTIAL CONVERT

The early Protestant missionaries to Asia were governed by an evangelical theology that made the conversion of people of other religions the primary

---

[2] Corrine G. Dempsey, *Kerala Christian Sainthood: Collisions of Culture and Worldview in South India* (Oxford: Oxford University Press, 2001), p. 5.

[3] Hugald Grafe, *History of Christianity in India, Vol. IV, pt 2: Tamilnadu in the Nineteenth and Twentieth Centuries* (Bangalore: Church History Association of India, 1990), p. 121.

agenda for their Christian discipleship. The ground-breaking publication of William Carey's *An Enquiry into the Obligations of Christians to Use Means for the Conversion of the Heathens*[4] clearly reflects a similar understanding of the other. Such a theology is prevalent among Christians in Asia even today. Therefore, many in Asia tend to view the people of other religions as potential converts and not just the followers of a different religious tradition. The contemporary scene is saturated with mission agencies started by individuals and groups of Christians in Asia and most of them reveal a similar posture towards the other.

THE OTHER AS PRIMITIVE SUPERSTITION

Some apply the rationality of the western Enlightenment to the religions of Asia and see them as primitive and superstitious. Missionaries, who were involved in educational ministry such as setting up schools, colleges and universities, saw their task as bringing the critical rationality of the Christian west to influence the people of Asia and, thus, help turn them away from religions full of primitive ideas and superstitious practices. One of the leading figures in this sort of encounter was Alexander Duff, who was a missionary in India during the nineteenth century.[5] Some western missionaries took the Hindu mythologies as a platform to argue for the rational character of the Christian faith. To cite one example, among many, John Murdoch maintains that the Hindu tradition 'cannot be accepted as the revelation from God, but as the invention of men in an enlightened age'.[6] Hindus, themselves, were weary of such a caricature of their religious tradition. As Sushil Madhava Pathak, an Indian historian, notes:

A careful reader is struck by the sense of missionary writers on the bright sides of Hindu thought and culture. The sublime philosophy of the Gita and the Upanishads was hardly discussed. The ideals enshrined in the characters of Ramayan which have captured Indian imagination from times immemorial, were never mentioned ... It was a favorite strategy of missionary writers to compare Krishna with Christ and show the superiority of the latter's character.[7]

---

[4] William Carey, *An Enquiry into the Obligations of Christians to Use Means for the Conversion of the Heathens* (London: Carey Kingsgate Press, 1961; originally published in 1792).
[5] See C. B. Firth, *An Introduction to Indian Church History* (Delhi: ISPCK, 1998), p. 182.
[6] John Murdoch, *Siva Bhakti: with an Examination of the Siddhanta Philosophy* (Madras: C. L. S., 1902), p. 61.
[7] Sushil Madhava Pathak, *American Missionaries and Hinduism* (Delhi: Munshiram Mnoharlal, 1967), p. 80.

THE OTHER AS AN UNFULFILLED SEEKER

Some of the Christians view the people of other religions as those who are on their way to finding Christ who is the fulfiller of all human longings and desires. For example, the idea of the 'Old Testament's' fulfilment in the New Testament is taken as the guiding principle in understanding the place of the 'other' in the overall economy of God. A supreme example of this approach is J. N. Farquhar's book, *The Crown of Hinduism*.[8] Farquhar picks up the various beliefs and practices of Hinduism, describes and examines each of them in detail and, finally, demonstrates how each of those find their fulfilment in Christ, who is thus to be known as the crown of Hinduism. In this approach there is a positive evaluation of other religions as those that are also on the same journey as Christianity yet without reaching the desired destination. Such a perception of the other is very common among the laity in Asian churches, and is especially manifested in the sermons of local preachers.

THE OTHER AS A STOREHOUSE OF CULTURE

From the middle of the twentieth century onwards there has been a movement among the churches in Asia called the inculturation of the gospel in Asian terms, symbols and spiritualities. Vatican II played an important part in promoting programmes of inculturation especially in the 'Third World' countries. As Felix Wilfred notes:

[The] most appropriate point of departure from the discussion of inculturation and mission in contemporary times in the Roman Catholic Church would be to begin with a very insightful observation of Karl Rahner, who was undoubtedly one of the foremost architects of Vatican II ... the Euro-centrism in which the church was caught up was broken, to enable all the peoples of the earth to live, celebrate, think and express the faith in their uniquely distinct ways.[9]

Hindu, Buddhist and other religious practices were adapted to serve Christian spiritual life and worship. Such a programme of inculturation sees the religious other as the storehouse of cultural symbols, linguistic tools and spiritual practices. In this move one detects a clear distinction between religion and culture. While religious beliefs and practices are shunned as non-Christian, the cultural milieu is accepted as that which

[8] J. N. Farquhar, *The Crown of Hinduism* (London: Oxford University Press, 1919).
[9] Felix Wilfred, *On the Banks of Ganges: Doing Contextual Theology* (Delhi: ISPCK, 2002), p. 30.

enhances the liturgical and spiritual life of Christian communities. Many Asian theologians view the religious traditions of Asia as those that provide the language, conceptual frameworks and resources for their own theological enterprise.[10]

THE OTHER AS A COMPANION IN STRUGGLE

Several nations in Asia gained independence from colonial rulers during the first half of the twentieth century. For example, India and Pakistan became independent nations in 1947 and Sri Lanka was to follow suit the following year. In such an ethos of nationalism, Christians in Asia found themselves standing alongside other religionists in the struggle for independence and in the arduous task of building a new nation. The writings of Paul Devanandan and M. M. Thomas of India influenced many in India to see the people of other religions as their companions in the task of building up a secular India. One of their early books, *Christian Participation in Nation-Building*,[11] ends with an invitation to probe the 'theological basis of Christian Non-Christian cooperation', and recommends a vision of the other as a partner in the struggle for justice and peace.[12] Such a vision of the other as a companion is not limited to patriotic activities alone. Today this companionship is expressed in the struggle to bring liberation and freedom to the marginalized peoples in Asia. For example, the liberation of women calls for such a companionship and so does the project to enable the Dalits to free themselves from the age-old bondage and oppression under the caste system in India.

THE OTHER AS A PARTNER IN DIALOGUE

The view of the other as a partner in inter-religious dialogue became a leading mode of encounter during the latter part of the twentieth century. The setting up of the Sub-Unit on Dialogue with People of Other Faiths and Ideologies at the World Council of Churches in 1971, under the leadership of Stanley Samartha from India, is indicative of this shift.

---

[10] See C. S. Song, *Third-Eye Theology: Theology in Formation in Asian Settings* (Maryknoll: Orbis Books, 1979); M. Thomas Thangaraj, *The Crucified Guru: An Experiment in Cross-Cultural Christology* (Nashville: Abingdon Press, 1994). And there are several more books of this kind which view the Asian religious traditions as the cultural backdrop for Christian theology in Asia.

[11] P. D. Devanandan and M. M. Thomas (eds.), *Christian Participation in Nation-Building* (Bangalore: Christian Institute for the Study of Religion and Society, 1960).

[12] *Ibid.*, p. 300.

Samartha, a great proponent and expositor of inter-religious dialogue, was influenced by P. D. Devanandan, who was a pioneer in inter-religious dialogue in India.[13] Wesley Ariarajah, a Sri Lankan theologian who succeeded Samartha as the Director of the sub-unit on Dialogue within the World Council of Churches, argues and promotes this view of the other in many of his writings.[14] Many of the seminaries in Asia have an active programme of inter-religious dialogue within their curricular landscape.

What I have outlined so far is an illustrative list of the various models of encounter between Christians and people of other religious traditions in Asia. This list is in no way comprehensive or exhaustive. It does, however, exemplify the variety of ways in which Asian Christians view their relationship with people of other religions. Our question now is: What are the theological themes and questions that emerge out of these encounters? In attempting to answer this question, one is again aware of the immensity of such a task. Therefore, I have chosen to highlight only four of the theological themes that arise out of Asian Christians' response to religious plurality in Asia.

THE BIBLE AMONG OTHER SCRIPTURES

When the Bible arrived in Asia, it had to discover its place within the many scriptures of Asia. Hindus, Buddhists, Muslims and others had their own scriptures and when the members of these traditions converted to Christianity they were given an alternative scripture: the Bible. Therefore, the new converts had to negotiate their new scripture within the existing scriptures of Asia. There are at least three distinct questions in such a process of negotiation.

First, how do Asian Christians understand and explicate the authority of the Bible in the midst of other scriptures? In addressing this question, one cannot but assess the relation of Asian Christians to the scriptural traditions of their former religions. For example, most of the Christians in India came from the lowest rungs of the caste ladder and thus did not have access to the Hindu scriptures, whether in Sanskrit or in their vernacular

---

[13] P. D. Devanandan, *Preparation for Dialogue* (Bangalore: CISRS, 1964). Stanley Samartha's works on inter-religious dialogue are numerous. Noteworthy among them for our purposes is Stanley J. Samartha, *Courage for Dialogue: Ecumenical Issues in Inter-Religious Relationships* (Geneva: World Council of Churches, 1981).

[14] These writings include Wesley Ariarajah, *Bible and People of Other Faiths* (Geneva: World Council of Churches, 1985) and *Not Without My Neighbour: Issues in Interfaith Relations* (Geneva: World Council of Churches, 1999).

language. Therefore, the authority of the Bible was not operating over against the authority of Hindu scriptures; but rather, it was a newly-found authority which was based on the early Indian Christians' actual possession of the Bible in their mother-tongues and holding it in their hands. Having their own copy of the Bible was a symbol of dignity and pride for Indian Christians.[15]

A related issue was the choice of a term to denote the Bible. The main Hindu scriptures were named *Veda*. Is the Bible a *Veda*? The Tamil Bible has gone through an interesting history of choosing the right term for *biblion*. Those who named the Bible as *Veda* had to argue it either as one of the *Vedas* of Hindu faith or as the true *Veda* replacing the Hindu *Veda*. For example, Robert De Nobili, a Roman Catholic missionary to India in the sixteenth century used *Veda* as the term for the Bible, arguing that the Bible was the fifth Veda which was lost in a flood, according to Hindu mythology.[16] Protestants, on the other hand, beginning with Bartholomew Ziegenbalg, who was the first Protestant missionary, have used variations of the term *Veda* such as *Vedapusthagam* (Veda-Book) and *Vedaagamam* (Veda and Agamas together), to claim a superior status for the Bible over and above the Hindu scriptures. More recently, Tamil Christians – both Roman Catholic and Protestant – prefer the term *viviliyam*, which is a transliteration of *biblion*.[17] In choosing *viviliyam* they have acknowledged the Bible as *one* among the many scriptures of the world, deriving its authority from the community of faith that claims it as its scripture.

Secondly, what is the relation between the Hebrew Bible, Asian Scriptures and the Bible, especially in relation to the canon? For the first-century Jewish Christians, it was a smooth, though not easy, transition from the Hebrew Bible to the New Testament since the Hebrew Bible was Jesus' Bible too. How do Asian Christians move from their earlier scriptures to the Christian Bible? Those who denied any scriptural authority to Hindu, Buddhist and other scriptures claimed the canonical books of the Bible as their scripture. However, for those converts who accorded scriptural status and authority to their earlier scriptures, a different

---

[15] See M. Thomas Thangaraj, 'The Bible as *Veda*: Biblical Hermeneutics in Tamil Christianity', in R. S. Sugirtharajah (ed.), *Vernacular Hermeneutics* (Sheffield: Sheffield Academic Press, 1999), pp. 133–43.

[16] For a detailed treatment of Nobili's use of *Veda*, see Soosai Arokiasamy, *Dharma, Hindu and Christian, According to Roberto De Nobili: Analysis of its Meaning and its Use in Hinduism and Christianity* (Documenta Missionalia, 19, Rome: Editrice Pontificia Universita Gregoriana, 1986), chapter 5.

[17] M. Thomas Thangaraj, 'The Bible as *Veda*', p. 139.

view of the biblical canon began to emerge. Arvind P. Nirmal, an Indian Christian theologian, puts this quandary in the following manner:

In spite of my desire to join in a recitation of the Deuteronomic Creed, 'A wandering Aramean was my father . . .', I really cannot identify myself with that Creed. This because I know for certain – historically – that this wandering Aramean was not my father. My father or forefathers were Indian Shudras and not Arameans.[18]

In dealing with this quandary, some Asian theologians have argued for viewing the Hindu, Buddhist, or Confucian scriptures as the 'Old Testament' for Asian Christians. For example, writing about the movement of Japanese Christianity during the Showa period, Yasuo Furnya mentions that 'for the Japanese, if not for Westerners, Shintoist ancient writings such as Kojiki and Nihonshoki are the Old Testament'.[19] In India, on the other hand, it was Pandipeddi Chenchiah, an Indian lay-theologian, who viewed the Hindu scriptures as the Old Testament for Indian Christians.[20] He was willing to view the New Testament as fulfilling some of the expectations and longings embedded in the scriptural writings of Hinduism – similar to the way in which early Christians interpreted the Hebrew Bible.[21]

Thirdly, how do Asian Christians negotiate the idea of the Bible as a source for theology in the midst of and in relation to other sources; such as, experience, the scriptural writings of Asians, folk stories, hymns and poems and art? One of most significant and distinctive elements in Asian theological enterprise is the place afforded to experience in the construction of Christian theology. In the Hindu philosophical traditions, *anubhava* (experience) plays a significant part in epistemology. Picking up on that significance, Asian theologians have argued for the primacy of experience as a source for theology. By the word 'experience' different theologians mean different things. After describing the context of Asia with its poverty, oppression, religiousness and so on, Peter Phan writes:

In an *Asian theology* whose form and method are moulded by and related to the historical context of Asia, as distinct from a *theology in Asia* whose structure and style are not shaped by such a context, the Asian reality as described above and not the Bible and/or tradition, is the starting point.[22]

---

[18] Arvind P. Nirmal, *Heuristic Explorations* (Madras: C. L. S., 1990), p. 53.
[19] Yasuo Furnya (ed.), *A History of Japanese Theology* (Grand Rapids: William B. Eerdmans, 1997), p. 56.
[20] Robin Boyd, *An Introduction to Indian Christian Theology* (Delhi: ISPCK, 2004), p. 158.
[21] *Ibid.*
[22] Peter C. Phan, *Christianity with an Asian Face: Asian American Theology in the Making* (Maryknoll: Orbis Books, 2003), p. 102 (original italics).

For Phan, experience signifies the whole of 'Asian reality' in all its joys, sufferings and struggles. For some others, it is the religious/mystical experience that takes precedence over the Bible in their theological thinking and articulation. For example, P. Chenchiah insists on his direct experience of Christ as gaining priority over the scriptures or tradition. For him 'the central fact of Christianity thus consists in the believer coming into a direct experiential touch with Christ; we must have the *anubhava* of the living Christ'.[23] In Chenchiah's words: 'Jesus is a cosmic fact – a crisis in creation. There can be no Christianity without this fundamental experience.'[24] In the writings of Abhishiktananda, Raymond Panikkar and other Roman Catholic theologians of Asia one discovers the same emphasis on experience. More recently, the idea of experience is related more closely with the experience of the poor, women and Dalits within Asia. It is their experience of both oppression and hope that serves as the source for theology and the basis for biblical hermeneutics.

Asian theologians have been foremost in the use of folk stories, poems, paintings and other such pieces as sources for theology along with the Bible. C. S. Song's writings are highly illustrative of this method of doing theology, especially his work, *Tears of Lady Meng: A Parable of People's Political Theology* (Geneva: World Council of Churches, 1981). He has been involved in a Programme for the Theology and Cultures in Asia (PTCA) that encourages Asian theologians to use their histories and stories of struggle as the source for constructing Asian theologies. The works of Masao Takenaka in Japan and Jyoti Sahi in India exemplify this creative move beyond the Bible to Asian art-forms.[25]

GOD AMONG GODS

Christianity did not arrive in a 'godless' Asia even though quite often Christian missionary rhetoric portrayed Asia as devoid of any knowledge of God. For example, Bishop Heber, who worked in India as an Anglican missionary and bishop, wrote the hymn 'From Greenland's Icy Mountains',

---

[23] Boyd, *Indian Christian Theology*, p. 147.

[24] P. Chenchiah, 'Wherein Lies the Uniqueness of Christ? An Indian Christian View', in R. S. Sugirtharajah and Cecil Hargreaves (eds.), *Readings in Indian Christian Theology*, vol. I (London: SPCK, 1993), pp. 83–92 at p. 92.

[25] Some of Masao Takenaka's works include *God is Rice: Asian Culture and Christian Faith* (Geneva: World Council of Churches, 1986); *Mission and Art*, co-edited with Godwin R. Singh (Singapore: Christian Conference of Asia, 1994); and *When the Bamboo Bends: Christ and Culture in Japan* (Geneva: World Council of Churches, 2002). For Jyoti Sahi, see Stefan Belderbos, 'Jyoti Sahi's Synthesis between Western Christianity and Traditional Indian Art', *Exchange* 31:2 (2002), 157–70.

in which he describes the people of Asia this way: 'The heathen in his blindness, Bows down to wood and stone.'[26] On the contrary, Asian religions had highly developed notions of God, albeit different from those of western Christianity. This means that Asian Christians' God-talk had to engage in a dialogue with the notions of God that were already present in a powerful way among the peoples of Asia. Such a dialogue, often, was compelled to address the following issues.

First, what is the dynamic equivalent for the term God of Christian faith – shaped by both *Yahweh* of the Hebrew tradition and *Theos* of the Greek tradition – in the local languages of Asia? This was a central and crucial question for all those who were involved in translating the Bible into Asian languages. Even though the Roman Catholics were not too keen on translating the Bible at the beginning of their missionary ventures in Asia, the Protestants saw the translation of the Bible as the first and primary task of missionary work and Roman Catholics were later engaged in it as well. Therefore, the work of translating the Bible demanded finding a dynamic equivalent term for God in local languages. The search for such an equivalent was not an innocent linguistic exercise; it was an exceedingly loaded theological task, primarily because of the presence of well-developed notions of God and the availability of a variety of terms for the Divine.

Let me offer a few examples. In Indonesia, whose population has a Muslim majority, one finds that the terms Allah and *Tuhan* are taken over and used in translating the biblical terms for God.[27] The use of Allah for God was based on the principle of finding a dynamic equivalent in the local language. Of course, the use of Allah in the Indonesian Bible may raise theological questions for other Christians in that geographical region. We see that:

> ... in the Javanese Bible, 'Lord' is 'Gusti' or 'Gusti-Pangeran', and 'God' is 'Yehuwah' which is a Javanization of 'Yehovah'. In the Batak Bible, 'God' is 'Debata' which is derived from the Hindu 'dewata' (deity), but 'Lord' is 'Jahoba' which is a Batak derivation from 'Yehovah'.[28]

One can notice a similar kind of struggle in China as well. The Chinese people had such a dramatically different view of the cosmos that the idea

---

[26] William Sterndale Bennett and Otto Goldschmidt, eds., *The Chorale Book For England*, congregational edn. (London: Longman, Roberts and Green, 1863, supp. 1865), no. 231.
[27] Emanuel Gerrit Singgih, *Doing Theology in Indonesia: Sketches for an Indonesian Contextual Theology*, ATESEA Occasional Papers 14 (Manila: ATESEA, 2003), p. 143.
[28] *Ibid.*

of God was not present in their thought; rather they had the Tao which was far beyond the conception of a personal Creator God. The Jesuits, Dominicans, Franciscans and Protestants suggested their own dynamic equivalents; such as, *tian* (heaven), *shangdi* (supreme ruler), *tianzhu* (Lord of Heaven) and so on.[29]

In India, however, the situation was more complex. The Hindu tradition had a host of names and terms for God. As far as the terms for God in the Indian languages were concerned, there were two levels of signification. The word *Brahman* signified the Ultimate Reality that was beyond the personal and can rightly be called suprapersonal. It was devoid of any attributes or forms. The other term was *ishvara*, meaning a personal God, very similar to the term *Theos* in the Greek language tradition. The missionaries rightly saw *Brahman* as different from the biblical view of God and hence rejected it as a possible equivalent term for God. So the only other alternative was the term *ishvara*. Here was another problem; namely, that *ishvara* seemingly had polytheistic overtones. This was repugnant to the missionaries in so far as they were looking for an equivalent for the biblical view of God. It was the genius of Roberto De Nobili that he saw *ishvara* as a live option and qualified it with a prefix meaning 'of all'. Hence he coined the term *saruveshvar*, God of God or God of all. The Protestants chose the word *Devan*, which is from the same root as Deus and has a masculine ending. Since the rise of women's criticism of the sexist character of Christian theological language, the word *kadavul*, which means 'the transcendent-immanent One', is preferred because of its gender-free character.

The numerous names of God in the Hindu tradition pose a problem for the Christian theological response to religious pluralism as well. Shiva, Vishnu, Ganesh and Murugan are all personal names of the Hindu pantheon. That means one cannot opt to use those terms for God. Moreover, the Hindu pantheon includes Goddesses too. As you can see the very act of naming God has such serious theological implications and consequences that one needs to tread carefully and cautiously in naming God in the Asian multi-religious situation. The theological concern behind all these various experiments in God-language is to avoid any trace of henotheistic implications and to maintain the radical monotheistic stance of the Christian faith.

---

[29] Kwok Pui-lan, 'Images of God in the Chinese Context', *Voices from the Third World*, vol. XXI, no. 2 (1998), 102–18 at 103. See also Hwa Yung, *Mangoes or Bananas? The Quest for an Authentic Asian Christian Theology* (New Delhi: Oxford University Press, 1997), p. 126.

Another concern that is linked to Asian Christians' God-talk is the Buddhist context in which the very talk of God is at odds with the Buddhist view of the cosmos. With its atheistic beginnings, Buddhism opts for the language of 'nothingness' (*sunyata*) when it comes to naming the ultimate context of human existence. How does one speak of the Christian view of God in such a setting? Jung Young Lee rejects the view of God as changeless and proposes that we see 'change' as an ultimate category to be used for God-talk, in light of the I-Ching of China. He writes: 'God is changeless because he is primarily Change itself. The ever-changing nature of God has in himself the unchanging pattern of change.'[30] In another work, Lee employs the yin-yang symbolic thinking as his theological method to expound the idea of God as Trinity.[31] He ends his discussion with these words:

As is true of DNA, I sense that the presence of the Trinity is the basic unit of life in everything from the microcosmic to the macrocosmic world. It is like the *ch'i*, the principle of energy, but it is more than the *ch'i*. Although I sense its presence, I have no way to identify it. The divine Trinity is more than what can be known.[32]

CHRIST AMONG OTHER SAVIOURS

One of the contentious issues in the Asian Christian response to religious pluralism in Asia is the Christocentricity of the Christian faith. While one can quickly discover points of contacts and instances of similarity in the concept of God or the view of scripture, the belief in the uniqueness of Jesus Christ is a matter of intense debate in Asia. This debate involves at least three major issues. One is the attempt by Christian theologians in Asia to discover a language that is relevant and meaningful to Asians in their specific contexts. The other issue is the apologetic side of Christ-ology where one is faced with questions such as 'Why Christ, why not Buddha, why not Krishna?' and 'What about the uniqueness and finality of Christ?' The third concern is the way in which non-Christian Asians have articulated the significance of Christ in relation to their own religio-cultural contexts. How may one christologically evaluate such attempts? Let us examine each of these.

---

[30] Jung Young Lee, 'Can God be Change Itself?', in D. J. Elwood (ed.), *What Asian Christians are Thinking* (Querzon City: New Day Publishers, 1976), pp. 173–93 at p. 189.
[31] Jung Young Lee, *The Trinity in Asian Perspective* (Nashville: Abingdon Press, 1996).
[32] *Ibid.*, p. 219.

First of all, what language may we borrow in this multi-religious setting of Asia to explain the significance of Jesus as the Christ? This is a question which almost all Asian theologians and Christians face. *Christos* is a Greek term backed by the notion of Messiah in the Jewish tradition. With all its 'scandal' and 'foolishness', it made sense to first-century Christians. What would it mean or entail to speak of *Christos* in the Asian religious setting? Are there equivalent 'salvific' figures or concepts/images in Asia that can provide a language or offer a helpful starting point for expounding the significance of Jesus as the Christ?

Asian theologians provide us with a wide variety of Christologies mainly because of the diversity of religious and cultural contexts in which they find themselves. One of the challenges for Asian theologians is to find a way to capture, in the Asian religious setting, the view of Christ as Logos-made-flesh. The concept of Logos, as used in the Johannine writings, comes from both Jewish and Greek philosophical–theological traditions. As such, it is foreign to the theological–philosophical framework of Asia. One of the concepts that comes closest to Logos is OM, the primordial sound in the Hindu tradition. This means that one could use the concept of OM-made-flesh as an exegesis of John 1:14. Yet interestingly, Indian theologians have not pursued this line of Christological construction, except in some passing references to Christ as OM in the writings of Sister Vandana and S. Jesudason. Vandana writes: 'In India its [Logos'] nearest equivalent is OM ... Jesus is the OM, the Logos.'[33] Jesudason also describes Christ as Eternal OM.[34] Christian poets and hymn-writers were freer to use the concept of OM to describe Christ. For example, Vedanayagam Sastriar, a prolific hymn-writer, refers to Christ as *Omanathi* (the eternal OM). One of the contemporary songs in praise of Christ goes like this: *OM Kristu natha, unaith tholuthen* (OM Christ, I worship you).[35]

Many theologians have appealed to the concept of *cit* in the divine triad: *sat, cit, ananda* (Truth/Being, Intelligence/Consciousness, Joy/Bliss). Brahmabandab Upadhyaya is prominent among them.[36] Discovering the concept of *sat-cit-ananda* to be a helpful category in expounding the

---

[33] S. Vandana and S. Jesudason, 'Water Symbolism in the Gospel of St. John in the Light of Indian Spirituality', in R. S. Sugirtharajah and Cecil Hargreaves (eds.), *Readings in Indian Christian Theology*, vol. I (London: SPCK, 1993), pp. 200–13 at p. 211.

[34] Sugirtharajah makes a passing reference to this in R. S. Sugirtharajah (ed.), *Asian Faces of Jesus* (Maryknoll: Orbis Books, 1993), p. 4.

[35] This song is said to have been composed by Fr. Chelladurai of Chennai. It is sung by Thirupamparam Shanmugasundaram in a cassette recording produced by the Tamilnadu Theological Seminary, Madurai, India.

[36] See Boyd, *Indian Christian Theology*, p. 63.

doctrine of Trinity, Upadhayaya describes Christ as *cit.* Jung Young Lee employs the *Tai chi t'u* (the diagram of the Great Ultimate in the *I-Ching*) and describes Christ as 'the perfect realization of change'.[37]

While the concept of Logos as such is foreign to Asian religio-philosophical traditions, the concept of incarnation is not, in any way, foreign to the Asian religious and philosophical traditions, especially the traditions of India. It is the twentieth-century western Christianity that has had some difficulty in dealing with the concept of incarnation. As Frances Young writes:

In the Western world, both popular culture and the culture of the intelligentsia has come to be dominated by the human and natural sciences to such an extent that supernatural causation or intervention in the affairs of the world has become, for the majority of people, simply incredible.[38]

There is a longstanding tradition of the idea of incarnation within the Vaishnavite tradition of Hinduism. Vishnu (Godhead) is said to take several incarnations to set right the course of the history of the universe. In Bhagavad Gita, Krishna (the incarnation of Vishnu) says:

> Whenever sacred duty decays
> And chaos prevails,
> Then, I create
> Myself, Arjuna.
>
> To protect men of virtue
> And destroy men who do evil,
> To set the standard of sacred duty,
> I appear in age after age.[39]

The word used to signify incarnation is *avatar*, which literally means descent. Vishnu is supposed to take ten *avatars* and the last one, Kalki, has not yet taken place. The idea of *avatar* is not confined to the religious and philo-sophical writings of Hinduism; it is popular among the people of India as well. Any and every religious or political leader of repute might easily be referred to as an *avatar* of God. One can see pictures of Jesus, Buddha and Gandhi together in one frame representing the multiple *avatars* of God. Thus in the popular Indian mind, Jesus the Christ is one of the *avatars* of God.

---

[37] Jung Young Lee, 'The Perfect Realization of Change: Jesus Christ', in R. S. Sugirtharajah (ed.), *Asian Faces of Jesus* (Maryknoll: Orbis Books, 1993), pp. 62–74.

[38] John Hick (ed.), *The Myth of God Incarnate* (Philadelphia: Westminster Press, 1977), p. 31.

[39] *The Bhagavad-Gita, Krishna's Counsel in Time of War*, trans. with Introduction and Afterword, Barbara Stoler Miller (New York: Bantam Books, 1986), p. 50.

While Indian Christian theologians have employed the concept of *avatar* in their Christological explorations, they are also aware of some inherent problems in doing so. For these theologians, the problem is not the mythical character of the idea of incarnation, rather the unique and once-and-for-all character of the incarnation of Christ, which is foreign to the Hindu idea of a multiplicity of incarnations. V. Chakkarai, a twentieth-century theologian, addresses precisely these issues in his book, *Jesus the Avatar*.[40] He finds that the Hindu understanding of incarnation is defective on two counts. First, the incarnation is temporary. God appears as the incarnate one, disappears and reappears, thus leading to a multiplicity of incarnations. The Christian understanding of incarnation views the Logos as a permanent God-Human, once the Logos had become flesh. Secondly, the Hindu view of incarnation is static, devoid of any further development or progress. The incarnation of Christ, on the other hand, is dynamic, in the sense that it progresses through several stages. Chakkarai writes: 'The Incarnation advanced from stage to stage, from the historical to the spiritual, from the external to the internal, from time to eternity.'[41] Thus he is able to state: 'Jesus Christ is the Incarnation of *Avatar* of God; the Holy Spirit in human experience is the Incarnation of Jesus Christ.'[42] Tamil hymn-writers, of course, have used the title *avatar* for Christ in many of their hymns. For example, M. Vedamanickam of Neyyoor sings:

> Holy *avatara*, I bow to you!
> Saviour of the world, I bow to you!

What I have touched upon is only a small fragment of the various Christological articulations of Asian theologians, both Christians and others. There is a wealth of resources for delving into this rich resource of Christology in a setting of religious pluralism.[43]

THE CHURCH AMONG OTHER COMMUNITIES OF FAITH

Christianity arrived in Asia not only as a theological option but also as a sociological option. In other words, the proclamation of the good news of

[40] V. Chakkarai, *Jesus the Avatar* (Madras: Christian Literature Society, 1932).
[41] *Ibid.*, p. 112   [42] *Ibid.*, p. 121.
[43] See Sugirtharajah (ed.), *Asian Faces of* Jesus; C. S. Song, *Jesus the Crucified People* (New York: Crossroad, 1990), *Jesus and the Reign of God* (Minneapolis: Fortress Press, 1993) and *Jesus in the Power of the Spirit* (Minneapolis: Fortress Press, 1994); M. M. Thomas, *The Acknowledged Christ of the Indian Renaissance* (London: SCM Press, 1969); S. J. Samartha, *The Hindu Response to the Unbound Christ* (Bangalore: CISRS, 1974); Thangaraj, *The Crucified Guru.*

Jesus Christ included an invitation to join a new community, a new voluntary association, called the church, in addition to one's vision of God. In most parts of Asia, a call to change one's religion was not a problem as long as it was accommodated within the given social order and arrangement. For example, there was a freedom to choose one's favourite God (*ishtadeva*) within the Hindu faith as long as one remained within the existing caste structure. The Eastern Orthodox tradition – the earliest to arrive in India – existed in peace and harmony with its Hindu neighbours mostly because it operated as a subcaste within the larger caste arrangement. The Roman Catholic and Protestant traditions faced an uphill task of creating a community of Christian disciples who transcended the boundaries of the caste system. The voluntary associational character of Christian faith was indeed a challenge to the close-knit, family-based and largely static (non-mobile) social arrangement of Asian societies. Moreover, the presence of western colonial rule in several parts of Asia created a situation in which the boundary lines between the church and the colonial political order were blurred. For example, the permission to engage in missionary work and the protection of Chinese Christians was an important part of the French Treaty with China.[44] This called for the difficult task of articulating the need, the pattern and the significance of the church.

What are some of the more appropriate ways of talking about 'church' in Asia? What are the issues at stake in the development of ecclesiologies within Asia? Among many the two most important issues are the following. How may the church in Asia envision itself and order its life as a church that is not simply a western church that is implanted in the lands of Asia, but expresses itself truly as a church of Asia? How may the church in Asia function as a separate voluntary association within the larger society in Asia without losing sight of its modest role in the establishment of the reign of God in Asia – an inclusive community of justice and peace, comprising the whole people of Asia?

The construction of a truly Asian church has happened in three distinct ways. The first is what is generally called the process of inculturation. The very process of communicating the Christian message to the people of Asia involved the discovery and use of Asian languages, symbols, thought-forms and conceptual tools. The translation of the Bible in vernacular languages was itself an act of inculturation. With the Bible in their hands, Asian Christians were able to imagine themselves into a new community of faith. The corporate worship life of Asian Christians is

---

[44] Wilfred, *On the Banks of Ganges*, p. 234.

another area in which the process of inculturation has been very active. To cite an example, the liturgical reforms within the churches in India are remarkable. Vatican II brought a significant change in the worship life of the Roman Catholic churches in India. These changes included the use of vernacular languages for liturgy, the employment of local musical traditions and the adoption of Indian architectural patterns in the building of churches. Protestants brought the worship patterns of the varying western Protestant denominations. Over the centuries, the Protestants themselves have gone through a liturgical renewal and now adopt local religio-cultural practices for Christian worship.

Apart from the Eastern Orthodox, Roman Catholic and mainline Protestant churches, Pentecostal and non-denominational churches have had their own modes and methods of inculturation of Christian worship. For example, Pentecostal churches were among the first to exploit the emerging light music tradition of India (a mixture of western and Indian musical traditions) for their worship and piety. What is common in these Christian churches is the conscious and intentional attempt to develop and practice the worship of the Christian community in local linguistic and cultural forms.

The ecclesial life of Asian Christians is shaped also by home-based religious practices. Asian Christians have adapted several local religious rites of passage into their religious life. These practices vary according to region and denominational affiliation. Indigenous elements are more conspicuously present in worship settings outside the church building. The prayer meetings held in people's homes, lyrical or musical preaching performed during festive occasions, prayer services at homes related to rites of passage such as puberty, marriages, funerals and other home-based worship services bear clear marks of indigenous elements and influence. All these point to a significant dialogue between Christianity and other religions of Asia that undergirds and promotes the emergence of a truly Asian church.

Another direction that Asian Christians have taken is to free themselves from western Christianity by imitating new movements or founding new churches. In India, the founding of indigenous churches began as early as the nineteenth century among Protestants. 'One remarkable Hindu believer in Christ at Madras was O. Kandaswamy Chetti, founder of the Fellowship of the Followers of Jesus, who openly confessed his faith in Christ as the only Saviour but declined baptism.'[45] Arumainayagam Sattampillai of South Tamilnadu founded the Indian Church of the Only

---

[45] Roger E. Hedlund, 'Indian Instituted Churches: Indigenous Christianity Indian Style', *Mission Studies* 16:1 (1999), 26–42.

Saviour (popularly known as the Hindu–Christian community) in 1857, in protest against western missionary domination.[46] Hedlund mentions a few others such as: the Indian Pentecostal Church of God, founded by K. E. Abraham around 1930; the Apostolic Christian Assembly, founded by Pastor G. Sundaram; the movement around K. Subba Rao in Andhra Pradesh; the New Life Fellowship in Bombay; Agape Fellowship churches in the state of Punjab and the Isupanthi movement in North Gujarat.[47]

In Japan, for instance, Kanzo Uchimura (1861–1930) envisioned a Non-Church (Mu-Kyokai) which led to 'clash with missionaries and estrangement from the established churches'.[48] The Three-Self Patriotic Movement in China was another example of a movement that attempted to release the Christian church in Asia from its captivity to western Christianity.[49]

Furthermore, the efforts at church union within Asia were directed towards establishing a church that was free from its dependency on the churches in the west and at the same time attuned to the multi-religious setting of Asia. For example, conversations toward unity emerged between the Anglican, Methodist, Presbyterian and Congregationalist churches in South India, ultimately leading to the formation, on 27 September 1947, of the Church of South India; an organic union of all four denominational traditions.[50] Similar conversations took place between Protestant churches in North India, which led to the formation of the Church of North India in 1970. There are continuing conversations even today among the three churches – the Church of South India, the Church of North India and Mar Thoma Church – toward a Bharath Christian Church.

The relation between the church and the reign of God is another crucial issue in the religiously plural situation of Asia. Peter Phan is greatly sensitive to this issue and outlines a new way of being church in Asia. He suggests an ecclesiology that is undergirded by four features.[51] The first feature is that of the church being 'a communion of communities'. Such a communion presupposes the equality of all and moves the church toward the reign of God. The second is that the church, in its

---

[46] M. Thomas Thangaraj, 'The History and Teachings of the Hindu Christian Community Commonly Called Nattu Sabai in Tirunelveli', *Indian Church History Review* 5:1 (1971), 43–68.

[47] Hedlund, *Indian Instituted Churches*, pp. 32–6.

[48] Yasuo Furnya, *A History of Japanese Theology*, p. 35.

[49] Yeo Khiok-Khng, 'The Rise of Three Self Patriotic Movement (TSPM): Chinese Christianity in the Light of Communist Ideology in New China', *Asia Journal of Theology* 6:1 (1992), 1–9.

[50] For a detailed study of the history of the formation of the Church of South India, see Bengt Sundkler, *Church of South India: The Movement Towards Union: 1900–1947* (London: Lutterworth Press, 1954).

[51] Phan, *Christianity with an Asian Face*, pp. 176–82.

structure, will be participatory and encourage mutuality. The third feature is the dialogical spirit that will pervade the church's relationship with three realities; namely, Asian cultures, Asian religions and Asians themselves. Fourthly, the church in Asia will find a new way of being the 'prophetic sign' emboldened to point the world to the coming reign of God.

To conclude, let me briefly mention some of the implications of the thrust of this essay. First, it is evident that Asian Christian responses to religious pluralism in Asia are complex in their variety. Some of the attempts in the west to see the 'Third World' churches as monolithic and primarily conservative are unfounded. The somewhat alarmist readings of Christianity in the Global South illustrate a failure to recognize the complexity and the variety of Asian Christian responses to religious plurality.[52] Asian Christians' struggles at articulating a theology of religions most often revolves around the question of Christian identity. For example, the question of Christian identity in a minority setting has a major impact on the way a theology of religions is articulated. One cannot simply approach other religions with exotic admiration, as is the tendency of most western academic students of Asian religions. Neither can one reduce Asian Christian attitudes to those of a minority complex as such. These theologians and thinkers from Asia bring a rich variety of approaches to the question of identity. The very use of the phrase 'Asian Christian' announces to world Christianity that to be a Christian is to be located in and shaped by one's geography, language, culture and religious landscape. Finally, Asian Christian responses to religious pluralism take their rightful place within the wide spectrum of theologies from all over the world and, in that process, relativize western theological viewpoints and refuse to take them as benchmarks for understanding and articulating the Christian faith in Asia today.

BIBLIOGRAPHY

Ariarajah, Wesley, *Bible and People of Other Faiths*, Geneva: World Council of
     Churches, 1985.
     Not Without My Neighbour: Issues in Interfaith Relations, Geneva: World
     Council of Churches, 1999.
Arokiasamy, Soosai, *Dharma, Hindu and Christian, According to Roberto De Nobili:
     Analysis of its Meaning and its Use in Hinduism and Christianity*, Documenta
     Missionalia, 19, Rome: Editrice Pontifica Universita Gregoriana, 1986.

---

[52] See Philip Jenkins, *The Next Christendom: The Coming of Global Christianity* (Oxford: Oxford
University Press, 2002).

The Bhagavad-Gita, Krishna's Counsel in Time of War, trans. with Introduction and Afterword, Barbara Stoler Miller, New York: Bantam Books, 1986.

Belderbos, Stefan, 'Jyoti Sahi's Synthesis between Western Christianity and Traditional Indian Art', *Exchange* 31:2 (2002), 157–70.

Bennett, William Sterndale and Goldschmidt, Otto (eds.), *The Chorale Book For England*, congregational edn., London: Longman, Roberts and Green, 1863, supp. 1865.

Boyd, Robin, *An Introduction to Indian Christian Theology*, Delhi: ISPCK, 2004.

Carey, William, *An Enquiry into the Obligations of Christians to Use Means for the Conversion of the Heathens*, London: Carey Kingsgate Press, 1961; originally published in 1792.

Chakkarai, V., *Jesus the Avatar*, Madras: Christian Literature Society, 1932.

Chenchiah, P., 'Wherein Lies the Uniqueness of Christ? An Indian Christian View', in R. S. Sugirtharajah and Cecil Hargreaves (eds.), *Readings in Indian Christian Theology*, vol. I, London: SPCK, 1993, pp. 83–92.

Dempsey, Corrine G., *Kerala Christian Sainthood: Collisions of Culture and Worldview in South India*, Oxford: Oxford University Press, 2001.

Devanandan, P. D. and Thomas, M. M. (eds.), *Christian Participation in Nation-Building*, Bangalore: Christian Institute for the Study of Religion and Society, 1960.

Devanandan, P. D., *Preparation for Dialogue*, Bangalore: CISRS, 1964.

Farquhar, J. N., *The Crown of Hinduism*, London: Oxford University Press, 1919.

Firth, C. B., *An Introduction to Indian Church History*, Delhi: ISPCK, 1998.

Furnya, Yasuo (ed.), *A History of Japanese Theology*, Grand Rapids: William B. Eerdmans, 1997.

Grafe, Hugald, *History of Christianity in India, Vol. IV, pt 2: Tamilnadu in the Nineteenth and Twentieth Centuries*, Bangalore: Church History Association of India, 1990.

Hedlund, Roger E., 'Indian Instituted Churches: Indigenous Christianity Indian Style', *Mission Studies* 16:1 (1999), 26–42.

Hick, John (ed.), *The Myth of God Incarnate*, Philadelphia: Westminster Press, 1977.

Hwa, Yung, *Mangoes or Bananas? The Quest for an Authentic Asian Christian Theology*, New Delhi: Oxford University Press, 1997.

Jenkins, Philip, *The Next Christendom: The Coming of Global Christianity*, Oxford: Oxford University Press, 2002.

Khiok-Khng, Yeo, 'The Rise of Three Self Patriotic Movement (TSPM): Chinese Christianity in the Light of Communist Ideology in New China', *Asia Journal of Theology* 6:1 (1992), 1–9.

Kwok, Pui-lan, 'Images of God in the Chinese Context', *Voices from the Third World*, vol. XXI, no.2 (1998), 102–18.

Lee, Jung Young, 'Can God be Change Itself?', in D. J. Elwood (ed.), *What Asian Christians are Thinking*, Querzon City: New Day Publishers, 1976, pp. 173–93.
'The Perfect Realization of Change: Jesus Christ', in R. S. Sugirtharajah (ed.), *Asian Faces of Jesus*, Maryknoll: Orbis Books, 1993, pp. 62–74.
The Trinity in Asian Perspective, Nashville: Abingdon Press, 1996.

Murdoch, John, *Siva Bhakti: with an Examination of the Siddhanta Philosophy*, Madras: C. L. S., 1902.

Nirmal, Arvind P., *Heuristic Explorations*, Madras: C. L. S., 1990.

Phan, Peter C., *Christianity with an Asian Face: Asian American Theology in the Making*, Maryknoll: Orbis Books, 2003.

Pathak, Sushil Madhava, *American Missionaries and Hinduism*, Delhi: Munshiram Mnoharlal, 1967.

Samartha, Stanley J., *Courage for Dialogue: Ecumenical Issues in Inter-Religious Relationships*, Geneva: World Council of Churches, 1981.

The Hindu Response to the Unbound Christ, Bangalore: CISRS, 1974.

Singgih, Emanuel Gerrit, *Doing Theology in Indonesia: Sketches for an Indonesian Contextual Theology*, ATESEA Occasional Papers 14, Manila: ATESEA, 2003.

Song, C. S., *Third-Eye Theology: Theology in Formation in Asian Settings*, Maryknoll: Orbis Books, 1979.

Jesus the Crucified People, New York: Crossroad, 1990.

Jesus and the Reign of God, Minneapolis: Fortress Press, 1993.

Jesus in the Power of the Spirit, Minneapolis: Fortress Press, 1994.

Sugirtharajah, R. S. (ed.), *Asian Faces of Jesus*, Maryknoll: Orbis Books, 1993.

Sundkler, Bengt, *Church of South India: The Movement Towards Union: 1900–1947*, London: Lutterworth Press, 1954.

Takenaka, Masao, *God is Rice: Asian Culture and Christian Faith*, Geneva: World Council of Churches, 1986.

When the Bamboo Bends: Christ and Culture in Japan, Geneva: World Council of Churches, 2002.

Takenaka Masao and Singh, Godwin R. (eds.), *Mission and Art*, Singapore: Christian Conference of Asia, 1994.

Thangaraj, M. Thomas, 'The History and Teachings of the Hindu Christian Community Commonly Called Nattu Sabai in Tirunelveli', *Indian Church History Review* 5:1 (1971), 43–68.

The Crucified Guru: An Experiment in Cross-Cultural Christology, Nashville: Abingdon Press, 1994.

'The Bible as *Veda*: Biblical Hermeneutics in Tamil Christianity', in R. S. Sugirtharajah (ed.), *Vernacular Hermeneutics*, Sheffield: Sheffield Academic Press, 1999, pp. 133–43.

Thomas, M. M., *The Acknowledged Christ of the Indian Renaissance*, London: SCM Press, 1969.

Vandana, S. and Jesudason, S., 'Water Symbolism in the Gospel of St. John in the Light of Indian Spirituality', in R. S. Sugirtharajah and Cecil Hargreaves (eds.), *Readings in Indian Christian Theology*, vol. I, London: SPCK, 1993, pp. 200–13.

Wilfred, Felix, *On the Banks of Ganges: Doing Contextual Theology*, Delhi: ISPCK, 2002.

CHAPTER 9

Cross-textual hermeneutics and identity in multi-scriptural Asia

Archie C. C. Lee

INTRODUCTION

The multi-scriptural phenomenon of Asian cultures and religions has presented a problem and a challenge to the reading of the Bible, by Asian Christians, from the time of the colonial era. In order to justify the existence of and uphold the credibility of the missionary movement, which was part of the whole colonial project of the empire, the basic missionary strategy was set to undermine and even condemn the living traditions of Asian religions and their respective scriptures. The impact of such a strategy was tremendous on the Asian Christian converts who could not afford to ignore the reality of the plurality of texts. Their new identity as Christians threw their Asian religio-cultural identity into confusion and head-on collision. In this historical situation of the spread of Christianity to the east, conflicts of the Bible with local religions and their scriptures gave rise to the suppression of the native. The very encounter of the different living scriptural traditions should have provided an exciting melting pot for the reading and re-reading of both the Christian Bible and the other Asian scriptures, if the Asian Christians were ever encouraged to interpret their cultural heritage in the face of the foreign canon and to appropriate the Bible in the context of a multiscriptural environment. The Bible and other Asian texts have attracted the attention of postcolonial research, since the Bible and its interpretation in Asia have been an enlightening topic ever since the colonial era.[1]

From the vantage point of postcolonial criticism, Sugirtharajah attempts to show the role of the Bible in the colonial conquest and to

---

[1] R. S. Sugirtharajah, *Asian Biblical Hermeneutics and Postcolonialism: Contesting the Interpretations* (Maryknoll: Orbis, 1998); *The Bible and the Third World: Precolonial, Colonial and Postcolonial Encounters* (Cambridge: Cambridge University Press, 2001); Pui-Lan Kwok, *Postcolonial Imagination and Feminist Theology* (Louisville: Westminster John Knox Press, 2005).

critically analyze the reality of the missionary position, which is not always completely innocent or without ignobility. He classifies three different modes of relating the Bible to Asian culture and religion in colonial history and champions the postcolonial reconfigurations as an alternative critical way of approaching the contested nature of the relationship between the Bible and other Asian texts. While the Anglicist mode endeavours to, on the one hand, replace the indigenous texts by integrating the colonized into the culture of the colonizer and, on the other hand, import the Enlightenment and the modernist conviction of grand-narrative as well as western reading techniques of historical criticism in order to ascertain the single objective meaning of the Christian Bible;[2] the Orientalist mode advocates the promotion and revival of the native texts and constructs local history and civilization as a preparation for biblical faith. In the case of India, Sugirtharajah observes that the Orientalist policy was 'instigated partly as a way of effectively controlling and managing the Indian people'.[3] He further notes that 'the Orientalist invocation of a lost Golden Age of Indian civilization based on ancient Sanskrit texts and Sanskritic criticism continues to act as a fertile cultural site for Indian Christian biblical interpretation'.[4] One of the consequences of the Orientalist effort is the re-moulding of India under the highly literary Brahman Hindu culture, which privileges the Sanskrit texts over the vernacular and folk tradition of the common people.

Both the Orientalist and the Anglicist also exercised their impact in China. The alleged 'manufacturing of Confucianism' by the Jesuits in China is a parallel case in point.[5] Not only does Chinese culture come to be equated almost exclusively with Confucian tradition, but also China possesses mainly a philosophical tradition that focuses on moral and ethical living with no substantive religious beliefs and practices. Buddhism is regarded as being imported from India and Taoism is mostly treated as a philosophy of nature and derogatively as a form of primitive religion. These misconceptions have given rise to the total neglect of the rich and elaborate indigenous religions of the people and consequently have done a lot of harm to an holistic understanding of Chinese culture. The Anglicist mode was operative in China at a time when 'Mr Science' and 'Mr Democracy' were warmly welcomed and put forward as the only

---

[2] Sugirtharajah, *Asian Biblical Hermeneutics and Postcolonialism*, pp. 8–12.
[3] *Ibid.*, p. 4.   [4] *Ibid.*, p. 5.
[5] Lionel M. Jensen, *Manufacturing Confucianism: Chinese Traditions and Universal Civilization* (Durham, NC: Duke University Press, 1997).

two saviours for the future of China, in the reconstruction of the nation in the face of defeats and humiliation under the colonial powers, in the earlier part of the twentieth century. Some liberal Christians under the influence of western science and democratic thought aspired to follow the scholarship of historical criticism in biblical studies. A liberal group of Christian intellectuals who established *Wenshe* (the shortened form in Chinese for National Christian Literature Association of China) attempted to introduce western literary and historical tools to China. Its members were in favour of not only a scientific examination of the Bible but also 'suggested that all myths and "superstitions" be deleted from the Bible'.[6] This belief in the objectivity of science also applied to the native culture and its texts.

Sugirtharajah's third mode of approach to the Bible and Asian texts is that of the nativist interpretation, which attempts to recover the vernacular forms as a corrective measure against the pitfalls of the first two modes. Though nativist interpretation has something to recommend it, Sugirtharajah rightly warns of its inherent tendency to idealize the indigenous tradition, privileging it as a pure, static and uncontaminated entity.[7] Sugirtharajah proposes that the postcolonial discourse assists the formerly colonized communities to resist the hegemonic claim of the Bible, to expose the implicit and explicit colonial codes in the text and to critique the imperial Eurocentric interpretation based on colonial ideology and practices. According to him, postcolonial reading is basically 'an emancipatory reading of the texts'[8] and he points out 'its advocacy of a wider hermeneutical agenda to place the study of sacred texts – Christian-Hindu, Christian-Buddhist, Christian-Confucian – within the intersecting histories which constitute them'.[9]

With Sugirtharajah's precise analyses of the three modes of relating the Bible to the Asian situation in colonial times and his passionate dedication to the postcolonial framework of reading as the backdrop, this chapter aims at exploring the hermeneutical issues of the encounter of 'the two texts' – the Bible and other Asian texts. Cross-textual biblical interpretation, which, I propose, is an appropriate approach to accommodate them and to facilitate a fruitful negotiation between them for the benefit

---

[6] Peter Chen-Mian Wang, 'Contextualizing Protestant Publishing in China: The Wenshe 1924–1928', in Daniel Bays (ed.), *Christianity in China: From the Eighteenth Century to the Present* (Stanford: Stanford University Press, 1996), p. 306.

[7] R. S. Sugirtharajah, *Asian Biblical Hermeneutics and Postcolonialism: Contesting the Interpretations* (Maryknoll: Orbis, 1998), p. 14.

[8] *Ibid.*, p. 19. [9] *Ibid.*, p. 23.

of the multi-scriptural Christian community of Asia, will be reiterated and expanded.[10]

The chapter is roughly divided into two parts. The first part will look at the Asian contexts through the two categories of socio-political aspects and religio-cultural dimensions. Biblical interpretation in terms of the socio-political struggle for liberation of the dalit and minjung will then be briefly presented, to be followed by an analysis of the multi-scriptural reality and its implications for biblical interpretation. The emphasis of the chapter will be placed on the proposal of cross-textual reading and its contribution to the issues of Christian identity and response to the plurality of religions in Asia. The focus on the written tradition in Asia does not intend in any way to undermine Asia's rich oral traditions, nor does it assume that hermeneutics in the textual framework is the only approach to the reading of the Bible.

Within the Asian pluralistic religious world, Asians have been used to having pluralistic scriptural traditions. The Indians and the Chinese in particular are in possession of numerous scriptural texts and have never established a doctrine of scripture that excludes others as pagan and unciv-ilized. Conversion to Christianity would not, therefore, present any serious conflict and dilemma to the local Christian converts, should there be enough space given to a spontaneous interaction and a mutual transformation without the imposition of the missionary's doctrinal prescription for a total submission to the absolute authority and exclusive claims of the Bible.

Asian Christians have been caught in the situation of having both the native scriptures (Text A) and a newly acquired biblical text (Text B), with great pressure from the Christian community to denounce the for-mer. They have to find ways to resolve the claims of the two texts which respects their loyalty as well as their identity.[11] It is imperative to accommodate the two texts in an appropriate way in order to ensure that the meaning of their life will not be fragmented or threatened by the conflict of the 'two worlds' embodied in them. The whole problematic of Asian hermeneutics is largely that while the newly-acquired Christian Bible began to provide them with a new meaning of life, Asian Christians could not completely sever their connection with their community and its

---

[10] A. C. C. Lee, 'Biblical Interpretation in Asian Perspective', *Asia Journal of Theology* 7.1 (1993), 35–9; A. C. C. Lee, 'Cross-Textual Interpretation and Its Implications for Biblical Studies', in Fernando F. Segovia and Mary Ann Tolbert (eds.), *Teaching the Bible: Discourses and Politics of Biblical Pedagogy* (Eugene: Wipf & Stock, 1995), pp. 247–54.

[11] A. C. C. Lee, 'Textual Confluence and Chinese Christian Identity: A Reading of Hanlin', *Duo Shu Chakana* 2 (2004), 93–107.

cultural–religious texts, which had nurtured and shaped their lives and continued to sustain and nourish their well-being.

THE ASIAN CONTEXT: SOCIO-POLITICAL STRUGGLES AND RELIGIOUS PLURALISM

When we approach the Asian context, there are two major observations: the socio-political reality of suffering and the religio-cultural characteristic of the plurality of religions and cultures. In this section, we will deal briefly with the social dimension first, to be followed by a more detailed analysis of the religious aspect.

Though suffering is universal and not exclusively the plight of Asian people alone, the reality of suffering in Asia in terms of its extensiveness, its magnitude and its far-reaching consequences on the bodies and minds of the people should not be overlooked or brushed aside lightly. Besides natural mishaps and hardships, there are economic exploitation, military violence and political oppression, coupled with the national machinery and the transnational corporations that deliberately violate human rights and transgress human dignity. There are romanticized views that have been presented to give a positive touch to sufferings in Asia. They attempt to uplift the rich spirituality and religiosity of Asian culture as being the result of a long history of experiences brought about by poverty and suffering. The representation of Asia as materially poor and spiritually rich should never be the excuse to push to the background the horrifying reality of pain and afflictions undergone and still being sustained by thousands of innocent human souls caught up in dehumanizing structures, and the ongoing colonial project still in active operation.

Because of the limit of space it is sufficient here just to look at two approaches to the reading of the Bible from the socio-political context of the suffering of the people: the dalit hermeneutics and the minjung interpretation of the Bible.

Dalit are the outcast and out-caste people of India who, under the religious sanction of Hinduism and its elitist monopoly, have been relegated to be the 'untouchables', inhumanly marginalized by society. Segregated social structures have been built to ensure that their rights are taken away from them and that they are cruelly pushed beyond the boundary of normal human community. Dalit Christians face the same oppression even within the Church.[12] In recent years dalit theologians

---

[12] James Massey, *Towards Dalit Hermeneutics: Re-reading the Text, the History and the Literature* (Delhi: ISPCK, 1994), pp. 38–68.

have attempted to re-read the Bible from the socio-cultural liberation perspective and to make sense of the text for the poor and oppressed dalits in their struggle to regain their freedom and humanity. Dalit hermeneutics is therefore a counter-hermeneutic, which challenges the classical religio-philosophical interpretation of Brahmanism that justifies the brutal caste system. Biblical interpretation that follows classical religions and philosophical principles, and uses their categories, has been heavily criticized by dalit interpreters as legitimizing the *status quo* and the social structure of India. The caste hierarchy, supported by Brahmin religious values, is usually endorsed by such an approach. Though similar to many other liberation hermeneutics based on Marxist economic analysis and class struggle, and on gender or racial discrimination, dalit hermeneutics is quite different in its Indian contextuality, in aiming at the dismantlement of the evil caste structure.[13]

While most of the dalit Christians are kept illiterate, the reading of the Bible as a written text with a logocentric orientation is inappropriate and irrelevant for them. Arul Raja, a dalit scholar, calls for orality as a model for approaching the Bible, in which 'the Bible should be carefully unencoded from the written text and uncoded in the form of oral dalit discourses'.[14] Such discourses are oriented towards an 'empirical mode of experiencing reality' and 'basically of the performative order'.[15] In terms of resources, dalits are accustomed to 'rich interpretations of the down-to-earth myths and symbols' and hence they are attracted to the world of apocalyptic literature which exhibits the symbolism of evil, the suffering of the marginalized and eschatological hopes.[16]

Korean minjung hermeneutics, taking seriously the historical experience of the people as the starting point of theological articulation, advocates an interactive socio-political interpretation of the Bible. Minjung interpretation has come to denote a theological construction that engages the plight and aspiration of the deprived and the exploited people, the minjung, a term which is not used to refer to the common folk in general. The specific theological usage constitutes the core concern of minjung theology, in the face of the raging brutality of post-war modernization, and the agonizing experience of the economic growth of Korea. Through an intensive study of the synoptic gospels, Ahn Byung-Mu (1921–97),

---

[13] M. Gnanavaram, 'Some Reflections on Dalit Hermeneutics', in V. Davasahayam (ed.), *Frontiers of Dalit Theology* (Delhi: ISPCK, 1997), pp. 329–35.

[14] A. Maria Arul Raja SJ, 'Some Reflections on a Dalit Reading of the Bible', in V. Devasahayam (ed.), *Frontiers of Dalit Theology* (Delhi: ISPCK, 1997), pp. 336–45 at p. 336.

[15] *Ibid.*, p. 338.   [16] *Ibid.*, p. 339.

a New Testament scholar, identifies the minjung tradition in the Bible. He avers that the *ochlos* surrounding Jesus in his day are the minjung. Concentrated research on the Gospel of Mark helps him to link this biblical minjung to the Korean minjung. Jesus' role with the minjung (*ochlos*) constitutes the focal point for understanding the minjung church of Korea in its striving for liberation and justice. Though the term 'cross-textual interpretation' has not been coined by minjung theologians and biblical scholars, they have recognized the importance of reading the biblical text in the Korean context, of using the notion of 'story' to describe the biblical material and the social experiences of minjung people suffering oppression and injustice. Being the subject rather than the object of history, the minjung must read the Korean socio-economic history from below.[17] A socio-scientific approach, coupled with a concern to take into account the present realities of the minjung, will certainly broaden the scope of the stories of the minjung, being retold in the light of the biblical story and minjung social biography, the living experiences of the minjung in their political struggle against the oppression of the ruling power.[18] The fusion of the story of the *han*-laden minjung and that of the struggle of the minjung in the Bible contributes to the process of mutual enlightenment of the two texts – the socio-political text of the social biography of the minjung and the portrayal of the minjung in the biblical text. The two stories illuminate one another in the retelling. Each of the stories are to be reread and reinterpreted, one in the light of the other.[19] Both the minjung and the biblical stories do exhibit 'the religious character' that enables them to be read together.[20] Nevertheless, there have

[17] The most helpful introductory book to the understanding of *minjung* theology is without doubt the collection of articles with an introduction by Daniel Preman Niles for the Commission on Theological Concerns of the Christian Conference of Asia, edited by Yong Bock Kim, *Minjung Theology: People as the Subjects of History* (Maryknoll: Orbis, 1983). For a very comprehensive summary of theological efforts in Asia, see the monumental volumes edited by John C. England *et al.*, *Asian Christian Theologies: A Research Guide to Authors, Movements, Sources from the Seventh to Twentieth Centuries*, vols. 1–3 (Maryknoll: Orbis, 2004).

[18] Y. B. Kim (ed.), *Minjung Theology: People as the Subjects of History* (Singapore: The Christian Conference of Asia, 1981), pp. 185–96.

[19] Daniel Preman Niles gives a brief summary of the varieties of minjung theologies and their biblical approaches in 'The Word of God and the People of Asia', in J. T. Butler, E. W. Conrad and B. C. Ollenburger (eds.), *Understanding the Word: Essays in Honour of Bernhard W. Anderson* (Sheffield: JSOT Press, 1986), pp. 281–313 at 284–95. Ahn Byung-Mu's identification of the *ochlos* (the motley crowd) in Mark's Gospel as the *minjung* over against the *laos*, a definable national or religious group, represents one of the ways of *minjung* appropriation of the Bible in a Korean context. See Ahn's article, 'Jesus and the *Minjung* in the Gospel of Mark', in Kim (ed.), *Minjung Theology*, pp. 138–52.

[20] Niles, 'The Word of God and the People of Asia', in Butler *et al.* (eds.), *Understanding the Word, Essays in Honour of Bernhard W. Anderson*, p. 296.

always been cautions from the minjung theological communities to guard against too fast a fusion of the two stories without a thorough examination of the tensions between them.

Dalit and minjung biblical interpretations are just two of those many approaches to the Bible from the perspective of the experience of the oppression of the people, who attempt to seek empowerment from their reading of the biblical text. Contextual socio-political sensitivity to the plight of the people is the point of departure, and the aim of biblical interpretation is largely communal liberation from social injustice imposed by oppressive socio-political structures. Biblical interpretations of the homeland theology of Taiwan, the theology of struggle in the Philippines and the tribal theology in northeast India operate within a more or less similar scope. The socio-political context has played a significant role in the understanding and criticism of the biblical text.

The second aspect of the notion of the Asian context is its plurality of living religions, which has caught the attention of Asian Christians, especially Christian intellectuals, from colonial times. Efforts have been made in various communities, in their own settings in Asia, to deal with the problematic of the hermeneutics of the encounter between Christianity and the Asian religions and their scriptures. Different solutions have been proposed, with a variety of terminology and conceptual frameworks. 'Indigenization', 'accommodation', 'acculturation', 'adaptation' and 'incarnation' are some of the well-known labels.[21] Since the independence movements of the fifties and sixties in the last century and the subsequent nation-building and social reconstruction projects in various Asian countries, these labels have given way to the more recent framework of 'contextualization', a term applied to theology by Shoki Coe of Taiwan.[22] With light shed by post-colonial and post-modern critical theories, this chapter attempts to re-visit the issue of the Bible and the plurality of religions, and to critically appropriate them in the proposed framework of a cross-textual reading process and the notion of identity.

It is a well-known fact that, when the Protestant missionaries brought the Christian Bible to Asia during the colonial enterprise in the nineteenth century, the Christian text was in the camp of the colonizer and was introduced to meet the multitude of scriptures through an imbalance

---

[21] Stephen B. Bevans, *Models of Contextual Theology* (Maryknoll: Orbis Books, 2002).

[22] S. Coe, 'Contextualizing Theology', in Gerald H. Anderson and T. F. Stransky (eds.), *Third World Theologies: Mission Trend No. 3* (New York: Paulist Press and Grand Rapids: Eerdmans, 2002), pp. 19–24; Virginia Fabella, 'Contextualization', in Virginia Fabella MM and R. S. Sugirtharajah (eds.), *Dictionary of Third World Theologies* (Maryknoll: Orbis, 2000), pp. 56–8.

of power, if the texts really met at all. The situation was very different from that of the earlier 'hidden history of Christianity'[23] when the Bible came mainly with believers in their individual capacity as merchants, traders, travellers or temporary settlers from west Asia, who usually did not mingle extensively with the local people nor present any military or cultural threat to the natives. Some of them stayed in small communities at the seaports in south Asia or along the Silk Road in central Asia. These Syrian forms of Christianity came to India (Mar Thoma Christians) and China (the Nestorians) in quite a peaceful manner with few reports of conflict. Both the Mar Thomas and the Nestorians adapted well to local religious forms. Buddhist concepts, Hindu ideas and Confucian terminology are used in their articulation of Christian doctrines. At the time of the Jesuit missions to Asia in the sixteenth century, accommodation to the native cultures was in general part of their policy, and the conflict between the Bible and Asian scriptures was not as severe as it became during the colonial era, since, among other socio-political reasons, the Catholics did not give the same significance to the Bible in their confession as compared with the Protestants, who were strongly influenced by the doctrine of *sola scriptura*.[24] Translation of the Bible into Asian languages was not therefore the primary task in the Jesuit mission, but it certainly constituted an indispensable part of the Protestant missionary endeavours.

Ever since the introduction of the Christian Bible to the pluralistic scriptural context of Asia, the hermeneutical issue of probing the meaning of 'the scripture and scriptures' has been one of utmost significance in Asian biblical interpretation.[25] The effects of the encounter of the Christian text with multiple religio-cultural texts in social relations and power dynamics were far-reaching. Most Protestant missionaries with a deep conviction of *sola scriptura* and a strong commitment to evangelical zeal would understandably claim the absolute authority and exclusive validity of the Word entrusted to them. They saw themselves as being commissioned by the Church to spread the Word to the 'heathens' and the 'pagan' world. Without attempting to learn and understand the other texts in context, they valiantly made the categorical proclamation of the idolatrous nature of all scriptures other than the Christian Bible, which alone

---

[23] John C. England *et al.*, *Asian Christian Theologies: A Research Guide to Authors, Movements, Sources*, 3 vols. (New Delhi: ISPCK; Quezon City: Claretian; Maryknoll: Orbis, 2002–2004).

[24] J. N. J. Kritzinger, 'The Function of the Bible in Protestant Mission', in Philip L. Wickeri (ed.), *Scripture, Community, and Mission: Essays in Honor of D. Preman Niles* (Hong Kong: CCA and London: CWM, 2002), pp. 20–45 at pp. 20–4.

[25] S. J. Samartha, *One Christ – Many Religions: Toward a Revised Christology* (Maryknoll: Orbis, 1991).

embodied the whole truth. The 'crash of authorities'[26] in the face of the plurality of scriptures was inevitable when the Christian text was proclaimed the sole authority over and against all other texts of scriptural status.[27]

Millions of Asian people have been nurtured and their lives sustained by the Asian scriptural traditions that provide ethical guidance and spiritual strength, not only to individual adherents of the religions concerned but also to the wider community. Fundamentally, the very social fabric and political order of these Asians are shaped by their scriptural insights. It is to no one's surprise that drastic political measures aimed at eradicating the power of traditional Confucian, Buddhist and Taoist claims on the mindset and practices of the Chinese people during the Communist Cultural Revolution (1967–77) did not succeed in getting rid of the age-old grip of Confucianism, Buddhism, Taoism and the syncretistic form of popular religion. The authority of the scriptures of these religio-cultural traditions, though being called into question and shaken at the very foundation, still functions to guide the social practices and the life orientations of most Chinese people. The fact of the matter is that the deep-rooted Chinese mentality has been formed by the syncretistic Chinese religious world.

Samartha, an Indian biblical scholar, comes to a succinct observation in his discussion of the Bible and the Asian multi-scriptural context, and his remarks are worthy of our serious pondering:

> To enter this multi-scriptural situation with the claim that the Bible 'is the only written witness to God's deeds in history' is to cut off all conversation with neighbors of other faiths in the world. This attitude makes it impossible for Christians to develop 'their own hermeneutics.' In a continent like Asia a claim for the supreme authority of *one* scripture can be met by a counter claim for similar authority for *another* scripture.[28]

Samartha's warning should be taken seriously in order to avoid having a detrimental effect on both the Asian scriptures and the Christian Bible. The multi-scriptural reality of Asia resists any claim of absolute authority and challenges the principles, purpose and practice of hermeneutics in the Asian context.[29] Most of the Asian scriptural traditions, be they Hindu, Buddhist, Confucian or Taoist, understand the notion of scripture and

---

[26] *Ibid.*, pp. 70–3.
[27] Samartha raises the highly complex hermeneutical concerns of the Asian churches and the larger Asian community in the chapter 'Scripture and Scriptures', *ibid.*, pp. 66–86.
[28] *Ibid.*, p. 76.
[29] S. J. Samartha, *The Search for a New Hermeneutics in Asian Christian Theology* (Bangalore: Board of Theological Education of the Senate of Serampore College, 1987).

scriptural authority differently from the Christian traditions, both Catholic and Protestant. The idea of a strictly closed canon with the final revelatory authority ascribed to a Christological understanding of the life and death of Jesus of Nazareth is basically foreign, if not totally strange, to the other Asian scriptural family members.[30]

It was not uncommon that in the historical processes of co-existence, quite a few of the Asian scriptures engaged with one another in constant inter-actions. Buddhist scriptures from India were translated into Chinese, accommodating Confucian conceptions and terminology. The Taoist canon and its scriptural commentaries employed Buddhist ideas. Even in conflict, criticism of and attacks on another tradition resulted in an interactive transformation and enriched articulations. Some commentarial works took a synthesized interpretive mode of reading other scriptural texts. The three religious traditions of China stand as good examples of cross-scriptural hermeneutics.[31] In the case of India, profound re-interpretations of the *prasthana-traya* (triple canon) of the *Upanishads, Brahmasutra* and *Bhag-avadgita* characterize the powerful renewal movements, bringing fresh meanings out of the text through the writing of commentaries.[32] The challenges from other religious texts coupled with the impact of contemporary political struggles shaped the commentarial world and enlarged the boundary of imagination.[33] The Qur'an also entered the religious worlds of India, Indonesia and China and produced rich and fruitful interactions with Asian texts. This observation on the interactive and dialogical relationship between Asian scriptures in historical processes will provide us with a critical stance to assess the current practice of reading the Bible in context.

THE PROBLEM OF THE TEXT–CONTEXT INTERPRETIVE MODE

The dynamics of text–context have gained currency in recent theology and biblical studies. Most scholars are familiar with this paradigm and assume

---

[30] Paul A. Rule, 'Does Heaven Speak? Revelation in the Confucian and Christian Traditions', in Stephen Uhalley Jr and Xiaoxin Wu (eds.), *China and Christianity: Burdened Past, Hopeful Future* (New York: M. E. Sharpe, 2001), pp. 63–79.

[31] Erik Zrcher, 'Buddhist Influence on Early Taosim: A Survey of Scriptural Evidence', *T'oung Pao* 66 (2002), 84–141.

[32] S. J. Samartha, *One Christ – Many Religions: Toward a Revised Christology* (Maryknoll: Orbis ,1991), p. 67.

[33] John B. Henderson, *Scripture, Canon, and Commentary: A Comparison of Confucian and Western Exegesis* (Princeton: Princeton University Press, 1991). The process of canonization of the Confucian scriptures in the time of the Han dynasty is characterized by the intense writing of commentary, see Sarah A. Queen, *From Chronicle to Canon: The Hermeneutics of the Spring and Autumn Annals According to Tung Chung-Shu* (Cambridge: Cambridge University Press, 1996), pp. 206–25.

that a text does not only have context of its own but also has to be interpreted in context. In a way this trend of thought should be readily recognized as it is beyond dispute that any language, history or cultural form which shapes our mindset is contextually formulated. But in the multi-scriptural Asian experience, the text–context interpretive mode has its intrinsic limitations and does not adequately address the reality of the plurality of scriptures and the co-existence of religious communities, since contextual biblical inter-pretation, as it is currently practised, embodies an ideological bias towards the mono-textual privileged status enjoyed by the Bible.

Taking the context of Asia seriously, George M. Soares-Prabhu, an Indian biblical scholar, invites us to be more sensitive to 'its frightening complexity and startling contrasts'.[34] He depicts the Indian context in terms of linguistic diversity, religious pluralism and massive economic poverty. He characterizes the enormous contrasts in this vivid portrayal:

The scandalous contrast between the great masses of India's poor and the tiny minority of the very rich finds a striking visual expression in Bombay's sprawling slums, stretching out endlessly in the shadow of high-rise luxury apartments and five-star hotels. Such economic disparity can lead to amusing juxtapositions of incongruous technologies. Bullock-carts trundle past atomic reactors; fortune-tellers ply a busy trade just outside institutes of advanced scientific research and scientists who split the atom and toss satellites into space arrange the marriages of their children by matching horoscopes, and celebrate them on astrologically determined auspicious days.[35]

The complexity of the Asian context exhibits both the impacts of modernization and globalization as well as traces of the traditional con-ceptions of the supernatural, human fate and social destiny, which are profoundly articulated in religious classics handed down from the past and still widely practised in daily rituals and rites. Context is not just a setting of the intersection of time and space; it is a conglomeration of texts in the conventional sense of written documents, as well as in the more elusive socio-scientific notion of historical events, peoples' movements, daily experiences and human actions in community as being 'social text'.[36]

The most acute criticism of the commonly practised mode of the interpretation of text and context in Asian biblical hermeneutics is

---

[34] G. M. Soares-Prabhu, 'Interpreting the Bible in India Today', in Francis D'Sa (ed.), *Theology of Liberation: An Indian Biblical Perspective: Collected Writings of George M. Soares-Prabhu, SJ*, vol. IV (Pune: Jnana-Deepa Vidypeeth, 2001), pp. 3–13 at p. 6.

[35] *Ibid.*, pp. 6–7.

[36] A. C. C. Lee, 'Engaging the Bible and Asian Resources: Hermeneutics of the Globalized in the Global-Local Entanglement', *Journal of Theologies and Cultures in Asia* 2 (2003), 5–30.

expressed in the following rhetorical questions formulated by D. Preman Niles, a Sri Lankan theologian trained in the Old Testament field: 'Is theology always a matter of relating text to context? Is it not also a matter of relating context to text so that the context may speak to the text? Is Asia there to receive? Has it nothing to contribute?'[37]

Niles succinctly pinpoints the pivotal debate in the Asian reading of the Christian Bible, whose exclusivity and hegemonic status presents itself not only as an unyielding giant, but also as an intolerant iconoclast, bringing massive destruction to Asian cultures and religions. The Asian context is usually pre-empted in its legitimate truth claims and religious contents. To many practitioners of the contextual interpretation of the Bible, the context only functions as the medium through which the meaning of the biblical text is to be understood. Translation of the text in the language of the context and communicating the gospel in terms of the cultural peculiarities become the two major preoccupations of most contextual work. Niles's implied concern with 'the Word of God' in Asian texts is most challenging and enlightening. In the questions: 'Is Asia there to receive? Has it nothing to contribute?' we hear an Asian quest for a full participation as the people of God in the world of God the creator and the God of history. Asia and its long history cannot be conceived as being denied the presence of God and divine revelation. The experiences of the people cannot be dismissed as 'pagan' and 'heathen' and therefore treated as being worthless and ignorant. The religious scriptures and classics which embody the spirituality of the people are not to be simply down-trodden as if of no value at all. To be true to the reality, the 'context' of Asia must be seen in terms of the profundity and richness of the cultural and religious quest of the Asian people in their long historical journey and the present reality of life in its struggle for humanness. In a word, the Asian context contains multiple texts and is itself a text, contributing to the reading and enriching the meaning of the biblical text.[38]

[37] Niles, 'The Word of God and the People of Asia', in Butler *et al.* (eds.), *Understanding the Word: Essays in Honour of Bernhard W. Anderson*, p. 282.

[38] A. C. C. Lee, 'Genesis 1 From the Perspective of a Chinese Creation Myth', in A. Graeme Auld (ed.), *Understanding Poets and Prophets: Essays in Honour of Professor George Anderson* (Sheffield: Sheffield Academic Press, 1993), pp. 186–98; A. C. C. Lee, 'Theological Reading of Chinese Creation Stories of Pan Ku and Nu Kua', in John C. England and Archie C. C. Lee (eds.), *Doing Theology and Asian Resources* (Auckland: Pace Publishing, 1993), pp. 230–37; A. C. C. Lee, 'The Chinese Creation Myth of Nu Kua and the Biblical Narrative in Genesis 1–11', *Biblical Interpretation* 2 (1994), 312–24; A. C. C. Lee, 'Death and the Perception of the Divine in Zhuangzi and Koheleth', *Ching Feng* 38 (1995), 68–81.

Reconciling the existence of the Asian text (Text A) and the biblical text (Text B) and seeking ways to appropriate them require us to construct a broader framework of meaning to accommodate different religious perspectives.[39] Niles sees in this a better chance of a deeper search for and an engendering of meaning in the interplay of these perspectives, which does not necessarily lead to polarization.[40]

Aloysius Pieris, a Sri Lankan Christian–Buddhist scholar, is convinced that biblical interpretation in Asia must acknowledge and take into account scriptures of other Asian religions in their search for the divine– human encounter and the 'God-experience' in the human concern for liberation praxis. He sees theology and biblical interpretation as oriented towards praxis ('theopraxis') and seeking mutuality and harmony between '*God-experience* which is silence and the *man-concern* which makes it heard'.[41] Pieris characterizes Asian religions in terms of mutuality of praxis and theory and further urges theological articulation in Asia to reconcile and engage with the plurality of Asian religions and the social-political struggle for liberation of the poor. Pieris has implemented *theopraxis* in reading the Bible and Tripitaka in seminars for Buddhist–Christian dialogue groups that he has conducted in Sri Lanka in the last twenty years or so. He summed up very well the different approaches to understanding the Bible and other scriptures under the suggested rubric of 'cross-scriptural reading', when he was invited to write on his experience.[42]

He proposed three major approaches, grouping together some present efforts at such a reading: the extra-contextual confrontation of text, the liturgical appropriation of text, and the symbiotic encounter of text. In the extra-contextual confrontation of text, Pieris underlines the easy equation of the two scriptures by de-contextualizing the two texts under study. He identifies the superficial comparison as an irenic approach, achieving similarity of ideas and messages without respecting the difference

[39] A. C. C. Lee, 'Cross-Textual Interpretation and its Implications for Biblical Studies', in Segovia and Tolbert (eds.), *Teaching the Bible*, pp. 247–54; A. C. C. Lee, 'Cross-textual Hermeneutics on Gospel and Culture', *Asia Journal of Theology* 10 (1996), 38–48; A. C. C. Lee, 'Weaving a Humanistic Vision: Reading the Hebrew Bible in Asian Religio-Cultural Context', in Leonard J. Greenspoon and B. F. Le Beau (eds.), *Sacred Text, Secular Times: The Hebrew Bible in the Modern World* (Omaha, Nebraska: Creighton University Press, 2000), pp. 283–95.

[40] Niles, 'The Word of God and the People of Asia', in Butler *et al.* (eds.), *Understanding the Word: Essays in Honour of Bernhard W. Anderson*, p. 301.

[41] Aloysius Pieris, 'The Asian Sense in Theology', in John England (ed.), *Living Theology in Asia* (London: SCM Press, 1981), pp. 171–6 at p. 175.

[42] Aloysius Pieris, 'Cross-Scripture Reading in Buddhist-Christian Dialogue: A Search for the Right Method', in Philip L. Wickeri (ed.), *Scripture, Community and Mission* (Hong Kong: Christian Conference of Asia, London: The Council for World Mission, 2003), pp. 234–55.

of paradigms in the two texts.[43] This approach to Asian biblical interpretation is therefore a superficial comparative method of bringing the
biblical text together with an Asian text, wherein a comparable situation,
event, or theme forms the contact point between the two texts. The
similarities in both texts are illuminated, but it is more often than not that
the philosophical concepts are compared and contrasted without
acknowledging their respective context.[44] Pieris's symbiotic approach to
the reading of texts stresses the living encounter of religions, 'resulting in a
further articulation of implicit meanings which these texts would not
reveal unless they are mutually exposed to each other's illuminating discourses'.[45] Examples are cited, by Pieris, for the reciprocal significance of
cross-scriptural reading in the mutual illumination of the biblical text by
the Buddhist scriptures and vice versa.[46]

Asian Christians inherit two textual traditions – that of the native Asian
scriptures and that of the newly acquired Christian Bible. This fact should
exert a great challenge to the hermeneutical task and compel Asian
Christians to develop a new interpretive approach. Samartha further infers
that 'if this fact is taken seriously Asian Christians could provide a bridge
through which the insights of different scriptures might be shared in the
larger community'.[47] The obstacle to the realization of an enriched religious world embodied in scriptures is, among other political and institutional factors, the preconceived presupposition of the supremacy of the
Bible in Christian understanding, which assumes an absolute authority
and an exclusive truth-claim of the Christian text that is set against the
unreality and idolatrous perversion of other religions. Such an antagonistic attitude makes it impossible for Asian Christians to quest for a new
hermeneutics that could both enhance Asian theological construction and
enrich the larger global community, in the search for an integrated human
spirituality and harmonious social order for humanity as a whole.

With the extended view of the notion of scripture that comes to terms
with the multiplicity of scriptural traditions in Asia, it is only natural that
the Bible entering the world of religion in Asia does by no means hold sway
over the other scriptural texts; and it is definitely imperative that it be read
cross-textually with other members of the scriptural family of humankind.

---

[43] *Ibid.*, p. 235.
[44] Khiok-Khng Yeo, 'Amos (4:4–5) and Confucius: The Will (Ming) of God (Tien)', *Asia Journal of Theology* 4 (1990), 472–88.
[45] Pieris, 'Cross-Scripture Reading in Buddhist-Christian Dialogue: A Search for the Right Method', in Wickeri (ed.), *Scripture, Community and Mission*, p. 244.
[46] *Ibid.*, pp. 244–53. [47] Samartha, *One Christ – Many Religions*, p. 75.

READER, IDENTITY AND CROSS-TEXTUAL INTERPRETATION

Reading scriptures, according to Soares-Prabhu, involves dialogical exchanges between the reader and the text, where each is open to the claims of the other. The reader, bringing his/her pre-understanding and contextual concerns to the Bible, must 'respect both the historical distance of the text and specificity of the religious experience it seeks to communicate'.[48] Soares-Prabhu advocates a different method of reading the biblical text when the alleged standardized historical critical method is shown to be 'ineffective, irrelevant and ideologically loaded'.[49] The inadequacy of historical criticism prompts him to seek for a 'cross fertilization of modern methods of biblical exegesis with the Indian exegetical tradition'.[50]

Based on Soares-Prabhu's discontent with historical criticism in interpreting the Bible and the multi-scriptural Asian milieu, Moon-Jang Lee proposes a fresh approach which aims at the fusion of the western academic historical–critical method and the Asian intuitive reading of the Bible.[51] In order to build a wider framework of interpretation to facilitate the reading of the Christian Bible in the midst of other Asian scriptures, this has been a constant call for making use of the principles of interpretation in the Asian philosophical and religious traditions.[52] Samartha also calls our attention to the long history of hermeneutical and exegetical traditions in Asia that have developed independently of the impact of western Christian interpretive tools.[53] There are, however, problems with these Asian hermeneutical tools, which originated from abstract philosophical traditions, born out of historical contexts that are mostly biased towards the ruling and the literary class, as revealed by dalit and minjung interpretation.

Asian biblical interpretation does not seek for mere information from the past, which historical criticism may shed relevant light upon. In a way,

[48] Soares-Prabhu, 'Interpreting the Bible in India Today', in D'Sa (ed.), *Theology of Liberation*, p. 5.
[49] George M. Soares-Prabhu, SJ, 'Toward an Indian Interpretation of the Bible', in I. Padinjarekuttu (ed.), *Biblical Themes for a Contextual Theology Today: Collected Writings of George M. Soares-Prabhu SJ* (Pune: Jnana-Deepa Vidyapeeth, 1999), pp. 207–22 at p. 208. The article was originally published in *Biblebhashyam* 6 (1980), 151–70.
[50] Soares-Prabhu, in D'Sa, (ed.), *Theology of Liberation*, p. 216.
[51] Moon-Jang Lee, 'A Post-Critical Reading of the Bible as a Religious Text', *Asia Journal of Theology* 14 (2000), 272–85.
[52] In the case of India, K. P. Aleaz has provided a summary of different efforts in understanding Christian ideas through Indian traditions: K. P. Aleaz, *Christian Thought Through Advaita Vedanta* (Delhi: ISPCK, 2000); and R. S. Sugirtharajah and Cecil Hargreaves have edited a collection of articles on Indian Biblical hermeneutics in part 4 of *Readings in Indian Christian Theology* (London: SPCK, 1993).
[53] Samartha, *One Christ – Many Religions*, p. 68.

historical criticism may lend a helping hand in the reconstruction of the past, but historical data are not all that readers are concerned with in reading a religious text. Furthermore, practitioners of the method often admit that 'what lies behind the text' (what really happened?) and 'what the authorial intention was' (what exactly was said?) are extremely difficult, if not impossible, to recover. The shift from the author to the reader and from the past to the present is a challenging movement that modern readers of the Bible, as a religious classic, in search of the meaning of existence and in quest of practical liberation, would be ready to affirm.[54]

David Tracy has shed some light on our understanding of religious classics, one of the characteristics of which is their 'excess of meaning'. He asserts that '[e]very classic lives as a classic only if it finds readers willing to be provoked by its claim to attention'.[55] The readers do not repeat but interpret a classic from their own contexts and with their pre-understandings. The act of interpretation is therefore considered absolutely necessary and fully public by Tracy, who acknowledges the process of retrieval of tradition and critical appropriation in the present. He further assumes that both text and reader are never static realities but realities-in-process.[56] Through the reading of classics the reader is confronted, surprised, shocked and challenged.[57] In the process of interpreting the classics the readers are interpreted as well. Classics embody the cultural experience of human reality and 'disclose a compelling truth about our lives'.[58] In them lies the realized experience, the memory of the past and the hope for the future.[59] There is, therefore, recognized 'remarkable resonances, even profound continuities, between many of the major literary and religious classics and expression in the culture'.[60] Religious classics open up a world of meaning and truth experienced in historical human context. The contextuality does not set a limit and constraint but profoundly relates to the whole of reality. With a continuous effort of interpretation, religious classics empower and transform the interpreters. Tracy uses the notion of conversation to bring out the dynamics of interpretation in reading scriptures. The quality of a demand for attention resting in a classic invites constant interpretation but resists a fixation of

---

[54] Soares-Prabhu, 'Interpreting the Bible in India Today', in D'Sa (ed.), *Theology of Liberation*, p. 4.
[55] D. Tracy, *The Analogical Imagination: Christian Theology and the Culture of Pluralism* (London: SCM Press, 1981), p. 103.
[56] *Ibid.*, p. 105. [57] *Ibid.*, p. 107. [58] *Ibid.*, p. 108.
[59] According to Tracy, the act of new interpretation is awaited by classics, and it is not only social and communal but also dialogical, *ibid.*, pp. 115–24.
[60] *Ibid.*, p. 134.

meaning and an absolute certainty. The excess of meaning and the radical otherness will open up the possibility of 'similarity-in-difference' and leads to 'an analogical imagination'.[61] The contemporary affirmation of plurality of lived experiences and diversity of contexts inevitably generate a variety of interpretations of the Bible.[62] Here the shift from the text to the reader must be underlined. Paul Ricoeur believed strongly that the process of composition was not completed in the text, but in the reader, in whom the reconfiguration of life is made possible by narrative. Ricoeur puts his position precisely and concisely in the following words:

I should say, more precisely: the sense or the significance of a narrative stems from the *intersection of the world of the text and the world of the reader*. The act of reading thus becomes the critical moment of the entire analysis. On it rests the narrative's capacity to transfigure the experience of the reader.[63]

While cross-textual interpretation aims at addressing the reader, for Asian Christians in the context of multi-scriptural Asia, neither the historicity nor the literary characteristics of the text is the primary concern. Simon Kwan, a young theologian from Hong Kong, rightly criticizes the inadequacy of both the literalist mode (text-oriented) and the contextual approach (context-oriented) in Asian hermeneutics. He summarizes the alternatives attempted by some Asian scholars under the rubrics of the interpreting subject 'who mediates between the text and the context'.[64] Cross-textual reading, which Kwan classifies under his framework of the interpreting subject, finds its primary location in the reader in community, which seeks to make sense of the Bible in the midst of a religiously plural neighbourhood facing both the impacts of globalization and the rising new forms of colonialism. The reading community is therefore the subject who has to negotiate meaning from the dialogical interactive interplay of the multiple texts under its custodianship. We must reiterate that the well-defined and restricted notion of text has been called into question and the boundary of any text must extend well beyond the traditional literary form and its immediate context. No text should hold sway over

---

[61] *Ibid.*, pp. 445–57; David Tracy, *Plurality and Ambiguity: Hermeneutics, Religion, Hope* (Chicago: University of Chicago Press, 1987), p. 20.

[62] David Tracy, 'Reading the Bible: A Plurality of Readers and a Possibility of a Shared Vision', in D. Tracy (ed.), *On Naming the Present: Reflections on God, Hermeneutics and Church* (London: SCM and Maryknoll: Orbis, 1994), pp. 120–30.

[63] Paul Ricoeur, 'Life in Quest of Narrative', in David Wood (ed.), *On Paul Ricoeur: Narrative and Interpretation* (London and New York: Routledge, 1991), pp. 20–33 at p. 26 (original italics).

[64] S. Kwan, 'Asian Critical Hermeneutics Amidst the Economic Development of Asia', *PTCA Bulletin* 11:1 (1998), 4–13 at 5.

other texts. The mono-textual supreme status of the Bible must be challenged and the local texts, too, should not have any overpowering claim. The two texts should be subjected to a vigorous and down-to-earth critical appraisal by readers who seek a renewed configuration of the identity of Asian Christians in a wider community.

Since the other Asian scriptures have been disgracefully pushed aside or embarrassingly discredited for some time, simply rescuing them from their present powerless status and enthroning them again is a hopelessly retro-spective effect. In an age of dynamic changes and fluidity a static authentic identity recovered from the past or simply constructed from a narrowly defined localized site is never a desirable alternative to the apparently ambiguous and multivalent identities that may have bothered some in this globalized village. But the fact of the matter is that, while almost everybody nowadays is in possession of dual, triple or multiple identities and reli-giously 'almost everybody is everywhere',[65] no one should dream of a pure identity fossilized or frozen in the past. The way forward in biblical studies for the Asian religious community is what Wai-Ching Angela Wong proposed in the inaugural address of the Congress of Asian Theologians (CATS). According to her, hybridity is the key to the Asian theological agenda of the twenty-first century and to the construction of the identity of Christian community in Asia. It helps theology and biblical interpretation to go beyond the binary opposite of east and west, which sees Asian identity in the category of difference constructed and designated by the west.[66]

Sugirtharajah also affirms the positive contribution of 'the post-colonial category of hybridity as a potential tool' in working out a Christian theological discourse in the Indian/Asian context. In his words, the pro-posal will address the issue of Christian identity in Indian theology and the Indian Church in responding to the challenge of religious pluralism:

The postcolonial notion of hybridity is not about the dissolution of differences but about renegotiating the structure of power built on differences. It is not synonymous with assimilation. Assimilation is something that the colonialists, and later the na-tivists, advocated. It is a two-way process – both parties are interactive, so something new is created. Living in multiple contexts means reforming the Christian identity. In this way, it will be accepted as complementary to other religious discourses in India and as a companion in the search for truth and religious harmony.[67]

---

[65] Mark Juergensmyer, *Global Religions: An Introduction* (Oxford: Oxford University Press, 2003), p. 4.

[66] W. C. Wong, 'Postcolonialism', in Fabella and Sugirthararjah (eds.), *Dictionary of Third World Theologies*, pp. 169–70.

[67] R. S. Sugirtharajah, *Postcolonial Reconfigurations: An Alternative Way of Reading the Bible and Doing Theology* (St. Louis: Chalice Press, 2003), p. 26.

As pastor of a grass-roots Christian church in a local parish of Hong Kong in the 1970s, I personally witnessed the dichotomy in the Christian community. At the times of birth, marriage and death, the congregation fell back to traditional values, customs, beliefs and ethoses. The Christian faith and its symbols just could not cope with the life situations at hand. Christianity failed to address the emotions and feelings of loss and bereavement; it did not adequately provide or contain the understanding of life fit for the life situation. I remember vividly funerals where the congregation reverted to traditional Chinese practices regarding veneration and the taboos of the dead. Beliefs in the world of the ancestors and its close link with the living were still alive despite years of vigorous Christian education. After these many years of Christianization and modernization, the religio-cultural texts supposedly eliminated from the community of Asian Christians are still in operation. They may be idling and inactive at times, when it comes to matters concerning the Christian faith, but they will pop up and claim their legitimacy in the daily interaction with the non-Christian world and in times of crisis.

In the religious world of the Chinese, the beliefs in the world of ghosts and spirits, *yin* and *yang*, *feng-shui*, fate and destiny as well as the realm of the dead and its impact on the living permeate different aspects of daily life and cultural practices.[68] Given the syncretistic approach to religion in the Chinese popular religious sphere, there is little wonder that in Christian funerals, wedding feasts and birth celebrations, traditional customs survive in various forms and creep into the supposedly triumphant world of the Christian gospel.[69] Should Chinese Christians continue to be in this situation of guilt, timidly hiding some of these unorthodox practices 'under the carpet'? Should the pastors go on pretending that they do not see or hear what happens behind the scenes in a Christian funeral? How long do we have to function as a split self, having to play with one 'text' at one time and the other in a different setting? Asian Christians can no longer live with integrity when the 'two texts' are held in different compartments. Somehow there needs to be an integrative process and a creative interface as well as a dialogical relation between

[68] A. C. C. Lee, 'The "Aniconic God" and Chinese Iconolatry', in Yeow Choo Lak (ed.), *Doing Theology with Religions of Asia* (Singapore: The Association for Theological Education in South East Asia, 1987), pp. 33–57; A. C. C. Lee, 'Syncretism from the Perspectives of Chinese Religion and Biblical Tradition', *Ching Feng: A Journal on Christianity and Chinese Religion and Culture* 39:3 (1996), 1–24.

[69] I understand that in the Christian west, the gospel has been variously contextualized, having local 'pagan' practices brought in to 'enrich' it; European Christianity can, therefore, in no way claim to be pure and original.

them. In the long run and for a healthy lived self, the 'suppressed text' must not be left unattended; the cross-textual interpretation is an attempt to address this issue concerning the Christian community in Asia. It attempts to achieve a new configuration of the identity of the reader and facilitate Asian Christians to live in an open community with active interaction with their multi-religious neighbourhood.

CONCLUSION

Literalism in an approach to the Bible and exclusivism in religious vision are dangerous in multicultural and pluralistic religious contexts; they only foster ethnic conflicts and terrorism. The three monotheistic faiths, which locate ultimate truth and divine revelation in the written word and its prescribed fixed meaning, have had in their collective history constant violence and strife. The expression 'your Book (Koran) against my Book (Torah) against her and his Book (the New Testament)'[70] vividly illustrates the power of the scriptures over their respective adherents and the crux of textual hegemony. A series of questions relating to the problem of the claim for absolute authority of the Christian Bible are raised further by David Miller: 'Why earthen vessels are then mistaken for golden bowls? Why my book, with my construction of its meaning, is paraded, in military-style, infallible, over against the books of others? Why human systems of meaning are granted divine status?'[71]

People of Asia actually experienced in their own history the destructive force of the 'divine word' coupled with a triumphant mentality nurtured by the religion of the book developed in Christianity. Although one should always seek ways to go beyond the tragic onslaught of one's historical experience, the assault of the Bible on Asian scriptures must not be taken too lightly or without thorough investigation into the problematic of book-based religion in the multi-scriptural reality of the Asian scene.

As has been shown, the boundaries of Asian texts, which serve as sacred religious texts to adherents of certain communities, are seldom clearly drawn. The ambiguity allows co-existence and invites cross-reading and confluence. To a greater or lesser extent adherents find borrowing and adaptation between texts of different religious traditions not only bearable, but also encouragingly fruitful. Conglomeration of diverse elements taken from these texts bespeaks not only a textual phenomenon

---

[70] David L. Miller, 'The Question of the Book: Religion as Texture', *Semeia* 40 (1987), 53–64 at 53.
[71] *Ibid.*, p. 62.

of cross-scriptural reading but also intense community neighbourliness. Harmonious inter-religious encounters are characterized by creative tension as well as effective resistance. At the end of a long interactive process, cross-textual enhancement and enrichment will revitalize the scriptural traditions concerned and transform them into new re-configured texts.

Biblical studies, taking on board the non-Christian scriptures of Asia, will make a strong declaration of the minority status of the Christian community in Asia in order to embrace the potential divine inspirational nature of other scriptures. This will eventually broaden the scope and renew the vitality of Christian biblical interpretation and theological discourse which, according to Soares-Prabhu, has remained 'disappointingly parochial'.[72] Commenting on the Catholic theologians (though this is equally true, if not more so, of the Protestant scholars), he states further:

Catholic theologians theologize in happy ignorance of religious traditions other than their own, almost as if the affluent, post-Christian world of the West were man's only achievement and God's only concern. Such ethnocentrism in Christian theology was understandable enough in the cultural isolation of the Middle Ages, or the cultural aggressiveness and arrogance of the colonial age. It is anachronistic today. For in our rapidly shrinking global village, the encounter of world religions is a sign of the times which no theologians can ignore with impunity.[73]

In this respect, cross-textual hermeneutics presses the religious community and the discipline of biblical studies for the acknowledgement of a plurality of embodiments of truth and meaning. The biblical text cannot force its way, as it once did under the colonial power, to ignore and undermine Asian cultures and their religious texts. Cross-textual reading aims at achieving an iconoclastic role for the Bible; it enables the Christian community to open itself up to multi-textuality and the plurality of faiths. The Bible has to constantly engage and negotiate with other scriptures in order to shape a Christian identity in a multi-scriptural context, which is, as it should be, ambiguously hybrid in a postmodern and postcolonial global setting; but still it is empowering and life-sustaining.

BIBLIOGRAPHY

Ahn, B-M., 'Jesus and the Minjung in the Gospel of Mark', in Y. B. Kim (ed.), *Minjung Theology: People as the Subjects of History*, Maryknoll: Orbis, 1983, pp. 138–52.

---

[72] Soares-Prabhu, 'Interpreting the Bible in India Today', in D'Sa (ed.), *Theology of Liberation*, p. 98.
[73] *Ibid.*, pp. 98–9.

Aleaz, K. P., *Christian Thought Through Advaita Vedanta*, Delhi: ISPCK, 1996.

Arul Raja, A. M., SJ, 'Some Reflections on a Dalit Reading of the Bible', in V. Devasahayam (ed.), *Frontiers of Dalit Theology*, Delhi: ISPCK, 1997, pp. 336–45.

Bevans, S. B., *Models of Contextual Theology*, revised edition, Maryknoll: Orbis, 2002.

Coe, S., 'Contextualizing Theology', in G. H. Anderson and T. F. Stransky (eds.), *Third World Theologies: Mission Trend No.3*, New York: Paulist Press and Grand Rapids: Eerdmans, 1976, pp. 19–24.

England, J. C., *Asian Christian Theologies: A Research Guide to Authors, Movements, Sources from the Seventh to Twentieth Centuries*, volumes 1–3, Maryknoll: Orbis, 2002–4.

Fabella, V., 'Contextualization', in V. Fabella MM and R. S. Sugirtharajah (eds.), *Dictionary of Third World Theologies*, Maryknoll: Orbis, 2002, pp. 56–8.

Gnanavaram, M., 'Some Reflections on Dalit Hermeneutics', in V. Devasahayam (ed.), *Frontiers of Dalit Theology*, Delhi: ISPCK, 1997, pp. 329–35.

Henderson, J. B., *Scripture, Canon, and Commentary: A Comparison of Confucian and Western Exegesis*, Princeton: Princeton University Press, 1991.

Jensen, L. M., *Manufacturing Confucianism: Chinese Traditions and Universal Civilization*, Durham, NC: Duke University Press, 1997.

Juergensmyer, M. (ed.), *Global Religions: An Introduction*, Oxford: Oxford University Press, 2003.

Kim, Y. B. (ed.), *Minjung Theology: People as the Subjects of History*, Maryknoll: Orbis, 1983.

Kritzinger, J. N. J., 'The Function of the Bible in Protestant Mission', in P. L. Wickeri (ed.), *Scripture, Community, and Mission: Essays in Honor of D. Preman Niles*, Hong Kong: CCA and London: CWM, 2002, pp. 20–45.

Kwan, S. M., 'Asian Critical Hermeneutics Amidst the Economic Development of Asia', *PTCA Bulletin* 11:1 (1998), 4–13.

Kwok, P-L., *Postcolonial Imagination and Feminist Theology*, Louisville: Westminster John Knox Press, 2005.

Lee, A. C. C., 'The "Aniconic God" and Chinese Iconolatry', in Y. C. Lak (ed.), *Doing Theology with Religions of Asia*, Singapore: The Association for Theological Education in South East Asia, 1987, pp. 33–57.

'Biblical Interpretation in Asian Perspective', *The Asia Journal of Theology* 7:1 (1993), 35–9.

'Genesis 1 from the Perspective of a Chinese Creation Myth', in G. Auld (ed.), *Understanding Poets and Prophets: Essays in Honour of Professor George Anderson*, Sheffield: Sheffield Academic Press, 1993, pp. 186–98.

'Theological Reading of Chinese Creation Stories of Pan Ku and Nu Kua', in J. C. England and A. C. C. Lee (eds.), *Doing Theology and Asian Resources*, Auckland: Pace Publishing, 1993, pp. 230–37.

'The Chinese Creation Myth of Nu Kua and the Biblical Narrative in Genesis 1–11', *Biblical Interpretation: a Journal of Contemporary Approaches* 2 (1994), 312–24.

'Cross-Textual Interpretation and Its Implications for Biblical Studies', in F. F. Segovia and M. A. Tolbert (eds.), *Teaching the Bible: Discourses and Politics of Biblical Pedagogy*, Eugene: Wipf & Stock, 1995, pp. 247–54.

'Death and the Perception of the Divine in Zhuangzi and Koheleth', *Ching Feng* 38 (1995), 68–81.

'Cross-Textual Hermeneutics on Gospel and Culture', *Asia Journal of Theology* 10 (1996), 38–48.

'The Recitation of the Past: A Cross-Textual Reading of Psalm 78 and the Odes', *Ching Feng* 38:3 (1996), 173–200.

'Syncretism from the Perspectives of Chinese Religion and Biblical Tradition', *Ching Feng* 39:3 (1996), 1–24.

'Lamentation in the Hebrew Psalter and the Chinese Shijing: A Cross-Textual Reading', *Ching Feng* 41 (1998), 249–73.

'Biblical Interpretation of the Return in the Postcolonial Hong Kong', *Biblical Interpretation: A Journal of Contemporary Approaches* 9 (1999), 164–73.

'Identity, Reading Strategy and Doing Theology', *Biblical Interpretation: A Journal of Contemporary Approaches* 9 (1999), 197–201.

'Weaving a Humanistic Vision: Reading the Hebrew Bible in Asian Religio-Cultural Context', in L. J. Greenspoon and B. F. Le Beau (eds.), *Sacred Text, Secular Times: The Hebrew Bible in the Modern World*, Omaha, Nebraska: Creighton University Press, 2000, pp. 283–95.

'Cross-Textual Hermeneutics', in V. Fabella, MM and R. S. Sugirtharajah (eds.), *Dictionary of Third World Theologies*, Maryknoll: Orbis, 2002, pp. 60–3.

'Engaging the Bible and Asian Resources: Hermeneutics of the Globalized in the Global-Local Entanglement', *Journal of Theologies and Cultures in Asia* 2 (2003), 5–30.

'Engaging Lamentations and the Lament for the South', in H. Hearon (ed.), *Distant Voices Draw Near: Essays in Honor of Antoneitte Clark Wire*, Collegeville: Liturgical Press, 2004, pp. 173–87.

'Textual Confluence and Chinese Christian Identity: A Reading of Hanlin', *Duo Shu Chakana* 2 (2004), 93–107.

Lee, M-J., 'A Post-Critical Reading of the Bible as a Religious Text', *Asia Journal of Theology* 14 (2000), 272–85.

Lenchak, T., SVD, 'The Function of the Bible in Roman Catholic Mission', in P. L. Wickeri (ed.), *Scripture, Community, and Mission: Essays in Honor of D. Preman Niles*, Hong Kong: CCA and London: CWM, 2002, pp. 3–19.

Massey, J., *Towards Dalit Hermeneutics: Re-reading the Text, the History and the Literature*, Delhi: ISPCK, 1994.

Miller, D. L., 'The Question of the Book: Religion as Texture', *Semeia* 40 (1987), 53–64.

Niles, D. P., 'The Word of God and the People of Asia', in J. T. Butler, E. W. Conrad and B. C. Ollenburger (eds.), *Understanding the Word: Essays in Honour of Bernhard W. Anderson*, Sheffield: JSOT Press, 1986, pp. 281–313.

Padinjarekuttu, I. (ed.), *Biblical Themes for a Contextual Theology Today: Collected Writings of George M. Soares-Prabhu SJ*, vol. I, Pune: Jnana-Deepa Vidyapeeth, 1999.

Pieris, A., SJ, 'The Asian Sense in Theology', in J. C. England (ed.), *Living Theology in Asia*, London: SCM Press, 1981, pp. 171–6.

'Cross-Scripture Reading in Buddhist-Christian Dialogue: A Search for the Right Method', in P. L Wickeri (ed.), *Scripture, Community and Mission*, Hong Kong: Christian Conference of Asia and London: The Council for World Mission, 2003, pp. 234–55.

Queen, S. A., *From Chronicle to Canon: The Hermeneutics of the Spring and Autumn Annals: According to Tung Chung-Shu*, Cambridge: Cambridge University Press, 1996.

Ricoeur, P., 'Life in Quest of Narrative', in D. Wood (ed.), *On Paul Ricoeur: Narrative and Interpretation*, London and New York: Routledge, 1991, pp. 20–33.

Rule, P. A., 'Does Heaven Speak? Revelation in the Confucian and Christian Traditions', in S. Uhalley Jr and X. Wu (eds.), *China and Christianity: Burdened Past, Hopeful Future*, Armonk: M. E. Sharpe, 2001, pp. 63–79.

Samartha, S. J., *The Search for a New Hermeneutics in Asian Christian Theology*, Bangalore: Board of Theological Education of the Senate of Serampore College, 1987.

One Christ – Many Religions: Toward a Revised Christology, Maryknoll: Orbis, 1991.

Soares-Prabhu, G. M., 'Toward an Indian Interpretation on the Bible', in I. Padinjarekuttu (ed.), *Biblical Themes for a Contextual Theology Today: Collected Writings of George M. Soares-Prabhu, SJ*, vol. I, Pune: Jnana-Deepa Vidyapeeth, 1999, pp. 207–22.

'Interpreting the Bible in India Today', in F. D'Sa (ed.), *Theology of Liberation: An Indian Biblical Perspective: Collected Writings of George M.Soares-Prabhu, SJ*, vol. IV, Pune: Jnana-Deepa Vidypeeth, 2001, pp. 3–13.

Sugirtharajah, R. S. and C. Hargreaves (eds.), *Readings in Indian Theology*, London: SPCK, 1993.

Sugirtharajah, R. S., *Asian Biblical Hermeneutics and Postcolonialism: Contesting the Interpretations*, Maryknoll: Orbis, 1998.

The Bible and the Third World: Precolonial, Colonial, and Postcolonial Encounters, Cambridge: Cambridge University Press, 2001.

Postcolonial Reconfigurations: An Alternative Way of Reading the Bible and Doing Theology, St. Louis: Chalice, 2003.

Tracy, D., *The Analogical Imagination: Christian Theology and the Culture of Pluralism*, London: SCM Press, 1981.

Plurality and Ambiguity: Hermeneutics, Religion, Hope, Chicago: University of Chicago Press, 1987.

'Reading the Bible: a Plurality of Readers and a Possibility of a Shared Vision', in D. Tracy (ed.), *On Naming the Present: Reflections on God, Hermeneutics and Church*, London: SCM Press and Maryknoll: Orbis, 1994, pp. 120–30.

Wang, P. C-M., 'Contextualizing Protestant Publishing in China: The Wenshe 1924–1928', in D. Bays (ed.), *Christianity in China: From the Eighteenth Century to the Present*, Stanford: Stanford University Press, 1996.

Wong, W-C. A., 'Asian Theology in a Changing Asia: Towards an Asian Theological Agenda for the Twenty-First Century', *CTC Bulletin*, special supplement (1997), 130–9.

  'Postcolonialism', in V. Fabella MM and R. S. Sugirtharajah (eds.), *Dictionary of Third World Theologies*, Maryknoll: Orbis, 2000, pp. 169–70.

  The Poor Woman: A Critical Analysis of Asian Theology and Contemporary Chinese Fiction by Women, New York: Peter Lang, 2002.

Yeo, K-K., 'Amos 4:4–5 and Confucius: The Will (Ming) of God (Tien)', *Asia Journal of Theology* 4 (1990), 472–88.

Zürcher, E., 'Buddhist Influence on Early Taosim: A Survey of Scriptural Evidence', *T'oung Pao* 66 (1980), 84–141.

CHAPTER 10

Re-constructing Asian *feminist theology:*[1] *toward a* glocal *feminist theology in an era of neo-Empire(s)*

Namsoon Kang

Feminism is a major philosophical, political, social and religious movement which requires a profound intellectual conversion ... It calls for a redefinition of power and authority and for a redistribution of power.

Kaye Ashe

To make the liberated voice, one must confront the issue of audience – we must know to whom we speak ... When I thought about audience – the way in which the language we choose to use declares who it is we place at the center of our discourse – I confronted my fear of placing myself and other black women at the speaking center.

bell hooks

PROBLEMATIZING 'ASIAN-WOMEN'

Asian feminist theology, like any other theology, is always in the making. The history of Asian theological engagement with feminism is in short supply and has not been explored in great detail in the various disciplines of theology over the last few decades. *Asian* feminist theology has emerged in the context of an ecumenical movement. Theologically trained women raised the issue of the invisibility of women in the Asian ecumenical

---

[1] I will use the word *Asian* in italics in *Asian* feminist theology to denote its contestable and stereotypical nature when it is used in different types of Asian theological discourses such as Asian feminist theology or Asian theology. As Asia can never be regarded as a monolithic entity, it is very often misleading and even distorting to define in a monolithic way that what constitutes Asia is 'overwhelming poverty' and 'multifaceted religiosity' in Asian discourse. For a more lengthy discussion of this issue, see Namsoon Kang, 'Who/What Is Asian: A Postcolonial Theological Reading of Orientalism and Neo-Orientalism', in Catherine Keller, Michael Nausner and Mayra Rivera (eds.), *Postcolonial Theologies: Divinity and Empire* (St. Louis: Chalice Press, 2004), pp. 100–117.

movement and its institutions. While western feminist theological discourse was developed by individuals with a theological and biblical critique of the sexist and patriarchal system both in theology and the
church,[2] *Asian* feminist theology did not raise a theological agenda *per se*
at the beginning of its development. The main issues were bringing
women out from invisibility to visibility in ecumenical organizations such
as the CCA (Christian Conference of Asia). The 'woman question' in
Christianity in Asia was first raised in 1977 at the Sixth Christian Conference of Asia (CCA) General Assembly in Penang with the following
statement:

Even though Christ restored the image of women, the church consciously and
unconsciously still refuses to accept the real status of women. It has almost
completely disregarded the wholeness which Christ has brought about.[3]

This statement was followed by an official request at the Seventh CCA
General Assembly in Bangalore, India, in 1981:

Asian women have remained backward and marginalized in all sectors of society.
Thus, women's concerns pose an enormous task for responsible Christians in
Asia. The Christian Conference of Asia can best respond to this challenge by
creating a specific program for women's concerns and appointing a full-time
executive staff.[4]

For the first time in the history of the CCA, the organization set up an
official Desk for Women's Concerns in 1981. The first anthology of Asian
feminist theology, *We Dare to Dream: Doing Feminist Theology As Asian
Women*, was published in 1990.[5] It is important to note, however, that
Asian feminist theological discourse written in English shows only a very
small part of what has been done in Asia simply because the majority of

---

[2] I do not intend to offer in this chapter an overall history of the development of feminist theological
discourse either in the west or in Asia. For more details on the historical development of the
women's movement and feminist theology in the west, see Rosemary Radford Ruether, *Women and
Redemption: A Theological History* (Minneapolis: Fortress Press, 1998), chapters 5, 6 and 7; and in
Asia, see Angela Wai Ching Wong, 'Women Doing Theology with the Asian Ecumenical
Movement', in Ninan Koshy (ed.), *A History of the Ecumenical Movement in Asia*, vol. II (Hong
Kong: CCA, 2004), pp. 85–114 and Pui-Lan Kwok, *Introducing Asian Feminist Theology* (Sheffield:
Sheffield Academic Press, 2000).

[3] Christian Conference of Asia, *Christian Conference of Asia Sixth Assembly, Penang* (Singapore: CCA,
1977), p. 103.

[4] Christian Conference of Asia, *Christian Conference of Asia Seventh Assembly, Bangalore* (Singapore:
CCA, 1981), p. 116.

[5] Virginia Fabella and Sun Ai Lee Park (eds.), *We Dare to Dream: Doing Theology as Asian Women*
(Maryknoll: Orbis, 1990).

Asians do not use English as their first language.[6] English, as an international language, privileges and benefits feminist theologians and scholars in the west and entitles them 'universal/global' and other people 'particular/local/vernacular'.

The major methodologies that Asian woman theologians adopted for their theological articulation, especially when writing in English as a second language, were case studies and storytelling of grassroots people. Storytelling can be used constructively to enable women to talk about personal experience. But it is meaningful only when such experience is placed in a wider theoretical and structural context. Such individual experience should be connected to a collective reality so that the storytelling and case studies can be a process of conscientization and politicization. What has been lacking in *Asian* feminist theological discourse is the theorization of such stories of Asian women. And there is a danger that this methodology of narrative can promote a construction of stories of Asian women's experience that becomes so normative that all experience that does not fit the model of 'normative' Asian women's stories is regarded as illegitimate.

In Asian feminist theological discourse, Asian feminist theologians have presented Asian women as a unitary group. Although this was politically unavoidable, especially at the initial phase of forming a coalition among them, there are underlying problems. The capacity to transform the concrete representations of women in theology and their condition in ministry has been hampered by an under-/mis-representation of the tremendously diverse reality of Asian women themselves. But in its primary stage of liberation from western discursive imperialism and in the process

---

[6] I am becoming more convinced that the use of English as an international language carries discursive imperialistic implications, especially in an era of globalization. The discursive hierarchy between English-speaking nations and non-English-speaking nations comes to take a form of discursive hegemony. Moreover, the strong tendency of the standardization of academic language only in the four former colonial languages – English, French, German and Spanish – in the US academia makes Asian look more inadequate for the production and reproduction of academic discourse. In the introduction to Asian feminist theology by Rosemary Radford Ruether, for instance, it is not even mentioned that the resources that are available in English must be only a part of the whole range of feminist discourse in Asia. For my criticism on this issue, see Kang, 'Who/ What Is Asian?', in Keller, Nausner and Rivera (eds.), *Postcolonial Theologies*, pp. 109–14.

In this era of globalization and of neo-imperialism, non-western academics do not have the luxury of ignoring what is happening in the US academy, because of its powerful influence on the global and local context of academic discourse and disciplinary structure. It seems hard to deny that English linguistic imperialism, by which I mean 'the dominance of English is asserted and maintained by the establishment and continuous reconstitution of structural and cultural inequalities between English and other languages', has been at work in the academy of the west. See Robert Phillipson, *Linguistic Imperialism* (Oxford: Oxford University Press, 1992), p. 47.

of its own theological construction, it is understandable that Asian women were characterized as a unified entity in terms of 'discriminated against, exploited, harassed, sexually used, abused',[7] who are pure victims of extreme poverty and exploitation. Asian women as 'pure victims' can be found in many early works by Asian feminist theologians. A typical example of this stereotyping of Asian women as 'pure victims' and Asian men as 'pure victimizers' is as follows:

Asian women are beaten by their fathers or sold into child marriage or prostitution. Asian women's husbands ... batter their wives ... Asian women's brothers ... often further their own higher educations by tacitly using their Asian sisters, ignoring the reality that their sisters are selling their bodies to pay for tuition.[8]

Ironically, these oversymplifying and homogenizing stories about Asian women, disseminated in English, seemed to enjoy a welcoming reception in the west rather than in Asian countries. For western readers, the satisfaction of these stories seems to derive from their depiction of the images of Asian women as totally different from the images of western women, but as entirely the same among Asian women themselves. Some Asian feminist theologians in the west cling, in their feminist theological discourse, to the stories and case studies of Asian grass-roots women and moralistically criticize 'the west' in the name of real 'Asian women's experience', while enjoying the privilege of living in the west. They become providers of knowledge about Asian women's 'authentic' experience and Asian culture, which is purported to be entirely different from the western version. In the process of discursive 'authenticization' of Asian women's experience, they contribute to the stereotyping of Asian women. As an Asian woman myself, I wish to problematize the very notion of 'Asian-women' and their stereotyped image as the point of ongoing struggle of liberation, because stereotyping a specific group of people is a primary form of oppression. It seems to me that the 'Asian-women' portrayed in the Asian feminist discourse, especially in English and not in vernacular language, are culturally essentialized.

Here it is worth noting that the gendered subject is 'simultaneously a racial, ethnic, and class-determined subject',[9] and that this subject occupies

---

[7] Virginia Fabella and Mercy Amba Oduyoye (eds.), *With Passion and Compassion: Third World Women Doing Theology* (Maryknoll: Orbis Books, 1988), p. 119.

[8] Hyun Kyung Chung, *Struggle to be the Sun Again: Introducing Asian Women's Theology* (Maryknoll: Orbis, 1990), p. 54.

[9] Teresa de Lauretis, *Technologies of Gender: Essays on Theory, Film, and Fiction* (Bloomington: Indiana University Press, 1987), p. 137.

different subject positions at different historical and cultural locations. Even among the same ethnic/gender/class group, heterogeneity, diversity and difference are hardly avoidable. When the notion of 'Asian-women' becomes a fixed image, Asian women's unified subjecthood can become more and more constraining rather than truly liberating.

DE-CONSTRUCTING THE MYTH OF ASIAN-WOMEN-NESS

When women began to realize that they had been silenced throughout human history, their first question was, Who are WE as women? In the early feminist movement in the west, this 'we-question' was based on the binary nature of 'men–the victimizer' and 'women–the victimized'. It did not take long, however, for them to realize that this 'we-question' was to be connected to the 'I-question'. Feminist women in the west soon realized that the 'we' – as the multiple 'I's – is not one but is divided by social class, race, sexual orientation, ethnicity, age, and religious affiliation, and that the 'We-ness' and 'I-ness' are inseparable. The articulation of the 'we-ness' of women was easily adopted by Asian feminist theologians because most Asian cultures have emphasized the significance of collectivity, the we-ness, rather than individuality, the I-ness. While feminist theologians in the west shifted their emphasis from the unified we-ness to the differentiated I-ness, *Asian* feminist theologians did not make such a shift.

In most Asian culture, especially Confucian culture, the individual is not central and there is no conception of individuality existing in the sense known to feminists in the west. In Confucian culture, the idea is not individual liberty or equality but order and 'harmony', not individual independence but communal 'harmony'. In this context, woman's claim for individual rights and freedom is against the purpose of society, which is not to preserve and promote individual liberty but to maintain the 'harmony' of the hierarchical and patriarchal order. This culture of patriarchal hierarchy, in the guise of harmony and communitarian virtue, makes it very hard for Asian women to make a shift from the unified, homogenized 'WE' into the multiple, heterogenized 'I's.[10]

Here I am not trying to perpetuate the stereotyped dichotomy of the individualist West versus communitarian Asia, especially as the very notions

---

[10] Cf. Louis Henkin, 'The Human Rights Idea in Contemporary China: A Comparative Perspective', in R. Randle Edwards, Louis Henkin and Andrew J. Nathan, *Human Rights in Contemporary China* (New York: Columbia University Press, 1986), pp. 7–40.

of individualism and communitarianism are contested. But it is undeniable, at least from my feminist perspective, that the individuality of Asian woman has been unthinkable, especially under Confucian culture. It is also significant to note that in Confucian practice, the notions of 'harmony' and 'relationality' between the members of the community are themselves very hierarchical in terms of gender, age, social status and familial rank, and are overtly androcentric.

A less visible but more critical problem in the positioning of 'Asian women' in a fixed image is related to the issue of 'representation', which deals with the question of whether Asian feminist theologians can truly represent less privileged Asian women by selecting particular stories of other 'oppressed' Asian women and telling 'their' stories on behalf of them. I agree with what Gayatri Spivak argues: that the authentic feelings of the subaltern once named will be misrepresented,[11] because of the multiple mediations of more powerful groups and institutions, both local and global.

If Asian women are portrayed as a unitary entity in Asian feminist theological discourse by feminist theologians both in the west and in Asia, feminist theologians are then repeating the 'misrepresentation' of women that they have criticized in patriarchal discourse, in which women have been named, portrayed as a unified subjecthood, and spoken on behalf of; women are thus misrepresented in their true situation as multiple and hybrid subjects. Women's life stories can be a powerful mechanism to convey authentic experiences and the relationship between the self and others, but only as long as the stories represent a 'process of struggling towards a particular consciousness'[12] that both reinterprets and remakes the world.

Asian feminist theology in the past did not succeed in offering theories of language, social location and gender capable of displaying the multiplicities of Asian women's being. Images of Asian women, the characterization of their 'authentic' experiences and the problematization of Asian women's reality as presented by Asian feminist theology in the past have been *geographically deterministic* and hence *culturally essentialist*. Hence, the tremendously diverse range of Asian women's experiences and

---

[11] Gayatri Chakravorty Spivak, 'Can the Subaltern Speak?', in Cary Nelson and Lawrence Grossberg (eds.), *Marxism and the Interpretation of Culture* (Urbana: University of Illinois Press, 1988), pp. 271–316.

[12] Susan Geiger, 'Women's Life Histories: Method and Content', *Signs*, 11:2 (1986), 334–51 at 348.

their theological quests were not portrayed. Two identities, 'woman' and 'Asian', dominated:

Asian women have also been raped, tortured, imprisoned, and killed for their political beliefs ... in the process of the struggle they are giving birth to a spirituality that is particularly *woman's* and specifically *Asian*.[13]

Asian women's theology is also *'very women.'* ... Asian women share all the blessings and the problems of being Asian and Third World people with Asian men. What distinguishes Asian women's struggle from the men of the continent is their *women-ness*. Asian women are oppressed economically, socially, politically, religiously, and culturally in specific ways just because they are women.[14]

This can be an example of the typical stereotyping of Asian women: either pure victims or heroic figures. Like all other forms of stereotypical images, the image of 'Asian-women' here has both an upgrading connotation and a degrading one. To imply that all Asian women suffer the same oppression simply because they are 'Asian women', is to lose sight of the many varied tools of patriarchy and to often unwittingly serve the patriarchal interest by failing to present a positive, alternative image of women except the victim-image. Making culturally essentialist overgeneralizations and a homogenization about Asian women's 'authentic' experience was the central weakness of Asian feminist theological discourse in the past. In this kind of Asian feminist theological discourse, which generalizes 'authentic' Asian women-ness, there are many 'theoretical diasporas'[15] among Asian women whose subjecthood is fundamentally overlooked, and who do not fit this 'authentic' image of Asian women. The huge discrepancy between the 'discursive Asian-women' and the 'real Asian-women' is hard to avoid.

AS-*DISCOURSE* AS A DISCURSIVE GROUND RECONSIDERED

> That she is herself
> Is more difficult than water is water
>
> *Kora Kumiko*[16]

Universality and particularity have been primary issues that feminist theories and practices have wrestled with from their inception. Feminists

---

[13] Mary John Mananzan and Sun Ai Park, 'Emerging Spirituality of Asian Women', in Fabella and Oduyoye (eds.), *With Passion and Compassion*, p. 79 (my italics).
[14] Chung, *Struggle to be the Sun Again*, p. 24 (my italics).
[15] Cf. Laura E. Donaldson, *Decolonizing Feminisms: Race, Gender and Empire-Building* (Chapel Hill and London: The University of North Carolina Press, 1992), p. 15.
[16] Cited in Kenneth Rexroth and Ikuko Atsumi (eds.), *Women Poets of Japan* (New York: New Directions Books, 1977), p. 123.

have emphasized the universality of women's victimization by patriarchy on the one hand, and the particularity of women, who are essentially distinctive from men on the other. Common ground among women and a universal sisterhood erupted in the late 1960s. In order to speak of women as victims of patriarchy, as being discriminated against on account of their biology, a woman has to be socially identifiable 'as-a-woman'. The underlying presupposition of this *as-discourse* is that underneath the possible differences among women there must be some shared experience and identity 'as-women' in a patriarchal world. The *as-discourse* appeared especially as a political pre-requisite for a coalition of the marginalized such as women. This *as-discourse* made women a collective entity 'as-victims' of patriarchy and 'as-sisters' in a universally patriarchal world. Feminist searching for a 'universal sisterhood' in the 1970s was therefore based either on a biological essentialism or on the social victimization of women under patriarchy.

But criticism emerged within the feminist circle, mostly on the part of black feminists who claimed that feminist searching for a universal sisterhood was in fact grounded on the experience of 'white' women and excluded the experience of 'non-white' women who suffer from racism and classism as well. In this regard, 'Black women are not white women with color.'[17] It is hard to deny that the search for the universal sisterhood in the 1970s tended to be *race-less* and *class-less*, as if the differences among women were threatening to the irrefutable fact that all women are some-how women, whereas racism and classism still overshadowed the everyday lives of the majority of women in the USA in particular and on the globe in general. Many began to call into question those feminisms that reduce domination to a single cause, focus exclusively on sexual difference and ignore women's differences as they intersect across other vectors of power, particularly with regards to race and class.[18] Non-white women began to raise their racial/ethnic voices using the same set of *as-discourse* but with a different focus – discourses of 'as-Asian', 'as-black' or 'as-Mujerista'.

The question of how to redefine difference for all women, which was raised in 1980 by Audre Lorde, came to the fore in feminist theological discourse. Lorde states that 'it is not our differences which separate women, but our reluctance to recognize those differences'.[19] Feminist difference

---

[17] Barbara Omolade, 'Black Women and Feminism', in Hester Eisenstein and Alice Jardine (eds.), *The Future of Difference* (New Brunswick: Rutgers University Press, 1985), pp. 247–57 at p. 248.

[18] bell hooks, *Talking Back* (Boston: South End Press, 1989), p. 23.

[19] Audre Lorde, *Sister Outsider: Essays and Speeches* (Trumansburg: Crossing Press, 1984), p. 122.

discourse emerging in the 1980s was twofold: women's difference from men, primarily based on biological essentialism, and the difference among women, primarily based on race and class. Multiple voices within the feminist theological discourse have been raised: feminist, womanist/black feminist, mujerista or Asian feminist theology.

The question of why racially white people, both men and women, do not use the discourse of 'as-white' even when white women express their victimization by sexism 'as-women', is very easy to answer: it is due to the mainstream-ness of their race in a national, regional and global level, even in the midst of the marginal-ness of their sex. It is like men not adopting the discourse of 'as-men'. What is it then to think of woman 'as-a-woman'? Is it really possible for us to think of woman's 'woman-ness' without taking her living in the US, France, Bangladesh, Korea, Kenya, Fiji, Britain or Palestine into our consideration? Or her being middle-upper class in Uganda or lower class in Germany? Any and all women can be identified 'as-women' but they can be identified also 'as' yellow, brown, white, black, professor, politician, housewife, actress, married, single, the first lady, factory worker, Queen, eastern, western, straight or lesbian and so on.

In this complexity around the discourse of *as-women*, justifying the claim in any particular case that it is sexism that has harmed a woman the most requires proving that the harm comes to her because she is a woman and not because of some other fact about her – her race or class, marital status, religious affiliation, cultural heritage, sexual orientation or physical disability. Moreover, even if a woman is oppressed by sexism, and even if we say that all women are victimized by sexism, we cannot automatically conclude that all discrimination and oppression by sexism is the same. It needs to be elaborated in detail what one's oppression 'as-a-woman' means in each case. In this context, producing an accurate picture of Asian women's lives and experiences requires not only reference to their identity *as-women* but also to other multiple factors which are deeply interlinked with one another.

Asian feminist theology has also started with 'as-discourse', like feminist theology in the west, but the *as-discourse* has dimensions unlike those of feminist theology in the west: 'as-woman' and 'as-Asian'.

We belong to different Christian denominations; we come from diverse and complex cultures and backgrounds, but we experience a common bond and a common bondage – *as Asians* and *as women*.[20]

---

[20] Fabella and Oduyoye (eds.), *With Passion and Compassion*, p. 118 (my italics).

Asian feminist theology has dealt with the 'as-discourse' as a form of difference-discourse in four ways: difference from men *as-women*, difference from western feminists *as-Asian-feminists*, difference from the western *as-Asian*, and difference from the other religions *as-Christians* in a religiously pluralist world. How then feminists, in Asia and other parts of the world, can relate to one another across difference, or despite difference, becomes one of the urgent issues that feminist theologians wrestle with.

There are of course political reasons for speaking about the shared experience of 'as-women' being oppressed by sexism, which can be the solid ground for a women's movement. However, speaking from and holding on to the perspective of *as-discourse* of Asian women continuously is politically dangerous because it can only lead to an ongoing 'balkanization' of feminist theological discourse.[21] If the coherency required for any political movement to get heard and to cause change requires a group to speak in a single voice of 'as-discourse', how will a single voice be shaped from the multiplicity of voices, and whose voice will predominate? Who has the rights, authority or ability to find a single voice from many as-women, as-Asians or as-Asian-women? Although they criticize the homogenized version of white women's experience as universal women's experience propagated by western feminists, Asian feminists tend to homogenize their own version of Asian women based on the same logic of 'as-discourse'. There is, naturally, always a danger in overemphasizing the difference:

The very theme of difference, whatever the differences are represented to be, is useful to the oppressing group ... [A]ny allegedly natural feature attributed to an oppressed group is used to imprison this group within the boundaries of a Nature which, since the group is oppressed, ideological confusion labels 'nature of oppressed person' ... [T]o demand the right to Difference without analyzing its social character is to give back the enemy an effective weapon.[22]

'As-discourse' in *Asian* feminist theological discourse has tended to claim essential *female-and-ethnic-difference* and to produce a standardization of the 'authentic' Asian women, wittingly or unwittingly. I would argue that the 'as-discourse' should be shifted to a 'with-discourse' and that the firm ground of 'with-discourse' is the radical realization of the interconnectedness

---

[21] Cf. Elisabeth Schüssler Fiorenza (ed.), *Searching the Scriptures: A Feminist Introduction* (New York: Crossroad, 1995), p. 17.

[22] E. Marks and I. De Courtivon (eds.), *New French Feminism* (Amherst: University of Massachusetts Press, 1980), p. 219.

of our lives across gender, race, region and class, and of the need for solidarity for the common good. I would also go on to argue that Asian feminist theology needs to make a shift from a *politics of identity* to a *politics of solidarity*. For an exclusive focus on the difference between identities based on culture, geopolitics or other factors of women's lives tends to overlook the interactive mediations between differences, and obscure the overlapping and hybridizing that takes place in the contact space in between differences. As a starting point, 'difference' means essentially 'division' in the understanding of many, and 'difference' can be no more than a tool of either self-defence or conquest. Minh-ha Trinh eloquently points out the problem of as-discourse of difference:

We (with capital W) sometimes include(s), other times exclude(s) me. You and I are close, we intertwine; you may stand on the other side of the hill once in a while, but you may also be me, while remaining what you are and what I am not ... 'I' is, therefore, not a unified subject, a fixed identity, or that solid mass covered with layers of superficialities one has gradually to peel off before one can see its true face. 'I' is, itself, *infinite layers*.[23]

Special identity as-Asian-women, which has been portrayed in Asian feminist theological discourse both by Asian and western feminists, is both limiting and in a way deceiving. If my identity as Asian woman, for instance, refers to the whole pattern of sameness within my life as Asian woman, how am I to lose, maintain or gain my identity as Asian-woman? Asian women can never be defined. Not every Asian woman can be a *real* and *authentic* Asian woman. 'As-discourse' in Asian feminist theology should be used only when understood socio-politically as a subversive force, not as a portrayal only as pure-victims. Otherwise Asian feminist theologians are contributing to their own homogenizing, romanticizing and stereotyping. In order to avoid this, we Asian feminist theologians should persistently wrestle with the following questions: How can we articulate Asian women's difference without having that difference turned into a cultural ghettoization of Asian women? How can Asian women 'speak'?

It is also important to note that Asian women are not inherently more life-affirming, nurturing, caring or non-violent than Asian man, as they are often portrayed as being in Asian feminist theological discourse. This is a very dangerous perspective because it leads to a focus on women's

[23] T. Minh-ha Trinh, *Woman, Native, Other: Writing Postcoloniality and Feminism* (Bloomington and Indianapolis: Indiana University Press, 1989), pp. 90 and 94.

biology and tends to reinforce the patriarchal notion that to be a woman means to be a mother as nurturer and care-giver. Asian women have not initiated wars simply because of our material and socio-political circumstances and not because we are 'innately' more moral and life-affirming than men. It is very clear that women's work, in either the private or public sectors, supports both war and peace activities. The socialization of Asian women and Asian men complements the needs of the culture in which they live, which is still very much patriarchal. As Gerda Lerner rightly points out, '[t]he system of patriarchy can function only with the co-option of women'.[24] A perpetuation of 'as-discourse' in Asian feminist theology is more constraining than empowering and weakens solidarity amongst feminists in the world. 'As-discourse' is needed only as a means of resistance but not as an end. The identity of *as-Asian-women* in Asian feminist theological discourse will have to be created through the action of resistance to any form of power that limits, exploits, distorts and degrades the lives of women and the marginalized.

A NEW CONTEXT FOR CONSTRUCTING *ASIAN* FEMINIST THEOLOGY IN AN ERA OF NEO-EMPIRE

Over the last decade, especially after the end of the Cold War, the so-called 'empire-discourse' has emerged in the context of neo-imperialism and globalization. A series of works has depicted the experience of American victory over Communism, and the field of American hegemony in geo-politics, economics and mass culture in the world. In their thought-provoking work, Hard and Negri interpret 'empire' as 'a *decentered* and *deterritorialising* apparatus of rule that progressively incorporates the entire global realm within its open, expanding frontiers'.[25] This is, in a way, a radicalized version of the 'globalization' that we experience today. This empire-discourse tries to set the economic, cultural and political world today within a political framework, and it further shows us how neo-colonialism and neo-imperialism become new forms of political/cultural/economic dependency on particular western nations such as the United States.[26]

[24] Gerda Lerner, *The Creation of Patriarchy* (New York: Oxford University Press, 1986), p. 217.
[25] Michael Hardt and Antonio Negri, *Empire* (Cambridge, MA: Harvard University Press, 2000), p. xii.
[26] Colonialism can be defined as the organized deployment of *racialized* and *gendered* constructs for practices of political rule over other racial/ethnic groups, which requires a territorial invasion. Imperialism shares with colonialism a tendency of domination over other peoples. However, imperialism can refer to an organized power's intention to institutionalize and expand its

Generally speaking, colonialism/imperialism is about power and ruling, and thereby about domination and subjugation. Therefore efforts to change the subordinate status of a certain group of people, like women, require a consideration of the nature of power. One must note at the outset that power is an elusive concept that must be characterized as essentially contested. Different theories of power rest on different assumptions about both the content of existence and the ways one comes to know it. That is, different theories of power rest on differing ontologies and episte-mologies, and a feminist rethinking of power requires attention to its epistemological groundings. Epistemologies, or theories of knowing, grow out of differing material contexts.

Feminism has often depicted women's oppression using the metaphor of the colonizer and the colonized. There exist certain similarities between the colonization of undeveloped countries and women's oppression within patriarchy: economic dependence, the cultural take-over, the identification of dignity with a resemblance to the oppressor.[27] Like the relationship of colonizer to colonized, patriarchal culture has defined women as different in kind from men, and denied women's right to own property and a share in the economic means of production. Therefore, it is argued that '[i]f we transpose the descriptions of colonized and colonizer to women and men, they fit at almost every point', and further that 'like slave-masters and colonizers they have expected women to identify their interests with their oppressors'.[28]

Just as colonization denies the colonized a voice in their own culture, feminists argue, most women in most patriarchal cultures have been deprived their own voices. But by adopting this 'men-colonizer and women-colonized homology' in my theorizing, I run the risk of over-simplifying the complexity of the empire-experience of neo-colonization/neo-imperialism today. I cannot, however, deny the fact that this meta-phor possesses power, particularly in articulating the oppression of Asian women today.

---

dominating/ruling power. So even though the terms colonialism and imperialism are used interchangeably, imperialism refers to the specific actions of colonizers to constitute their power as a political machine that rules from the centre and extends its control to the peripheries. Cf. Robert J. C. Young, *Postcolonialism: An Historical Introduction* (Oxford: Blackwell, 2001), p. 27, and also see Keller *et al.* (eds.), *Postcolonial Theologies*, p. 42.

[27] Sheila Rowbotham, *Women, Resistance and Revolution: A History of Women and Revolution in the Modern World* (New York: Vintage Books, 1971), p. 201.

[28] Marilyn French, *Beyond Power: On Men, Women and Morals* (New York: Ballantine Books, 1985), p. 121 and p. 122.

THE HEGEMONIC TWINS: THE HOMOLOGY
OF KYRIARCHY AND EMPIRE

Women in patriarchy, as the colonized in colonization, are *Othered* in
many different ways. The creation of *Other* is the necessary precondition
for the justification and legitimation of both imperialism and patriarchy.
The colonized is portrayed as opposite to the colonizer. The colonized is
purported to carry all the negative qualities.[29] In this *Othering*, the desire
to dominate gains its end. Empire-building is therefore all about power-
building by creating a devalued *Other*. The Othered subject is then
dominated by the empire. Interestingly, in the construction of the empire,
the colonized is often feminized. A ruling being is created that sees itself
as located at the centre and possessed of all good qualities. As Memmi
rightly elaborates:

[T]he colonized is always degraded and the colonialist finds justification for
rejecting his [sic] subjectivity ... The colonialist removes the factor from history,
time and therefore possible evolution. What is actually a sociological point
becomes labelled as being biological, or preferably, metaphysical. It is attached to
the colonized's basic nature.[30]

Here I would like to use a neologism coined by Elisabeth Schüssler
Fiorenza, *kyriarchy*, instead of patriarchy, simply because patriarchy does
not show the complex system of domination and subordination in a
contemporary neo-imperial, empire-building situation. Schüssler Fiorenza
argues that the concept of patriarchy needs to be redefined when it is
understood, as usually, as simply the rule of men over women in the sense
of gender dualism. It is limited because a social pyramid of domination
and subordination is quite complicated. Kyriarchy means, according to
Schüssler Fiorenza, 'the rule of the emperor/master/lord/father/husband
over his subordinates'.[31] It should be noted that women are neither the
'pure victims' nor are men the 'pure victimizers'. This exclusive gender
dualism does not reveal the power imbalance among women of different
race, ethnicity, class or sexual orientation. By adopting the term kyriarchy
instead of patriarchy, I would like to reveal the underlying epistemology
of empire-building in relation to women's subjugation and, furthermore,

---

[29] Cf. Albert Memmi, *The Colonizer and the Colonized* (Boston: Beacon Press, 1967), p. 82.
[30] *Ibid.*, p. 85.
[31] Elisabeth Schüssler Fiorenza, *Jesus: Miriam's Child, Sophia's Prophet: Critical Issues in Feminist Christology* (New York: Continuum, 1995), p. 14.

to emphasize the fact that not all men dominate and exploit all women without difference. Not all women are oppressed by men, simply on the ground of their biology.

THE MULTIPLE COLONIZATION OF ASIAN WOMEN IN RELIGION

It is claimed that theologians in the west have written more books about 'animals and environment than about colonialism or race', and have not taken a serious theological interest in empire. Empire was even justified as inevitable by Reinhold Niebuhr.[32] There is a blind spot in theological construction in the west, what might be called *sanctioned ignorance*. The term *sanctioned ignorance* comes from Spivak in her powerful critique of Michel Foucault's position as a self-contained western intellectual.[33] She criticizes Foucault, focusing on his blind spot concerning the techniques for the appropriation of space that ravaged the colonies during precisely the same historical period that held his attention, because he was distracted by other matters. Her point alerts us to the production/reproduction of *sanctioned ignorance* not only amongst theologians in the west but amongst us in Asia as well.

Those Asian intellectuals and social activists who have criticized the supremacy of the west often overlook their own supremacy in relation to Asian women. In this sense, Asian women are colonized not only by western imperialist power but also by Asian kyriarchal domination. Those who have been treated as *the other* by western neo-imperialism are practising their own hegemonic powers on women and the powerless in their own local context. In this sense, 'localist opposition' to western empire-building may well be politically well-intentioned but it rests on false assumptions and is therefore damaging. It assumes that the local is 'outside' empire-building. The local however cannot represent a stable barrier against the emerging western empire. Any 'locale' is rarely unproblematic and any simple celebration of local culture against western hegemony for its own sake cannot be the solution to the problem of

---

[32] R. S. Sugirtharajah, 'Complacencies and Cul-de-sacs: Christian Theologies and Colonialism', in Keller *et al.* (eds.), *Postcolonial Theologies*, pp. 22–38 at p. 22. Here Sugirtharajah points out that Reinhold Niebuhr, in his book *Nation and Empire*, sees colonialism as an inevitable stage, morally neutral though open to misuse, in the development of civilizations, and triggered by three motivations: missionary, economic, and political. Cf. Reinhold Niebuhr, *Nations and Empire: Recurring Patterns in the Political Order* (London: Faber and Faber, 1959).

[33] Spivak, 'Can the Subaltern Speak?', in Nelson and Grossberg, *Marxism and the Interpretation of Culture*, pp. 271–313.

empire. Asian men, for instance, can be colonized by the western empire, but at same time they can be the colonizers in practising their kyriarchal power in their local culture. It is also true that Asian middle- and upper-class women can be the colonizers of lower-class men and women. The locality should be scrutinized also from the perspective of the marginal-ized, from those below, from the least.

Here I would suggest differentiating the *Empire* from *empires* to identify the Empire with the west as a master-narrative and the empires in our own locales as a small-narrative. In this context, the real question would not be *whether* Empire but *whose* Empire.[34] And this question is not only to check the abuses of power by others, but also to check our own abuses of power, and therefore to bring us into critical awareness of and engagement with the interests of all our relations.

In this context I would say that Asian women in religion have experienced multiple colonization: colonization by the socio-politico-cultural hegemony of the west; colonization by the discursive hegemony of feminists in the west; colonization by the kyriarchal hegemony of Asian men; and colonization by the kyriarchal value systems in religions. Empire from a feminist perspective should not be singular in form but plural, simply because there is not only one form of Empire but many different forms of Empires. Asian women must be alert to the multiple faces of Empires: not only Empire-out-there, but also Empire(s)-in/among-us. I think that a comprehensive discourse of empire would help us to figure out not just 'what to do' but 'who we are'. It would help us Asian women to identify our socio-geopolitical and religious location in terms of power relations: who is oppressor, who is oppressed and in what sense one can be both the oppressor and the oppressed at the same time. The comprehensive empire-discourse would help us further to understand that many are multi-dimensionally oppressed and colonized. It also highlights the multiple and often contradictory elements of who 'WE' are as-Asian-women. The we-they binarism is not as self-evident as we usually suppose: The 'they' would disguise itself as 'us' and is secretly invading us. There is colonization by 'them', the west, but also colonization by 'us' – Asian men, feminists in the west, and fellow men and women within the same religion. It is therefore true that the once colonized is not immune to becoming the colonizer on another level.

---

[34] Sharon Welch, *After Empire: The Art and Ethos of Enduring Peace* (Minneapolis: Fortress Press, 2004), p. xvi.

TOWARD A *GLOCAL* FEMINIST THEOLOGY AS A DISCOURSE OF RESISTANCE AND LIBERATION

One of the threatening things in feminist theological movements for me is when we feminists refuse to change ourselves while we try to change the world. Many people, whether men or women, or western or Asian, exist in a painful ambiguity both as colonizers and colonized. Those who ignore the multiple power relations involved in empire-building fail to provide an epistemology for the task of the transformation of existing reality. In a postcolonial context, we cannot deny that ' "[w]e" do not quite know who is "us" and who is "them" '. In an era of globalization, it is also undeniable that '[n]either race nor language can any longer define nationality'.[35] Although an Empire through one nation's hegemony is dominating the rest of the world, it is our reality that we in fact are both a part of the Empire and have our own empire(s) within/among ourselves.

In this context, one's geographical location is no longer a parameter in constructing feminist theological discourse. Rather, a feminist theological construction today need not be in accordance with a specific geographical territory. In an era of globalization, geographical boundaries are beginning to blur through the displacement of peoples. Through the dislocation, relocation, and translocation of peoples with diverse cultures and religions, the old context for Asian feminist theology has been changed. The direction of this theology, which has invested so much in geographical locations, the fixed identity of 'as-Asian-women' and Asian indigenous cultures and resources, should be radically redirected. The old paradigm of Asian feminist theology has been a 'localist/nativist position' in which the major resources for theological construction are directed only at local culture and tradition. In this localist/nativist approach, Asian feminist theology has had a tendency to romanticize, idealize and glorify the local and discredit the west. A sharp contrast between Asia and the west has been its typical approach. I would argue that this kind of theological nativism still functions and continues to imprison not only the 'other culture' but also its own 'vernacular culture' within entirely *geographically deterministic* and *culturally essentialist* discursive boundaries.

Feminist theological discourse in Asia must commit itself to two simultaneous projects: an internal critique of the hegemonic kyriarchy of the theologians' own local cultures and societies, and the formulation of historically and contextually grounded feminist theological concerns and

---

[35] Keller *et al.* (eds.), *Postcolonial Theologies*, p. 1.

strategies for overcoming gender injustice in theological discourse, theological and ecumenical institutions, and the church, which can provide an alternative vision of the world and of Christianity. While the first project is a process of deconstruction, the second one is a process of reconstruction. Asian feminist theological discourse has a further task on a global level: to present the complex reality and hybrid experience of Asian women in their respective contexts and their feminist theological quest, enquiries and hopes to the peoples of the globe.

I would like finally to propose a *glocal* feminist theology, in which the global context and the local context are proactively combined to resist Empire(s) of all forms and to strengthen solidarity with the women and the marginalized who are dislocated and displaced, either physically or ontologically, and whose lives have been destroyed and diminished by the power of various forms of Empire(s). What I envision for a *glocal* feminist theology is trans-national, trans-regional, trans-cultural and trans-religious. In order to carry out this vision for a *glocal* feminist theology, the following tasks are to be taken into account.

First, Asian feminist theology as *glocal* feminist theology needs to articulate a comprehensive empire-discourse that recognizes that Asian feminist theologians' local activities are interlinked with a global geopolitical reality. Asian women must not give up the claim that material life not only structures but sets limits on the understanding of social relations, and that, in systems of domination and subjugation, the vision available to the emperors/rulers will be both partial and will reverse the real order of things. The ruling Empire(s), in terms of race, class and gender, actively structure the material–social relations in which we all are forced to participate, wittingly or unwittingly. We have to acknowledge, as Antonio Gramsci points out in his theory of hegemony, that empire-building has been possible not just by force but by our consent as well.[36] The vision of ruling Empire(s), therefore, cannot be dismissed as simply false or misguided. A binary position of 'us versus them' can be a misreading of our ambivalent reality. The colonized/oppressed group must struggle for their own understandings, which will represent achievements

---

[36] In his *Prison Notebooks*, Gramsci writes, 'It seems clear … that there can, and indeed must be hegemonic activity even before the rise of power, and that one should not count only on the material force which power gives in order to exercise an effective leadership.' His theory of hegemony shows how dominant groups or individuals can maintain their hegemony by persuading the governed to accept, adopt and internalize their values and norms, which is considered one of the great lessons taught by Gramsci. Antonio Gramsci, *Selections from the Prison Notebooks of Antonio Gramsci*, Quintin Hoare and Geoffrey Nowell Smith (eds.) (London: Lawrence & Wishart, 1971), p. 57.

requiring both theorizing and the education which grows from political struggle and engagement.

Second, Asian feminist theology as *glocal* feminist theology needs fiercely to engage in the historical, socio-political and theoretical process of constituting us women as subjects as well as objects of our specific history – both local and global, which are inextricably interlinked especially in an era of globalization. *Glocal* feminist theology needs to sort out who Asian women really are. We Asian women need to dissolve the false 'WE' into its real multiplicity and variety. And out of this concrete multiplicity of 'I's, we need to build an account of the world as seen from the margins, an account which can expose the falseness of the view from the top and can transform the margins as well as the centre. The history of the marginalization of Asian women will work against creating a totalizing discourse both by Asians and westerners. Asian women need to name and present/ represent continuously and persistently their diverse experiences of multiple colonization and struggle.

Third, Asian feminist theology as *glocal* feminist theology needs to construct a discourse of power for women, and for the colonized of various types, that is a call for transformation and participation in altering the power relations of domination and subjugation in multiple forms. Through this comprehensive power-discourse, this theology is able to offer a better illustration of how neo-imperialism works, and how neo-Empire and Empire(s) as ideological domination succeed the best without physical coercion, without territorial invasion, without actually capturing the bodies and the minds of Asian women. The apparent absence of the 'enemy' in an era of neo-Empire(s) as such requires more sophisticated and comprehensive power-discourse.

Fourth, Asian feminist theology needs to shift from a *politics of identity* to a *politics of solidarity*, from *as-discourse* to *with-discourse*. *With-discourse* requires adopting 'we-hermeneutics', which interprets life and its opportunities and challenges in the light of the self and the community.[37] 'We-hermeneutics' is a challenge to acknowledge our embeddedness in community: 'I am because we are; and we are because I am.'[38] Here 'we' is not based on a hierarchical/vertical relationship as is the case in Confucian culture, but on an egalitarian/horizontal democratic relationship between

---

[37] Jace Weaver, *Other Words: American Indian Literature, Law, and Culture* (Norman: University of Oklahoma Press, 2001), pp. 303–4.

[38] Karen Baker-Fletcher and Garth Kasimu Baker-Fletcher, *My Sister, My Brother: Womanist and Xodus God-Talk* (Maryknoll: Orbis, 1997), pp. 203–4.

and across gender, age, race, ethnicity, class, sexual orientation and religious/cultural background.

Constructing feminist theological discourse as a discourse of resistance and liberation is not just for identifying common 'victimizers', for the self-justification of as-women as the victimized, or for mutual-recognition among Asian women as victims under patriarchy. Instead, it should be for an ongoing contestation and change, ongoing learning, unlearning, and de-learning to work for change for an alternative world. *Asian* feminist theologians are those who are in-between. They are in-between the west and Asia, in-between women and men, in-between Christians and people of neighbouring faiths, and eventually in-between the world of *already* and the world of *not-yet*. Their 'in-between consciousness' makes them day-dream. They dream of an alternative world where all forms of domination and subjugation are overcome and where no one is alienated on the ground of sex, race, ethnicity, class, age, religion, sexual orientation, physical ability or appearance, and where an authentic peace prevails. Feminist theologians are permanent 'resident aliens'[39] who reside in this existing world but are alien because of their day-dream. Through this day-dreaming, they can form the 'solidarity in multiplicity and diversity' which is necessary for the survival of *Asian* feminist theology as a revolutionary discourse and movement.

BIBLIOGRAPHY

Baker-Fletcher, K. and Baker-Fletcher, G. K., *My Sister, My Brother: Womanist and Xodus God-Talk*, Maryknoll: Orbis, 1997.
Christian Conference of Asia, *Christian Conference of Asia Sixth Assembly, Penang*, Singapore: CCA, 1977.
  Christian Conference of Asia Seventh Assembly, Bangalore, Singapore: CCA, 1981.
Chung, H. K., *Struggle to be the Sun Again: Introducing Asian Women's Theology*, Maryknoll: Orbis, 1990.
Donaldson, L. E., *Decolonizing Feminisms: Race, Gender and Empire-Building*, Chapel Hill and London: The University of North Carolina Press, 1992.
Edwards, L. and Roces, M. (eds.), *Women in Asia: Tradition, Modernity and Globalization*, St. Leonards, Australia: Allen & Unwin, 2000.

---

[39] Cf. Janet Wolff, *Resident Alien: Feminist Cultural Criticism* (New Haven and London: Yale University Press, 1995); and Elisabeth Schüssler Fiorenza also adopts the metaphor of 'resident alien' to denote 'a "doubled" insider/outsider position' in her *Discipleship of Equals: A Critical Feminist Ekklēsia-logy of Liberation* (New York: Crossroad, 1994), p. 335.

Fabella, V. and Oduyoye, M. A. (eds.), *With Passion and Compassion: Third World Women Doing Theology*, Maryknoll: Orbis Books, 1988.

Fabella, V. and Park, S. A. L. (eds.), *We Dare to Dream: Doing Theology as Asian Women*, Maryknoll: Orbis, 1990.

French, M., *Beyond Power: On Men, Women and Morals*, New York: Ballantine Books, 1985.

Geiger, S., 'Women's Life Histories: Method and Content', *Signs*, 11:2 (1986), 334–51.

Gramsci, A., *Selections from the Prison Notebooks of Antonio Gramsci*, Quintin Hoare and Geoffrey Nowell Smith (eds.), London: Lawrence & Wishart, 1971.

Hardt, M. and Negri, A., *Empire*, Cambridge, MA: Harvard University Press, 2000.

Henkin, L., 'The Human Rights Idea in Contemporary China: A Comparative Perspective', in R. Randle Edwards, Louis Henkin and Andrew J. Nathan, *Human Rights in Contemporary China*, New York: Columbia University Press, 1986, pp. 7–40.

hooks, b., *Talking Back*, Boston: South End Press, 1989.

Kang, N., 'Creating Dangerous Memory: Challenges for Asian and Korean Feminist Theology', *The Ecumenical Review* 47, 1 (1995), 21–31.

'Who/What is Asian?: A Postcolonial Theological Reading of Orientalism and Neo-Orientalism', in C. Keller, M. Nausner and M. Rivera (eds.), *Postcolonial Theologies: Divinity and Empire*, St. Louis: Chalice Press, 2004, pp. 100–17.

'Confucian Familism and Its Social/Religious Embodiment in Christianity: Reconsidering the Family Discourses from a Feminist Perspective', *Asia Journal of Theology*, 18:1 (2004), 168–89.

'A Bridge of Inclusiveness of Gender, Race and Culture: Women of Color Scholars in the Construction of Theology of Inclusiveness', *Quarterly Review* (Summer 2000), 173–84.

Keller, C., Nausner, M. and Rivera, M. (eds.), *Postcolonial Theologies: Divinity and Empire*, St Louis: Chalice Press, 2004.

Kwok, P-L., *Introducing Asian Feminist Theology*, Sheffield: Sheffield Academic Press, 2000.

De Lauretis, T., *Technologies of Gender: Essays on Theory, Film, and Fiction*, Bloomington: Indiana University Press, 1987.

Lerner, G., *The Creation of Patriarchy*, New York: Oxford University Press, 1986.

Lorde, A., *Sister Outsider: Essays and Speeches*, Trumansburg: Crossing Press, 1984.

Marks, E. and De Courtivon, I. (eds.), *New French Feminism*, Amherst: University of Massachusetts Press, 1980.

Memmi, A., *The Colonizer and the Colonized*, Boston: Beacon Press, 1967.

Mohanty, C. T., Russo, A. and Torres, L. (eds.), *Third World Women and the Politics of Feminism*, Bloomington and Indianapolis: Indiana University Press, 1991.

Feminism without Borders: Decolonializing Theory, Practicing Solidarity, Durham and London: Duke University Press, 2003.

Niebuhr, R., *Nations and Empire: Recurring Patterns in the Political Order*, London: Faber & Faber, 1959.

Omolade, B., 'Black Women and Feminism', in H. Eisenstein and A. Jardine (eds.), *The Future of Difference*, New Brunswick: Rutgers University Press, 1985, pp. 247–57.

Phillipson, R., *Linguistic Imperialism*, Oxford: Oxford University Press, 1992.

Rexroth, K. and Atsumi, I. (eds.), *Women Poets of Japan*, New York: New Directions Books, 1977.

Rowbotham, S., *Women, Resistance and Revolution: A History of Women and Revolution in the Modern World*, New York: Vintage Books, 1971.

Ruether, R. R., *Women and Redemption: A Theological History*, Minneapolis: Fortress Press, 1998.

Schüssler Fiorenza, E., *Discipleship of Equals: A Critical Feminist Ekklēsia-logy of Liberation*, New York: Crossroad, 1994.

   Jesus: Miriam's Child, Sophia's Prophet: Critical Issues in Feminist Christology, New York: Continuum, 1995.

Schüssler Fiorenza, E. (ed.), *Searching the Scriptures: A Feminist Introduction*, New York: Crossroad, 1995.

Spivak, G. C., 'Can the Subaltern Speak?', in C. Nelson and L. Grossberg (eds.), *Marxism and the Interpretation of Culture*, Urbana: University of Illinois Press, 1988, pp. 271–316.

Trinh, T. M., *Woman, Native, Other: Writing Postcoloniality and Feminism*, Bloomington and Indianapolis: Indiana University Press, 1989.

Weaver, J., *Other Words: American Indian Literature, Law, and Culture*, Norman: University of Oklahoma Press, 2001.

Welch, S., *After Empire: The Art and Ethos of Enduring Peace*, Minneapolis: Fortress Press, 2004.

Wolff, J., *Resident Alien: Feminist Cultural Criticism*, New Haven and London: Yale University Press, 1995.

Wong, W. A., *'The Poor Woman': A Critical Analysis of Asian Theology and Contemporary Chinese Fiction by Women*, New York: Peter Lang, 2002.

Wong, A. W. C., 'Women Doing Theology with the Asian Ecumenical Movement', in Ninan Koshy (ed.), *A History of the Asian Ecumenical Movement*, vol. II, Hong Kong: CCA, 2004, pp. 85–114.

Young, R. J. C., *Postcolonialism: An Historical Introduction*, Oxford: Blackwell, 2001.

CHAPTER 11

The ecumenical movement in Asia in the context of Asian socio-political realities

S. Wesley Ariarajah

THE 'ECUMENICAL' IN THE CONTEXT OF ASIA

The word 'ecumenical' has many shades of meaning and is used in a variety of ways. Therefore, it is important to understand the special meaning it has acquired in the Asian context. The original Greek word 'oikoumene' in the Roman world simply meant, 'the whole inhabited earth'. At the height of Roman power, the occupied territories of the empire were equated with 'the whole inhabited earth'. Ecumenism, therefore, had to do originally with what happened in the territories of the empire. However, ever since the church became a prominent part of the empire, successive emperors had to deal with the problem of divisions within the church over the interpretation of the Christian faith. They feared that disunity and divisions within the church would harm the unity and coherence of the empire itself. Thus, the emperors themselves wanted to preserve the unity of the church and from time to time brought the bishops of the oikoumene (the occupied territories) together, if need be by the use of force, and put pressure on them to come to agreements on questions of doctrine so that the 'unity of the oikoumene' might be preserved. These councils that the Emperors organized were the ancient 'ecumenical councils' that drew up many of the classical doctrinal statements and the Creeds – like the Nicene Creed.

Since these ecumenical councils were organized to maintain and at times enforce the unity of the church, the word 'ecumenical' came to be associated with the search for church unity. The modern ecumenical movement, in its early expressions as the Missionary and Life and Work Movements, for instance, were primarily concerned, respectively, with 'unity' among Christian mission agencies for the spread of the gospel and for the churches to speak with 'one voice' on issues faced in the world.

The Faith and Order Movement, which eventually became the primary symbol of the ecumenical movement in the western world, concerned itself almost exclusively with the search for the visible unity of the church. It is significant that when the World Council of Churches came into existence in 1948, incorporating Faith and Order and Life and Work (the Missionary Movement was to come in later), the mottoes that were chosen were from John 17:11 (RSV) 'that they may be one' and from John 17:21 'that the world may believe'. The concern was for Christian unity so that 'the world may believe' the Christian message. The ministry of the World Council of Churches, of course, developed into something much larger and the WCC has an impressive record of concern for the world and its unity. But it had become difficult to disassociate the word 'ecumenical' from the internal life of the church.

Wilfred Cantwell Smith points out the distortion that had taken place. The word that was intended to mean the unity of the peoples on the earth, he says, has 'been appropriated lately to designate rather an internal development within the ongoing Church'.[1] He argues that the word should apply to the search for the wider unity in a religiously plural world. The word, as we have seen, however, originally meant much more than even the unity and harmony among religious traditions.

As we shall see in the discussions that follow, it is significant that it is in the Asian context that the word 'ecumenical' has gradually begun to recover its original meaning of concern for 'the whole inhabited earth'. Christian unity has been one of the dimensions of the understanding of the 'ecumenical' in Asia as well; but the emphasis has more clearly been on the peoples, social movements, economic realities and socio-political revolutions in the Asian continent. It could be said that the ecumenical movement in Asia is about 'the People of God in the midst of All God's People', and its mission is about the 'healing of the nations'. This reality gives a new flavour and a solid grounding to Asian ecumenism.

ASIAN REALITIES THAT IMPACT ON ASIAN ECUMENISM

Several factors have affected the nature of ecumenism in Asia. Of the many local, regional and global factors, six features can be lifted up as features common to the whole region that have left their mark on Asian ecumenism.

---

[1] Wilfred Cantwell Smith, 'Christians in a Religiously Plural World', in John Hick and Brian Hebblethwaite (eds.), *Christianity and Other Religions* (Oxford: Oneworld, 2001), pp. 44–58 at p. 45.

Diversity and plurality

It is often said that the diversity and plurality of the peoples of the Asian land mass is so pronounced that 'Asia' can only be a geographical notion. The ethnic, cultural, religious and social plurality within and between nations are so great that no religion, political ideology or cultural tradition, however powerful, has been able at any time in history to encompass the entire region designated as Asia. The early missionary movement, for instance, was reasonably confident that by domesticating China and India for Christianity, the Asian region would be 'won for Christ', as was Europe and the North and South American continents. Enormous resources were poured into these two countries. But Christianity, despite powerful colonial backing, could not imitate even the limited, yet impressive, success of Buddhism and Hinduism. The irreducible plurality of Asia and its indigestible diversity were at odds with the grand design of 'unity' (meaning: 'one'-ness) embraced by the ecumenical impulses in the western hemisphere. This reality has left an indelible mark on the nature of ecumenism in Asia.

Christianity and colonialism

Christianity, according to established evidence, was present in Asia, especially in China, Tibet, India, Burma and Java, from the very early centuries of the Common Era. It was brought by Jewish, Arab, Persian and Armenian traders who had embraced Christianity to the settlements of their communities in different parts of Asia. The Nestorians, who were fleeing persecution in Europe, for instance, were among the first to introduce Christianity into China. But many of these eastern Christian traditions, with the exception of the Syrian church traditions in Kerala, India, died out.[2] The predominant Christianity in the Asia of today came with the colonizing forces from Portugal, Spain, the Netherlands, France and Britain. This introduced three factors that affected ecumenism in Asia. First, the Christian confessional and denominational differences, rivalries and divisions in Asia had nothing to do with the history of Christianity in Asia; they were 'imported divisions' and the doctrinal problems made little sense in the Asian context. Second, Christianity was associated with power and privilege and had to face the crisis of disempowerment and

---

[2] For a good account of this history, see John C. England, *The Hidden History of Christianity in India: The Church of the East Before 1500* (Delhi: ISPCK, 1996).

dependence in the post-colonial situation. Third, the Christianity that came with colonialism had a very negative appraisal of the religious and cultural traditions of Asia and had done much to isolate the Christians religiously and culturally from the rest of the community. At the end of the colonial era, churches had to struggle to gain credibility, to overcome alienation and to find a meaningful place in the post-colonial efforts at nation building. The Asian agenda for ecumenism, therefore, was vastly different from that of the mainstream ecumenical movement in the western hemisphere.

Asian poverty, deprivation and oppression

The Sri Lankan theologian Aloysius Pieris speaks of 'poverty' and 'religiosity' as the two Asian realities that should inform Christian theological reflections. Endemic poverty, certainly, is one of the most glaring features of the Asian continent. Much of the poverty rises from entrenched structural injustices that have been built into the social fabric expressed in the overt oppression of large sections of people based on class, caste, ethnicity and gender. The political liberation from the colonial powers did not assure social and economic liberation to the masses. Therefore issues of justice, human rights, gender equality, and human and economic development are among the highest priorities in Asia. Asian ecumenical consciousness, programmes and priorities are shaped by this reality.

The influence of religious and cultural traditions

The fourth prominent feature of Asia in general is what Pieris has described as 'Asian spirituality'. Asia is the home of most of the major religious traditions of the world. Hinduism, Buddhism and Confucianism still have a strong grip on the vast majority of people. Other religious traditions, from numerous localized tribal traditions to nationalistic Shintoism, diffused Taoism, Sikhism that sought to bring the best of Hinduism and Islam together, and Jainism that embraced radical non-violence, were born and are deeply entrenched in Asia. Christianity and Islam, although brought from outside, have a significant presence, especially in Indonesia, the Philippines and Korea. Unlike in Europe, no one tradition had been able to dominate the Asian scene or displace its inherent plurality. More significantly, most of the religious traditions in Asia are 'ways of life' that find expression as cultural traditions. The Christian churches, mostly built up as alternate communities and taught to reject these traditions, needed to find their place within them in the post-colonial era.

The issue of building a new relationship is further complicated for the churches by the fact that some of the religio-cultural traditions are closely related to the structural oppression in Asia. The Confucian tradition, for instance, is based on a strict hierarchy of relationships and much of classical Hinduism is caste-based. Uncritical loyalty to the emperor based on Shintoism brought about devastation to the Japanese nation. This meant that the ecumenical movement in Asia has been very ambivalent about Asian religious traditions. On the one hand, the movement has been at odds with the oppressive dimensions of Asian religions; on the other, it had to enable the churches to respond creatively to the religious and cultural traditions of Asia, to shake off their 'foreignness', and to win the hearts and minds of the Asian people.

Revolutionary upheavals

The last issue that influenced the development of the ecumenical movement in Asia has to do with the social, political and cultural revolutions that marked its history for over a century. The Japanese imperial expansion, its involvement in the Second World War with the devastating consequence of atom bombs on Hiroshima and Nagasaki, the Korean War that separated a people into two nations, the struggle of most of the Asian nations to free themselves from the shackles of colonialism, the subsequent internal turmoil in nation building, the rise of Communism in China and its impact on Taiwan, Indo-Pakistan and Sino-Indian wars, the Cold War fought out in Indochina, and the resurgence of religious and cultural nationalisms are only some of the upheavals that provided the context for ecumenism in Asia. For the churches, the additional problem was to assert their independence from their parent churches in the west, without abandoning the commitment to see the church as a universal fellowship of believers. All these struggles, played out at local, national and regional levels, have left a deep impact on the way the ecumenical movement has developed in Asia.

It is little wonder that issues of justice, people-centred development, human rights, church-state relations, indigenization, women's concerns, and rural and urban missions dominated the Asian ecumenical agenda. Today additional concerns like facing the negative impact of the globalization of the economic and financial markets, the search for peace and reconciliation, the social liberation of oppressed groups, the reunification of the Korean peninsular, an adequate theological basis to meet the challenge of religious plurality, the challenges brought by the rapid economic advances in the Far East, and the emergence of China and India as global powers demand the attention of the Asian ecumenical agenda.

To these we shall return in the closing comments on ecumenism in Asia. In the meantime, it is important to note that ecumenism in Asia has also developed and grown in the classical sense of the 'search for the unity' of Christians and churches. The earliest impetus toward this, however, did not come from the established churches but from lay movements, where Christians of many confessions and denominations were thrown together to face the challenges of living the faith in concrete situations of daily life. The foremost among these were the YMCA, YWCA and the student movements expressed as the Student Christian Movement (SCM) locally and as the World Student Christian Federation (WSCF) globally.

ECUMENICAL BEGINNINGS

Lay movements

It is significant that the modern ecumenical movement finds its beginnings, not only in Asia but also in all parts of the world, not in churches but in lay movements; it shows that the impetus for the movement came not so much from the inner faith dynamics of the life of the churches, but from the need for relevance in the world. The urgency for this relevance was felt most acutely in two areas: the mission of the church and the students' search for a relevant faith in a multi-religious and increasingly secular world.

John R. Mott, a Methodist layman from the United States, stands as a towering figure in the modern ecumenical movement because he became acutely aware of the need to transcend confessional and denominational differences both in the task of bringing the Gospel message to the nations and in student witness in school and especially university settings. In 1897 he published a book on his missionary journeys entitled *Strategic Points in the World's Conquest: The Universities and Colleges as Related to the Progress of Christianity*. In the Preface to his book he laid out his vision: 'It is hoped that this record [of his missionary journeys] will lead to a wider recognition of the universities and colleges in the spiritual conquest of the world and awaken larger interest in the [missionary] movement to make all institutions of higher learning strongholds and propagating centres of the Christian faith.'[3]

---

[3] John R. Mott, *Strategic Points in the World's Conquest: The Universities and Colleges as Related to the Progress of Christianity* (London: Nisbet, 1987), as cited by Ninan Koshy, *A History of the Ecumenical*

Mott followed up his vision with the creation of the World Student Christian Federation (WSCF) in 1895 and the establishment of SCMs in universities around the world. The YMCA and YWCA, also committed to having a relevant lay Christian presence in society, had already been established in 1844 and 1854 respectively in Britain. Although the ecumenical impact of these three movements was worldwide, in the predominantly multi-religious context of Asia they played a significant role in initiating and promoting ecumenism. Hans Reudi Weber rightly observes that, 'While for some Western countries an ecumenical history might perhaps be written without mentioning the work of SCMs, YM/YWCAs, this is impossible for Asia. In Asian ecumenical history it was these ecumenical youth movements which pioneered to set the pattern.'[4]

The missionary societies were also conscious of the need to avoid competition and duplication of efforts in the mission fields of Asia and Africa. One way to resolve the problem was to come to 'comity' arrangements by which the missionary societies agreed to partition areas of the mission fields among themselves as distinct areas where specific missions would carry out their work. Mott went on to create, as extensions of the missionary movement, National Christian Councils (NCCs) that brought together all the Christian agencies and churches that worked in a country. These also became the places where Christians and churches met and where the ecumenical spirit was fostered.

Disquiet in local churches

While the lay movements were primarily interested in crossing confessional barriers for the mission of the church, there was also disquiet in some parts of the church in Asia over the imported divisions and the foreignness of Christianity in local settings. Some of this disquiet found concrete expression, for instance in China. A study of the history of Christianity in China would show that the main concern of those who dissented with the classical missionary enterprise was two-fold. The first concern related to cultural alienation and the second to the European divisions that were imported into the life of the church in China. Many thinkers like T. C. Chao, L. C. Wu and Y. T. Wu, among other notable figures, spared no energy in attempting to 'sinicize' Christianity in the context

Movement in Asia, vol. I (Hong Kong: World Student Christian Federation Asia Pacific Region, Asia and Pacific Alliance of YMCAs and Christian Conference of Asia, 2004), p. 39.
[4] Hans Reudi Weber, *Asia and the Ecumenical Movement* (London: SCM Press, 1966), p. 111.

of the Confucian and Taoist cultures. At the Centenary Conference of 1907 that marked one hundred years of Protestant missions in China, for instance, the decision was made to bring about a 'Federal Union of the Churches' under the title Christian Federation of China. In so doing, they laid the foundations for the evolution of the China Christian Council and the patriotic 'Three-Self Movement' of self-support, self-governance and self-propagation. It is also on this basis that the mainline churches in China, after China opened itself to the outside world, presented themselves as the 'post-denominational' Church of Christ in China.

Disquiet with the classical missiology and patterns of church planning was also evident in India, even though much early effort here concentrated on indigenization and on issues of the Christian attitude to other religious traditions.[5] However, through the very attempts to go beyond the classical teachings to reach out to Hinduism and Buddhism these pioneers relativized the significance of confessional differences within Christianity. In any case, the leaders of the churches in India, as also many missionaries working with them, found the divisions within the church a scandal and an obstruction to mission. It is this line of thinking that eventually led to church union negotiations in south India, resulting in the formation of the Church of South India in 1947. The church union in south India was quite revolutionary at that time because it was the first occasion in history when Episcopal and non-Episcopal churches were brought into an organic unity. The inspiration of the creation of the CSI led to church union negotiations in north India, Sri Lanka and several African countries.

Asian involvement in global ecumenism

The impetus for ecumenism in Asia was also fostered by the rise of the modern ecumenical movement at the global level. Mott, as mentioned earlier, felt that much of the Christian effort at 'winning the world for Christ' was being frustrated by the uncoordinated activities of independent missionary societies. He believed that if only the missionary agencies would get their act together they would be able to 'evangelize the world in their generation'. Believing that the 'decisive hour for Christian

[5] Early pioneers in the field include: Rajah Rammohan Roy (1772–1833), Keshab Chander Sen (1838–84), Brahmabanhab Upadhyaya (1861–1907), Nehemiah Goreh (1825–95). Within the Roman Catholic Church the well-known scholars are Jules Monchanin (1895–1957), Henri Saux, renamed Swami Abhishiktananda (1910–73) and Bede Griffiths. In their very attempt to reach out to Hindu culture and religion they disregarded the confessional labels.

missions' had come, he called a meeting of missionary societies and mission agencies in 1910 for a World Missionary Conference in Edinburgh, Scotland. In fact, William Carey, the pioneering Baptist missionary in India, had already made the call for such a conference to the Baptist Missionary Society in Britain; he had suggested that it be held at the Cape of Good Hope in 1810. The Baptist Missionary Society, however, had dismissed the suggestion as a difficult one. A century later, Mott was able to call just such a conference, but there were only seventeen persons from the 'third world', most of them from Asia. Despite their small numbers, the Asians made a significant contribution. A much quoted speech came from V. S. Azariah from India who called for partnership in mission, challenging the missionaries to look upon their local partners as 'friends', pointing to the glaring inequality of the treatment of 'foreign nationals' and 'native workers' in the mission field: 'Through all the ages to come the Indian Church will rise up in gratitude to attest the heroism and self-denying labours of the missionary body. You have given your goods to feed the poor. You have given your bodies to be burned. We also ask for *love*. Give us FRIENDS.'[6] Voices from Japan and China called upon the missionary movement to be sensitive to local cultures and religious traditions. Thus, although tentatively, the Asian involvement in global ecumenism had begun in earnest.[7]

In the two subsequent World Mission Conferences in Jerusalem (1928) and Tambaram (1938) the Asian voices became much more prominent, primarily because of the uncertainties within the missionary movement about the Christian approach to other religious traditions.[8] At Tambaram, the Missionary Movement attempted, through the Dutch missiologist Hendrik Kraemer's preparatory volume, *The Christian Message in a Non-Christian World*, to re-establish biblical and theological foundations for the classical missionary understanding of mission as conversion of others to the church and to make the church the primary agent of mission.[9] There were strong Asian voices of dissent at Tambaram and the

---

[6] V. S. Azariah, *World Missionary Conference, Edinburgh*, vol. IX (London: Oliphant Anderson & Ferrier, 1910), p. 315.

[7] Cf. Reports of the Conference, *World Missionary Conference, Edinburgh*, vol. IX (London: Oliphant Anderson & Ferrier, 1910).

[8] For details, see S. Wesley Ariarajah, 'Christianity and People of Other Religious Traditions', in Ninan Koshy (ed.), *A History of the Ecumenical Movement in Asia*, vol. II (Hong Kong: World Student Christian Federation Asia Pacific Region, Asia and Pacific Alliance of YMCAs and Christian Conference of Asia, 2004), pp. 139–65.

[9] Hendrik Kraemer, *The Christian Message in a Non-Christian World* (London: Edinburgh House Press, 1938).

'Tambaram Controversy' gave rise to significant ecumenical exploration of the issues of the 'Christian Approach to Other Religions' and of the relationship between 'The Church and the Kingdom of God' in the Asian region.[10]

THE FORMATION OF A REGIONAL BODY FOR ECUMENISM

At the global level, the outbreak and the aftermath of the two World Wars forced the churches in the west to bring their search for Christian unity into a concrete institutional expression, so that they might together serve the world in turmoil. The Faith and Order Movement and the Life and Work Movement came together to inaugurate the World Council of Churches in Amsterdam in 1948. The Missionary Movement was to become part of this fellowship at a later stage. In the meantime, there was also interest in the Asian region to give institutional expression to the unity of Asian Christians and churches. In 1949 a meeting of church leaders from all over east Asia was called under the leadership of Rajah B. Manikam of India and S. C. Leung of China. This meeting, which gave an opportunity to church leaders to consider the common issues facing the Asian churches, led first to the formation of a secretariat to work among churches and Christian councils in Asia, and eventually to the creation of an Asian ecumenical instrument, the East Asia Christian Conference (EACC), later to become the Christian Conference in Asia (CCA). D. T. Niles, one the primary architects of the EACC, did much in its formative stages to keep the EACC a genuine part of the global ecumenical movement and yet an authentic regional body committed to tackling the hard issues faced by Christians and churches in the Asian region. The Asian ecumenical body became one of the active, vibrant, relevant ecumenical bodies within the ecumenical scene inspiring the creation of such regional bodies in other parts of the world.

THE ROMAN CATHOLIC CHURCH IN ASIAN ECUMENISM

In the meantime, within the Roman Catholic Church (RCC), Pope John XXIII decided that a 'Second Sacred Ecumenical Synod of the Vatican'

---

[10] The debate over the issue was so intense that after the Tambaram meeting Kraemer's presentation and that of those who dissented were collected as a volume of the proceedings of the conference: see *The Authority of Faith: International Missionary Council Meeting at Tambaram, Madras,* 12–29 December 1938 (London: Oxford University Press, 1939).

should be called to consider the issues that the Roman Catholic Church was facing in a new era. The Council, popularly known as Vatican II, examined several issues pertaining to the life of the RCC. Ecumenism, or its relationship to other churches and ecclesial communities, became one of its priorities. For the first time Protestant and Orthodox observers were invited to the Council. In 1960 a Secretariat for Promoting Christian Unity was created to serve the Council in its ecumenical deliberations. *The Decree on Ecumenism* and the document on the *Dogmatic Constitution of the Church* opened the possibility for ecumenical advances, and successive Popes have been committed to the ecumenical spirit that emanated from Vatican II.

Many within the RCC in the Asian region made full use of the new openings that Vatican II presented, especially in the areas of theology, liturgy and ecumenism. One of the most significant developments, from the perspective of ecumenism, is the coming together of the National Episcopal Conferences in Asia into the Federation of Asian Bishops' Conference (FABC), officially constituted in 1972. Thus, the RCC had an umbrella organization in Asia, like the CCA that brought together the churches and Christian agencies of the Protestant and Orthodox traditions in the region. Further, the FABC created an Office of Ecumenical and Interreligious Affairs (OEIA) with the mandate to promote Roman Catholic relations with the churches and religious traditions in the region.

Virginia Fabella points out that the new office was initially more concerned with other religious traditions than the other churches in Asia. She notes that 'despite the FABC's stand on ecumenical collaboration, given the multi-religious reality of Asia, the bishops focused more on interreligious rather than ecumenical dialogue. Dialogue is key to the Catholic bishops, but as often stated, it is a triple dialogue with Asian religions, Asian cultures and Asia's poor.'[11] The two large bodies, representing between them most of the Asian Christians, however, could not remain in mutual isolation. The growing contacts at personal and institutional levels resulted in a historic meeting in Singapore on 9-10 July 1987 on the theme 'Living and Working Together with Sisters and Brothers of Other Faiths in Asia'.[12]

---

[11] Virginia Fabella, 'The Roman Catholic Church in the Asian Ecumenical Movement', in Koshy (ed.), *A History of the Ecumenical Movement,* vol. II, p. 116.

[12] D. D. Rosales Gaudencio and C. G. Arevalo (eds.), *For All the Peoples of Asia: Federation of Asian Bishops' Conferences Documents from 1970 to 1991,* vol. I (Quezon City, Philippines: Laretian Publications, 1997), p. 303.

Even though this was the first official meeting sponsored by the two bodies, there had already been significant participation of leaders and scholars across the confessional lines in numerous conferences and meetings on issues affecting the Asian region. The Singapore meeting, however, precipitated interest in having more formal cooperation between the CCA and the FABC, resulting initially in the formation of an Asian Ecumenical Committee (AEC) to promote greater cooperation and later in a more ambitious Asian Movement for Christian Unity (AMCU). The activities carried out under this umbrella and the mutual participation in CCA–FABC meetings and consultations have brought Asian Christians closer together. It must be noted, however, that much of the togetherness of Christians and churches in Asia is inspired more by the urge to witness to and be of service in the world than by the urge to seek the institutional unity of the divided churches. This orientation of both the CCA and the FABC towards Asia's peoples, traditions, issues and historical developments continues to inspire the greater Asian ecumenical scene. We should, therefore, examine the role of ecumenism in the social, political, economic and religio-cultural context of Asia.

THE CHURCH, THE WORLD AND MISSION

The greatest challenge that faced the Asian churches in the early stages of the post-colonial era was the question of identity, which related to three distinct issues. First, having gained some measure of independence from their 'mother churches' in the west, they had to find their 'selfhood' as churches in Asia. What did it mean, to use Pieris's words, to transform themselves from being the 'church *in* Asia' to the 'church *of* Asia'? This was a difficult issue because most of the denominational and confessional churches were still closely related to the parent churches in the west and were still dependent on them for human and financial resources. The structures of the church that had been uncritically adopted from the parent churches, the institutions built by mission agencies to promote education, health and social welfare, and the methods of missionary out-reach were enormous and expensive and needed external resources to maintain. Hence it was difficult for the Asian churches suddenly to cut their dependence on their western partners. More importantly, the task of becoming the 'church *of* Asia' involved a radical change in the 'ethos' of the church, a rethinking of theology, a building of new relationships with peoples of other faith traditions and a more committed participation in nation building. The Asian churches were the least prepared for the political independence of the Asian nations and were in a state of confusion. The newly constituted Asian ecumenical instrument, EACC, under the leadership of Niles, did much to enable the churches to grapple with the question of 'selfhood' in ways that helped to maintain their links with the universal church and yet to assert their identity and independence as Asian churches. Even though the Churches found it difficult to shed their colonial heritage and transform themselves into the churches *of* Asia, a task yet to be completed, the ecumenical movement in Asia should be credited with keeping the issue constantly at the forefront of the churches' endeavour.

The second and equally difficult issue of identity had to do with the churches' relationship to the world. The 'world' in Asia meant a multi-religious and multicultural world, a world that was beset with poverty, oppression and deprivation. Even though the rank and file of church membership in Asia came from the poor masses, the leadership of the church, for a long time in the hands of the missionaries, had the colonial ethos built into it. The Asian 'world' in the missionary era was primarily a 'mission field' and an arena for Christian service and humanitarian mission. The biggest struggle for the churches in Asia was to re-discover themselves as part of that world, to identify with it, to suffer with it and to be ready to participate in its destiny. This, to quote Pieris again, demanded nothing less than a 'baptism by immersion in the Asian spirituality and poverty'. This too was hard for the churches, but the ecumenical movement in Asia did much to enable the churches to understand the extent of the challenge they faced on this question in the post-colonial context.

The third issue of identity related to the churches' understanding of the evangelistic mission of the church in the new context. Even though the missionary movement in Asia had done much to liberate and humanize Asian societies in general, the classical missionary paradigm was 'church planting', where evangelization was seen as a task of calling peoples out of their communities to become part of the Christian community, which lived as an alternative community. The ecumenical movement in Asia helped the churches to expand their understanding of mission and evangelism for the new context. In fact, Asian ecumenism helped the churches in this struggle not only in Asia but also at the global level. As seen earlier, the Asian voices had challenged the classical understanding of mission and the approach it promoted toward other religions and cultures at the World Mission Conferences in Jerusalem and Tambaram. Further thinking on mission was facilitated in the assemblies, consultations and conferences of the EACC/CCA.

Niles, as the General Secretary of the EACC, has written several books and articles that reinterpret the missionary task in ways that respect the integrity and reality of other religious traditions.[13] The primary move made on the issue by the ecumenical movement in Asia was to affirm all people as God's people and to see the church as the servant of God's mission in the world. A further move was to see the risen Christ as already present and at work in the movements and events in Asia that had brought about healing and wholeness to the people. Niles introduces the concept of the 'previousness of Christ' to affirm that the risen Christ was already present and active in Asia long before the missionary out-reach. We do not bring Christ into Asia, he argues, but we witness to him by pointing out his healing grace at work in the world. He popularizes the image of evangelism as one beggar telling another where food may be found, thereby striking at the roots of the triumphalism that had been part of the missionary enterprise.

M. M. Thomas goes further, interpreting the meaning of salvation as humanization and interpreting mission as the humanization of the life of the Asian people, thereby presenting a theological rationale for the Christian participation with people of other faiths and ideologies in post-colonial nation building.[14] Even though Niles and Thomas are given here as examples of the new thinking of the time, the urgency for rethinking mission was felt by those committed to the ecumenical vision all over Asia and is reflected in the statements and documents of the EACC/CCA, FABC assemblies and consultations. 'The Christian Community within the Human Community' was already the focus of the first EACC assembly in Bangkok (1959); and the tradition had continued, as reflected in the title of the report of the CCA Mission Conference in Osaka (1989) 'Peoples of Asia, People of God', and in the theme of the eleventh assembly of the CCA in Tomohon, Indonesia (2000) 'Time for Fullness of Life for All'.

---

[13] Among D. T. Niles's significant works are: *Sir, We Would See Jesus* (London: SCM press, 1938); *Preacher's Calling to be Servant* (London: Lutterworth Press, 1959); *Preachers Task and the Stone of Stumbling* (New York: Harper and Brothers, 1958). He also drafted many of the statements on mission and evangelism of the EACC and conducted studies on mission. For a comprehensive statement on mission that resulted from these consultations, see D. T. Niles, *Upon the Earth: The Mission of God and the Missionary Enterprise of the Church* (London: Lutterworth Press, 1962).

[14] See M. M. Thomas, *Salvation and Humanization: Some Crucial Issues of the Theology of Mission in Contemporary India* (Bangalore: CISRS, 1971) and M. M. Thomas, *The Secular Ideologies of India and the Secular Meaning of Christ* (Madras: CLS, 1976).

RELIGIONS, CULTURES AND THEOLOGY

The other area in which the ecumenical movement in Asia has made considerable strides is in the field of theology. In the missionary era the classical confessional theologies were handed over by the missionary movement as the theology of the Asian churches; the respective missions also transplanted confessional brands of liturgy and church structures. Even though individual missionaries and small groups of Asian Christians had rebelled against this reality from the very beginning, there had been no real avenue to rethink the Christian faith in Asia. As mentioned earlier, church leaders in China were keen on the 'sinicization' of the faith and related this to Confucian and Taoist culture. In India a 'Rethinking of Christianity in India' group emerged, seeking to rethink Christianity in the Hindu context. Similar movements, less recognized and visible, were in action in other parts of Asia also. Much of the work of rethinking Christianity in thought and practice happened in ashrams, study centres and amongst small groups of scholars, but these were marginal to mainstream Christianity and unable to make any impact on the theology and missiology that had come with the original missions. Real possibilities for effective rethinking opened up after the formation of the EACC/CCA and the openings provided by Vatican II for tentative, yet bold, experiments with liturgy, theology and missiology within the RCC.

The new theological thinking developed along four lines within Asian ecumenism. First were attempts to rethink the faith in the context of religions and cultures. Many of the Asian theologians who worked on this area in the first phase of Asian ecumenism, like Kosuke Koyama and Sachi Yagi in Japan, C. S. Song in Taiwan, Lynne A. de Silva and Aloysius Pieris in Sri Lanka, and M. M. Thomas, P. D. Devanandan, Stanley Samartha and others in India were given a platform for their rethinking in the ecumenical arena. These were later followed by several younger theologians of all church traditions (too many to name) that have begun to push the theological boundaries of the church in the area of relating the faith to the religious and cultural traditions of Asia.

Masao Takenaka and Ron O'Grady, under the umbrella of the EACC/CCA, provided leadership in making these theological explorations concrete by enabling people to express the indigenization of the Gospel message in Asian art, music, dance, architecture and new forms of worship.[15]

---

[15] See Masao Takenaka, *Christian Art in Asia* (Tokyo: Kyo Bun Kwan and CCA, 1975); Masao Takenaka, *The Place Where God Dwells: An Introduction to Church Architecture in Asia* (Hong Kong: CCA, 1995).

The need for Asian Christians to sing each other's songs was recognized at the beginnings of the EACC. The first attempt to bring together Asian songs in an *EACC Hymnal* (Bangkok 1964) was undertaken by Niles. The creation of the Asian Institute of Liturgy and Music (AILM) in Manila, Philippines, with Francisco Feliciano as its head, gave a much-needed institutional base to this concern. I-to-Loh, who assisted him at that time, an ethnomusicologist from Taiwan, did much work on collecting and setting to music songs from all parts of Asia. A revised version of the *Sound of the Bamboo*, edited by Feliciano, I-to-Loh and Jim Minchin of Australia and published by the CCA in 2000, had three hundred and fifteen hymns from twenty-two countries representing forty-three languages.[16] Interesting experiments have been done also in the pastoral and liturgical centres of the RCC, on indigenizing the liturgy, music and symbols of the Christian tradition in Asia.

The second line along which the Asian ecumenical theological tradition developed related to the Christian faith in the context of Asian socio-political realities. Here the movement facilitated streams of theological thinking like peoples' theology in the Philippines, minjung theology in Korea, Asian liberation theologies, dalit theology and the like. The greatest contribution of the ecumenical movement to individual Asian theologians and schools of theology was to facilitate the meeting of people who were until then working in isolation, by publishing their thinking and making it widely available in Asian countries and outside. Several theological consultations organized by the CCA and the FABC, individually and jointly, helped the Asian theologians to test their thinking with colleagues; there was cross-fertilization of ideas across national and confessional lines. The CCA's Commission on Theological Concerns and its *CTC Bulletin* did much to further ecumenical theological thinking in Asia. The Congress of Asian Theologians (CATS) that meets periodically to explore relevant theological themes has been successful both in furthering theological thinking in Asia and in introducing new theologians to the movement.[17] The creation of the Ecumenical Association of Third World Theologians (EATWOT) opened the way for Asian theologians to

---

For the history, see Ron and Alison O'Grady (eds.), *Twenty Years: A Celebration of the Asian Christian Art Association* (Hong Kong: ACAA, 1998).

[16] Cf. Ron O'Grady, 'Indigenization and Asian Culture', in Koshy (ed.), *A History of the Ecumenical Movement*, vol. II, p. 380.

[17] Formed by the CCA in 1997, CATS has organized four Congresses up to 2005. Even though the Roman Catholic Church (FABC) is not a co-sponsor, Catholic theologians and the observers from the FABC play a significant role in the Congress as leaders and keynote speakers.

be in conversation with those doing theology in African, Latin American and other marginalized contexts.

The third line of theological development within Asian ecumenism related to the plight of women in Asia and in empowering women to do theology of their own. The CCA was slow in getting issues relevant to women on its ecumenical agenda. Initially it took the form of promoting 'Cooperation of Men and Women in Home, Church and Society' (1959), but gradually the questions of discrimination and oppression became part of the ecumenical agenda. More importantly, the movement began to provide the space necessary for women to speak for themselves. CCA's sixth assembly in Penang (1977) and seventh assembly in Bangalore (1981) were places where women were able to bring their concerns as theological concerns affecting the practice of the faith of the church. The CCA formed a Committee on Women's Concerns and also set up a 'desk' for women's concern within its staff structure. The programmes carried out under this desk and the evolution of a 'Women's Commission' within the EATWOT have helped in the evolution of a distinct Asian feminist theology in Asia, with persons like Virginia Fabella, Angela Wong, Mary John Mananzan, Sun Ai Lee Park, Sook Ja Chung and Pui-Lan Kwok giving the lead. The Asian women's journal *In God's Image* and the Asian Women's Resource Centre for Culture and Theology (AWRCCT) enhances the participation of women in the Asian theological task.[18]

The fourth line of development was in ecumenical social thought. From the very beginning, the Asian ecumenical movement has seen socio-economic-political issues as questions of faith. The task of post-colonial nation building presented stark alternatives to the political–economic scene. The pressures on Asian nations to move towards capitalism, socialism or communism were enormous and the churches had to deal with hard choices in the context of Asia's extreme poverty and deprivation. Wars and internal turmoil in several countries forced the movement to think about issues of violence and non-violence, peace and reconciliation, and religion and state. The emphasis on development brought questions of the kinds of development that are appropriate for the region. The plight of women in Asian societies raised fundamental questions about the Christian understanding of human worth and dignity. The oppression and marginalization of several groups of people raised ethical issues about the nature of the community we seek. Asian

---

[18] For a more detailed account, see Angela Wai Ching Wong, 'Women Doing Theology with the Asian Ecumenical Movement', in Koshy (ed.), *A History of the Ecumenical Movement*, vol. II, pp. 85–114.

ecumenical social thought was firmly based on three theological pillars. First, the world belongs to God and God is active in it to bring about its healing; Christian discipleship entails our willingness to participate with God in this work of liberation. Secondly, economic, social and political issues are questions of faith; involvement in them is part of the test of faith and witness. Thirdly, social ethics has to do primarily with human worth and dignity; nothing that diminishes the worth of a human person can correspond to the will of God.

JUSTICE, HUMAN RIGHTS AND RELIGIOUS LIBERTY

Concrete programmes and activities to promote justice and reconciliation accompanied the theological reflections on issues. Born in the midst of revolutionary changes, social upheavals, wars and inter-ethnic and inter-religious conflicts, the Asian ecumenical movement has had much to say about international affairs, human rights, rights of communities, religious liberty and the relationship between religion and state. More importantly, the movement has been engaged with action groups, social movements, liberation struggles and groups engaged in bringing about relief, rehabilitation and development. The Urban and Rural Mission (URM) is instrumental in expressing solidarity with marginalized groups. The Asian Christian Service, formed to minister to the people of Vietnam, did much to bring relief and rehabilitation to the whole of Indochina, and similar movements have been active in promoting efforts at unification in the Korean peninsula, giving pastoral support in areas where communities are in conflict on religious or ethnic issues. In fact the strength of Asian ecumenism lies in its capacity to strike a healthy balance between action and facilitation and its ability to promote thought, advocacy and action on a variety of issues that affect the life of the Asian churches and the peoples of Asia.

CHALLENGES FACING THE ECUMENICAL MOVEMENT IN ASIA

Given the complexity and plurality of the Asian continent, it must be said that the record of the ecumenical movement in Asia in the past, despite the shortcomings that necessarily accompany any such movements, is quite impressive. The movement has not only been of service to the Asian continent but has also made an enormous contribution to global ecumenism in terms of both ideas and persons; Asian leadership in global ecumenism has an impressive record. But, what are the prospects for ecumenism in Asia? What are some of the challenges it needs to face as it looks to the future? This question of course can be answered from a variety of perspectives. I shall briefly highlight seven issues that will affect the future development of ecumenism in the decades ahead.

The impact of globalization

Much has been said about the positive and negative impacts of the globalization of economic and financial markets, the radical changes that are being brought about by the communications revolution and the demographic impact of the massive movements of population in our day. In one sense, the ecumenical movement aims also at building a 'global community' where nations and peoples will live together in peace and justice; the 'oikoumene' of the ecumenical vision is indeed the 'whole inhabited earth'. Several Asian countries and sections of the population in all Asian countries, however, are deeply affected by the negative effects of economic globalization. Widespread and ever-deepening poverty, economic dependence, the loss of the power of the state, the imposition of a materialistic consumerist ideology, and the loss of the sense of identity and community are matters that continue to draw the attention of the Asian ecumenical movement. The effect of the unregulated liberalization of the financial markets hit Asia when Japan, South Korea, Thailand, Malaysia and Indonesia suddenly found themselves in financial ruins in the Asian financial crisis of 1997.

Globalization, as a process of drawing the human community closer together, however, is likely to stay with us; people of the world need to find ways of harnessing its positive elements for the good of the wider community; they need to find ways of providing space for each other and learning to live together in peace and justice. While it may not be possible to prevent the globalization of the human community, it should indeed be possible to enable the Asian people and nations to have a better understanding of the issues involved, to expose its negative effects on nations and people and to help find avenues that will channel the globalizing forces to move in creative directions. One of the problems presented by the impact of globalization is that many issues are no longer clearly confined to specific geographical regions nor can they be tackled by the commitment of people in any one region or religion. The Asian ecumenical movement has been engaged in several studies on the effects of globalization on people's lives, but neither they nor the ecumenical movement at the global level have found adequate ways of addressing this difficult issue. This remains a challenge to the movement as it looks to the future.

Affluence and poverty

The second issue relates to the gradual blurring of the lines between the 'north' and the 'south' as categories that denote the developed and developing worlds, especially as this relates to Asia. Some of the Asian countries like Japan, Korea, Singapore and Taiwan have achieved economic prosperity in general and have become major trading partners with the countries of the north. China, India and Indonesia have the potential economically to rival any of the western nations in the near future. At the same time, several other Asian countries struggle to live above the poverty line. Further, in almost all Asian countries the gap between the rich and the poor within the countries has been growing. The attitude of seeing economic prosperity as the sole goal of life has been on the increase. This reality has raised several questions for the classical north–south framework within which economic issues are discussed in the Asian context. At the political level, there have been attempts to build up the relationships among nations in Asia and to create adequate economic and political instruments to protect Asian interests from falling prey to the predatory capitalism of the north. At the same time bewilderment over the impact of a consumerist, secular culture on Asian people is shared by the leadership of all the major religious traditions of Asia, which have consistently taught the limitations of material benefits and the need to place greater emphasis on a spirituality that affirms nobler values in life. New initiatives are necessary within Asian ecumenism to deal with this multi-faceted question.

The rise of China and India

The Asian ecumenical movement also needs to prepare itself for the emerging new geopolitical reality in which China and India are likely to emerge as major economic and political powers of the twenty-first century. Even though Chinese churches have played a significant role and provided much leadership to the ecumenical movement in the early stages, political developments in China have prevented the churches, for decades, from having any meaningful involvement in it. When China opened up to the world outside, the mainline Church of Christ in China was not able to play a significant role because of its need to concentrate on rebuilding the church internally and training and equipping a new generation of leadership. The unresolved issue of the China–Taiwan relationship also plagues the Chinese relationship with the Asian ecumenical movement. There have, of course, been many attempts on the part of the Asian and global ecumenical movements to facilitate the involvement of the Chinese churches in their programmes and to help the church in China in its reconstruction, but more needs to be done to facilitate the fuller involvement of China in Asian ecumenism. Likewise, in India the Christian relationship with Hinduism has been under pressure and much needs to be done to lay a more secure and solid foundation for a good relationship.

The movement also needs to ask the question: What kind of global leaders will China and India become? Will they simply imitate the example of the western powers that dominate and exploit the world, or will they pave the way for new ways of building international relationships, international security and the people's economic wellbeing? The Asian ecumenical movement is well placed to initiate and foster discussions over these issues in the church and in secular circles.

Strains in interfaith relations

The fourth concern for Asian ecumenism is the deterioration of the relationships between religious traditions and the conflicts that they have engendered. The rise of conservative and militant expressions of religion, insensitive and aggressive methods of evangelizing, the increasing role of religion in political affairs, issues of religious liberty and the loss of impact of religious values in general are matters that call for concerted attention.

The perceived confrontation between the west and Islam, aggravated by the unwarranted invasion of Iraq, the unrestrained war on terror and the proliferation of militant groups within Islam have begun to have an impact in Asia also. The Philippines, Indonesia, Thailand, India, Pakistan, Bangladesh and several other nations in the region face the prospect of a worsening inter-religious situation unless timely measures are taken to contain the problems and to meet legitimate grievances.

The incomplete social revolution

Even though the Asian region underwent a social revolution at the end of the colonial era, this revolution remains partial, especially in relation to women, children and marginalized groups within most Asian societies. Discrimination against the dalits in India, the tribal and aboriginal peoples in several countries and ethnic and religious minorities in others, continues to frustrate the building of a truly human community in Asia. While there is a greater consciousness of the need to treat women with equality and dignity, in reality women in most Asian countries still suffer the discrimination they have suffered for centuries. Much of the discrimination against women is still entrenched in religious and cultural norms. There is also deep concern over the widespread prevalence of child labour, child prostitution, child soldiers and child abuse in the Asian region. Here too the ecumenical movement in Asia has been active, but these concerns should continue to dominate the agenda. Asian societies can never be truly free until the rights and dignity of women, children and minority groups are secured.

A changing religious consciousness

It is no secret that the ecumenical movement in all parts of the world is in some measure of crisis in terms of leadership, resources and agenda. Much has been said and written to analyse the reasons, but some of it has to be attributed to a changing religious consciousness in the context of a global culture that promotes individualism and consumerism. Conservative religious movements that place an emphasis on individual salvation, promise prosperity as God's gift and give definitive answers to difficult questions have made many inroads into the religious consciousness of people. Ecumenism, increasingly, appears to be a luxury that individuals can ill afford. Happily, there is still considerable commitment on the part of the churches towards ecumenism, but it can no longer be taken for granted; hence, the need to rebuild the ecumenical movement from the base on new foundations has become urgent. This also requires programmes that involve and include the progressive elements within 'evangelical' circles. The moves that have been made in this direction in the CCA and the conversations about a 'larger ecumenical instrument for Asia' are good beginnings and need to be pursued.

The search for a wider ecumenism

The churches in Asia will remain minorities in most Asian societies in the foreseeable future. Their lives are inextricably bound up with those of the people of other religious and secular traditions. Christians cannot hope to resolve any of the intractable problems of the continent on their own or with their own resources. In any case, a creative, positive and genuine relationship with the people of other religious traditions is absolutely essential for Christian life and witness in Asia. All this points to the inadequacy of an ecumenism that relates only to the divided churches.

The churches should still work together to grow in their own unity and to bring the best of their resources to serve the larger community, but they also need to seek to build a 'new' or 'wider' ecumenism that will bring people across all religious traditions into the service of humanizing and liberating Asian societies as a whole. There is every reason to believe that the Asian churches and the ecumenical movement are able to discern the urgency of this need; they also need to begin to act on it.

BIBLIOGRAPHY

The Authority of Faith: International Missionary Council Meeting at Tambaram, Madras, 12-29 December 1938, London: Oxford University Press, 1939.

England, J. C., *The Hidden History of Christianity in India: The Church of the East Before 1500*, Delhi: ISPCK, 1996.

Koshy, N., *A History of the Ecumenical Movement in Asia*, vol. I, Hong Kong: World Student Christian Federation Asia Pacific Alliance of YMCAs and Christian Conference of Asia, 2004.

Koshy, N. (ed.), *A History of the Ecumenical Movement in Asia*, vol. II, Hong Kong: World Student Christian Federation Asia Pacific Alliance of YMCAs and Christian Conference of Asia, 2004.

Kraemer, H., *The Christian Message in a Non-Christian World*, London: Edinburgh House Press, 1938.

Mott, J. R., *Strategic Points in the World's Conquest*, London: Nisbet, 1987.

Niles, D. T., *Upon the Earth: The Mission of God and the Missionary Enterprise of the Church*, London: Lutterworth Press, 1962.

O'Grady, R. and O'Grady, A. (eds.), *Twenty-Years: A Celebration of the Asian Christian Art Association*, Hong Kong: ACAA, 1998.

Pieris., A., SJ, 'The Asian Sense in Theology', in J. C. England (ed.), *Living Theology in Asia*, London: SCM Press, 1981.

Smith, C. W., 'Christians in a Religiously Plural World', in J. Hick and B. Hebblethwaite (eds.), *Christianity and Other Religions*, Oxford: Oneworld, 2001, pp. 44–58.

Takenaka, M., *Christian Art in Asia*, Tokyo: Kyo Bun Kwan and CCA, 1975.
The Place Where God Dwells: An Introduction to Church Architecture in Asia, Hong Kong: CCA, 1995.

Thomas, M. M., *Salvation and Humanization: Some Crucial Issues of the Theology of Mission in Contemporary India*, Bangalore: CISRS, 1971.
The Secular Ideologies of India and the Secular Meaning of Christ, Madras: CLS, 1976.

Weber, H. R., *Asia and the Ecumenical Movement*, London: SCM Press, 1966.

World Missionary Conference, Edinburgh, vol. IX, London: Oliphant Anderson and Ferrier, 1910.

CHAPTER 12

Mission and evangelism: evangelical and pentecostal theologies in Asia

Hwa Yung

The church in Asia has been growing at a phenomenal rate, doubling twice in the last century. This chapter will first examine the beginnings of evangelical and pentecostal theologies up to the middle of the twentieth century; secondly their further developments over the last fifty years; and thirdly the challenges posed for understanding Christianity and mission in Asia and globally.

First we need to clarify our use of the terms evangelical and pentecostal. 'Evangelical' refers to those who are theologically conservative, subscribing to traditional Christian doctrines and affirming the ultimate authority of the Bible, the importance of personal conversion and the need to obey the Great Commission of Matthew 28:18–20. 'Pentecostal' is used in a broad sense to refer to all who emphasize the supernatural work of the Holy Spirit and take seriously 'signs and wonders' in the life and ministry of the Christian church; hence, it applies collectively to 'classical Pentecostals' and 'charismatics' who trace their roots to Azusa Street in 1906, as well as to many varieties of indigenous Asian churches.[1]

THE NINETEENTH CENTURY AND THE FIRST HALF OF THE TWENTIETH CENTURY

India

Nehemiah Goreh (1825–95) is an important example of evangelical theology in nineteenth-century India. Goreh was a Brahmin who converted to Christianity in 1848. His most significant work, *A Rational Refutation of*

---

[1] The term pentecostal (lower case 'p') is used as defined above and distinguished from classical Pentecostals (upper case 'P') here. See further David B. Barrett, *et al.* (eds.), *World Christian Encyclopaedia* (Oxford and New York: Oxford University Press, 2001), vol. I, pp. 27–30; and Hwa Yung., 'Pentecostalism and the Asian Church', in Allan Anderson and Edmund Tang (eds.), *Asian and Pentecostal: The Charismatic Face of Asian Christianity* (Oxford: Regnum, 2005), pp. 37–57.

the Hindu Philosophical Systems,[2] is a conscious apologetic directed at the six traditional systems of Hindu philosophy, including a lengthy critique of *Advaita Vedanta* (non-dualism). He employs the *reductio ad absurdum* against Vedantic epistemology and the concept of *maya*.[3]

Vedantic philosophy affirms that there is only one reality, *Brahman*; *Brahman* has true existence in contrast with the practical existence of the world, human souls and the personal God (*Isvara*). Yet the true Vedantin knows that practical existence is illusory. The phenomenal world and God appear to be real because of *maya* (ignorance or illusion). Only when one sees beyond these to *Brahman*, one truly sees reality. Goreh, however, proceeds to demonstrate the incoherence of this epistemology. He states: 'Such is the waywardness of the Vedantins' intellect, that, though they consider a thing to be false, and call it practical and apparent, yet, as soon as they have called it so, it begins to look to them real.'[4] That is, while on the one hand the world is said to be false and illusory, on the other hand it is equated with *Brahman*. But, Goreh argues, either the world actually exists (implying dualism), or everything apart from *Brahman* is *maya* (illusion arising from ignorance). Yet, if cosmic-illusionism is true and the phenomenal world is *maya* (illusion), we cannot know anything in it to be true, including the whole Vedantic philosophical worldview of which the idea of *maya* is a part. Thus, cosmic-illusionism makes nonsense of all our empirical experiences and, as Goreh shows, one cannot consistently claim to be an absolute non-dualist and try to smuggle in some kind of existence for that which is not *Brahman*.[5]

Among those influenced by Goreh was Pandita Ramabai Sarasvati (1858–1922) or simply Pandita Ramabai, probably the most well known of Indian Christian women.[6] Like Goreh, she was born a Brahmin. She became a noted Sanskrit scholar as a child, but converted to Christianity in 1883, becoming a radical advocate of women's rights and social reform in modern India. Ramabai is also significant for her role in pentecostal beginnings, following a spiritual revival that began on 30 June 1905 at the Mukti Mission in Pune, of which she was the founder. Accounts of the

[2] Nehemiah Goreh, *A Rational Refutation of the Hindu Philosophical Systems*, trans. Fitz-Edward Hall (Calcutta: Bishop's College Press, 1862).
[3] *Ibid.*, pp. 156–280; cf. Robin S. Boyd, *An Introduction to Indian Christian Theology*, revised edition (Madras: Christian Literature Society, 1975), pp. 46–50.
[4] Goreh, *A Rational Refutation of the Hindu Philosophical System*, p. 251.
[5] Hwa Yung, *Mangoes or Bananas?: The Quest for an Authentic Asian Christian Theology* (Oxford: Regnum, 1997), pp. 133–5.
[6] For a useful introduction to her writings, see M. Kosambi (ed.), *Pandita Ramabai Through Her Own Words: Selected Works*, trans. M. Kosambi (New Delhi: Oxford University Press, 2000).

revival reported weeping and speaking in tongues, preceding the so-called 'original' appearance of classical Pentecostalism in 1906 in Azusa Street, Los Angeles, and acted as a catalyst for the beginnings of Pentecostalism in Chile.[7] Furthermore, for Ramabai, this revival was one way by which the Spirit was creating an indigenous Indian Christianity.[8] This is fairly typical of other examples of indigenous Christianity in Asia, as well as in Africa and Latin America; that is, in the absence of a rationalistic Enlightenment worldview, indigenous Christianity tends towards pentecostalism.

This brings us to Sadhu Sundar Singh (1889–1929), probably the most famous of Indian Christians. Born a Sikh, he was brought up under the strong influence of his mother in both the Sikh and the Hindu *bhakti* traditions. But following her death he converted to Christianity in 1904. He embarked on an evangelistic preaching ministry across India, into Tibet and, finally, all over the world. Eric Sharpe classifies Sundar Singh's theology as 'evangelical orthodoxy' and asserts that 'no Indian Christian has exercised an influence even remotely comparable to Sundar Singh's'.[9]

Sundar Singh experienced many visions, which he tested against the Christian scriptures,[10] in addition to overseeing the miracles and healings that were apparently commonplace in his ministry.[11] Moreover, his approach was firmly rooted in his culture. His sermons and writings constantly used parables drawn from everyday life in India.[12] In his arguments, he regularly employed a recognized Indian pattern of reasoning, which dealt with issues, not by precise logic, but by use of vivid analogy.[13] Similarly, by living as a *sadhu* and a *sannyasi*, he used a contextual model of preaching and teaching which Indians were familiar with and readily accepted. Further, as with Justin Martyr, Sundar Singh saw the Logos at work everywhere, even in non-Christian cultures and scriptures. He sums up his passionate concern to proclaim Christ contextually as follows: 'Indians do need the Water of Life, but not in the European Cup.'[14]

---

[7] Allan Anderson, *An Introduction to Pentecostalism* (Cambridge: Cambridge University Press, 2004), pp. 36–7 and 173–5.

[8] *Ibid.*, p. 173; see also Roger E. Hedlund, *Quest for Identity: India's Churches of Indigenous Origin: The 'Little Tradition' in Indian Christianity* (Delhi: ISPCK, 2000), pp. 157–63.

[9] Eric J. Sharpe, 'The Legacy of Sadhu Sundar Singh', *International Bull. Miss. Research* 14:4 (1990), 161–7 at 165.

[10] Boyd, *An Introduction to Indian Christian Theology*, p. 95.

[11] See A. J. Appasamy, *Sundar Singh: A Biography* (Madras: Christian Literature Society, 1966), pp. 97–100.

[12] See his writings in T. D. Francis (ed.), *The Christian Witness of Sadhu Sundar Singh: A Collection of His Writings* (Madras: Christian Literature Society, 1989).

[13] Boyd, *An Introduction to Indian Christian Theology*, pp. 96 and 231.

[14] From a personal interview with the authors, cited in B. H. Streeter and A. J. Appasamy, *The Sadhu: A Study in Mysticism and Practical Religion* (London: Macmillan, 1921).

Japan

The two most important thinkers from Japan in this period are Kanzo Uchimura (1861–1930) and Toyohiko Kagawa (1888–1960); the former is the pioneer of the 'non-church' concept and the latter is known for holistic mission.

Kanzo Uchimura, from the *samurai* class, grew up with a combination of Confucian morality and Japanese folk religion. In 1877 he enrolled in the Sapparo Agriculture School, where he converted to Christianity, although, during the Meiji Restoration, Christianity was often deemed to be incompatible with traditional Japanese values. Uchimura attempted to reconcile patriotism and Christianity. He went to America in 1884 and became more evangelical while studying at Amherst College. He studied further at Hartford, before returning to Japan in 1888 and devoting his life to education, journalism and evangelistic ministry.[15]

Uchimura's distinctive contribution to Japanese Christianity is his *mu-kyokai* or 'non-church' concept, which was a major initiative towards indigenization, or a unique Japanese form of Christianity. He rejected the institutional church as 'a kind of government or political party, which tries to expand its power and save the people, not by faith but by public opinion'.[16] He disliked creeds and traditional doctrines, and was indifferent towards the sacraments. For him, the Gospel is 'Jesus Christ and him crucified. I protest against any doctrine or set of doctrines which go beyond ... this simplest of all doctrines'[17] and the non-church is the natural expression of the community of the coming kingdom; it is the true church, the church of those who are without an institutional church. However, Uchimura never rejected the church *per se* as a community of God's people, unlike some of his more radical followers. He and his followers formed small Bible study groups, meeting weekly in homes. Widely published, he had a major and lasting impact on the Japanese church and society.

Toyohiko Kagawa converted to Christianity at fifteen, subsequently training in the Presbyterian College, Tokyo, followed by Kobe Theological Seminary and, later, Princeton. He moved to Shinkawa, the appalling Kobe slums, in 1909 in order to begin a credible programme of evangelism and social outreach as an insider. As a Christian socialist, he

---

[15] Akio Dohi, 'The First Generation: Christian Leaders in the First Period', in Yasuo Furuya (ed.), *A History of Japanese Theology* (Grand Rapids: Eerdmans, 1997), pp. 11–42 at pp. 18 and 35–42.

[16] Kanzo Uchimura, *The Study of the Bible*, no. 11 (1921), cited in Dohi, 'The First Generation', p. 37.

[17] Kanzo Uchimura, *Protestantism*, no. 5 (1916), cited in Dohi, 'The First Generation', p. 40.

cared for the sick and destitute, unionizing both industrial workers and peasants (at a time when unions were illegal), espousing non-violence and opposing Japanese military aggression overseas. He was often in trouble with the police and sometimes imprisoned, until, at the height of the 1930s depression, he was made chief adviser to Tokyo's welfare bureau, subsequently serving as special adviser to the government on public welfare.

As an indefatigable evangelist, Kagawa coordinated the Kingdom of God Movement in Japan from 1929–32, netting 62,460 'decisions', although only a fraction of these actually joined the church. His goal, in his own words, was to effect 'the salvation of 100,000 poor, hasten the day of the emancipation of 9,430,000 labourers toiling in various fields and liberate 20,000,000 tenant farmers'.[18] Perhaps the greatest difficulty in assessing Kagawa lies with his theology. Charles Germany places him among the key exponents of modern Japanese liberal theology.[19] Nevertheless, he held fundamentalist theological beliefs, such as the virgin birth, the incarnation and the Cross as penal substitution. Yet, his extreme optimism about post-conversion humanity and his view of the Kingdom of God as fully realizable in history, through an ethic of love and human brotherhood, clearly place him amongst proponents of the social gospel. He maintains respect amongst Japanese Christians today.

China

The three most notable revivalist figures of China in the 1920s and 1930s are Wang Ming-Dao (1900–91), John Sung (1901–44) and Watchman Nee (1903–72). In 1927 Wang Ming-Dao began building the Christian Tabernacle, an indigenous church in Beijing, in addition to which he produced a quarterly magazine, *Spiritual Food*. Between 1927 and 1940 John Sung brought revival to hundreds of churches across China and Southeast Asia, leading to tens of thousands of conversions, and exercised a powerful healing ministry. At the same time Watchman Nee (or Nee To-Sheng) was building a network of churches called 'Little Flocks' throughout China. Both Wang and Nee suffered long years of Communist incarceration, with the latter dying in prison.

By the beginning of the twentieth century, there was widespread opposition towards Christianity and its perceived links with imperialistic

---

[18] Cited in William Axling, *Kagawa* (London: SCM, 1932), p. 112.
[19] Charles H. Germany, *Protestant Theologies in Modern Japan* (Tokyo: International Institute for the Study of Religious Responsibility, 1965), pp. 32–7.

western powers. In response to the anti-Christian attacks one group of
Chinese Christians, many of them modernist, responded quickly with
apologetic arguments and indigenization efforts, shaped by the social
gospel of the time.[20] The conservatives, while agreeing with the modernists on the need for national salvation and the revitalization of the
church, however, rejected the social gospel in favour of a soteriological
focus emphasizing personal conversion. For them, repentance and faith in
Christ was the first step towards real transformation. Only then could the
church exemplify the life of Christ, and China's hope of building a truly
ethical society materialize. As Thomas Harvey states, 'Beneath the harsh
rhetoric, the true divide between Chinese modernists and fundamentalists lay
not in the goal of social improvement but in the means for achieving it.'[21]

Wang, Sung and Nee agreed upon the need for an independent Chinese
church, recognizing that western control and dependency on foreign funds
were stunting church growth; hence, they advocated the three-self principle
(two decades before the Three-Self Patriotic Movement of the Communist
era). Sung, for example, urged the church 'to be self-propagating, self-
governing and self-supporting',[22] and Wang built his Beijing church on
that basis. Nee went further by challenging the division between clergy and
laypersons, and promoting local autonomous and non-denominational
churches, freed from external organizational control. In practice, however,
his 'Little Flock' movement became an indigenous denomination of its
own, having grown, by 1949, to seven hundred congregations with seventy
thousand members. The movement remains a significant force amongst the
contemporary house church movement in China. Nevertheless, Sung was
the most effective Chinese evangelist and revivalist of that period and
operated most freely in the realm of 'signs and wonders', including healing
and prophecy, even though he was not a classical Pentecostal.[23]

All three men borrowed much from the theologies of conservative
western missionaries, which, at the time, prioritized the spiritual over

---

[20] Wing-Hung Lam, *Chinese Theology in Construction* (Pasadena: William Carey Library, 1983);
Chun Kwan Lee, 'The Theology of Revival in the Chinese Christian Church, 1900–1949: Its
Emergence and Impact', unpublished PhD thesis, Westminster Theological Seminary (1988),
pp. 94–173 and 237–48.

[21] Thomas A. Harvey, *Acquainted with Grief: Wang Mingdao's Stand for the Persecuted Church in
China* (Grand Rapids: Brazos Press, 2002), p. 8.

[22] Cited in Leslie Lyall, *A Biography of John Sung* (Singapore: Armour, 2004), p. 98. Similar
statements can be found in his diary entries; cf. John Sung, *The Diaries of John Sung: An
Autobiography*, trans. Stephen L. Sheng (Brighton, MI: Luke H. Sheng and Stephen L. Sheng,
1995), pp. 34, 54 and 183.

[23] Lyall, *A Biography of John Sung*, pp. xv and 168–73; on 'tongues' see Sung, *The Diaries of John Sung*,
p. 29.

socio-cultural matters. Hence, despite the inadequacy of the modernists' alternative, these Chinese leaders failed adequately to address the socio-cultural challenges of their world. Nevertheless their legacy has helped shape the ethos of the Chinese house church movement, as well as that of many overseas Chinese churches today.

THE SECOND HALF OF THE TWENTIETH CENTURY

The Second World War disrupted the life of the Asian churches, only to be followed by two decades of regional wars and widespread poverty. Through these times the church grew steadily, albeit slowly, in most places. It was some time before a more mature evangelicalism began to detach itself from its earlier fundamentalist tendencies, and for indigenous pentecostal movements to come into their own. From the late 1960s onwards there has been a gradual growth and strengthening such that, by the end of the twentieth century, Asian Protestant Christianity was largely evangelical and/or pentecostal.

Asian Christianity has always been broadly conservative, although some western missionaries and western-trained national leaders attempted to steer it in a liberal direction. In order to fight this trend, evangelicals banded together increasingly after the Second World War, initially forming the Evangelical Fellowship of Asia and the Asia Theological Association (ATA), and followed later by the Asia Lausanne Committee on World Evangelization. Notable individuals associated with these movements include Bong Rin Ro, Ken Gnanakan and Vinay Samuel; the first two were General Secretaries of the ATA. Ro's contribution has been mainly through his editorial work of multi-authored volumes on evangelical Asian contextual theology.[24] Similarly, Gnanakan has produced some important volumes on mission-related issues, while Samuel, in conjunction with his British colleague, Chris Sugden, has produced important literature on holistic mission.[25]

Similarly, within pentecostal circles, some very significant thinking in mission and evangelism has been emerging. For example, among

---

[24] These include Bong Rin Ro and Ruth Eshenaur, *The Bible and Theology in Asian Contexts* (Taichung: ATA, 1984); Bong Rin Ro (ed.), *Christian Alternatives to Ancestor Practices* (Taichung: ATA, 1985); Bong Rin Ro and Mark C. Albrecht (eds.), *God in Asian Contexts* (Taichung: ATA, 1988).

[25] See for example Ken Gnanakan, *Proclaiming Christ in a Pluralistic Context* (Bangalore: Theological Book Trust, 1989 and 2000); Vinay Samuel and Christopher Sugden (eds.), *The Church in Response to Human Need* (Grand Rapids: Eerdmans and Oxford: Regnum, 1987); and Vinay Samuel and Christopher Sugden (eds.), *Mission as Transformation* (Oxford: Regnum, 1999).

non-classical Pentecostals, Bakht Singh of India, who founded a cluster of 'Assemblies' with more than 200,000 members, has been referred to as a 'biblical indigenous prophet'.[26] Also, important theological work on evangelism, mission, pastoral leadership and spirituality is emerging among classical Pentecostals, such as Simon Chan, Wonsuk Ma,[27] Young-Gi Hong, and, most notably, David Yong-Gi Cho, the pastor of Yoido Full Gospel Church in Korea, all of whom come from the Assemblies of God tradition.

From a rather different angle, the Korean Presbyterian, Moonjang Lee, has made some innovative evangelical contributions to hermeneutics, mission and theology in an Asian and religiously plural context.[28] We shall look at ATA, Samuel and Cho in more detail below.

Asia Theological Association (ATA)

The Asia Theological Association was formed out of the concern that the Asian church leadership was being increasingly influenced by liberal theology. It was first constituted in 1968 at the Asia South-Pacific Congress of Evangelism in Singapore, with the goal of developing evangelical scholars and thinkers for the leadership of the Asian Church. Since its inception it has helped develop theological education all over the continent, up to doctoral level, and it has acted as the accreditation body for evangelical seminaries.

Theologically, its 'Statement of Faith' indicates that it follows mainstream evangelicalism in the west, as opposed to sectarian fundamentalism.[29] At the same time, in its concern for contextualization, it demonstrates that it is no mere western clone. Without minimizing the dangers of religious syncretism, universalism and accommodation in contextualization, it nevertheless affirms that 'these ... should not excuse evangelical theologians from taking responsibility for their cultural context seriously'.[30] In line with this concern, it has pioneered efforts to

---

[26] Hedlund, *Quest for Identity*, pp. 175–9.

[27] In addition to his writings, Ma co-edits the *Asian Journal of Pentecostal Studies* and *Asian Journal of Mission*.

[28] See for example Moonjang Lee, 'Experience of Religious Plurality in Korea: Its Theological Implications', *International Review of Mission* 88:351 (1999), 399–413; and 'Identifying an Asian Theology: A Methodological Quest', *Asia Journal of Theology* 13:2 (1999), 256–75.

[29] ATA, 'Statement of Faith', in *ATA Accreditation Manual for Residential and Non-Residential Schools* (Tiachung: ATA, 1985), p. 1.

[30] ATA, 'The Bible and Theology in Asia Today: Declaration of the Sixth Asia Theological Association Theological Consultation, 1982', in Ro and Eshenaur (eds.), *The Bible and Theology in Asian Contexts*, pp. 3–20 at p. 10.

relate the gospel to the different Asian religions and cultures; such as, theologizing within the different Asian contexts, responding to ancestral practices in Asia and constructing the doctrine of God in the midst of Asian religious plurality.[31] These are clearly solid pioneering efforts, but much more in-depth work needs to be done if we are to see the emergence of a genuinely Asian Christian apologetics in relation to other cultures, philosophies and religions, and also to contextualized systematic theologies.

ATA's understanding of mission is founded on evangelism and church-building. For example, in their 'Hong Kong Declaration' it states: 'Until men are brought to put their trust in Jesus Christ as Lord and Savior, God's good news has not come home to them in any biblical and meaningful sense ... In giving priority to evangelism we emphasize the transcendence of God.'[32] Nonetheless, in using the language of holistic mission instead of only emphasizing evangelism, the ATA has moved quite some distance from the conservatism of the earlier half of the century. Its 'Statement of Faith' speaks of 'the total mission of the church to the whole man [or woman] in society in the contemporary context'.[33] This is further elaborated in the 'Hong Kong Declaration', which states:

We are burdened with ... Asia's need, a need with physical, social and political aspects as well as spiritual. We see ourselves as responsible for proclaiming the gospel in all its breadth as well as its depth. We confess our past failures to ... identify with Asian man [woman] in his [her] personal and social suffering.[34]

Moreover, another document insists that personal conversion is not the end of the Christian life; rather, Christian transformation 'has to be brought into the socio-cultural sphere'; that is, contextualization needs to take into account socio-political issues as an essential part of the agenda for theology.[35]

In summary, ATA's theology is basically orthodox but largely reflects western evangelical theology. The ATA has made forays into the realms of contextualization and holistic mission, but these remain rather tentative; although Gnanakan, for example, has attempted to take them further.

---

[31] See Ro and Eshenaur (eds.), *The Bible and Theology in Asian Contexts*; Ro (ed.), *Christian Alternatives to Ancestor Practices*; Ro and Albrecht (eds.), *God in Asian Contexts*.

[32] ATA, 'Hong Kong Declaration', in *Voices of the Church in Asia: Report of Proceedings, ATA Consultation, Hong Kong, 27 December 1973–4 January 1974* (Singapore: ATA, 1975), pp. 165–8 at p. 167.

[33] ATA, 'Statement of Faith', p. 1.   [34] ATA, 'Hong Kong Declaration', p. 168.

[35] ATA, 'The Bible and Theology in Asia Today', p. 9.

Vinay Samuel

Vinay Samuel (1939–) trained first in India and then at Cambridge. As a presbyter of the Church of South India, he has engaged in parish work, social out-reach and theological training ministries. In addition, he was involved with the World Evangelical Alliance and the Lausanne movement. However, his theological identity is probably most clearly defined by his present position as the Executive Secretary of the International Fellowship of Evangelical Mission Theologians (INFEMIT). INFEMIT is the umbrella body for three indigenous evangelical movements from the two-thirds world, the Latin American Theological Fraternity, the African Theological Fraternity and Partnership in Mission Asia. It is primarily concerned with articulating an evangelical theology out of the context of mission in the two-thirds world. Two of its more significant ministries are the Oxford Centre for Mission Studies and *Transformation*, which is an international journal on holistic mission and social ethics.

Samuel's theology is first and foremost an evangelical reflection on mission among the poor in the Indian context.[36] His convictions emerged out of personal involvement in grassroots ministry to the poor in India, including living in Lingarajapuram, one of the slums in Bangalore. The experience of living in the slum convinced Samuel that the meaning for the poor of the good news in the Bible defines the meaning of the good news for all. He writes:

In the New Testament, the poor ... [are] the focus of the gospel. As the poor are called; as the multitude rejoice and experience the gospel, the real nature of the gospel becomes evident to others. This in no way means that the gospel is not for other groups. It does mean that it has to be mediated through what it means to the poor.[37]

The second distinctive element of Samuel's theology is that, according to Sugden, he is a 'theologian of dignity'.[38] In India, the relationship between the social structure, the caste system and the Hindu tradition is intimately bound to extreme poverty, robbing the poor of dignity and a proper sense of identity. By contrast, dignity requires a proper sense of

---

[36] Christopher Sugden, *Seeking the Asian Face of Jesus* (Oxford: Regnum, 1997), pp. 155–82. Sugden has produced the only detailed systematic study of Samuel's thought; see also Hwa, *Mangoes or Bananas?*, pp. 96–205.

[37] Vinay Samuel and Christopher Sugden, 'The Gospel of Transformation', unpublished manuscript (1984), p. 30, cited in Sugden, *Seeking the Asian Face of Jesus*, p. 159.

[38] Sugden, *Seeking the Asian Face of Jesus*, pp. 183–209.

self-worth and self-respect, mediated through equality and justice, which in turn requires freedom of self-determination, such that the previously marginalized – the vulnerable, the disabled and women – have their humanity affirmed. In Samuel's opinion, the restoration of dignity and the end to dehumanizing tendencies only transpires through the gospel of grace. The gospel of grace promotes a new identity, rooted in the image of God-in-us and the Christian calling to be God's children.

Thirdly, Samuel was one of the earliest advocates for holistic mission theology. For him, the relation between evangelism and social responsibility is not a matter of either/or, but one of inseparability. He holds that the prioritization of humanity's vertical relationship over the horizontal pre-supposes a 'dualistic understanding of existence'.[39] This dualism assumes that humans live in two separate realms: an inner and an outer realm, where the former is an individual's relationship with God and the latter is the physical and social realm. Samuel maintains that this dualism cannot be justified on either biblical or philosophical grounds; conceptually, therefore, we cannot prioritize personal over social change or vice versa. Hence, he states: 'Any discussion of priority in the focus of the church's mission will depend not on the concept of mission, but on the context.'[40]

Fourthly, as part of his overall concern for holistic mission, Samuel seeks to develop a coherent theory of social change from an evangelical perspec-tive.[41] His theory consists of three significant elements: first, unlike those who minimize the role of the church, Samuel sees the church as 'central in any program of Christian social change', since it is both the place where the kingdom is at work and also the instrument and sign of the kingdom; secondly, his theology of social change is rooted in both the doctrines of creation and redemption; and thirdly, he recognizes the problematic place occupied by social analysis and human ideologies in Christian approaches to social change. Samuel does not reject analysis and ideology altogether, but rather suggests that we evaluate them rigorously in light of 'biblical criteria for a just society which are acceptable to the east and west'.[42]

Furthermore, Samuel takes the issue of contextualization or inculturation seriously. This is seen most clearly in his concern to relate the salvation

---

[39] Vinay Samuel and Christopher Sugden, 'Evangelism and Social Responsibility: A Biblical Study on Priorities', in Bruce J. Nicholls (ed.), *In Word and Deed: Evangelism and Social Responsibility* (Exeter: Paternoster, 1985), pp. 189–214 at p. 195.

[40] *Ibid.*, p. 211.

[41] Vinay Samuel and Christopher Sugden, 'Towards a Theology of Social Change', in Ronald Sider (ed.), *Evangelicals and Development: Towards a Theology of Social Change* (Philadelphia: Westminster, 1981), p. 46.

[42] *Ibid.*, p. 64.

history of the Bible to that of the histories and cultural identities of all nations. Despite the historical differences recorded in the biblical account between God's relationship with Israel and God's relationship with other nations, Samuel insists that both sets of relationships took place within one history, in the sense that God was equally concerned with all nations. When 'gentiles' were invited into the community of God's people, they did not lose their particular histories by becoming Christians; rather: 'They were incorporated into the people of God and took the history of Israel and their Messiah as theirs also, not as a replacement for but as an addition to their own national history.'[43] Consequently, neither the early Jews nor later western Christianity has the monopoly on salvation history and, therefore, the histories and cultural identities of nations and peoples are vital for affirming and recovering their own Christian identities, which is 'crucial for the discovery of African, Asian, or Latin American Christian identity'.[44]

Thus, while Samuel has stayed within the evangelical circle, his strong affirmation of holistic mission has taken him beyond the traditional western conservative view of mission that focused primarily on the spiritual. In so doing, he has sought consistently to advance evangelical social thought, criticizing traditional western evangelical theology when necessary, in this respect as well as in relation to contextual theology and inter-religious dialogue. He maintains that the Bible is distinctive, whilst asserting that the fear of syncretism, being misunderstood and the decline of evangelism have led to too much hesitation surrounding inter-faith dialogue. Hence, he chides the evangelicalism in the 'Lausanne Covenant'[45] for having little or no inclination to question whether God is at work in other faiths. Samuel argues that serious inter-faith dialogue is necessitated by the current religiously plural context, both for the sake of social transformation and the effectiveness of evangelism.[46]

David (Paul) Yong-Gi Cho

David (Paul) Yong-Gi Cho (1936–), a Korean, trained at the Assemblies of God Bible College in Seoul and, except for a brief stint in the army

---

[43] Samuel and Sugden, 'God's Intention for the World', p. 133.   [44] *Ibid.*, p. 135.

[45] LCWE, *The Lausanne Covenant*, Declaration of the International Congress for World Evangelization, Lausanne (1974), para. 3, available at http://www.lausanne.org/Brix?pageID=12891 [accessed 11 April 2005].

[46] Vinay Samuel and Christopher Sugden, 'Dialogue with Other Religions: An Evangelical View', in Ro and Eshenaur (eds.), *The Bible and Theology in Asian Contexts*, pp. 265–89.

in 1961, has been ministering since 1958. Today he pastors the largest church in the world, the Yoido Full Gospel Church in Seoul, which claims to have eight hundred thousand members. With an international preaching ministry and over a hundred books to his name, he is certainly one of the best known classical Pentecostal ministers in the world.

Evangelism and church growth are clearly central to Cho's concerns. In a paper entitled 'The Secret Behind the World's Biggest Church', he states that his 'ultimate purpose ... is winning souls' and his desire is 'that churches all around the world may grow so that they can glorify God through their ministries'.[47] The commitment to evangelism is seen clearly in the ministry of the Yoido Full Gospel Church, which has founded numerous churches in Korea and elsewhere and has six hundred missionaries engaged in international evangelism. Further, Cho recognizes that church growth requires proper and effective structures for nurturing new converts; hence, among the various discipling programmes he has initiated, the most important is the use of homogeneous cell groups meeting in homes or places of work.[48] In fact, the Yoido Church is made up of tens of thousands of cell groups, meeting under lay leadership.

Similarly, prayer is also central to Cho's church-growth. When asked, 'How have we maintained such unusual growth in our local church?', he replied: 'The real answer is prayer.'[49] Prayer, for Cho, includes private and group prayer, fasting and extended sessions at 'Prayer Mountains'. In addition, Cho is known for his teaching on 'faith-incubation', which claims that, through prayer, the Christian can access what Cho calls the 'fourth-dimension': the spiritual realm that controls the physical. The four basic steps of the faith-incubation process are: 'envisioning a clear-cut objective', 'having a burning desire', 'praying for assurance' and 'speaking the word'. Cho holds that, through the process of 'faith-incubation' in prayer, we can change circumstances in the physical world leading to miraculous healing and material blessings from God.[50]

In Cho's opinion, divine healing through prayer is inseparably linked to church growth, such that the usual lack of emphasis on the miraculous often disguises the powerlessness of the church. Cho states: 'Signs, wonders

---

[47] Y. Cho, 'The Secret Behind the World's Biggest Church', in L. Grant McClung Jr (ed.), *Azusa Street and Beyond: Pentecostal Missions and Church Growth in the Twentieth Century* (South Plainfield: Bridge Publishing, 1986), pp. 99–104 at p. 104.

[48] Y. Cho with Harold Hostetler, *Successful Home Cell Groups* (South Plainfield: Bridge Publishing, 1981).

[49] Y. Cho, *More Than Numbers* (Waco: Word Books, 1984), p. 99.

[50] Y. Cho, *The Fourth Dimension* (South Plainfield: Bridge Publishing, 1979), pp. 9–66.

and the power of the Holy Spirit are essential for successful preaching of the gospel.'[51] Cho's ideas are resonant with classical Pentecostal teaching concerning healing; although, unlike some Pentecostal teachers, he is careful to point out that sometimes it may not be God's will to heal.[52]

Moreover, Cho's emphasis on divine healing is part of his teaching on 'treble blessings'.[53] Cho sees the Christian message as one of hope based on 3 John 2 and, following some American Pentecostal preachers, interprets this to mean salvation of the soul, healing of the body and material blessings from God; hence, a 'triple salvation'. Consequently, Cho has been criticized for preaching a Korean version of the 'prosperity gospel', but he has sought to distance himself from this, since he equates the prosperity gospel with the materialism of western society. Thus, whilst emphasizing that we can expect God to bless us materially, Cho insists that his teaching arose contextually out of the widespread poverty and physical suffering left by the Korean War. Indeed he has suggested that his teaching is a 'gospel of need', in contrast to the 'gospel of prosperity' which is a 'gospel of greed'.[54]

Nevertheless, Cho's twin emphases on the miraculous and God's blessings have also led to the charge that he is 'shamanizing' Christianity, an accusation that focuses especially on his healing and exorcism ministries. The criticism is misplaced however, and Cho's response is that he sought 'to show the miraculous power of God to those who still believed in shamanism'.[55] Even so, one critic argues: 'The only difference is that a shaman performs his wonders in the name of spirits while Rev. Cho exorcizes evil spirits and heals in the name of Jesus.'[56] Yet, such criticisms only reinforce Cho's defence that he does not exercise shamanistic power, but the power of the Holy Spirit. From a missiological perspective, Cho is merely providing a 'functional substitute' to meet a need experienced by his people in the context of Korean culture. In essence, Cho serves to illustrate the increasingly recognized fact that pentecostalism often serves as a powerful tool for contextualizing the Christian gospel.

[51] Y. Cho, *Salvation, Health and Prosperity: Our Threefold Blessings in Christ* (Altamonte Springs: Creation House, 1987), p. 143.
[52] Y. Cho, *How Can I Be Healed?* (Seoul: Seoul Logos, 1999), pp. 35, 62 and 135–40.
[53] Cho, *Salvation, Health and Prosperity*.
[54] Hwa Yung, 'The Missiological Challenge of David Yonggi Cho's Theology', in Wonsuk Ma *et al.* (eds.), *David Yonggi Cho: A Close Look at his Theology and Ministry* (Baguio: APTS Press and Seoul: Hansei University Press, 2004), pp. 69–93 at p. 87.
[55] Y. Cho, 'The Secret Behind the World's Biggest Church', p. 100.
[56] Boo Woong Yoo, 'Response to Korean Shamanism by the Pentecostal Church', *International Rev. Miss.* 75:297 (1986), 70–74 at 74.

Finally, while Cho's church engages with social concerns through widely recognized welfare programs, he has not been noted for his advocacy of active socio-political involvement. For example, during the difficult years of the sixties and seventies military dictatorship in South Korea, Cho stayed away from all anti-government protests, unlike the *minjung* theologians. Hence, while there are indications that his theology is changing in the direction of advocating more meaningful participation in social justice issues, Cho is still in the process of emerging out of the fundamentalist antipathy to socio-political involvement. In summary, therefore, Cho's theology can be described as a classical Pentecostal theology, with its respective strengths and weaknesses, as well as distinctively Korean elements.

THE WAY FORWARD

The above survey of evangelical and pentecostal theologies in Asia sums up the most important trends in the past hundred years or so. These trends also broadly represent the current place of Asian churches and many of the key issues they are struggling with, since the vast majority of the churches are evangelical and pentecostal in outlook.[57] In addition, it shows that evangelical and pentecostal thought in Asia is maturing rapidly and has begun to mount serious challenges to more traditional theologies, both in Asia and elsewhere. In particular, this is true in the following four key areas: holistic mission, the supernatural and the miraculous, contextual theology, and the theology of religions.

Holistic mission

The twentieth-century debate on mission centred on whether mission is primarily about evangelization or humanization. Increasingly it is recognized that both positions represent extremes which are not entirely true of the classical Christian tradition. Many practitioners now prefer the language of holistic mission, refusing to draw sharp divisions between the spiritual and the socio-cultural and physical. As discussed above, the Chinese revivalists of the 1920s and 1930s were caught up in the traditional divisions, and some like Cho and the ATA still struggle to emerge from the old paradigm. At the same time, others like Ramabai and Kagawa

---

[57] Philip Jenkins, *The Next Christendom: The Coming of Global Christianity* (Oxford: Oxford University Press, 2002), p. 7.

have no problems combining a revivalist and/or evangelistic theology with a genuine concern for social justice. Samuel, of course, has moved furthest in pursuing a robust theology of holistic mission.

Now, it is acknowledged frequently that at the heart of the traditional division is a dualistic worldview that has become endemic in western theology.[58] The early incorporation of the Platonic body–soul distinction into Christian theology laid the foundation for a pervasive dualism in western thought. Indeed, Carver Yu, a Chinese theologian, has asserted that the roots of this dualism can be traced even further back to the pre-Socratic Greeks. The adoption of a pre-Socratic understanding of reality as 'reality-in-itself', uncontaminated by anything other than itself, led to the view that reality is made up of discrete self-subsistent things, with dynamic interaction and interpenetration of being categorically excluded.[59] Further, the perception of the unrelatedness of the world gives rise to a dualistic model of reality in the western mind, in contrast to a holistic biblical one.[60] The overall result is that the universe is dichotomized into dualistic categories at every point: the individual and the external world, soul and body, spirit and matter, the religious as against the secular and evangelism versus socio-political concerns. Generally speaking, if liberals have been guilty of 'horizontalizing' mission, conservative Christians have been equally guilty of spiritualizing mission. In other words, both schools have been dominated by the same dualism, although they have opted for opposite sides of it.[61] It is the dualistic view of mission that Asian Christians, unburdened by the Greek tradition, are rejecting increasingly, paving the way for a more holistic understanding of mission.

The supernatural and the miraculous

Largely because of the impact of the Enlightenment and its naturalistic worldview, modern western Christianity had little or no place for the supernatural, the miraculous and the demonic. Yet most Asian Christians, with their supernaturalistic worldviews have no problems taking the miraculous in the Bible seriously. Thus, Asian supernaturalism, together with African and Latin American Christianity, poses a fundamental challenge to western theology. In addition, the western anti-supernaturalistic

---

[58] David J. Bosch, *Transforming Mission: Paradigm Shifts in Theology of Missions* (Maryknoll: Orbis Books, 1991), pp. 215–17.

[59] Carver T. Yu, *Being and Relation: A Theological Critique of Western Dualism and Individualism* (Edinburgh: Scottish Academic Press, 1987), pp. 64–114.

[60] *Ibid.*, pp. 147–235.   [61] Hwa, *Mangoes or Bananas?*, pp. 49–55.

mindset has been strongly challenged by the rise of classical Pentecostalism and the charismatic movement from within the western church. Consequently, in the future the church worldwide will have to give the gifts of the Spirit and the healing and deliverance ministries a greater role in its mission and theology.

Contextual theology

The overwhelming predominance of western culture in the modern world (at least until the middle of the twentieth century) meant that almost every impulse towards contextualizing or indigenizing Christianity in the non-western world faced entrenched opposition, both active and passive. Some efforts at contextualizing succeeded nonetheless and after the Second World War attempts to contextualize Christianity became more conscious and intentional. Apart from the emphases on holistic mission and the supernatural, we have also noted the emergence of various indigenous versions of apologetics and ecclesiology. Hence, it is almost certain that the Protestant world will be vastly reshaped theologically and ecclesiologically in twenty-first-century Asia.

Theology and religions: addressing cultural and religious plurality

Finally, for mature forms of indigenous Christianity to blossom in Asia, it must address the challenge posed by cultural and religious plurality. Unfortunately, the approach that has often been taken by liberals presupposes a religious pluralism that asserts that all religions are essentially expressions of the same reality. What is often not recognized at the moment, even by many Asian writers, is that religious pluralism is a western problem defined by western culture's captivity to the Enlightenment.[62] Tom Driver, who is a religious pluralist, openly admits that the whole discussion 'belongs to Western liberal religious thought at the present time ... couched in Western terms, addressed to Western audiences and aimed at the Western conscience'.[63] If this is so, then Asian scholars need to find a different way of approaching the issue. Asian Christians can learn much from the Apologists, whose writings formed

---

[62] *Ibid.*, pp. 115–21.
[63] Tom Driver, 'The Case for Pluralism', in John Hick and Paul F. Knitter (eds.), *The Myth of Christian Uniqueness: Towards a Pluralistic Theology of Religions* (Maryknoll: Orbis Books, 1987), pp. 203–18 at p. 206.

one of the earliest corpuses of indigenous theology in the Early Church; but to accomplish the same in the church today, we need to master the various cultural and religious traditions of Asia.

At the other extreme, some Asian conservatives, who reject religious pluralism in favour of rigid exclusivism, treat almost everything in their indigenous cultures and traditional religions as demonic, or at least as unworthy of being incorporated into Christianity, resulting in an essentially western Christianity. What is needed therefore is the development of a fully satisfactory theology of cultural and religious plurality, as opposed to one of religious pluralism, which takes seriously Christian and biblical distinctiveness on the one hand, and recognizes both evil and goodness in human cultures and religious pursuits on the other. This work has begun,[64] as we have seen above, but more is required in order to lay an adequate foundation for mission and evangelism in the twenty-first century.

BIBLIOGRAPHY

Adhav, S. M., *Pandita Ramabai*, Madras: Christian Literature Society, 1979.
Anderson, A., *An Introduction to Pentecostalism*, Cambridge: Cambridge University Press, 2004.
Anderson, A. and Tang, E., *Asian and Pentecostal: The Charismatic Face of Asian Christianity*, Oxford: Regnum, 2005.
Appasamy, A. J., *Sundar Singh: A Biography*, Madras: Christian Literature Society, 1966, originally published by London: Lutterworth Press, 1958.
ATA, 'Hong Kong Declaration', in *Voices of the Church in Asia: Report of Proceedings, ATA Consultation, Hong Kong, 27 December 1973 – 4 January 1974*, Singapore: ATA, 1975, pp. 165–8.
'The Bible and Theology in Asia Today: Declaration of the Sixth Asia Theological Association Theological Consultation, 1982', in B. R. Ro and R. Eshenaur (eds.), *The Bible and Theology in Asian Contexts*, Taichung: ATA, 1984, pp. 3–20.
'Statement of Faith', in *ATA Accreditation Manual for Residential and Non-Residential Schools*, Taichung: ATA, 1985, p. 1.
Axling, W., *Kagawa*, London: SCM, 1932.
Barrett, D. B. *et al.* (eds.), *World Christian Encyclopaedia*, 2 vols., Oxford and New York: Oxford University Press, 2001.
Bosch, D. J., *Transforming Mission: Paradigm Shifts in Theology of Missions*, Maryknoll: Orbis Books, 1991.

---

[64] See: Samuel and Sugden, 'Dialogue with Other Religions: An Evangelical View' and Hwa Yung, 'Towards an Evangelical Approach to Religions and Cultures', *Transformation: An International Evangelical Dialogue on Mission and Ethics* 17:3 (2000), 86–91.

Boyd, R. S., *An Introduction to Indian Christian Theology*, revised edition, Madras: Christian Literature Society, 1975.

Chan, S., *Spiritual Theology*, Downers Grove: Inter-Varsity Press, 1998.

Pentecostal Theology and the Christian Spiritual Tradition, Sheffield: Sheffield Academic Press, 2000.

Cho, Y., *The Fourth Dimension*, South Plainfield: Logos International, 1979.

Cho, Y. with Hostetler, H., *Successful Home Cell Groups*, South Plainfield: Bridge Publishing, 1981.

Cho, Y., *More Than Numbers*, Waco: Word Books, 1984.

'The Secret Behind the World's Biggest Church', in L. G. McClung Jr (ed.), *Azusa Street and Beyond: Pentecostal Missions and Church Growth in the Twentieth Century*, South Plainfield: Bridge Publishing, 1986, pp. 99–104.

Salvation, Health and Prosperity: Our Threefold Blessings in Christ, Altamonte Springs: Creation House, 1987.

How Can I Be Healed?, Seoul: Seoul Logos, 1999.

Dohi, A., 'The First Generation: Christian Leaders in the First Period', in Y. Furuya (ed.), *A History of Japanese Theology*, Grand Rapids: Eerdmans, 1997, pp. 11–42.

Driver, T., 'The Case for Pluralism', in J. Hick and P. F. Knitter (eds.), *The Myth of Christian Uniqueness: Towards a Pluralistic Theology of Religions*, Maryknoll: Orbis Books, 1987, pp. 203–18.

Francis, T. D. (ed.), *The Christian Witness of Sadhu Sundar Singh: A Collection of His Writings*, Madras: Christian Literature Society, 1989.

Germany, C. H., *Protestant Theologies in Modern Japan*, Tokyo: International Institute for the Study of Religious Responsibility, 1965.

Gnanakan, K., *Kingdom Concerns: A Biblical Theology of Mission Today*, Leicester: Inter-Varsity Press, 1989.

Proclaiming Christ in a Pluralistic Context, Bangalore: Theological Book Trust, 2000.

Goreh, N., *A Rational Refutation of the Hindu Philosophical Systems*, trans. F-E. Hall, Calcutta: Bishop's College Press, 1862, original gives author's name as Nehemiah N. S. Gore.

Hedlund, R. E., *Quest for Identity: India's Churches of Indigenous Origin: The 'Little Tradition' in Indian Christianity*, Delhi: ISPCK, 2000.

Harvey, T. A., *Acquainted with Grief: Wang Mingdao's Stand for the Persecuted Church in China*, Grand Rapids: Brazos Press, 2002.

Hioshi, M., *The Life and Thought of Kanzo Uchimura, 1861–1930*, Grand Rapids: Eerdmans, 1996.

Hong, Y-G., 'Nominalism in Korean Protestantism', *Transformation: An International Evangelical Dialogue on Mission and Ethics* 16:4 (1999), 135–41.

'Dynamism and Dilemma: The Nature of Charismatic Pastoral Leadership in the Korean Mega-Church', unpublished PhD thesis, University of Wales, 2000.

'The Impact of Charismatic Pastoral Leadership on Religious Commitment and Church Growth in the Korean Mega-Churches', *Mission Studies* XVIII:2:36 (2001), 22–49.

Hwa, Y., *Mangoes or Bananas? The Quest for an Authentic Asian Christian Theology*, Oxford: Regnum, 1997.

'Towards an Evangelical Approach to Religions and Cultures', *Transformation: An International Evangelical Dialogue on Mission and Ethics* 17:3 (2000), 86–91.

'The Missiological Challenge of David Yonggi Cho's Theology', in W. Ma *et al.* (eds.), *David Yonggi Cho: A Close Look at his Theology and Ministry*, Baguio: APTS Press and Seoul: Hansei University Press, 2004, pp. 69–93.

'Pentecostalism and the Asian Church', in A. Anderson and E. Tang, *Asian and Pentecostal: The Charismatic Face of Asian Christianity*, Oxford: Regnum, 2005, pp. 37–57.

Jenkins, P., *The Next Christendom: The Coming of Global Christianity*, Oxford: Oxford University Press, 2002.

Kennedy, N. L., *Dream Your Way to Success: The Story of Yonggi Cho and Korea*, South Plainfield: Logos International, 1980.

Kinnear, A., *Against the Tide: The Story of Watchman Nee*, Fort Washington: Christian Literature Crusade, 1973.

Kosambi, M. (ed.), *Pandita Ramabai Through Her Own Words: Selected Works*, trans. M. Kosambi, New Delhi: Oxford University Press, 2000.

Koshy, T. E., *Brother Bakht Singh of India: An Account of Twentieth Century Apostolic Revival*, Secunderabad: OM Books, 2003.

Lam, W-H., *Chinese Theology in Construction*, Pasadena: William Carey Library, 1983.

Lee, C. K., 'The Theology of Revival in the Chinese Christian Church, 1900–1949: Its Emergence and Impact', unpublished PhD thesis, Westminster Theological Seminary, 1988.

Lee, J. T-H., 'Watchman Nee and the Little Flock Movement in Maoist China', *Church History* 74:1 (2005), 68–96.

Lee, M., 'Experience of Religious Plurality in Korea: Its Theological Implications', *International Review of Mission* 88:351 (1999), 399–413.

'Identifying an Asian Theology: A Methodological Quest', *Asia Journal of Theology* 13:2 (1999), 256–75.

'A Post-Critical Reading of the Bible as a Religious Text', *Asia Journal of Theology* 14:2 (2000), 272–85.

LCWE, *The Lausanne Covenant*, Declaration of the International Congress for World Evangelization, Lausanne, 1974, available at http://www.lausanne.org/Brix?pageID=12891 [accessed 11 April 2005].

Lyall, L., *A Biography of John Sung*, Singapore: Armour, 2004, originally published as *John Sung: Flame of God for the Far East*, fourth edition, London: OMF, 1961.

Ma, W. and Ma, J. C. (eds.), *Asian Church & God's Mission: Studies Presented in the International Symposium on Asian Mission in Manila, January 2002*, Manila: OMF, and W. Caldwell, NJ: MWM, 2003.

Ma, W. *et al.* (eds.), *David Yonggi Cho: A Close Look at his Theology and Ministry*, Baguio: APTS Press and Seoul: Hansei University Press, 2004.

Myung, S-H. and Hong, Y-G. (eds.), *Charis and Charisma: David Yonggi Cho and the Growth of Yoido Full Gospel Church*, Oxford: Regnum, 2003.

Paradkar, B. A. M., *The Theology of Nehemiah Goreh*, Banglore: CISRS and Madras: Christian Literature Society, 1969.

Ro, B. R. (ed.), *Christian Alternatives to Ancestor Practices*, Taichung: ATA, 1985.

Ro, B. R. and Albrecht, M. C. (eds.), *God in Asian Contexts*, Taichung: ATA, 1988.

Ro, B. R. and Eshenaur, R. (eds.), *The Bible and Theology in Asian Contexts*, Taichung: ATA, 1984.

Samuel, V. and Sugden, C., 'Towards a Theology of Social Change', in R. Sider (ed.), *Evangelicals and Development: Towards a Theology of Social Change*, Philadelphia: Westminster, 1981, pp. 45–68.

'Dialogue with Other Religions: An Evangelical View', in B. R. Ro and R. Eshenaur (eds.), *The Bible and Theology in Asian Contexts*, Taichung: ATA, 1984, pp. 265–89.

'The Gospel of Transformation', unpublished manuscript, 1984.

'Evangelism and Social Responsibility: A Biblical Study on Priorities', in B. J. Nicholls (ed.), *In Word and Deed: Evangelism and Social Responsibility*, Exeter: Paternoster, 1985, pp. 189–214.

'God's Intention for the World', in V. Samuel and C. Sugden (eds.), *The Church in Response to Human Need*, Grand Rapids: Eerdmans and Oxford: Regnum, 1987, pp. 128–60.

Samuel, V. and Sugden, C. (eds.), *Mission as Transformation*, Oxford: Regnum, 1999.

Schildgenm, R., *Toyohiko Kagawa, Apostle of Love and Social Justice*, Berkeley: Centenary Books, 1988.

Sharpe, E. J., 'The Legacy of Sadhu Sundar Singh', *International Bull. Miss. Research* 14:4 (1990), 161–7.

Streeter, B. H. and Appasamy, A. J., *The Sadhu: A Study in Mysticism and Practical Religion*, London: Macmillan, 1921.

Sugden, C., *Seeking the Asian Face of Jesus*, Oxford: Regnum, 1997.

Sung, J., *Forty John Sung Revival Sermons*, 2 vols., trans. T. Tow, Singapore: Alice Doo, 1978 and 1983.

The Diaries of John Sung: An Autobiography, trans. S. L. Sheng, Brighton, MI: Luke H. Sheng and Stephen L. Sheng, 1995.

Uchimura, K., *Kanzo Uchimura Memorial Collection*, Tokyo: International Christian University Library, 2005, available at http://www-lib.icu.ac.jp/Uchimura/index-e.htm [accessed 30 April 2005].

Wang, M-D., *Spiritual Food*, trans. A. Reynolds, Southampton: Mayflower Christian Books, 1983.

Yoo, B. W., 'Response to Korean Shamanism by the Pentecostal Church', *International Rev. Miss.* 75:297 (1986), 70–4.

Young, R. F., 'Enabling Encounters: The Case of Nilakanth-Nehemiah Goreh, Brahmin Convert', *International Bull. Miss. Research* 29:1 (2005), 14–20.

Yu, C. T., *Being and Relation: A Theological Critique of Western Dualism and Individualism*, Edinburgh: Scottish Academic Press, 1987.

CHAPTER 13

Subalterns, identity politics and Christian theology in India

Sathianathan Clarke

PUZZLES ON THE GROUND, REMEMBERING THE CONTEXT

Let me start by stating how I have come to forge a relationship between subalternity, identity politics and Christian theology in India. In 2001 I took my class of twenty-four students to spend three days with a dalit Christian community in a Tamilnadu village in south India.[1] I made this a requirement for my course on 'dalit theology', which I taught from 1996 to 2004 at the United Theological College, Bangalore. This pilgrimage was designed to enable all of us to journey into the community we studied in our classrooms. But it was also a journey into ourselves: our notions of self and other, our conceptions of mission and our realization of the nature of the Indian Church. During this visit, as is our custom, we slept and prayed in the church, ate, sang and danced with the families and spent our time visiting the various communities that made up this village.

Through our time there we discovered that the Indian community seemed to be divided along several lines. To begin with there was the caste community and the dalit community partition: there existed the obvious conventional division between the caste community and the dalit community. Apart from geographical distance, the lives of these two respective communities revolved around their own deities, their own cultural festivities and their own socio-economic network of interaction. Then, as is true of much of rural India, there was the intra-dalit community division. The Paraiyar was numerically the largest dalit community, which is traditionally engaged in agricultural labour. The Arundhathiyar was numerically the smaller dalit community, which is traditionally engaged with the leather business. The latter community was responsible for

---

[1] A version of this chapter was first presented at a public lecture at Princeton Theological Seminary, New Jersey, in October 2002.

curing leather and manufacturing various leather articles (from footwear to buckets used for agriculture). Finally, and also quite characteristic of Indian social life, there was the dalit community and the Adivasi community separation. The two dalit communities were deliberately distanced from another oppressed and marginalized community. The Irrullar, an outcast Adivasi community, was considered so low in rank and status that they were also looked down upon by the dalits. They traditionally live from harvesting the natural world and hunting birds and small animals.

These divisions have a long and complex history. However, while the division between the caste community and the dalits and Adivasis, on the one hand, has been addressed and dealt with in a variety of ways, the rupture between the dalit communities themselves and between the dalits and the Adivasis, on the other, has hardly been deliberated. Most alarming is the fact that in recent years the rift between the two dalit communities has deepened. Further, both the dalit communities have almost nothing to do with the Adivasis. Thus, the Irrullar community was not considered part of the 'reality' of the dalits.

I noted three things from my visit, which are relevant to this reflection. First, the animosity of the Paraiyars was directed against the Arundhathiyars rather than the caste communities. This stemmed from a recent panchyat election in which the Arundhathiyars supported a caste Hindu man against the dalit Christian women from the Paraiyar community. The Christian dalits tried to dissuade us from visiting the Arundhathiyar colony. In discussions it was clear that they did not think that anyone else shared the dalit identity with them. Second, the temple in the Arundhathiyar area, which was built over the last two years, was crowded with icons of non-dalit gods and goddesses. The goddess Mariyamman, who they claimed was their territorial deity, was there, but she was one among many others without any prominent position in the small temple. The person who functions as the priest was deliberately ambiguous in answering my question concerning this, and said: 'We had to please the many caste Hindus that gave us most of the money to build this temple, but only Mariyamman is taken out and made to bless our colony during the yearly religious festival.' In contrast to the Arundhathiyar, the Christians from the Paraiyar community have constructed a large Church with a tall bell-tower. The church building has nothing in it that reflects any local religious or cultural art forms or architectural styles. The cross and the church bell are the most conspicuous symbols that are lifted high on this edifice; a concrete signifier, perhaps, of the Paraiyar community's aspiration to pursue a new and different identity. Third, the indifference of the Christian dalits to the plight of the Adivasis was overt. There was an air of superiority that they communicated when talking about the Irrullar. The Paraiyar community confidently asserted that the caste communities treat them with much greater respect than the Irrullar because the latter were 'dirty' and 'unclean'. Ironically, these were the same terms that caste communities have traditionally used to distinguish themselves from the dalits.

All three communities outside the caste society (Paraiyar, Arundhathiyar and Irrullar) are socially marginalized and economically exploited, currently working as agricultural labourers on the lands owned by the caste community, and yet their inter-relationships among themselves are played out as if they have internalized the mindset of caste society. They live in their own separate geographical spaces and have their own cultural and religious shrines and festivals. Moreover, they tend to view their social interactions within a hierarchical framework. Thus, there is an implicit aversion to inter-dining and there is an explicit rejection of inter-marriage between themselves as communities. In fact, they informed us that some of the major clashes between these communities emanated either from differences about interpretations of the role that one of these communities ought to have played in the other's religious festivals or from romances that had taken place across their conventionally defined community lines. All three of these communities were treated as being outside the caste society. Thus, they were equally inferior to the populace of the main village, which made up the caste communities, but still they constantly vied for a more favourable status in their relationship with the caste community.

The situation that I have just described is not atypical. Let me underscore one finding at this juncture: dalit Christian communities may have concretized and contextualized the Christian gospel into their own particular historical context but this has not enabled them to broaden the scope of this good news to build community solidarity with similar oppressed communities. Nevertheless, in the doing of contextual theology, which is also liberational in objective, much has been achieved; for example, from the early 1980s a voice has been given to local, thus far excluded, communities and the particular cultural resources of marginal communities have altered the contours and the contents of theology. Dalit theology and tribal theology are the concrete expressions of such a needed trajectory, and yet there may be reasons to deliberate on a different course of direction.

The time is ripe, I believe, to re-examine Indian Christian theology. The twenty odd years of dalit and tribal theology have succeeded to some extent in re-locating God. God was unsettled from the security of the heavens and brought low down to be touched, heard and seen among a broken people. God was released from various forms of Brahminic captivity and rehabilitated into the everyday struggles of a striving and resisting out-caste people. God was debugged of all the conceptual and metaphysical riddles of reason and scattered into the body politics of specific marginalized communities. Even so, all these theologies appear to have moved in one particular direction: linking God preferentially with one marginalized community without any consideration for links with other communities for whom God would have the same preferential option. Thus, there is the contracting of God to be with one specific local community, that is, the Paraiyars in this case, without the effects that would be produced by flowing sideways, that is, to the Arundhathiyar in this case. Hard questions are not to be evaded: might there be some connection between the particularizing and localizing of Indian contextual theology and its propensity toward parochialism and provincialism? Or to put the issue more bluntly, must concretizing theology lead inevitably to a form of communalization? There can be no doubt that more on-the-ground study must go into this question before it can be answered one way or another.

This chapter is an interim and constructive effort to address this issue. First, I suggest that we seriously invoke a roomier conception of community, which is less prone to becoming insular and more open to plugging into the Jesus as the Christ momentum. This of course I will do without surrendering the contextual and liberative objectives of theology. Second, after the process of working out my contention that 'subaltern' be accepted as such a candidate and relating its implication for identity politics in India, I reflect on the theological affiliations that lie between and betwixt the deliberation. This culminates in a self-reflexive effort to define Christian theology.

SUBALTERN AS AN INTERPRETIVE POSTURE AND A CATEGORY OF INTERPRETERS

I suggest that we employ the category of 'subaltern' to make space for the solidarity of various particularized and parochialized identities among the marginalized peoples of India. I utilize the term 'subaltern' in the activity of theology both as an interpretive posture and as a category of interpreters; in both cases, it qualifies the subjectivity that the theologian embraces.

Let me first comment on subaltern as an interpretive posture. The pre-supposition underlying such a declaration of a definite interpretive standpoint (or professed subjectivity) includes at least two components. On the one hand, it asserts that even if there is an objective viewpoint it is not achievable in the realm of theology. This liability for the discipline of theology stems from the fact that because it deals with the symbol of God in relation to human beings it cannot be done outside of human experience. Theology is not a recording or photographing of God's reflection on God followed by a duplicating of this knowledge to all human beings; rather it is reflection done about God by human beings. It is thus a discourse about God as related to human beings and the world undertaken by human beings; for the glory of God no doubt, but not without being saturated by the various aspects of human beings in their search for their own wholeness before God and in relationship to all of creation. On the other hand, the taking on of a specific viewpoint pre-sumes a capacity to transcend the notion that theology is the testimony of each individual's experience concerning God, as though soliloquy is the only possibility open for this discipline. Rather, theology is understood to be inter-subjective; it cannot eliminate the community that exists around the individual theologian. To put it another way, since the 'I' that projects itself as the subject is socially constructed and committed, it is not pos-sible to distil and craft a solipsistic worldview on God. A certain tension can be detected at the intersection between claiming one's own human situatedness in theological discourse and seeking to express that in com-munitarian ways, which is further complicated by the fact that such an interpretive standpoint is not chosen in a vacuum. Antonio Gramsci (1891–1937) is relevant in determining the place of the 'subaltern' in the midst of the intricate mechanisms of power.

Gramsci, an Italian Marxist writing to counter Fascism in the 1920s and 1930s, substituted the much-used phrase 'proletarian classes' with the word 'subaltern'. In proposing this term Gramsci was referring to the working classes, which were the objects of the economic and ideological exploitation of the dominating elite. He concentrated on the non-economic dimensions that the elite utilized to sustain their domination over the subaltern. He suggested that in order to sustain their control over the working masses, the dominating elite had to weave convincing and all-embracing worldviews, which would make it acceptable and meaningful to live under such repressive conditions. Hegemony, the name that Gramsci gave to this process, operates both to legitimize the conditions of domination and to offer a rationale for encouraging the dominated to participate in their own domination. Even a cursory reading of Gramsci's notion of hegemony will suffice to throw light on the vulnerability of theology; that is, it could easily serve the purposes of hegemony. Liberation theology was well aware of this propensity of theology and, in order to counter this tendency, it therefore calls for theologians to make a preferential option for the poor and the excluded, thereby undercutting any hegemonic propensity in theology. The theological rationale however stemmed from God's own preferential option for the poor as symbolized by Jesus as the Christ. Theologians imitate God's own bias toward the poor by committing themselves to the view-point of the marginalized and oppressed.

In the Indian context, however, one of the draw-backs in this process that I have pointed to has to do with the parochializing and commu-nalizing of the working out of such a preferential option. Thus, God's preferential option is actualized in essentialist terms, as though there is an ethnic boundary that must contain this privileged relationship between God and God's people. This in no uncertain terms negates the dynamic that was initiated and mediated by Jesus as the Christ: he ended the traditional understanding of God's covenant with people in terms of ethnicity and opened a new pattern of relationality. Again a Gramscian insight might help us in retaining the idea of a preferential option for the subaltern without limiting its ramifications to any one specific ethnic community. One way that Gramsci interprets the concept of subaltern accentuates the negative: people as objects of the process of hegemony, which is instrumentalized by the elites. But one can also tease out a positive reading from Gramsci's commentary on the subaltern: the emergence of a 'contradictory consciousness' in subalterns as they forge solidarity among themselves in order to live in freedom and dignity. Thus the subaltern are the working classes that are connected together, not by any ethnic or essentialist traits, but by their 'good sense', which seeks to escape the hegemonizing scheme of the elites in order to live in freedom and dignity. Dalits, Adivasis and other subordinated communities are bound together by a consciousness rather than an ethnicity.

What does this mean for the task of theology? Taking the cue from Gramsci, I contend that Indian Christian theology needs to interrogate and reinterpret God's preferential option in terms of process rather than in substantive ways. To put this in the language of physics: in the dynamics of energy rather than the stuff of mass. Thus, in advocating God as preferentially opting to covenant with subalterns we are stressing that God is aligned with the activity of people who participate in countering hegemony and embracing their own authentic freedom and dignity. This thrust calls for experiencing and expressing God's presence through the dynamic movement of people struggling for life and liberty. In line with this way of thinking, dalits and Adivasis and other marginalized groups are challenged to move beyond the claim that God is on their side because of their ethnicity. Rather, the emphasis is on participatory knowing, which involves a struggle alongside God in the cooperative journey toward authentic and free life. Thus, there is no claim to an ontological privilege in their relationship with God; rather, claiming God is conceived of as participating in God's working to bring about free and dignified life. For dalits and Adivasis, just as for all human beings, God is known as the source, sustainer and goal of life. Nonetheless, in an indirect way, because it is primarily the oppressed and exploited (dalits and Adivasis as the case in India suggests) that want to subvert the unjust and oppressive socio-economic and religio-cultural structures, they will more likely join in the working of God to bring about such a life of freedom and dignity for all, especially the subaltern. So implicitly participation in solidarity with God's liberative working is in a particular way more appealing and germane to the oppressed and alienated. Within this logistic scheme the issue is not set up in a manner whereby God is seen only on the side of dalits and Adivasis; rather, the argument seems to hinge on the practical possibility that if knowledge of God is conceived of in terms of participatory knowing through commitment to God's working in the world, then it is most plausible that the oppressed and alienated will inevitably take the side of God.

For the dalits, Adivasis and the other oppressed communities, this theological position, which does not presuppose the privileging of any human collective in terms of their ethnic reality, is a move away from the hierarchical mindset that leads to claims of exclusive priority of God's favour. First, it saves communities from the politics of measuring their own worth before God in direct proportion to the weight of their suffering; a trend that resorts to quantifying oppression in terms of once- or twice- or thrice-alienated, as if the more one accumulates the affects of marginalization the more one is preferred by God. Secondly, it retains the inclusive character of God while at the same time formulating a crucial role for the marginalized based on their participation in their own liberative struggles. Thirdly, it proposes an understanding of God's relationship with God's people which is based on participation in God's activity of restoring human freedom and dignity, so that all marginalized groups cannot expect anything apart from their own involvement. Finally, it reiterates the principle of self-help and self-worth in the process of liberation; total or adequate liberation is indeed a gift from God to all of creation but it is something which must be appropriated and shared in. This last point in itself frees dalits, Adivasis and the other oppressed groups from the false hope that liberation is a gift that can be received through God by the good will of the caste communities. The only hope for all exploited people lies in the working of God, who is the source, sustainer and goal of free and authentic life for all, and their own willingness and commitment to participate alongside God in this purposive and ongoing activity.

Even while making the point that one can create more space for thinking about subalternity in terms of process rather than substance, one must be careful not to disembody the subaltern. Thus, much more needs to be said about subaltern as a category of interpreters, particularly in relation to theology. What or who are the subalterns that energize human contrary consciousness in the activity of resisting hegemony and positing versions of authentic and free life? As I have already suggested, subaltern is the most suitable term to gather together various groupings in India through which theologians can commit themselves to reflectively view and critically re-view notions of God, world and the human being and their inter-relationships. In the discussion that follows I shall make a case for why the term 'subaltern' is the most fitting and appropriate for the present Indian context and how it becomes serviceable for the ongoing task of liberation and contextual theology.

Let me start by admitting that this is not a radically innovative suggestion in Indian historical and political theory. The term subaltern has been brought to the centre of theoretical discourse by a group of scholars referred to as the Subaltern Studies Collective. From 1986 onward the Collective has published eleven substantial volumes on south Asian history and society from a 'subaltern perspective'. In the Preface to *Subaltern Studies*, volume I, Ranajit Guha proposes the following definition: 'The word "subaltern" ... stands for the meaning as given in the *Concise Oxford Dictionary*, that is, 'of inferior rank'. It will be used ... as a name for the general attitude of subordination in south Asian society whether this is expressed in terms of class, caste, age, gender and office or in any other way.'[2] In a clarificatory note, at the end of this same Preface, he further opines, 'The terms "people" and "subaltern classes" have been used synonymously throughout this note. The social groups and elements

---

[2] Ranajit Guha, 'Preface', in Ranajit Guha (ed.), *Subaltern Studies I: Writings on South Asian History and Society* (New Delhi: Oxford University Press, 1982), pp. vii–viii at p. vii.

included in this category represent *the demographic difference between the total Indian population and all those whom we have described as the elite.*[3]

It is important to point out that Guha symbolizes the search for a category of interpreters through which to write history in India within a context that had become used to opting between the Colonialist and the Nationalist schools of historiography. Historiography in India, according to Guha, 'has been dominated by colonialist elitism and bourgeois-nationalist elitism'.[4] In a sense the Subaltern Collective engenders an alternate perspective that puts common people back into historical narratives. Subalterns 'constitute the mass of the labouring population' as distinguished from the elite in India.[5] Their historical truths have been suppressed or discounted in forming historiography. It is such a subaltern standpoint that is professed by scholars of subaltern studies. One can notice some similarities in the history of theologizing in India. Until the 1980s the struggles in Indian theology seem to have been between missionary-advocated and nationalist-promoted theologies. The former school of theology was mainly preoccupied with fitting Indian theological expressions into the universal doctrines that characterized the essence of Christianity while the latter school of theology was principally concerned with valorizing a unitary Indian Christian vision that would be both comprehensive and contextual in order to function as an alternate 'master narrative' to the missionary-advocated Christian worldview. The subalterns, who form the largest section of interpreters, were missing in most of this theologizing. In the section that follows I want to interrogate this category of interpreters against the backdrop of the Indian theological movements by arguing how this could best contain the directionality of theology.

SUBALTERNS AS POST-DALIT AND POST-ADIVASI COMMUNITY

The Subaltern Collective has popularized the term subaltern by clubbing together various categories of differentiation ('class, caste, age, gender and office and any other way') because of which people suffer subordination. There is no doubt that if we use the criteria of dominated versus dominating we could identify a host of groups that share in an assortment of debilitations and subjugations. As is clear from my initial case study, and

---

[3] *Ibid.*, p. viii (original italics).
[4] Ranajit Guha, 'Introduction', in Ranajit Guha (ed.), *A Subaltern Studies Reader: 1986–1995* (New Delhi: Oxford University Press, 1998), pp. ix–xxii at p. xiv.
[5] *Ibid.*, p. xv.

previous systematic work on the Indian context, we cannot be involved in any micro and macro analyses of social, economic, cultural, political and religious life without taking the structure and functioning of the caste system into primary consideration. Correspondingly I contend that any workable and germane configuration and exposition of this category cannot be fleshed out apart from excavating the caste dimensions of subalternity. The words of Partha Chatterjee are relevant here: 'No matter how we choose to characterize it, subaltern consciousness in the specific cultural context of India cannot but contain caste as a central element in its constitution.'[6]

The subordination and subjection that marks the life of Dalits in India bring them into the contours of a particularly contextual assembly of subalternity. 'Untouchables [Dalits] have retained their identity as a subordinated people within Indian society, and by this we mean to identify a condition that is far more severe than merely being bottom of an inevitable hierarchy.'[7] This is not to deny that collectives held together by commonality of age, gender, class and office do not share in the state of subalternity; rather I am containing the scope of this analysis of domination and exploitation to reflect upon the specific manner by which the institution and ideology of caste engenders a contextual manifestation of subalternity that is tied intrinsically to the task of theology in India. Keeping this in the background, let me put forward a more restricted and focused definition of subaltern, which goes beyond the generalities of thinking of this category in terms of subordinated labouring people (as distinguished from the dominant elite) that are held together by an emerging contradictory consciousness in their search for a free and authentic life. The term subaltern signifies communities that are cumulatively and comprehensively disadvantaged and subordinated through the structure and agency of the caste system, which operates to benefit the dominant groups in retaining their social, economic, political and religious privilege. However, this formal definition will have material implications, which raises the following question: Based on a definition contingent on the caste system, which specific groupings need to be incorporated into the subaltern?

---

[6] Partha Chatterjee, 'Caste and Subaltern Consciousness', in Ranajit Guha (ed.), *Subaltern Studies VI: Writings on South Asian History and Society* (New Delhi: Oxford University Press, 1989), pp. 169–209 at p. 169.

[7] Oliver Mendelsohn and Marika Vicziany, 'The Untouchables', in Oliver Mendelsohn and Upendra Baxi (eds.), *The Rights of Subordinated Peoples* (New Delhi: Oxford University Press, 1994), pp. 64–117 at p. 115.

There will be general consensus that all communities outside of the caste society will form the substratum of the subaltern. Thus, dalit and Adivasi communities form the foundation of the subaltern. The various dalit communities, which have historically been cast outside human society by the Hindu caste social order, form the majority of the subaltern. It is important not to forget that this is not a homogeneous grouping. On the one hand, dalit is a symbol that embraces over four hundred different communities that are differentiated from each other in spite of sharing in the overall condition of being ejected from the social and religious interactions of Hindu caste society. On the other hand, much of the distinctiveness of the various dalit communities is played out within the framework of cautious repulsion rather than congenial solidarity. Thus, it is often almost impossible to bring together two different dalit communities that live in the neighbourhood of a common village for a common issue. The mutual suspicion and hostility, leaving aside the lack of solidarity, between the Paraiyar and the Arundhathiyar in Tamilnadu and the Malas and the Madhigas in Andhra Pradesh, have led to numerous sociological and theological studies.

The various Adivasi communities have also been kept outside the contours of the caste society. It is only the caste communities that can live within the borders of the main village. The Adivasis, like the dalits, live beyond the boundaries of the village. They have been exploited and marginalized by the caste communities both economically and socially. Adivasis too comprise over four hundred distinct tribes spread all over the country. Apart from the tribes of north east India, where many live in some autonomy from the Hindu caste social order, the Adivasis live in subservience to the caste communities and in tension with local dalit communities. Yet, both these communities share in the common experience of being economically exploited by the caste communities and being ostracized by its social and geographic world. The dalits and the Adivasis represent the underside of Indian society and the refuse of the caste system.

But what about sections of the caste community that share in some of the debilitations and marginalizations that affect dalits and Adivasis? Is there room in the subaltern community for them? The component of the caste community that I am referring to forms the lowest rung of the caste hierarchy, called the asat-Shudras (not-so-pure Shudras). In the four-fold hierarchical caste system the Brahmins, Kshatriyas and Vaishyas were considered the twice-born and the Shudras were designated as the once-born. This primarily meant that the caste system conferred certain religious and social privileges on the first three castes, which it did not extend to the fourth caste. For example, the Shudras were traditionally not allowed into temples, were not permitted to read sacred scripture, and were not included in the social intercourse of the twice-born castes. There was a categorical status divide between these two segments within Hindu caste society. In the historical course of their interaction, however, because of the absence of Kshatriyas and Vaishyas in many regions, some sub-castes among the Shudras were able to acquire social and religious rights that were reserved for the twice-born caste communities; they were designated as the sat-Shudras (pure-Shudras) and they gradually took on the social and religious functions of the Kshatriyas and Vaishyas. The asat-Shudras thus continue to be exploited and marginalized by the twice-born caste communities and also dominated and subjugated by the sat-Shudras. The asat-Shudras are usually landless labourers like the dalits and the Adivasis, and they are at the base of the caste system.

Kancha Ilaiah, an influential contemporary political scientist, proposes that the dalits and the Shudras are bound together not only by their alienation and exploitation from the Brahminic caste communities but also by an alternate set of religious and cultural values that rebut the values of caste communities.[8] Ilaiah polarizes Indian society along the lines of Hindu caste community versus dalitbahujan: while the former is inspired and directed by the Brahminic tradition (Hindutva), the latter is funded by its counter values that are drawn from the socio-economic and cultural heritage of labouring people. Such a dalit–Shudra worldview both critiques 'Hindutva philosophy, culture and political economy' and offers a more integrated, inclusive and egalitarian way of collective living. While there are many problems with such an easy binary notion of Indian society, for our purposes I merely want to point to the notion of 'dalitbahujan', which means 'dalit majority', as one contextual offering that seeks to build a cultural and economic basis for a more spacious identity for oppressed and marginalized communities in India.

Ilaiah has not included the Adivasis and has not problematized adequately the distinction between sat-Shudras and asat-Shudras. Nonetheless, his suggestion of the possibilities of the outlines of a civilizational pattern from the underside of Indian society and the forging of a cultural

---

[8] Kancha Ilaiah, *Why I am not a Hindu: A Sudra Critique of Hindutva Philosophy, Culture and Political Economy* (Calcutta: Samya, 1996) and Kancha Ilaiah, 'Productive Labour, Consciousness and History: The Dalitbahujan Alternative', in Shahid Amin and Dipesh Chakrabarty (eds.), *Subaltern Studies IX: Writings on South Asian History and Society* (New Delhi: Oxford University Press, 1996), pp. 165–200.

and economic commonality between the dalits and segments of the Shudras are important for our deliberations. I suggest that the category of subaltern be open to the inclusion of asat-Shudra segments with certain caveats. First, the cornerstone of the subaltern is taken to be the dalit and Adivasi communities; their historical experience of being the refuse of the caste society constitutes the basic building blocks of the subaltern community. Secondly, asat-Shudra segments of the caste community can be accommodated if they are willing to both renounce casteist customs (this would involve practising inter-dining and an openness to inter-marrying) and embrace dalit and Adivasi emancipation as the primary agenda. Thirdly, the collective is defined by its 'labouring classes' self-identity, which means that the subalterns set themselves up to be vigilant against co-option by the dominant caste communities, on the one hand saving them from the vested interests of the owner class and on the other hand guarding against the uninterest of the middle class. In other words, the subaltern is a collective of labour- or productivity-based and dalit- and Adivasi-identified communities, which forge solidarity through contradictory consciousness in order to live in freedom and dignity. Thus the prefix 'post' does not mean the eclipse of the dalit and the Adivasi marker; rather, it is a pointer to a future that negotiates difference and construes solidarity without denouncing the richness and depth of significations that are communicated by these identities. Further, it protects such identities from becoming essentialized and parochialized, and it is to this issue that we shall turn our attention in the next section.

SUBALTERNS AS AN ANTI-CASTE COMMUNITY

The historical crystallization of dalit identity formation cannot be seen in a religio-cultural vacuum. Dalit notions of self and other, of the historical and metaphysical worlds and of God and goddesses are configured within an ongoing interaction with the all-embracing or, more realistically, all-invading inclinations of the Hindu worldview of the caste community (which I referred to earlier as 'Brahminic or Hindutva' world-visions). Let me be clear that I am not endorsing Moffatt's thesis.[9] He, after an in-depth study of the dalits' and the caste communities' various deities, festivals, leadership patterns and transactional rituals, concludes that 'every fundamental entity, relationship, and action found in the religious

---

[9] Michael Moffatt, *An Untouchable Community in South India: Structure and Consensus* (Princeton: Princeton University Press, 1979).

system of the higher castes is also found in the religious system of the Untouchables'.[10] He further adds, 'Untouchables and higher caste actors hold virtually identical cultural constructs ... they are in nearly total conceptual and evaluative consensus with one another.'[11] He calls this 'structural replication'; that is, according to Moffatt, the dalits replicate structurally, in an interdependent manner, what the caste communities manifest. Thus, Moffatt deduced that dalits religiously, culturally and socially express their own collective identity in conformity with the overall rationale and workings of the essence of the Hindu–Indian ideology based on purity and pollution.

I am critical of Moffatt's research,[12] since he represents dalits as submissively living their individual and collective lives by 'replicating' (copying/duplicating/cloning/mirroring) the religious and social ideals and practices of the caste community, and as compliant and passive objects in a worldview that is cleverly devised by the caste community for their own benefit and welfare. He thus characterizes the dalit communities as incapable of self-reflective human agency that would tend to advance collective self-interest. Yet, Moffatt's study contains an element of truth that cannot be discounted, in as much as the formation of dalit identities within the historical context of the overarching and over-reaching worldview of Hindu caste communities is constantly exposed to casteist configurations. My own work has attempted to rectify this lapse by delving into the resistive and constructive aspects of the dalit world-view in order to comprehend and circulate elements of this collective self-representation by analysing the symbols of the goddess and the drum. However, this was done against the backdrop of the powerful and persuasive dynamics of the worldview of the caste communities, which was actively involved in co-opting dalit communities to understand themselves within the structure and functioning of the caste system.

Even through the task of valorizing the self-representational and self-reflexive trajectories of the dalits' own worldview one cannot ignore the various ways in which the pervasive logic and practice of this caste-based worldview affects dalit identity formations. I started this reflection by locating such an example in a village in Tamilnadu, where the label dalit is invoked and yet it is appropriated in terms of a sectarian, or, most contextually, a sub-caste-like manner. However, construal of collective

[10] Ibid., p. 289. [11] Ibid., p. 291.
[12] Sathianathan Clarke, Dalits and Christianity: Subaltern Religion and Liberation Theology in India (New Delhi: Oxford University Press, 1998), pp. 97–108.

identities in specific historical settings is constantly prone to caste-oriented cultural patterns, even if this takes place under the veneer of liberation. Many of the political movements in south India that have mobilized under the banner of emancipation and justice for the marginalized have calculatingly and candidly taken on sectarian ('sub-caste-like') identities. Thus, within Tamilnadu the notion of a dalit identity is without doubt subservient to the more organized and more vocalized Pallar or Paraiyar or Arundhathiyar identities, each of which clearly represents a caste-based valuation of one's collective distinctiveness. In this context, the notion of subaltern could steer collective solidarity formation among the various dominated and exploited communities away from the community world-view that interprets all configurations of body politics along caste lines.

The rationale of this caste-based ideational framework for interpreting identity must have some links to local Indian anthropology. The following ethno-sociological worldview on human identity is compelling and significant in this regard. The native Hindu view of caste, as developed by McKim Marriott and Ronald Inden in their 'individual-particle' theory, is based on the belief that all human beings are born with a coded-substance that relates to their caste, sex, and personality.[13] These substances are constituted by particles containing the same coding, which can be detached from the body and become annexed to another body. Herein lies the difference from a western notion of 'individual', which implies a kind of enduring indivisibility of the human person. Due to the potential for dividuation in the Hindu view, physical interaction must be socially controlled to enable individuals possessing the same substance coding to exchange compatible particles and restrict individuals having disparate substances from coming together. It is crucial that these coded-substances be kept from mixing. This logic feeds the dynamic of Hindu caste society, which seeks to maintain auspiciousness, order and purity as against its opposite state of inauspiciousness, disorder and pollution, thus explaining the underlying reason that prevents various communities in India, including dalit communities, from interacting with each other in freedom and solidarity. In Dipankar Gupta's words:

According to the native Hindu theory, individuals belonging to a particular caste share identical particles. These particles are different from the particles that

[13] For further reading see Marriot McKim and Ronald B. Inden, 'Towards an Ethnosociology of South Asian Caste System', in Kenneth A. David (ed.), *The New Wind: Changing Identities in South Asia* (Chicago: Aldine Publishers, 1977), pp. 227–38; and Pauline Kolenda, *Caste and Contemporary India: Beyond Organic Solidarity* (Prospect Heights: Waveland Press, 1985).

constitute other individuals in other castes. This is why it is necessary to maintain distance between castes, lest these particles commingle ... unlike racial strati-fication where visible differences govern social interaction, the caste system has to rest eventually on the belief in natural differences.[14]

Subaltern as an anti-caste community denounces and renounces such an essentialist conception of human identities. It seeks to posit an alternate ideational framework that undercuts biological justification for forging collective identities in ethnic terms and creates space for inter-sectarian and inter-parochial transfigurations of corporate human identities. This conception of subaltern ceases to think of human beings in terms of magnets that either attract or repel substances, which feeds into the idea that identities are essentially an assembly of similar particles. Rather, it posits human beings as socially constructible according to common struggles and aspirations, conceiving of identity formation across trad-itionally dividing categories. Thus, dalits, Adivasis and asat-Shudras can find themselves in a movement toward configuring a collective identity that subverts the logic and the functioning of the caste-based worldview from extending itself among those who are beaten down by its working.

SUBALTERNS AS THE FIRST FRUITS OF GOD'S RELATIONAL POLITY OF JUST WHOLENESS

Let us not delude ourselves that there exists such a community in con-temporary India. There may be instances of the temporary and strategic banding together of such collectives; but this has been transitory and far from integrated. In this final section I shall first comment on the theo-logical model of community that informs this reflection of the subaltern (even in dialogue with sociological or political theory my commitment as a Christian theologian permeates much of my arguments); secondly, I shall sum up this section by proposing a definition of theology that appears to have emerged from this exercise.

I cannot escape the accusation that 'subaltern', as I have explicated it in these pages, is a projected community, which is tinged with eschatological interpolations even if contrived to manifest concrete actualizations. When I look back at these reflections I am acutely aware how much my inter-pretation of this term 'subaltern' has been funded by the theological concept of the reigning of God as mediated through the Jesus as the Christ dynamic. Jesus as the Christ is presumed to be distinctly and

---

[14] Dipankar Gupta (ed.), *Social Stratification* (New Delhi: Oxford University Press, 1991), p. 25.

inextricably related to the reign of God; that is, God's relational polity of just wholeness. I believe that Jesus as the Christ transforms this eschatological frame of reference into a historical momentum; hence, in the energy that Jesus expends in being the Christ the rule of God is let loose in the world. Jesus as the Christ concretely and decisively instrumentalizes God's polity of just wholeness and invites all human beings to realize the proximity and appropriateness of this rule of God, expressed in Jesus' proclamation at the commencement of his ministry: 'The time is fulfilled, and the Kingdom of God has come near, repent, and believe in the good news' (NRSV Mark 1:15). Also, in the Jesus as the Christ momentum, the ethnic and the geographical contours of the promise and fulfilment of the reign of God are redefined to include all peoples everywhere; thus, it moves far beyond the nation of Israel to include all people living in the whole inhabited world, with a special relationship carved out for the poor and the excluded. Let me attempt to extrapolate the significant nuances with which I have critically appropriated and constructively employed this conception to mean God's relational polity of just wholeness with reference to subalterns.

First, Jesus' invitation to the reigning of God is the subalterns' hope for a relational polity of just wholeness. The momentum that is instrumentalized by the Jesus as the Christ dynamic opens up new and liberative ways for subalterns to move away from the politics of domination towards the politics of freedom and liberty. A discerning reader of the synoptic Gospels will discover that Jesus' main objective was neither to communicate knowledge about God or knowledge of himself; rather he came to announce, inaugurate and invite his hearers to enter into the dynamics of the reigning of God, which I have construed to signify a relational polity of just wholeness. On the one hand, the reigning of God is a gift of God to all creation; it is always waiting to break into history. In the Jesus as the Christ movement the polity appears as an actual and actualizing force attracting all human beings to repent and enter into the relationship that God intends for God's people. It is important to stress the notion that this polity of just wholeness is a gift and creation of God, which is built into the structures of a God-intended and God-activating order. The reigning of God thus is the processes of configuring just wholeness, which presupposes God's promise and purposive activity for God's creation. On the other hand, the subalterns become God's hope for a relational polity of just wholeness, as is testified to by the masses that surrounded Jesus and the persons that decided to follow in his way. The Jesus movement was not as attractive to those dominant communities that needed to retain their own privileges. On the contrary, it was the poor and the excluded that gravitated towards its pronouncement and engagement. Hence, the objective of God and the hope of the subaltern find commonality in the reign of God.

Secondly, Jesus renders the reigning of God as a kinship based on water rather than on blood. The subaltern, accordingly, is conceived of in terms of a relationship of engagement rather than a commonality of substance. This has direct relevance to formations of identity; that is, it rejects the Hindu caste worldview, which proposes that human beings are to think of identity in essentialist and substantial ways, as if a person is a conglomeration of specific particles that have a coding predetermining one's caste, gender and persona. Rather subaltern identity is constructed as a relationship that emerges through the active participation in the dynamic of striving toward a life of freedom and dignity. Without doubt this representation as I elucidate it is categorically Christian, in the sense that the exchange of a blood-based identity with a water-interpreted one can be explained by pointing to the baptism of Jesus, symbolizing the point at which he renounces his blood-based identity and embraces his water-based identity.

To clarify, let me start by saying that Jesus' baptism was deliberately chosen. In the midst of a host of voices in Israel Jesus chose the baptism of John. There were the Essenes, the Zealots, the Pharisees and the Sadducees, but Jesus came to be baptized by John; John, the fierce and irritating prophet, who chose to live outside the borders of society. In John's own mind he was offering a baptism of repentance; this was the unique characteristic of John's baptism, and yet Jesus sought out John in order to be baptized. In a sense, one can assert that Jesus repented; thus his baptism symbolized turning around from an ethnic identity that involved some privileges and some restrictions to a new identity that was defined by solidarity with the community that would be bound together with God in bringing about the relational polity of just wholeness. Jesus turns around in the same way that he turns away from blood-based identity and towards water-based identity. On the one hand, at baptism Jesus was turning away from the privilege of his race and his status because of being a pure Jew and a strong male in what we would call a racist and patriarchal system. Jesus, I think, repented of all that he had gained for many years from this privilege, which was rooted in a society that interpreted his identity in essentialist and substantive ways. He repented of the entrenchment of his life in the world; he turned away from all of its entrapment so as to be the agent of the rule of God. Jesus' baptism then was a genuine act of repentance; it was a sign that he was decisively turning around. From this point on it becomes clear to the world that Jesus' blood-based identity has terminated; hence, from then on his mother and brothers and sisters are those who do the will of God, and there is no more bonding based on birth, race and gender. His descent into the waters of the Jordan is a form of dying to the old self and his rising from the water is the configuration of a new self, based in another kind of identity. Thus, on the other hand, Jesus' baptism as an act of repentance also was a turning toward the sole privilege of being the mediator of the community based on water and a willingness to live fully within God's relational polity of just wholeness. Blood was no longer thicker than water; in fact water was now thicker than blood. This identity is constructible and can be freely chosen, and yet this water baptism, as instantiated by Jesus as the Christ, lifts up the prophetic challenge for those incorporated into the new identity based on water. To sum up this discussion let me restate that at baptism Jesus became wholly disobliged to the identity that was derived from blood and became wholly obliged to his chosen identity, which was symbolized by water. In so doing he offers a model for the formation of subaltern identity in its journey toward freedom and dignity.

Thirdly, Jesus' idea of the reigning of God was far removed from the idea that it merely involved the ruling of God in the heart of the indivual believer. The domain of the reign of God is not only within the Christian person. Instead Jesus teaches that the kingdom of God is a social entity; a commonwealth of God's humanity organized in all its aspects according to the will of God. The idea that the kingdom of God is solely linked up with the internal being of the individual is not consonant with Jewish thought in general, rather it is much more typical of Greek philosophical thought. Jesus was a Jew and his thought-world was predominantly corporate and social. Thus, in accordance with his Jewish tradition, Jesus locates the dynamics of the reign of God within the spiritual, social, political and economic realities of the excluded people; consequently, he took the corporate identity formation of the subaltern seriously. The words of Jesus found in Luke 17:21 are important: 'For, in fact, the kingdom of God is [not merely within you or merely without you, but] among you'; that is, the reign of God as propounded by this passage addresses the social and earthly dimensions of life in all its fullness. Therefore, it is no wonder that the subaltern had much to gain from the drawing near of this reign of God, which had social and earthly implications for human society. Thus, calculatingly, Luke's version of the beatitudes has Jesus saying: 'Blessed are you who are poor for yours is the kingdom of God' (Luke 6:20). It is the reigning of God as a new community of relationships intended by God, energized by Jesus as the Christ and celebrated by the poor and excluded, that seeks to break in among us as a concrete entity.

Consequently, the notion of Christian theology that emerges can be articulated in this way: Christian theology is a critical and constructive reflection on the symbols of God, world and human being and their interrelationships as interpreted through the Jesus as the Christ momentum that is contextually mediated and liberationally steered by the power of the Holy Spirit.

BIBLIOGRAPHY

Chatterjee, P., 'Caste and Subaltern Consciousness', in R. Guha (ed.), *Subaltern Studies VI: Writings on South Asian History and Society*, New Delhi: Oxford University Press, 1989, pp. 169–209.

Clarke, S., *Dalits and Christianity: Subaltern Religion and Liberation Theology in India*, New Delhi: Oxford University Press, 1998.

Guha, R., 'Preface', in R. Guha (ed.), *Subaltern Studies I: Writings on South Asian History and Society*, New Delhi: Oxford University Press, 1982, pp. vii–viii.

    'Introduction', in R. Guha (ed.), *A Subaltern Studies Reader: 1986–1995*, New Delhi: Oxford University Press, 1998, pp. ix–xxii.

Gupta, D. (ed.), *Social Stratification*, New Delhi: Oxford University Press, 1991.

Ilaiah, K., 'Productive Labour, Consciousness and History: The Dalitbahujan Alternative', in S. Amin and D. Chakrabarty (eds.), *Subaltern Studies IX: Writings on South Asian History and Society*, New Delhi: Oxford University Press, 1996, pp. 165–200.

    Why I am not a Hindu: A Sudra Critique of Hindutva Philosophy, Culture and Political Economy, Calcutta: Samya, 1996.

Kolenda, P., *Caste and Contemporary India: Beyond Organic Solidarity*, Prospect Heights: Waveland Press, 1985.

McKim, M. and Inden, R. B., 'Towards an Ethnosociology of South Asian Caste System', in K. A. David (ed.), *The New Wind: Changing Identities in South Asia*, Chicago: Aldine Publishers, 1977, pp. 227–38.

Mendelsohn, O. and Vicziany, M., 'The Untouchables', in O. Mendelsohn and U. Baxi (eds.), *The Rights of Subordinated Peoples*, New Delhi: Oxford University Press, 1994, pp. 64–117.

Moffatt, M., *An Untouchable Community in South India: Structure and Consensus*, Princeton: Princeton University Press, 1979.

Index